Solidarity and the Palestinian Cause

Also Available from Bloomsbury:

Continental Philosophy and the Palestinian Question: Beyond the Jew and the Greek, Zahi Zalloua
Žižek on Race: Toward an Anti-Racist Future, Zahi Zalloua
Traces of Racial Exception: Racializing Israeli Settler Colonialism, Ronit Lentin
Plural Maghreb: Writings on Postcolonialism, Abdelkebir Khatibi, trans. P. Burcu Yalim

Solidarity and the Palestinian Cause

Indigeneity, Blackness, and the Promise of Universality

Zahi Zalloua

BLOOMSBURY ACADEMIC
LONDON • NEW YORK • OXFORD • NEW DELHI • SYDNEY

BLOOMSBURY ACADEMIC
Bloomsbury Publishing Plc
50 Bedford Square, London, WC1B 3DP, UK
1385 Broadway, New York, NY 10018, USA
29 Earlsfort Terrace, Dublin 2, Ireland

BLOOMSBURY, BLOOMSBURY ACADEMIC and the Diana logo are trademarks of
Bloomsbury Publishing Plc

First published in Great Britain 2023
This paperback edition published 2024

Copyright © Zahi Zalloua, 2023

Zahi Zalloua has asserted his right under the Copyright, Designs and Patents Act, 1988, to be identified as Author of this work.

For legal purposes the Acknowledgments on p. viii constitute an extension of this copyright page.

Series design by Charlotte Daniels
Cover image: *Conclusion*, acrylic on canvas, 100x150cm, 2018 (© Saher Nassar)

All rights reserved. No part of this publication may be reproduced or transmitted in any form or by any means, electronic or mechanical, including photocopying, recording, or any information storage or retrieval system, without prior permission in writing from the publishers.

Bloomsbury Publishing Plc does not have any control over, or responsibility for, any third-party websites referred to or in this book. All internet addresses given in this book were correct at the time of going to press. The author and publisher regret any inconvenience caused if addresses have changed or sites have ceased to exist, but can accept no responsibility for any such changes.

A catalogue record for this book is available from the British Library.

A catalog record for this book is available from the Library of Congress.

ISBN: HB: 978-1-3502-9019-8
PB: 978-1-3502-9023-5
ePDF: 978-1-3502-9020-4
eBook: 978-1-3502-9021-1

Typeset by Deanta Global Publishing Services, Chennai, India

To find out more about our authors and books visit www.bloomsbury.com and sign up for our newsletters.

To all of the Palestinians who refuse to disappear.

Contents

Acknowledgments — viii

Introduction: Critique of Indigenous Reason — 1

1. Look, a Palestinian! — 37
2. Thinking under Occupation — 67
3. *Ressentiment*/Paranoia — 95
4. ~~Sovereignty~~ — 125

Conclusion: The Palestinian Cause — 159

Notes — 169
Bibliography — 238
Index — 265

Acknowledgments

This book is in some respects a sequel to my *Continental Philosophy and the Palestinian Question: Beyond the Jew and the Greek* (2017). If my earlier book traced the Palestinian question in the changing field of continental philosophy, with an eye for the dynamics of particularism and universalism, *Solidarity and the Palestinian Cause* centers on the challenging debates in Critical Black Studies and Indigenous and Settler Studies about thinking Palestine and Palestinian resistance. Critically dialoguing with these fields made it clear to me that to respond to the question "Can the Palestinian matter?" necessitates a whole set of reflections on the meanings of the human and sovereignty, the nation and its Others. The subtle shift from the Palestinian question to the Palestinian cause suggests that to respond ethically and politically to the former entails taking up the latter. The Palestinian cause solicits and is enriched by solidarity. There is no Palestinian cause without making the Palestinian question a universalist concern.

In forming and forging my ideas, I have immensely benefited from the exchanges with Whitman students, particularly those in my spring 2022 seminar on the Palestinian question. Their excitement, curiosity, and commitment to justice constantly reminded me that this new generation is well equipped to deal with ruthless attempts to silence both Palestinian and Jewish voices speaking out against the Occupation, along with their supporters. They exemplify a promising trend; students in the United States and across the world are refusing ready-made answers, interrogating the meaning of Zionism, and rejecting the stereotypical images of Palestinians so often propagated by mainstream political discourse. Student activists are defiantly asking for more. This book emerges from a similar place and shared commitment.

Writing this book was all-encompassing. I was in the middle of preparing it during the last Gaza war in May 2021. I could neither stop writing nor talking about the media coverage, enraged by the failure of Western powers to curtail Israel's slaughter of Palestinians—whose fundamental fault was simply being Palestinian and refusing to disappear. During this time, my brother Mounir was as usual an immeasurable source of comfort, listening to me rant about liberal hypocrisy and political cowardice. I'm also deeply thankful for the emotional and intellectual support of my colleagues at Whitman and especially grateful for my conversations with Susanne Beechey, Shampa Biswas, Matt Bost, Chetna Chopra, Arash Davari, Tarik Elseewi, John Johnson, Kazi Joshua, Camilo Lund-Montaño, Gaurav Majumdar, Lydia McDermott, Libby Miller, Lauren Osborne, Kaitlyn Patia, Jason Pribilsky, Daniel Schultz, Lisa Uddin, and Xiaobo Yuan. Vlad Voinich provided invaluable research assistance in the early stages of the book project.

For generative encounters outside of Whitman, I want to thank Robert Beshara, Jake Blevins, Clint Burnham, Claire Colebrook, Jeffrey Di Leo, Jennifer Kwon Dobbs, Matthew Flisfeder, Agon Hamza, Peter Hitchcock, Derek Hook, Ilan Kapoor, Jamil Khader, Sophia McClennen, Todd McGowan, Paul Allen Miller, Christian Moraru, Brian O'Keeffe, R. Radhakrishnan, Debarati Sanyal, Russell Sbriglia, Rob Tally, Calvin Warren, and Cindy Zeiher. I would like to thank Liza Thompson and Lucy Russell from Bloomsbury for their strong commitment to this project. Most of all, I'm thankful for Nicole's presence in my life—her endless kindness means everything to me.

Portions of Chapters 1 and 3 appeared elsewhere in a revised form: "'*Il faut bien détruire ensemble*,' or Solidarity after Afropessimism," *symplokē* 29, 1–2 (2021): 547–8 and "Palestinian Paranoia and the Colonial Situation," *symplokē* 29, 1–2 (2021): 281–300, respectively. I thank Lina Abojaradeh and Saher Nassar for sharing their powerful artwork with me. I also would like to thank the various publishers for granting me permission to reproduce my epigraphs. This project was supported in part by a Louis B. Perry Summer Research Grant.

Introduction

Critique of Indigenous Reason

I define relative humanity as the belief that certain human beings, to the extent that they share a common religious, ethnic, cultural, or other similarly substantial identity attribute, lack one or more of the necessary attributes of being human and are therefore human only in a relative sense—not absolutely and not unequivocally.

—Omar Barghouti[1]

Indigeneity has become constitutive of the Palestinian question. Indigenous and Native American Studies have opened a much-needed grammar for recognition and redress in Palestine. To perceive Palestinians as the Indigenous people of this contested land is already to overcome—or at least to push back against—the view that (all) Jews are the timeless victims of history, incapable of victimizing others. Foregrounding Palestinian Indigeneity recasts Israeli Jews as dispossessors and settlers—those who have historically wronged Palestinians and still continue to do so under the brutal occupation of the West Bank and Gaza, and in Israel proper. To claim Palestinian Indigeneity is to respond directly to Israel's own claim of Jewish priority, to its connection to the "land of milk and honey," to its ideological fantasy of continuous spatial and temporal presence on the Promised Land. It stubbornly affirms the antecedence of Palestinians' being and world, rejecting what we might call Israel's mythic nativity, its phantasmatic identity, deployed to legitimize and justify Palestinian dispossession on the grounds that it is Israel's ontological entitlement, its right to inhabit the "Holy Land," the land of *Judea and Samaria* as described in scripture.[2] In Saidian parlance, Jewish Indigeneity is "divine" or metaphysical; it appeals to "origins," as in the narrative of "Israeli Manifest Destiny," whereas Palestinian Indigeneity is "historical" or worldly, dealing rather with "beginnings."[3] The former dreams of transcendence and redemption, the latter is born of contingency and resilience.

At the same time, in a global context marked by liberal democratic ideology, formulating Palestinian identity in terms of Indigeneity tends to confine it, to fix it at the level of culture. It effectively risks casting the Palestinian dilemma exclusively as a problem of cultural management. Casting Indigenous Palestinians as a cultural minority in Israel leads to calls to protect, preserve, and accommodate the Palestinian way of life: Israel ought to be more tolerant and so on. This approach campaigns against an apartheid Israel and in favor of civic justice, a more democratic state capable of including cultural minorities without fundamentally altering its framework. When Indigeneity is construed instead as intimately linked to questions of land and sovereignty, Palestinians can be thought as a majority surrounded by hostile settlers and Israeli Occupation Forces[4] (in the West Bank), reduced to dwelling in the world's largest open-air prison (in Gaza); in this framework, Palestinian lives can be conceived as mattering and deserving of the same right to self-determination. Yet, this tack leads to calls for national independence and collective sovereignty typically—and problematically—embodied in the two-state solution. The Western nation-state framework lives on in this model, and Indigeneity is reappropriated, neutralized, and translated into preconceived notions of racial separatism, neatly aligning Jews and Arabs with their respective nations.

Solidarity and the Palestinian Cause insists that any analysis of Indigeneity's purchase must keep this problem of translation in mind and consider what an appeal to Indigeneity means for those within (Palestinians themselves and their competing claims) and what it signifies to those without (most particularly, Western political powers). Do these align? Or is there friction? What gets eclipsed when the idea of Indigeneity travels, when its audience is liberal multiculturalists—who desperately hunger for (the imago of) Indigeneity, eager to save the endangered Palestinians—is precisely the question of politics. When the demand for stolen land is surpassed by arguments foregrounding the recognition of Palestinian rights (allocated by the Israeli nation-state), what, then, are the counter-politics of Indigeneity? When does the culturalization of Indigeneity empower the colonized? And when does it lead to a suspension of politics, understood as "the space of litigation in which the excluded can protest the wrong or injustice done to them"?[5] Does Indigeneity become a form of identity category through which Palestinians are able to make political demands and declare their desire for collective self-determination?[6] Does privileging Indigeneity lock Palestinians in their particularity, obscuring the universality of the *Palestinian cause*?[7] Is "Indigenous reason"—the interminable thinking, desiring, or interpreting what is deemed Indigenous—capable of inciting revolutionary change, of dismantling the master's, or settler's, house?

This book takes this last question to heart—considering especially how this plea is (mis)heard by liberal Zionists and Western powers who want to save

Israel from itself, to protect its democracy from the state's increasingly racial and racist policies without ever questioning the idea/l of a Jewish state. And yet, rejecting the nation-state can lead all too easily into the traps of a pristine *time before the settler*:[8] to the commitment of reviving a Palestine prior to the Nakba, the catastrophe of 1948, protected from the wounds and ravages of colonialism. Against this understanding of Indigenous insularity, this book puts Palestinian Indigeneity in dialogue with Critical Black Studies as a way to meditate on the full force and concrete provocations of the Chilean precept, "Another end of the world is possible" (*Otro fin del mundo es possible*).[9] We ask: How does Palestinian Indigeneity relate and speak to current global reactions to racial injustice fueled in large part by the Black Lives Matter movement? Isn't an emancipatory movement worthy of its name not predicated upon interrogating Indigeneity and its complicity with anti-Blackness? Are struggles against settler colonialism and anti-Blackness incommensurable, prone to distortion, confusion, and instrumentalization? Or, if we choose, as I believe we should, not to condemn these cross-racial efforts in advance, might they foster acts of solidarity, be imagined as constitutive of a new global anti-capitalist and anti-imperialist Left that avoids the separatist temptation (isolating tribal interests and fetishizing particularism) and the elimination of difference (the claim that all subjugations are the same)? If so, how does Indigeneity *with* Blackness signal a struggle not only against cultural domination (anti-Blackness, Islamophobia, neo-Orientalism, etc.) but also against economic exploitation (the instrumentalization of human life and the naturalization of neoliberal values)? How does this emergent global demand for racial and economic justice recast and retrieve Indigeneity and the question of Palestine anew as a universal cause?

Whither Indigeneity?

The signifier "Indigenous" is part and parcel of a general logic of othering the colonized, the Native of the land. Countering this logic, decolonial thinker Walter Mignolo ingeniously turns the table on the colonizers by applying the signifier to them: "European indigenous peoples."[10] Mignolo dispels the strangeness of saying *Europeans are indigenous*, observing: "You will find that the word is an adjective referring to those 'born or originating in a particular place.' It comes from the late Latin *indigenus*, which means 'born in a country, native.' So, if Europeans are not indigenous, where did they come from?"[11] This move is intended to question the universalism and epistemic superiority of the

Western subject, and its alignment with civilization and the privileges of culture. It denaturalizes the Europeans' naturalization of their heroic overcoming of nature, reframing the Western subject as irremediably marked by its positionality and geography. Europeans are not born exemplars of humanity and civilization; they ideologically and phantasmatically become them. In other words, there is nothing ontologically special about the *being* of Europeans.

While in support of the desire to demystify European exceptionalism, Anishinaabe curator Wanda Nanibush, in her dialogue with Mignolo, cautions against such blanket deployments of the term; asserting *we are all indigenous* misses something. Nanibush draws attention to the position of the enunciation, to the one who utters the word:[12]

> I think our difference is that I use words after re-centring Anishinaabe ways of being and thinking rather than from within a critique of Eurocentrism. Yes, you are right that the dictionary definition does in fact mean that to somewhere everyone is indigenous. It is also true that indigenous is a word not of our own creation, much like most geopolitical markers in the world today. However, I did not appropriate "indigenous." Instead, I use "Indigenous" ... Indigenous with a "capital I" is about sovereignty movements, land rights, the rights of the earth, return to Indigenous women's role in our societies and much more dreaming that cannot be contained in a policy document. It seems there are differences we name with the word Indigenous that is not part of the European definition and that create breaks in a colonial framework.[13]

Indigenous at once indexes people who preceded the colonial encounter and emerges as a response to that the encounter. Indigeneity is an invention and a *process*, a form of becoming, rather than a mere *product* of settler colonialism. If Europeans effaced their own "indigeneity" when they subjected the non-European inhabitants of the land to a racialized mode of classification (Mignolo), the same subalternized non-Europeans are now speaking and writing back, reimagining "Indigeneity" on their own terms (absent humanitarian intervention), altering, or rather politicizing, what it means to be Indigenous (Nanibush). Such is the case of the native Palestinians.

Settler colonialism, not unlike slavery, is not a historical relic. It has a thriving afterlife. Indigenous identities across the globe bear the ontological marks of their dreadful encounter with European settlers. As Edward Cavanagh and Lorenzo Veracini observe, an analysis of settler colonialism that does justice to its complexities must adopt a disjunctive temporality, and grasp this "global and transnational phenomenon" at its beginnings and in its current forms, "as much a thing of the past as a thing of the present."[14] Like other settler-colonial projects, Zionism is not primarily about the *exploitation* of Palestinians (what would be expected under colonialism) but their *elimination*; the target is not Indigenous labor but native land. "Unlike European colonisation," Sayez Sayegh argued in 1965, "the Zionist colonisation of Palestine was essentially incompatible with the continued existence of the 'native population' in the coveted country."[15] Under Zionism, settler colonialism took the most brutal form: "If *racial discrimination* against the 'inferior natives' was the motto of race-supremacist European settler-regimes in Asia and Africa, the motto of the race-supremacist Zionist settler-regime in Palestine was *racial elimination*."[16] The Zionist settler did not seek the Native's exploitation ("You, work for me"); he sought her disappearance ("You, go away").[17] In its inception, then, Zionism equated territory with national sovereignty, and thus created the Indigenous inhabitants of the land as a "problem": an existential obstacle for the realization of its people.

Claiming Palestinian Indigeneity jams the settler's ongoing discursive and epistemic domestication of the Native—the project of rendering the Indigenous docile and inexistent. *Existence is resistance*. It thwarts the settler's playbook, the Zionist desire to Judaize Palestinian land: to naturalize dispossession and the removal of the Indigenous inhabitants, to implement racist housing policies and accelerate home demolitions, and, of course, to aggressively pursue the extraction of natural resources. Claiming Palestinian Indigeneity also points to something unassimilable, residing outside Israel's "web of imperial knowledge."[18] Read through the prism of settler colonialism, "1948 Arabs"/Israeli Palestinians are *Nakba survivors*. This designation linguistically registers both the historical trauma of the settler conquest—its "profound epistemic, ontological, cosmological violence,"[19] as Eve Tuck and K. Wayne Yang put it—and the persistence of Palestinians, their refusal to disappear: "the presence of Indigenous peoples—who make *a priori* claims to land and ways of being—is a constant reminder that the settler colonial project is incomplete."[20] Indigeneity evokes not only the people's prior existence to the land (Palestinians were here first), it also denaturalizes the political scene, insisting, as Mark Rifkin points out, on the necessity "to interrogate the legitimacy of the legal and administrative frameworks of the settler-state while also attending to the presence and contours of actual or aspirational political formations by indigenous peoples."[21]

Palestinian Indigeneity is clearly a problem for settler Zionism, an affront to it, a remainder and reminder of Israel's *failed* eliminative project. Palestinians are still struggling against the Occupation and the rest of the world is waking up to the justice of their cause. At stake here are two narratives of what we might call "Indigenous reason," after Achille Mbembe's notion and treatment of "Black reason":

> "Black reason" names not only a collection of discourses but also practices—the daily work that consisted in inventing, telling, repeating, and creating variations on the formulas, texts, and rituals whose goal was to produce the Black Man as a racial subject and site of savage exteriority, who was therefore set up for moral disqualification and practical instrumentalization. We can call this founding narrative the *Western consciousness of Blackness*. In seeking to answer the question "Who is he?" the narrative seeks to name a reality exterior to it and to situate that reality in relationship to an *I* considered to be the center of all meaning. From this perspective, anything that is not identical to that *I* is abnormal.
>
> Let us call this second narrative the *Black consciousness of Blackness*. It nevertheless had its own characteristics. Literary, biographical, historical, and political, it was the product of a polyglot internationalism. It was born in the great cities of the United States and the Caribbean, then in Europe, and later in Africa. Ideas circulated within a vast global network, producing the modern Black imaginary.[22]

Indigenous reason similarly establishes two diametrically opposed attitudes to settler colonialism. The first narrative of Indigenous reason serves as settler colonialism's raison d'être, essentializing and hierarchizing both the settler and the Native—the latter's land is the former's "Manifest Destiny."[23] This Indigenous reason is "constituted from the outside."[24] Indigenous reason degrades native lives. It produces a biased ontology that hierarchizes the being of the settler above that of the Native and the enslaved: "the settler positions himself as both superior and normal; the settler is natural, whereas the Indigenous inhabitant and the chattel slave are unnatural, even supernatural."[25] Indigenous reason expels Palestinian Indigeneity from the designation "human." In this narrative, the Native is an artifact of settler colonialism and Zionist ideology. You are not born Native, you become racialized as one. This Indigenous reason is a settler-colonial reason obsessed with (neutralizing/killing) the Native. It celebrates Israel's racial and ethnic domination over the Indigenous population, while proclaiming the latter's mental and moral inferiority: they are (rendered) primitive, unreliable, wicked, suspicious, and dangerous. What we have here is the *Zionist consciousness of Palestinian Indigeneity*.

The second narrative posits Indigenous reason as "self-constituting";[26] it reappropriates and rearticulates Indigenous reason as the consciousness of the harrowing experiences that have forged Indigenous identities across the globe from 1492 to the present—of all the native peoples who have been, and continue to be, touched by the machinery of settler colonialism. In the case of Palestine/Israel, it questions settler ontology, Jewish exceptionalism, and seeks colonialism's demise by reinventing and reviving Indigenous modes of being: this is *Palestinian consciousness of Palestinian Indigeneity*. This consciousness emanates from Palestinians in the Occupied Territories, in Israel proper, and from the diaspora. Needless to say, the narratives of Palestinian Indigeneity that such a consciousness produces are marked, dismissed, and/or criminalized as anti-Semitic by the Israeli settler state and its staunch Western supporters. In both instances, Indigenous reason (for consistency, and because they are entangled, I capitalize Indigenous in referring to both modes) names an array of discourses and practices invested in peoples whose relation to the land is in question or an object of concern.

Indigenous reason is also a hermeneutic. It interprets the autochthonous, the Native, as either given or a colonialist construction. Anti-colonial theory has long attended to the latter and cautioned against accepting the colonizer's terms, or hegemonic script. (Self-)endowed with the power to name and categorize, the colonizer, after all, does not so much discover Indigenous people as fix and narrate them. "Imperialism is the export of identity,"[27] as Edward Said succinctly put it. Western powers project an identity, an ontology, onto Indigenous populations, simultaneously essentializing them and producing knowledge about these non-Europeans. In the case of Palestinians, what is produced by the settler is paradoxically a knowledge of their nonbeing, of their status as a non-people. The concept of *terra nullius*—"a land of no one," an eighteenth-century legal notion deployed to authorize the European expropriation of Indigenous peoples' lands—plays a crucial role in the production of this knowledge. Indigenous reason conceives of the Native as primitive, deceitful, and a pest to eliminate.

Claiming Palestinian Indigeneity foregrounds *Palestinian consciousness of Palestinian Indigeneity*. It puts the settler-colonial framework front and center in the discussion of Palestine, countering two major objections to its use by critics keen to question its rhetorical utility and accuracy: first, that the evocation of settler colonialism hardens the will of your interlocutors, alienating those whom you're trying to convince and open up to the Palestinian question (a version of "Nobody likes to be called a racist"), and second, that no one actually believed in *terra nullius* (Jewish settlers knew that Palestinians lived on the disputed land).[28] The first reproach smacks of bad faith; it represents a betrayal of integrity and conscience. The theft of land and freedom is sidestepped in favor of accommodating the sensibilities of the oppressors/settlers and their supporters who would be disturbed or vexed by any queries into Zionism's colonial ambitions (then and now). The second's rendering of the situation simplifies the affective and ideological appeal of *terra nullius*, downplaying the "fetishist disavowal" of the early settlers: *they knew very well that Palestinians live on this land, but they didn't believe it.* "By emptying 'the Other' from the head of the colonizer,"[29] Zionism mythically de-substantializes Palestinian presence (then and now), treating the inhabitants *as if* they came from elsewhere, making them "Arab" outsiders provisionally occupying the land until its "true" inhabitants returned. Zionism's epistemic classification of Arabs as Indigenous (unlike the true Indigeneity of the "Chosen People") was and is meant to facilitate their subjugation, control, and liquidation. In historic Palestine and modern Israel, Palestinians/Arabs remain brute nomadic trespassers on their own land, and "poor in world,"[30] in Heideggerian parlance, whereas Jewish settlers are white, Western, and world-forming.

Edward Said's *Orientalism* helps to trace the becoming white/colonial of the Jewish people to the emergence of the late nineteenth-century Zionist movement in Europe and the splitting of the figure of the Semite: "By a concatenation of events and circumstances the Semitic myth bifurcated in the Zionist movement; one Semite went the way of Orientalism, the other, the Arab, was forced to go the way of the Oriental."[31] Post-Second World War, Western powers and Zionists worked in tandem.[32] The former wanted Jews out of Europe (viewing their loyalty as a constant source of suspicion) and the latter wanted Jews in their own homeland (believing that only a Jewish nation could counteract the "degeneration"—the ontological effects of alienated existence in Europe—that Jews were experiencing). The founding of Israel became the preferred Zionist solution.[33] European anti-Semitism, reaching its apogee in the Shoah, provided the sociopolitical conditions for the Zionists' pitch to their fellow Jews and the rest of the world.[34]

In preparing the grounds for a future Jewish state in Palestine, Zionist leaders eagerly formulated their understanding of Jewish belonging around the fetish of the modern European nation-state. By successfully exporting the nation-state to Palestine and committing to the notion of its superior values and racial matrix ("one nation, one state"), political Zionism not only phantasmatically whitened Jews but, more important, racialized Palestinians as non-white, permanent nonnationals of the land. Israel's 2018 Nation-State Law confirmed this vision, making it abundantly clear that "the right to exercise national self-determination" is "unique to the Jewish people."[35] In "ascending to whiteness,"[36] Zionist settlers depicted the Indigenous population as wild animals, devoid of any moral worth, which, in turn, facilitated their killing, dispossession, and mass expulsion (the well-trodden path of settler colonialism!). Long self-promoted as a beacon of civilization, ever since Theodor Herzl, the father of Zionism, strategically framed the Jewish state as "a part of a wall of defense for Europe in Asia, an outpost of civilization against barbarism,"[37] Israeli leaders have continued to remind the Western world that Israel constitutes their "protective wall" (from fanatic Arabs), faithfully securing and serving the geopolitical interests of its unwavering imperial sponsors (namely, the United States and England). Israel stood and still stands as a "villa in the middle of a jungle,"[38] in the memorable but shamelessly self-serving words of the former Israeli prime minister Ehud Barak.

But as with Orientalism, it is crucial to note that the "knowledge" that Indigenous reason produces has less to do with Palestine and Palestinians than it does with the Western world. Its knowledge (let's say about "the Arab mind") is indeed "a kind of Western projection,"[39] marked by the knower/subject's own anxieties, insecurities, and vulnerabilities (the Zionist perspective, of course, also supplements and mediates the West's already expansive colonial/Orientalist imaginary, thus compounding the ideological distortions of Palestinian life and ways of being). Simply put, Indigenous reason—in its proliferations of racist and Orientalist tropes about the Natives—always tells us more about the knower than the known, the narrator than the narrated, the colonizer than the colonized.

Deeply enmeshed in necropower, Indigenous reason produces and rationalizes the racial divide between the West and the rest. Achille Mbembe moves to unsettle this divide by provincializing Giorgio Agamben's Eurocentric grammar of suffering, laid out in his analysis of the Holocaust as the ultimate paradigm for exceptional violence and the making of "bare life."[40] Though following Agamben in maintaining that sovereign power exists in the capacity to eradicate political existence (to strip individuals of their legal rights, for instance), reducing life to biological existence, Mbembe, not unlike Hannah Arendt and Aimé Césaire before him,[41] supplements or enlarges the analytical scope of biopolitics by looking at European colonialism and racial slavery. In this context, European colonial sovereignty takes from the start a different form; it is not enough to say that biopolitics takes a turn for the worse "when the state of exception starts to become the rule."[42] "The notion of biopower," Mbembe writes "does not suffice to account for the contemporary ways in which the political, under the disguise of war, of resistance, or of fights against terror, makes the murder of its enemy its primary and absolute objective."[43]

A biopolitical investment in *all* lives—in the regulation and expansion of life as such—is utterly foreign to the settler-colonial project. There is a necropolitics at the core of settler colonialism. The settler state does not manage death for the sake of life; rather, settler-sovereignty is constitutively necropolitical. Necropolitics in the colony is after "*the generalized instrumentalization of human existence and the material destruction of human bodies and populations*."[44] It quickly becomes clear, however, that colonial experimentation or variation in biopolitics is *not* a feature of the past, *as if* chattel slavery and the genocidal conquest of the New World were only a couple of "dark" episodes in European modernity, mere hiccups in the teleological march of progress. The legacy of European colonial sovereignty persists, and it is fully visible in Palestine/Israel. "The contemporary colonial occupation of Palestine" testifies to the singular entanglement of the disciplinary (the disciplining of bodies), the biopolitical (the regulating of bodies), and the necropolitical (the destroying of bodies). There and elsewhere Mbembe unearths a sovereign logic characteristic of late modern colonial occupation, at work in "seizing, delimiting, and asserting control over a physical geographical area—of writing on the ground a new set of social and spatial relations."[45] Colonial sovereignty, Mbembe claims further, "define[s] who matters and who does not, who is *disposable* and who is not."[46]

We can reformulate Mbembe's observation about necropower in the colony in terms of the paradigm of immunology: Lives that matter are immunized (from the racialized Other), purified, and nourished, while those that don't are contaminated, left exposed and impoverished at best, and, at worst, judged a securitization problem and thus marked for destruction or debilitation. Necropolitical sovereignty introduces a firm hierarchy of lives/races. Its use of biopower is destructive rather than productive. Indigenous reason does the bidding of the sovereign settler, who decides which lives are worthy of immunization and protection and which ones are neglected and left vulnerable. Israel's decision to put Gaza on a "diet"[47] reflects the state's necropolitical logic at work in managing Palestinian Indigeneity: "Counting calories in order to avoid a disaster" constitutes, for Nadia Abu El-Haj, "the calculus of Israel's necropolitical regime."[48] At its most basic level, then, immunizing life in the colony is first and foremost a racist technology of domination; its racial calculus solidifies the self as it purifies it from any unwanted excess, from any exposure to undesirable racial foreignness. *The Jewish state must be defended.* If starving the enemy is not an option (a humanitarian crisis would trigger too much attention from Western powers and media), then psychically and physically weakening her through a cruel diet, one that keeps the Native alive only to better contain her, becomes the settler's preferred alternative. Under the quasi-speciesist horizon of Zionism, Jewish life enjoys the security and pleasures of national citizenship whereas Palestinian life is racialized, made to reside in "a third zone between subjecthood and objecthood,"[49] figured as a "savage life," that is, "just another form of *animal life*."[50]

Settling the Human, or the Un-Mattering of Palestinians

Indigenous reason divides land, erects racial classifications, and disciplines Palestinian Indigeneity. Palestinians are deemed *in but not of*[51] the human world. They arouse a mixture of fear and disgust in the Zionist settlers; their sheer presence is an existential threat and an offense to these settlers' demographic advantage and exclusive right to belong. In the Zionist order of things, for Jewish life to matter, Palestinian life must un-matter. An "un-mattered life," here, is clearly not one that enjoys all of the privileges of being human/white, but neither is it a life that simply "doesn't matter" (the lot of not-humans, of those who lie outside humanity, subject to human neglect or indifference).[52] Rather, it is a life haunted by an anterior self (whose life would have presumably mattered if circumstances were different), whose humanity has been ontologically undone or negated, the source of un-care, rendered inhuman or faceless—the fruits of a cruel and racist assemblage. An "un-mattered life" bears the traces of its ripped subjectivity, congealed in a fixed order, racialized to the point of monstrosity/animality, and condemned to "death-in-life."[53]

If "humanity is a racial signifier,"[54] as Denise Ferreira da Silva points out, the Zionist settler's message to the West is clear: *Don't be fooled by their appearance, Palestinians aren't like us (white/human)*. They are intrinsically wicked and cannot be trusted; they are more animal than human. Don't blame us for taking strong, disproportionate measures—for defending Jewish collectivity. We are only defending Israel and/as the West from the inhuman Arab next door. Settler ideology predicts a set future, a reproduction of the status quo; it espouses a heartless futurology, which, as Slavoj Žižek defines it, is "a systematic forecasting of the future from the present trends in society. And therein resides the problem—futurology mostly extrapolates what will come from the present tendencies."[55] Zionist futurology is driven by a Manichean logic; Jews and Palestinians are stuck in implacable positions, foreclosing the possibilities of "'historical miracles,' radical breaks which can only be explained retroactively, once they happen."[56]

Futurology is the settler's temporality of choice. It normalizes what's to come, projecting a foreseeable future: more Zionist expansion, more Palestinian dispossession. Israel's political decisions are effectively depoliticized by making them appear predictable, even necessary, rather than the result of callous deliberation. Why? It is the fixed *being* of Palestinians that dictates Israeli *doing*. Indigenous reason denies the anti-colonial frame for reading the Palestinian struggle, replacing it with an anti-Semitic one, ruling out armed struggle as a legitimate mode of resistance against the illegal Occupation.[57] For the settlers, Palestinians are bloodthirsty terrorists; anti-Semitism is in their cultural DNA; they refuse to recognize Israel's right to exist (since a Jewish state would entail no Palestinian right of return, guaranteeing a demographic advantage for Jews); they embrace a culture of death, displaying no care for life or for the innocent. Israel claims that it can only react, lamenting how the Jewish people lack a genuine peace partner: there is no Palestinian Gandhi or Mandela to put an end to the "conflict."[58] This is an instance of Israeli *hasbara* (a term meaning *explanation* and used euphemistically in Hebrew to refer to propaganda), a rhetorical performance for its Western audience: if Palestinians had opted for nonviolence in their pursuit of national sovereignty, goes this line of thought, then things would have unfolded differently.

Conservative columnists peddle this narrative wholesale. The late Charles Krauthammer, for example, lamented Palestinians' unwillingness to make peace with Israel:

> Israel wanted nothing more than to live in peace with this independent Palestinian entity. After all, the world had incessantly demanded that Israel give up land for peace. It gave the land. It got no peace. The Gaza Palestinians did not reciprocate. They voted in Hamas, who then took over in a military putsch and turned their newly freed Palestine into an armed camp from which to war against Israel. It has been war ever since.[59]

Bret Stephens similarly reads the current situation as one of Arabs' own doing:

> Nearly every time the Arab side said no, it wound up with less. . . . It was true in 2000, when Syria rejected an Israeli offer to return the Golan Heights, which ultimately led to U.S. recognition of Israeli sovereignty of that territory. It was true later the same year, after Yasir Arafat refused Israel's offer of a Palestinian state with a capital in East Jerusalem, which led to two decades of terrorism, Palestinian civil war, the collapse of the Israeli peace camp and the situation we have now.[60]

This Arab-blaming narrative abstracts and dehistoricizes Palestinians, removing them from their environment and the settler-colonial context; the impact of the Occupation on their being and psyche is irrelevant or of no concern. Moreover, it is as if Israel is offering or giving up land out of generosity, and not because it is in violation of international law and illegally occupying Palestinian territory. And yet, this ideological narrative resonates with Western liberals. Progressive counternarratives reframing the discussion from a Palestinian perspective have yet to gain wide circulation and traction, while those dubbed Progressives except for Palestine (PEP) go with the flow.[61] American politicians on both sides of the aisle repeatedly affirm the "unbreakable bond" between Israel and the United States, and mechanically insist on Israel's right to defend itself (= its right to remain an illegal occupying force), aping Israel's talking points about security (= its land grab). The move of the US embassy in Israel to Jerusalem, which constituted a slap in the face of Palestinians, was also overwhelmingly supported by both Democrats and Republicans—then Senate minority leader Chuck Schumer even personally applauded Donald Trump for his decision. Given this widespread pro-Israel sentiment,[62] the Palestinian-blaming narrative offers a superficial "explanation" for the deadlock (the recourse to violence indicates that Palestinians aren't really interested in peace with Israel), and an excuse for doing nothing about it.

Settler ideology, which converts anti-colonial resistance into anti-Semitic hate, is thus in the business of keeping the possible *possible* and the impossible *impossible*. The political projects of a Free Palestine and a decolonized Israel are excised from the Western/Zionist political imaginary. Futurology points to more occupation, more annexation, and a looming "Greater Israel," that is, a racist one-state solution under the nervous eyes of a liberal West, still delusionally invested in a two-state solution, one that recognized the national yearnings of both peoples. But when *all* Palestinians are increasingly tagged as enemies—we are, for example, told by the Israeli defense minister Avigdor Lieberman that "there are no innocent people in the Gaza Strip"[63]—political myopia unavoidably sets in. Western-backed solutions to the "Palestinian problem," which de facto require as a precondition Israel's approval to move forward, narrow significantly.

Settler ideology not only fixes the identity of its Indigenous population, it's also responsible for their racialized creation as non-white and inhuman (inhuman *because* non-white). Many Zionist settlers brought with them to historic Palestine a Western metaphysics that conditioned if not overdetermined their encounter with the native inhabitants. Of course, not all Zionists adopted an exclusionary stance in relation to the land. Though the majority never questioned the biases shaping the project of settler colonialism as a "civilizing mission"[64] (bringing culture and modern knowledge to savages and backward people) nor doubted the "virtuous" character of settlement and expansion— even displaying a Lockean enthusiasm for working the land and realizing God's plan—some early Zionists like Martin Buber favored cultural Zionism and urged cooperation and coexistence with their Arab neighbors.[65] But it would be an understatement to say that cultural Zionists lost the struggle over the meaning of Zionism after the creation of Israel in 1948. With the 1967 Six-Day War, political Zionism cemented its authority and its control over the signifier "Jew," naturalizing the identification of Jewishness with the state of Israel. The implications of this move are chillingly clear: a critique of Israel is a critique of the Jewish people and is thus anti-Semitic or, if uttered by a Jewish dissenter, pathological or self-hating. According to the International Holocaust Remembrance Alliance (IHRA), "claiming that the existence of a state of Israel is a racist endeavor" qualifies as an instance of anti-Semitism.[66] Questioning Israel's status as a settler state is tantamount to questioning the legitimacy of the Jewish people and casting all Jews as oppressors. Along with this ideological naturalization of Jewishness, political Zionism invested its efforts in producing the Arab of the land as *otherwise than human*. In this respect, Indigenous reason fulfills the agenda of political Zionism.

Zionist consciousness of Palestinian Indigeneity traffics in what Alexander Weheliye dubs "racializing assemblages."[67] Expanding the ways we imagine "race," Weheliye stresses how this elusive signifier is neither a biological nor cultural taxonomy, but operates as "a set of sociopolitical processes that discipline humanity into full humans, not-quite-humans, and nonhumans."[68] After Gilles Deleuze and Félix Guattari, assemblages are thought of as provisional, contingent associations of human and nonhuman entities.[69] Assemblages follow an anti-identitarian logic; nothing could be more foreign to assemblage thinking than the essentialization of bodies or objects; indeed, assemblages "de-privilege the human body as a discrete organic thing," writes Jasbir Puar.[70] Assemblages foreground complexity and process, drawing their "agentic capacity" from "the vitality of the materialities that constitute it."[71] If assemblages are, in principle, unfinished and unstable bodies, always ontologically open to transformation and reconfiguration, racializing assemblages produce bodies in order to keep them in their proper place, divested of mobility and fluidity:

> In the context of the secular human, black subjects, along with indigenous populations, the colonized, the insane, the poor, the disabled, and so on serve as limit cases by which Man can demarcate himself as the universal human. Thus race, rather than representing difference, comes to define the very essence of the modern human as "the code through which one not simply *knows* what human being is, but *experiences* being."[72]

The purpose of racializing assemblages is to differentiate, hierarchize, and include/exclude. In Zionism's socio-spatial order, racializing assemblages frame the Palestinian native corporeality as the Other of the human/white/settler, assigning full symbolic and material value to the latter while denying it to the former.

Zionist settler consciousness inscribes the figure of the Palestinian in its *racial theater*, this "space of systematic stigmatization."[73] Palestinians have been thingified as "rocks of Judea" (Israeli president Chaim Weizmann),[74] but the stigma of choice is clearly animalization: the making of the Natives into another *species*. Israeli political and military leaders have, for example, described Palestinians "beasts walking on two legs" (Israeli prime minister Menachem Begin),[75] "drugged cockroaches in a bottle"[76] (General Rafael Eitan), "human animals"[77] (Israeli prime minister Netanyahu), or "snakes"[78] (justice minister Ayelet Shaked) to be eradicated or driven out from the Holy Land. David Theo Goldberg sums up succinctly the portrayal of the "Palestinian problem" as one of foreign infestation: "Palestinians have been increasingly animated as 'snakes in tunnels' squirming their way into Israel to carry out terroristic plots, or as insects crawling across the landscape. They are deemed maggots, cockroaches, and vermin out to infect Israel's body politic, a decaying rot eating at the nation's democratic social fabric."[79] What is Israel to do? How do you deal with infestation? Violently, with extermination on the table.

This racist imaginary is also gendered, and the bestialization of Palestinian bodies comingles with the feminization of their collective body. During *Operation Protective Edge*, the 2014 Israel-Gaza war, the patriarchal side of settler ideology was on full display. In a post addressed to prime minister Netanyahu that reached a broad audience on Israeli social media, we see "a veiled woman labeled 'Gaza', naked from the waist down, holding a message: 'Bibi, finish inside this time! Signed, citizens in favor of a ground assault.'"[80] The massacre of Palestinians is phantasmatically transfigured into a violent, sexualized spectacle akin to a snuff film. Hyper-masculinization symbolizes the humanity of the Israeli Jew while the less-than-human Palestinian is objectified, reduced to violable flesh awaiting military intervention and domination.[81] In this collective rape fantasy, Gazans are ventriloquized, obscenely cast as willing participants in their own violation/elimination, starring Benjamin Netanyahu as the rapist-in-chief.

Zionist settler consciousness at once mystifies and simplifies the relationship between Jew and non-Jew. Whereas Jews are made to stand exclusively for the human, non-Jews are consigned to the categories of the "not-quite-humans" (the second-class Palestinian citizens of Israel) and the "nonhumans" (the Palestinians of the West Bank and Gaza—the eternal enemies).[82] The coherence of Zionist identity is predicated on the undoing or un-mattering of Palestinian humanity, on relativizing it, producing what Omar Barghouti dubs "*relative* humans," those who are deemed "human only in a relative sense—not absolutely and not unequivocally,"[83] alien in their own homeland and undeserving of the protection and privileges of Jewish nationality. Zionist reason precludes Indigenous entry into the privileged orbit of the human. The Palestinian is said to exemplify the Zionist's antithesis, the "not-quite-human," at best, the "nonhuman," at worst. Forever relativized, Palestinian humanity is never more than a remote possibility. Infinitely caught between the taxonomies of "not-quite-human" and "nonhuman," Palestinians are overdetermined not to count, while Israeli Jews know they matter, enjoying the absolute certainty and coherence of their humanity. Are the differences between "humans," "not-quite-humans" and "nonhumans" bridgeable? Can racial becoming be halted and redirected? Can racist assemblages be undone and re-signified? Is a reassemblage of Palestinianness possible? If so, what would it take? And what would it look like?

We can start by interrogating the difference between the Palestinians in the Occupied Territories and Israel proper. Let's imagine a hypothetical scenario in which a liberal Zionist government has been elected on a platform advocating kinder treatment of the Palestinian people. We could get: a suspension of the long-running blockade of the "Gaza gulag,"[84] an expansion of cultural rights over religious sites in Jerusalem, a release of political prisoners, an increase in the political sovereignty of the Palestinian Authority (PA) over the West Bank, and even a decriminalization of Nakba Day—the commemoration of Palestinian dispossession. All of these overtures would surely bridge the gap between the two Palestinian groups, but it would be mere window dressing, leaving untouched the Zionist settler belief in the depraved inhumanity of *all* Palestinians. Again, it is the *being* of the Natives that is the threat, not what they do. If the latter, actions, are changeable (if, for instance, an atmosphere of trust and collaboration ever sets in between Arab Palestinians and Jewish Israelis), the former is not. To subscribe to this vision of Indigenous ontology is to condemn Palestinians to a "*death-world*,"[85] to a Zionist world that defines life as Jewish/white, against what it is *not*: Palestinian. Raising Palestinian lives to the standard of Israeli Palestinians might seem like a breakthrough, or at least progress, to a Western/liberal audience, but these ontical upgrades would do little to disrupt what Sylvia Wynter calls the "genre of the human."[86]

In Palestine/Israel, the "genre of the human"—what constitutes the human as such—is captured by the Israeli Jew, or more precisely, the Ashkenazi, or

European-born, Jew who "overrepresents itself as if it were the human itself."[87] A "one mode of being human"[88] mentality invariably breeds an apartheid logic, a segregationist attitude, a walling off of the Jew from the non-Jew. Indigenous reason aligns Jewishness with the Enlightenment, with humanity and civilization. Within this Eurocentric regime of the human, Zionist settlers stand as the self-appointed representative of the West/whiteness in the jungle of the Middle East. And the corollary: Indigenous reason aligns Palestinianness with an innate inhumanity/savagery, splitting the Palestinian from the human. Palestinians stand for what is other than civilization. To be Palestinian/Arab—Indigenous reason dictates—is to be plagued by an alien propensity for violence. Indeed, the core of Palestinian subjectivity is always already traversed by an inhuman excess, a radical extremism, so that bloodlust is not a deviation from their character or exception to it, but rather signals a predilection for cruelty and hate, making anti-Semitism integral to being Palestinian. The inhuman Arab neighbor must be contained, controlled, and dealt with (and, as in the rape imagery above, is fantasized as asking for it). Palestinophobia stems, in part, from this disfiguration of the Palestinian as bloodthirsty—the terrorist par excellence. The image of the Palestinian as terrorist was, of course, only exacerbated and amplified, to the point of becoming a fully naturalized Arab stereotype in the "righteous" global War on Terror. Israel all too easily adopted the US playbook on "terrorism," which "becomes another word for savagery and nihilism, for the negation of the West and everything it ostensibly stands for: freedom, democracy, and the American way."[89] *A safe Palestinian is a debilitated Palestinian*, to adapt a genocidal saying from the Western frontier.

We ought to keep in mind here Walter Benjamin's poignant remark, "Every document of civilization is also a document of barbarism."[90] Anti-Palestinian prejudice, then, is not some regrettable or embarrassing attitude of a few racist Israelis but a foundational and permanent feature of Israeli normativity. Palestinophobia is constitutive of so-called Zionist civilization; the Zionist settler state remains always already obsessed with the opposition between Jew and non-Jew: "*racial self-segregation, racial exclusiveness* and *racial supremacy . . .* constitute the core of the Zionist ideology."[91] And yet the state does on occasion register and admonish the inhuman(e) treatment of Palestinians by the IDF or police. Take, for example, the fatal shooting of Eyad Hallaq, an unarmed 32-year-old autistic Palestinian man, by an Israeli border police officer, on his way to the special-needs school that he attended in the Old City of East Jerusalem on May 30, 2020.[92] The event produced national and international outrage, forcing Netanyahu to make a statement: "What happened with the Hallaq family, with

Eyad Hallaq, is a tragedy. A person with disabilities, with autism, who was suspected we now know unjustly of being a terrorist in a very sensitive place. We all share in the grief of the family."[93] Netanyahu performed the semblance of accountability, signaling that an error was committed (the officer's suspicion of terrorism was not borne out) while also implying that the significance of the location (East Jerusalem) accounted for the officer's tragic overreaction to the situation. Clearly wanting to avoid a George Floyd-scale response to this unlawful killing, Israeli prosecutors, who typically look the other way, charged the border officer with reckless manslaughter.[94]

Will Hallaq and his family receive justice? It is unlikely, since the charge of reckless manslaughter already pales in front of what seems to have been a callous execution.[95] Does the Hallaq example pose a problem for Indigenous reason? Yes and no. The event put on display Israel's collective fantasies of Palestinians as phobic objects. The benign Hallaq gave the lie to Zionist consciousness of Palestinian Indigeneity. The fallout is potentially immense. Israel's legitimacy is at stake. The legitimacy of any state (for its people and the world at large) lies in its capacity to administer the law justly. With Hallaq, the world witnessed the Israeli police as an agent of injustice.[96] "When representatives of law commit crimes in their very enforcement of the rule of law," writes Žižek "the rule of law is not just weakened but undermined from within—it directly appears as its own self-negation."[97] This legitimacy crisis is, however, recuperated and given an ideological spin. Predictably, Israel neutralizes the incident by treating it as an exception to its habitual practice. Israel prides itself with having the "most moral army"; its police force is cut of the same cloth. But perhaps more important, it uses this error of judgment to produce a phantasmatic image of the Palestinian. Nir Hasson perceptively notes:

> Eyad Hallaq is a convenient case, too convenient. His helplessness, his nature as a child in a man's body, managed to allow the public to see him in his humanity. Unlike Hallaq, Israelis do distinguish between Jews and Arabs. Only when the victim is sufficiently helpless so as to completely dismiss any possibility that he harbored malicious intentions, are they viewed beyond their national category. It's the justified outcry in Hallaq's case that underscores the roaring silence in all the others.[98]

The "humanity" of Palestinians discloses itself, or rather is imputed to them by Western eyes, only when their docility is assured. We might say that Hallaq's "humanity" is retroactively granted, involving a kind of double negation—a non-nonhumanity, which is never truly identical to humanity as such. Saidiya

Hartman critiques this type of identificatory impulse—"Only if I can see myself in that position can I understand the crisis of that position"[99]—among white liberals when it comes to the victims of anti-Blackness. Such a phantasmatic/narcissistic identification becomes a precondition for white liberal outrage: "that is the logic of the moral and political discourses we see every day—the need for the *innocent* black subject to be victimized by a racist state in order to see the racism of the racist state."[100] For racialized bodies to be seen as "innocent" they have to be emptied out and libidinally rewritten as white bodies.[101] Cleansed of his Palestinianness, and thus depoliticized, Hallaq is no longer marked as a phobic object, the inhuman stain the Israeli police imagined him to be; his innocence is ironically secured now that he is dead—rendered an absolute victim—and alchemically turned "white": *a human Palestinian is a dead/whitened Palestinian.*

If political Zionists and right-wing nationalists are undisturbed by Israel's rule of force, Palestinophobia, and shamelessly continue to engage in fearmongering by casting Arab Israelis/Palestinians as enemies from within and without—endlessly peddling in Orientalist stereotypes—liberal Zionists disavow this reality, and ignore the state's racial practices, whenever they insist that they want "peace" with the Palestinians in exchange for nonviolence: we're tired of air raids; please no more rockets into Israel, no more Gaza wars, goes their public plea to the other side. Liberal Zionists feel ashamed and cringe when they hear the ultranationalist Ayelet Shaked speak about Palestinians in genocidal terms. As former justice minister, Shaked infamously endorsed the perspective that Palestinian mothers and children are fair game in the defense of Israel, favorably quoting on her Facebook page the late Uri Elitzur, a speechwriter and adviser to Netanyahu:

> They are all enemy combatants, and their blood shall be on all their heads. Now this also includes the mothers of the martyrs, who send them to hell with flowers and kisses. They should follow their sons, nothing would be more just. They should go, as should the physical homes in which they raised the snakes. Otherwise, more little snakes will be raised there.[102]

For liberal Zionists, Shaked becomes the face of the intolerant/authoritarian Zionist,[103] the excessive racist who doesn't speak for them or *their* Israel. But this "moral" reaction creates a distinction without substance. In practice, liberal Zionists actually enjoy and benefit from Shaked's brazen Palestinophobia.[104] She distracts from their complicity with the settler system, from their shared practice of "altruicide": the constitution of the Palestinian "not as similar to oneself but as a menacing object from which one must be protected or escape, or which must simply be destroyed if it cannot be subdued."[105] Liberal Zionists purport to be different (when you think of Israel, identify with us, not Shaked), since they are not after a "Greater Israel"; they are anti-settlements and their endorsement of the two-state solution signals that they are not racists or even settlers (since settler colonialism belongs to the past; modern Israel is different—its citizens, on the whole, are not allergic to Palestinians, etc.). In fact, liberal Zionists assure Western powers that Israel wants peace. But what kind of peace do they really want? It is a peace understood as the absence of disruptions, the suspension of anti-colonial struggle (armed or otherwise); it is a form of peace that serves the interests of the occupiers and their staunch supporters, because a "peaceful" condition obfuscates the nonspectacular reality of the Occupation; it distracts from the numbing "hyperregulation" governing Palestinian mobility, as Saree Makdisi describes it, matched with the life-draining reality of "curfews, checkpoints, roadblocks, ditches, walls, fences, closures, whose very randomness helps keep Palestinians off-balance."[106] Signaling Jewish liberalism—a purported openness to the Indigenous Other—illustrates what Tuck and Yang describe as "settler moves to innocence": "those strategies or positionings that attempt to relieve the settler of feelings of guilt or responsibility without giving up land or power or privilege, without having to change much at all."[107] Liberal, "woke" Zionists feel absolved of any responsibility for state violence/terror. They can go on ignoring the debased condition of everyday Palestinians, willfully oblivious to what is happening to the Natives when nothing (spectacular) is happening. Worse, this move gives liberal Zionists a surplus enjoyment in hating the haters, which, also, casts them as "good" for "feeling bad"[108] while narrowing what is objectionable about Jewish exceptionalism.

Edward Said rightly challenged the validity of the distinction between liberal and political Zionisms, between dovish and militaristic Zionisms. The former's "views are routinely aired in the western media as representative of the peace camp, and do a brilliant job of concealing their real views of Palestinians (not so different from Likud's) beneath a carpet of conscience-rending, anguished prose."[109] For liberal Zionists, the "Palestinian problem" is a '67 problem. The reality of the Occupation more or less exhausts what is wrong with Israel. The ethnic cleansing of 1948 is whitewashed, rarely factoring into any form of accountability. Zionism as a settler-colonial project, which firmly aligns its leaders and supporters with Western imperial powers, is never acknowledged.[110] Rather, liberal Zionists are keen to underscore how Zionism was at its origin a democratic project, a national liberation movement: Jews fleeing anti-Semitism in Europe for a safer and better life in historic Palestine. As victims themselves, they profess sympathy for the Palestinian people. They feel bad about their mistreatment. But this gesture of symmetry—"we (Israelis and Palestinians) are all victims of trauma"—is ideologically dubious, a more sophisticated move to innocence, a variant of "we are all colonized," which as Tuck and Yang point out, "may be a true statement but is deceptively embracive and vague, its inference: 'None of us are settlers.'"[111] The peace-loving guise of liberal Zionists protects them from the label of settlers. They want justice without justice. They want peace without sacrificing Jewish privilege, that is, without confronting its racist and hierarchical logic. They want change (better treatment of Palestinians) without actual change (don't ask me to give up power, accept the right of return, renounce my Jewish privilege, and de-Zionize Israel). Liberal Zionists don't want to see themselves on the wrong side of history, supporting a state that is in the process of losing its global legitimacy. As Teodora Todorova notes, "disavowal [is] one of the key characteristics of settler psychology."[112] But liberal Zionists, of course, know about Palestinophobia—they are quite cognizant of institutional racism, that Palestinians/Arabs as a class are systematically racialized, demonized, and neglected by the Jewish state—but they act as though they did not know that anti-Palestinian prejudice and discrimination structure and give coherence to the Jewish state, a state that must perpetually wage a "demographic war" to maintain and protect its Jewish majority (especially from the Palestinian right of return).

In their everyday mode of existence, liberal Zionists believe that the problem lies squarely in the "visible" violence, in the type of violence that interrupts the socioeconomic order, the habitual routine of Israeli Jews. The absence of flare-ups with Hamas animates and sustains the belief in Israel's legitimacy; it justifies pride in the nation, that is, in the idea of a pristine, democratic Jewish state. This understanding of the conflict, sustained by fetishist disavowal or willful amnesia, resolves the inconsistencies of liberal Zionists and keeps Palestinians in their subordinate place. Woke Zionism leaves unquestioned the ubiquitous, life-draining, and naturalized violence of the repressive Occupation, and the colonial settler framework that underpins it, unacknowledging, in turn, the full terror and implications of the ongoing un-mattering and social death of Palestinians.

Unsettling the Settler's House, or the Anti-Colonial Fight for Recognition

The liberal approach to Palestinian Indigeneity fails to change the coordinates of the Occupation. Worse, its intervention reinforces rather than alleviates the socioeconomic and cultural domination of Palestinians. The liberal attitude coexists with Zionist consciousness of Palestinian Indigeneity. And for this reason, the liberal script has been disastrous for Palestinians, freezing them in a state of "subaltern humanity."[113] With *Palestinian consciousness of Palestinian Indigeneity* a new optic emerges. Standing in front of the Zionist/Western gaze, the Palestinian asks: "Am I, in truth, what people say I am?"[114] We shift from the reasoning *about* Palestinians to the reasoning *of* Palestinians.[115]

If the reasoning about Palestinians produces the Indigenous population as primitive, anti-Semitic, and violent (and whose violence is condemned as illegitimate and irrational), the reasoning of Palestinians contests the framing of resistance (self-defense, returning fire) as a series of hateful terrorist acts. The former considers anything short of absolute compliance a threat, a provocation; the latter adopts an anti-colonial vantagepoint: *Zionist settler colonialism is the problem*. And Palestinian violence is deemed by no means irrational but a form of resistance to domination, a stubborn survival strategy in the face of colonial erasure, the incessant Zionist desire to transform Palestinians into a vanished or vanishing people. Reclaiming Palestinian violence also jams the Western liberal framework that makes (the recognition of) Palestinian humanity contingent on the colonized's unconditional embrace of nonviolence.[116] As Jamil Khader recalls, this Western demand is not unproblematic because "the right to resist an occupying force . . . is enshrined in international law."[117] Liberals may be enamored with the ethics of nonviolence, but living under settler colonialism impacts your options of resistance so that, at times, the path of nonviolence appears less as a valiant moral stance than a narcissistic liberal privilege, the privilege of choosing nonviolence over violence.[118] The Native's *unqualified* claims to humanity and nonviolence will never dismantle the settler's house.[119]

Indigenous reason returns us, again, to the settler-colonial situation. To paraphrase Max Horkheimer: *Whoever is not willing to talk about settler colonialism should also keep quiet about armed struggle*.[120] Those who are not willing to talk critically about Israel's egregious policies of dispossession should also keep quiet about the form that Palestinian resistance takes. From the vantage point of anti-colonialism, Palestinian violence is both a bold message of noncompliance and an inventive source of psychic replenishment—a view of rehumanization that eschews moralization.[121] As Fanon pointedly observes: "at the individual level, violence is a cleansing force. It rids the colonized of their inferiority complex, of their passive and despairing attitude. It emboldens them, and restores their self-confidence."[122] This is why, as Lara Sheehi and Stephen Sheehi note, we should not collapse the violence of the occupied with that of the occupier: "Equating the violence of the Israeli state with violence as a means of liberation is an unethical equivocation that erases the difference in conditions between the colonizer and the colonized, settler and native."[123] Palestinian consciousness is through and through combative;[124] it yearns to remedy colonial devastation and rehabilitate the image of the Native beyond its designation as infrahuman. Indigenous reason, with or without armed struggle, is an ontological reset; it constitutes "a *declaration of identity*,"[125] an identity at odds with the Western/Zionist one imputed to the Palestinian people.

As Edward Said pointed out, Zionism looks quite different when the perspective shifts to its victims, when Palestinians are no longer *narrated* but become the *narrators* of their tragic history. Claiming Palestinian Indigeneity announces and enacts their permission to narrate, to reframe the ways in which they have been wronged by Israel, whose own permission to narrate—to tell their story of exceptional suffering—has been key in its colonial success, immunizing it from significant critique from Western powers. It allows for a retailing of "Zionism's *other* aspects."[126] Indigenous reason now serves as an antidote to native *epistemicide*: the silencing of Palestinians, denial of their agency and barring of their involvement in any hermeneutical endeavor and official knowledge production.[127] "The reclaimed visibility of my people,"[128] as Palestinian historian and essayist Elias Sanbar puts it, exemplifies this mission and desire for a Palestinianness set against the dehumanized image engineered by Zionism. This anti-colonial narrative restores native dignity and delivers Palestinians (back) to humanity. Simply put, the tools of Indigenous reason are put in the service of rehumanizing the Palestinian people. Anti-colonialism, then, aspires to an alternative humanism, promising a rebirth for Fanon's "wretched of the earth."

In foregrounding settler colonialism, Indigenous reason—the reason of the wretched—contests the colonial order of things, preaches epistemic disobedience, and restages the native Palestinian as a contesting subject, no longer functioning as the screen onto which Western/Zionist settler consciousness projects its racist desires and fears about the Orient and Arabs:

> the place where writing seeks to exorcise the demon of the first narrative and the structure of subjection within it, the place where writing struggles to evoke, save, activate, and reactualize original experience (tradition) and find the truth of the self no longer outside of the self but standing on its own ground.[129]

Palestinian consciousness re-Indigenizes the Palestinian people; they were here before the Israeli state. It proceeds to redefine Palestinianness on its own terms by reappropriating Palestinians' self-image, untainted by the gaze and judgment of Zionist settlers. This is indeed the other side of Indigenous reason. It boldly summons an Indigeneity recovered/fashioned in opposition to Zionism's racist assemblages, jamming the social processes that invent and isolate the essential, native Palestinian (dwelling outside the Green Line), as infrahuman, expendable, marked for killing or injuring. If Zionist consciousness defaces the native population, disfiguring them as a sight/site of abjections, Palestinian consciousness reframes Indigeneity as desirable and a locus of agency. It aims to rescue Palestinian humanity, to free Palestinians from their Zionist enclosure. Palestinian citizens of Israel pursue this struggle as a *cultural* fight for equality, calling for a better biopolitics, better management of their lives. Amal Jamal, for example, stresses the relevance of the category of Indigeneity for Israeli Palestinians "because it provides a vocabulary beyond conventional liberal citizenship rights with which they can articulate their demands."[130] Palestinians in the Occupied Territories, for their part, strive to survive, to avoid getting killed or maimed by Israel's necropolitics as they struggle to remove the colonizers from the land taken after "The Six-Day War" in 1967 and to politically reclaim the space for their collective sovereignty. Hamas and the PA struggle in different ways to achieve the same end: a Free Palestine. The former engages mostly in a politics of refusal, adopting a hostile attitude toward its occupiers; the latter plays the Western game of diplomacy, and maintains security collaboration with the occupying force, abiding by the terms to which the Palestinian leadership agreed in the Oslo Accords, in the cruel hope that Israel will deliver on its part, on the Oslo principle of "land for peace."

Palestinian consciousness of Palestinian Indigeneity thus appears split: one narrative fights for the rewards of recognition and equality, while the other yearns for national independence and collective sovereignty. The former operates within an apartheid apparatus, pursuing its reform if not overcoming; the latter adopts a settler-colonial framework of analysis, seeking to drive out the occupying presence. But this split distracts from what they have in common: both imagine native remedy via the logic of the nation-state. Recognition of Palestinians within a Jewish state will always by definition be qualified. Racial inequality is part and parcel of the Zionist social order: can the Israeli state be both Jewish *and* democratic? Indigenous reason here tacitly accepts the idea of a Jewish and democratic Israel. As a "democracy," Israel is redeemable; it holds the power to end segregation (internal racism), halt institutional state violence, and be more inclusive by extending full rights to its "Arab" citizens. Israel can reform itself from *within*: it must promote Arab assimilation and integration, and reverse its apartheid policies, which are doing harm to the idea/l of citizenship. Basically, ending Israel's apartheid logic is good for Jews and Arabs alike. No need for Indigenous anti-colonial nationalism, then, if Indigenous reason can restore dignity and deliver Arab rights—and thus move from "separate and unequal" to "separate but equal" (despite what we know of this dubious principle's history in the United States).

On a first read, Indigenous anti-colonial nationalism gets a strong endorsement from Palestinians in the Occupied Territories. The remedy to Palestinian injury does not operate along "the axis of inclusion/exclusion."[131] Inclusion is not the answer to the situation of West Bankers, Gazans, and Jerusalemites. Palestinians living under Occupation are after true sovereignty, not inclusion or recognition. There is no settler Occupation with dignity or a human face. Settler colonialism is the problem, not how it is being managed. As Chickasaw scholar Jodi Byrd perspicaciously notes, settler narratives of inclusion, the liberal push for a politics of recognition, systematically fail "to grapple with the fact that such discourses further reinscribe the original colonial injury."[132] The Indigenous claim for land repatriation and the liberal fight against racism or anti-Blackness in the United States are fundamentally "incommensurable."[133] But here again Palestinian nationalism purporting to break from the liberal axis of inclusion/exclusion ironically ends up following a colonial path when it is realized and realizable only in the would-be two-state solution. Palestinians are caught up in the prison house of the nation-state. To be sure, the Palestine Liberation Organization (PLO) did not naively embrace the two-state solution; its leaders acknowledged that their concessions were significant, that the two-state solution constituted a great compromise. The late Saeb Erekat, who served as secretary general of the PLO, wrote: "We recognized Israel over 78 percent of historic Palestine in what has been the most significant concession made by any party in the context of Middle East peace. To embrace the two-state solution on the 1967 border was the Palestinian adoption of an international position."[134] An Indigenous reason nurtured by the dream of "a time before the settler," that is, a Palestine without Zionist settlers, is willing to limit collective sovereignty to one-third of Palestinians, to those dwelling inside the '67 borders (the West Bank, the Gaza Strip, and East Jerusalem), dividing the Indigenous people of a future state from both their kin in Israel and refugees whose internationally sanctioned right of return Israel continues to belligerently deny.

Haidar Eid perceptively calls the two-state solution the "opium of the Palestinian people."[135] The two-state solution is not only an ideological drug that distorts Palestinian consciousness of Palestinian Indigeneity, it also, and more important, attests to a real suffering. Accordingly, a demystification of the two-state solution is of limited value if the conditions for the suffering are left unaddressed. The two-state solution has been treating *symptoms* ever since the Oslo process in 1993 (by giving Palestinians hope for a better future), but what is needed is a "de-Osloisation of the Palestinian mind,"[136] which would clear the space for a genuine solution to emerge, one that would reorient us to the *causes* of Palestinian misery and hopelessness: Zionist settler colonialism and Israel's apartheid logic. Such de-Osloisation is visible in the Palestinian reaction to the 2021 Gaza war, *Operation Guardian of the Walls*. The world witnessed an unexpected "Unity Intifada" among Palestinians. Frustrated, angry, and defiant Palestinian protesters in Israel proper stood unified in solidarity with their brethren in Occupied Palestine, against the ongoing Nakba. As Palestinian-American congresswoman Rashida Tlaib reminds us in a pointed tweet: "The Nakba never ended. From Jaffa in 1948 to Sheikh Jarrah, Jerusalem today, we must recognize the forced displacement and violent dispossession faced by Palestinians for over 70 years."[137]

The two-state solution vision of "land returned, identity regained" leaves additional questions unanswered. Aside from the serious problem of fragmenting its people, the other Palestinians that Indigenous reason sidelines, what role do economic structures play in the repatriation, restitution, and rehabilitation of Palestinian Indigeneity? Yellowknives Dene scholar Glen Coulthard supplements the anti-colonial struggle for land and independence with a strong anti-capitalist sentiment: "For Indigenous nations to live, capitalism must die."[138] The same holds true for Indigenous Palestinians. As Noura Erakat observes: "To adequately remedy institutionalized discrimination and subjugation, reformed state institutions should also be imbued with an ethos of socioeconomic dignity for all its citizens and residents."[139] The fight against capitalism, however, is not undertaken in isolation or withdrawal but in universalizing the Palestinian plight.

Here we have to abandon the classic Marxist category of the proletariat and its exclusive identification with the white working class. To take up the Palestinian question is thus to "trouble" the traditional subject of the revolution. I agree with Žižek that we have to look elsewhere for revolutionary subjects: "a 'predestined' revolutionary subject,"[140] as in the days of Marx, is not an option. We need to turn to those who are systematically excluded, disprivileged, and racialized by society's laws and norms, falling outside the liberal and humanist umbrella. They occupy what Žižek dubs a "proletarian position."[141] What we have now are "different *proletarian positions*. It means those people who are deprived of their substance, like ecological victims, psychological victims, and, especially, excluded victims of racism, and so on."[142]

This account of the proletarian position jars with Mignolo's decolonial suspicion of the Marxist critique:

> Class consciousness means a "critical consciousness," which like the one generated by colonial difference and the colonial wound (e.g., critical border thinking), generates, in the first case, projects of *emancipation* and, in the second, projects of *liberation*. However, in Marx and in the Marxist tradition, the idea of "class consciousness" hides the fact that the paradigmatic model of the proletarian is white, male, European.[143]

If Marxist critical consciousness is still compromised by a latent Eurocentrism, then it not only fails to deliver on its full political potential, but compounds and prolongs the subordination of Indigenous and disenfranchised peoples. Žižek's formulation, however, changes the ontological make-up of the proletariat, which is now multiple and precisely at odds with its reduction to white, male, European subjects. But Mignolo would surely not be satisfied with a mere update regarding who counts as a subject of the revolution if the main target of the critique remains global capitalism as opposed to coloniality (the afterlife of colonialism[144]). A focus on capitalism puts the focus back on modernity and its vaunted legacy. For Mignolo, this critical orientation toward modernity—as an unfinished or redeemable project—can only "keep on reproducing coloniality."[145] The Left's championing of communism discards non-European ways of being: "there cannot be only one solution simply because there are many ways of being, which means of thinking and doing. Communism is an option and not an abstract universal."[146] Mignolo insists that capitalism is *not* an unavoidable problem (to which communism is the solution), but a Western leftist obsession, and that one can, in fact, fight against "the necessity of war," the logic of "success and competition which engender corruption and selfishness," and pursue the goals of "harmony" and "the plenitude of life" without effectively ending capitalism.[147] But Mignolo's ideals of "harmony" and "plenitude of life," as Žižek rightly notes, are empty abstractions lacking any content and can lend themselves too easily to ideological manipulation, mobilized to obfuscate society's social antagonism.[148] It is also unclear how affirming a non-European way of life or a decolonial project of liberation actually shields you from the tentacles of global capitalism. Neoliberalism is not a Western problem that Palestinians and other non-European communities can simply opt out of. To believe that Indigenous peoples can is to peddle the ideological fantasy of a faultless or frictionless world untouched by the evils of capitalism. In any case, Occupied Palestine is clearly already feeling neoliberalism's debilitating encroachments; any genuine alternative to the national frame cannot be seriously entertained without reckoning with the circulation and globalization of capital in Palestine/Israel.

To be sure, Marxists have, on the whole, neglected both settler colonialism and racial slavery, treating them as preconditions or historical moments of "primitive accumulation"[149] in the emergence of capitalism. Against this predominant view of capitalism as unfolding in a linear temporal fashion, Coulthard importantly reorients the Marxist critique back to colonial dispossession—land grabs, extractivism—in order to recast it as an ongoing and urgent problem. Colonial dispossession is a structural problem rather than a series of discrete events that (temporarily) incite media attention, gaining the status of a spectacle.[150] Dispossession is by no means a *relic* of the past nor a minority concern but intrinsic to "racial capitalism"[151] and its reproduction, making the life of both (Indigenous peoples and capitalism) inextricably and antagonistically linked. Against Mignolo's decoupling of this link, in a way that would preserve the existence of both (Indigenous communities free of capitalism and Western capitalism), I want to attend more closely to the ways the former wages its collective struggle against the latter.

What Palestinians, other Indigenous communities, and Black folks have in common is that they occupy a "*proletarian* position, the position of the 'part of no-part.'"[152] They are the "'supernumerary' elements" of their respective societies: "those who belong to a situation without having a specific 'place' in it; they are included but have no part to play in the social edifice."[153] Since their interests are not predetermined by their positionality, when these subjects seek to remedy a wrong (inequality, for example), they speak to universal concerns. "Precisely because Palestinians have been reduced to this undead position in the global capitalist system," Khader notes, "Palestinians can be said to represent the truth of the system, its constitutive injustice and inequality. In their inherent exclusion and abjection, therefore, Palestinians can be considered, in Žižek's words, the 'very site of political universality.'"[154]

Indeed, when Said expresses his motto "equality or nothing,"[155] he never limits it to the wronged Palestinians alone or fetishized Indigenous grievance: the call for egalitarian justice, "equality or nothing," is precisely *open to all*. He follows it, in fact, with "for Arabs and Jews." Palestinians must meet the challenges of political justice, and *not* exceptionalize themselves and take refuge in Palestinocentrism: "If one people enjoys a right of return, the other one must also. Otherwise the conflict continues—in the real interests of no one at all. No one, not even those who seem to be profiting in the short run."¹⁵⁶ But Indigenous reason in its practice is prone to foster racial forms of belonging, and to bolster exclusionary and separatist mindsets—"to *secession* from the world"¹⁵⁷—which ultimately benefit and unwittingly reproduce the settler-colonial matrix.

In arguing that Indigenous Palestinians embody a proletarian position, I propose to recast what *Palestinian consciousness of Palestinian Indigeneity* might look like. The wager: for the struggle of collective freedom to become truly transformative—and effectively break with liberal/colonial scripts and their authorized social relations—Palestinians cannot content themselves with the phantasmatic and nostalgic lure of an atavistic "time before the settler,"¹⁵⁸ absent a confrontation with the global economy and racial capitalism (most notably, the structural role of anti-Blackness in the formation of modernity's human subject and its claims of sovereignty). As a counter to the ideological traps of rootedness and purity (a life prior to or free from the trauma of Zionism), this book reads Palestinian Indigeneity dialectically in an effort to dislodge the current impasse between the settler and the Native, the Jew and the Palestinian, moving beyond identitarian solutions. To paraphrase Fanon, *the white Israeli is locked in his whiteness. The Palestinian in his Indigeneity*.¹⁵⁹ Whence the need to decolonize the mind and rethink anew Palestinian Indigeneity.

"Decolonizing the mind" is not a mere metaphor/symbol, something that should give way to demands for actual/material change. Tuck and Yang mistakenly downplay the political force of the Fanonian injunction from *The Wretched of the Earth*: "Fanon told us in 1963 that decolonizing the mind is the first step, not the only step toward overthrowing colonial regimes.... Until stolen land is relinquished, critical consciousness does not translate into action that disrupts settler colonialism."¹⁶⁰ This is obviously true: critical consciousness is, in of itself, *insufficient* to end settler colonialism. But Tuck and Yang go further, repeatedly questioning its importance or emancipatory value by degrading it to a "first step" among more important ones in the project of decolonization. Fanon would hardly characterize decolonizing the mind a "first step," as if once accomplished the colonized can move to the more serious matter of land repatriation. On the contrary, we might say that decolonizing the mind is Indigenous reason at its rigorous best: the self is at "war against consciousness";¹⁶¹ self-critical/self-violent and transformative—the latter because of the former. Decolonizing the mind complicates the relationality between the Native and the settler, so that the problem of occupation is not only located or embodied in the latter but in the former as well.

First of all, decolonizing the mind registers the degree to which symbolic violence degrades the *ontology* of the Indigenous population. Indeed, it is not at all clear that decolonizing the mind is a metaphor. Or if it is a metaphor, it is a metaphor that discloses something about the powers of language, and exposes the limits of a liberal anti-racist critique that remains at the representational level—believing that words affect *thinking*, but not *being* itself. In the struggle against racial domination, racist *words* must be given their full material weight. Words penetrate bodies; they produce abject monsters. This is Hortense Spillers's point in her powerful rewriting of an old schoolyard adage: "Sticks and stones *might* break our bones, but words will most certainly *kill* us."[162] Decolonizing the mind—refusing the settler's symbolic rules and demands—must be understood here as a materialist or ontological project. It is not enough to reject the settler's ways. Excising the colonizer's ideology from the colonized's mind/being involves the dialectical and arduous task of undoing what has been done *to* the Native, what has been produced *in* the Native. For this reason, overcoming Israeli anti-Arab prejudice and Palestinophobia cannot be achieved by a retreat into one's (restored/revived) cultural particularity. Though the affective comfort of identity, of feeling at home, ought not to be ignored or underestimated, this culturalization of Indigeneity—the territorialization of Palestinianness—always risks prolonging the settler's essentialization of the Natives, homogenizing and sealing the latter in their ethno-religious identity. Decolonizing the mind is a vital counter to this temptation of authenticity, symbolized by the racist desire for a Palestine exclusively for the Palestinian people (alongside the equally racist desire for a Jewish state exclusively for the Jewish people, or simply Israel); it is an act of self-violence, a "self-beating"[163] of sorts, which begins with a disruption of the Native's affective investments in rooted identity, in self-identity: in what the settler has enjoyed but systematically denied the Indigenous population.

Coulthard, following Taiaiake Alfred and Leanne Simpson,[164] offers an alternative—and a decidedly *non-dialectical*—relation to one's past, involving doubling-down on tradition, recasting it as "self-conscious traditionalism"[165] and opting "to 'turn away' from the assimilative reformism of the liberal recognition"[166] and its complicity with capitalism writ large. Culture is an archive and endless source of/for "Indigenous resurgence."[167] Countering a sanctioned politics of recognition with a politics of refusal might weaken capitalism's hold on Indigenous communities—halting its dispossession of land and extractivist logic, and exposing its complicity with the liberal white state (the promise of change, without real change)—but would it actually bring about its global demise? To recall Coulthard's bold declaration: "For Indigenous nations to live, capitalism must die." Which he follows with: "for capitalism to die, we must actively participate in the construction of Indigenous alternatives to it."[168] Yes, but can Indigenous nations truly live if capitalism thrives everywhere else in the world (assuming one can even manage to kill it at home via sustainable and self-sufficient Indigenous economies)? Doesn't global capitalism benefit if Indigenous communities keep their anti-capitalism, their nonexploitative alternatives, local?[169] Jamming "the interests of settler capital,"[170] Coulthard's libidinal investment in "Indigenous practices of the past,"[171] discloses here the limits of Indigenous reason. Psychic investment in these practices is not *a priori* problematic (they can, of course, be a source of pride or invention—compelling us, in an important fashion, to think culture *with* economics, the "mode of production as a *mode of life*"[172]) but they are also all-too-prone to fetishization, *locking* communities in their (anti-capitalist) Indigeneity.[173]

To mobilize the Palestinian cause, national belonging, polity, and insurgency itself must be imagined *otherwise*. Palestinian Indigeneity must be both defended (it is not backward, primitive, underdeveloped, etc.) and reinvented by infusing it with a diasporic and transnational sensibility. I echo here Fanon's call for a more generous affective and identificatory field:

> I am a man, and I have to rework the world's past from the very beginning. I am not just responsible for the slave revolt in Saint Domingue. Every time a man has brought victory to the dignity of the spirit, every time a man has said no to an attempt to enslave his fellow man, I have felt a sense of solidarity with his act.[174]

Fanon kept his distance from the lures of identity and sameness, always attentive to the wretched's cries of injustice. As Bashir Abu-Manneh argues, "For Fanon, ending racism and exclusion had to be done not through reifying oppressed identities and celebrating national or ethnic particularism, but through common struggle for freedom and equality."[175] A care for another ought not to be limited to your putative kin, nor prioritized over and above any other engagements. Palestinian Indigeneity is not only what/where you are (a fixed/rooted state of being), it is also what you do (becoming/relationality); becoming Indigenous—Indigeneity as an antiracist assemblage—is "born out of the sites and processes of struggles that Palestinians in different locations and times are and have been inhabiting."[176] The struggles that Palestinians inhabit are multitude. In this light, to stand in solidarity with the Palestinian cause does not entail an exercise in identitarian identification. If there is an affective call in the Palestinian cause, which I believe there is, it is one that identifies with the Palestinians' emphatic *no*, that affirms the inscrutable refusal to be subjugated and bears witness to the emancipatory force behind this political act of indocility: Indigenous resurgence as such! This staging of the Palestinian cause clears a space for the universal, for political innovation and a reimagining of universality as the possibility for cross-racial/revolutionary solidarity—as an emancipatory project of "the repressed, the exploited and suffering, the 'parts of no-part' of every culture . . . com[ing] together in a shared struggle."[177] As both a call for Indigenous resurgence and an enactment of it, the Palestinian cause manifests itself in unexpected ways and places. The spontaneous support of activists in Occupied Palestine for the Black Lives Matter (BLM) movement—along with BLM's reciprocal gesture—attests to this miraculous (im)possibility, where politics exceeds any faction's immediate goals.[178] These Palestinians displayed to the world that the Palestinian cause is not limited to Palestinian matters. This Black-Palestinian solidarity in the making—this "universality-in-becoming"[179]—disrupted and is disrupting a futurology grounded in narcissistic identity politics and the cynical calculation of self-interest. For the Palestinian cause is global or it is not.

The chapters that follow make the case that the Palestinian cause, in its incitement to solidarity, is a universal proposition. In Chapter 1, "Look, a Palestinian!," I explore the Zionist gaze and its devasting impact on Palestinian bodies. Analogous, but not identical, to the experience famously related by Fanon—who describes how the white gaze obliterates his very being, barring him from the category of the human (the subject, par excellence) and reducing him to an inert object—to be (un)seen as Palestinian is to be on the receiving end of a racialized colonial logic that determines your presence as an existential threat to Israel and Jewish Israelis. From the Zionist vantage point, being Palestinian is always already a crime: to be guilty of "Palestinianness." Palestinian Indigeneity is a cause for suspicion and dehumanization: witness the Israeli military checkpoints, buffer zones, Apartheid Wall.

At the same time, Black Studies critics emerging from the Afropessimist movement have cautioned against this analogy between Blackness and non-Black people of color, insisting on their incommensurability. Afropessimists warn against the tendency to see a common cause between Blacks and Palestinians, as if they are resisting the same thing. They underscore the necessity of sustaining the difference between Blacks and Palestinians not only because it is wrong to collapse the two (different histories, different enemies) but also because it obfuscates a consideration of conscious and unconscious Palestinian anti-Blackness. Against Afropessimism's Manichean reason, which insists on the Black/non-Black divide, the chapter argues that what jams the gaze of Jewish supremacy is not an intervention that serves to promote a zero-sum approach to the struggle against racial injustice: Indigeneity or Blackness? Two competing narratives of social death? No, the challenge is to see how Indigeneity *and* Blackness are both ensnared in a multifaceted matrix of racialization. The fate of one is invariably dependent on that of the other.

Chapter 2, "Thinking under Occupation," delves into the challenges of innovation when Palestinians are silenced, denied agency, and excluded from knowledge production: when, that is, *they are cast as the known, not the knowers*. Decoloniality, in its endeavors to empower native cultures and make Indigenous knowledges visible, relevant, and comprehensible, seems well poised to speak to Palestinians' needs and desires, safeguarding their Indigeneity against Israel's hegemonic narrative. Decoloniality rightly casts Zionism as complicit with the "dark side of modernity," aligning it with coloniality and the racial domination of non-Europeans. This chapter takes up Mignolo's decolonial thesis, "I am where I think," which significantly departs from Descartes's abstract formulation, "I think therefore I am," and assesses its appeal, relevance, and ultimately limits for understanding Palestinian identity.

Decoloniality lays out a path forward for Indigenous Palestinians. The imperative is to delink from coloniality and reconstitute, or relink to, precolonial ways of thinking and living. And yet decoloniality's response to the Palestinian question tends to fetishize the local, to homogenize and romanticize the Natives' precolonial roots. It imagines the spaces of Indigeneity as untouched by coloniality, conceiving of a Palestinian identity freed from Zionist enclosure. Against decoloniality's nativist penchant and frictionless account of Indigenous identity/community, I turn to the notion of exile, as elaborated by Edward Said and Mourid Barghouti. Thinking Indigeneity with exile (and vice versa)—to conceive of them contrapuntally—is a way to resist the lures of both rootedness and abstraction.

Chapter 3, "*Ressentiment*/Paranoia," situates the affect of *ressentiment* and the mood or orientation of paranoia in the material reality of the Occupation. I do so in order to decouple Zionism's ideological pairing of *ressentiment* and paranoia with anti-Semitism. If the Zionist script constantly casts *ressentiment* and paranoia as defects of the Palestinian mind, I try to map an alternative meaning for both terms. In exploring Palestinian *ressentiment*, I first turn to Elia Suleiman's *Divine Intervention*, which stages Palestinian communities as full of friction and *ressentiment* coming not only from without (living under the Occupation) but also from within (living with fellow Palestinians). While Suleiman puts on full display the sickness of Palestinian communities—how the collective Indigenous body is striking at itself; how Palestinians are striking at their kin—*Divine Intervention*'s magical moments recast Palestinians as striking at their occupiers. Palestinian *ressentiment* breaks from its containment as an exclusively bitter affect, becoming the ground for what I call the "public use of *ressentiment*," akin to Kant's "public use of reason." The "public use of *ressentiment*" transmutes the existential suffering of Palestinians, transforming it into a collective moral feeling founded on the shared but unacceptable condition of exclusion and dispossession. The public of *ressentiment* situates this affect not within the personal realm of blame and hatred but the public sphere of anger and politics.

Next, I take up the possibility of an "anti-Zionist hermeneutic" that short-circuits the Zionist machinery reducing Palestinian paranoia to a manifestation of the eternal hatred of Jews. As a case study, I examine the so-called controversy regarding Jasbir Puar's talk at Vassar College about her ethnographic research in the West Bank. Her remark that some West Bankers believed that the Israeli government harvested Palestinian organs became a lightning rod (despite government officials' acknowledgment that the practice in question happened in the recent past). Some critics manufactured outrage, quickly accusing Puar of recycling and disseminating "blood libel," and manipulatively tying the "anti-Semitism" of the Left to a narrow and ideological-loaded understanding of Palestinian paranoia.

In Chapter 4, "Sovereignty," I address the desire for collective or national sovereignty that fuels the Palestinian struggle against settler colonialism. The return of land would in principle signal the end of the settler-colonial regime and the start of self-determination. In the contemporary scene, the idea of the two-state solution continues to enjoy wide support among Western powers, Arab neighbors, liberal Zionists, and the PA itself. Palestinian sovereignty appears exclusively legible through the paradigm of the two-state solution. But critics and activists have declared this solution both impossible and undesirable. The former because of the ongoing land grab by the Israeli government; the latter because it feeds a racist vision, a partition of the land based on ethnonationalist investments.

This chapter first critically unpacks the ideological appeal and affective spell of the two-state solution, captured in Bartlett Sher's film *Oslo*, which creates nostalgia for the Oslo Accords and the peace process. It then turns to Larissa Sansour's science-fiction short film, *Nation Estate*, for its staging of a dystopian and hopeless rendering of the two-state solution. Next, I take up binationalism as an ethico-political project that undertakes to imagine sovereignty differently.

If the concept of sovereignty serves both as a reminder of sovereignty's damning colonial genealogy and as a warning against Palestinians' ongoing complicity with neoliberalism's insatiable and perverse logic, which instrumentalizes humans and deprives them of their rights and protection, engendering, in turn, a new class of slaves, ~~sovereignty~~ interrogates its relation to the category of the human, and underscores the intricate labor of decolonization and abolition.

1

Look, a Palestinian!

Any act of defiance on our part is rejected outright. Unlike Mandela and King, we are Palestinian Arabs with an intrinsic tendency for terrorism.

—Haidar Eid[1]

Palestinianness occupies a space of ambivalence in Palestine/Israel. The Zionist gaze isolates the Palestinian body only to negate it and disavow it. The disavowal of Palestinianness is particularly true in Israel proper, where Palestinians face the challenges of living under a Zionist regime that structurally works to evacuate their being and reality. In the eyes of the Israeli government, the factual claim of Palestinian Indigeneity is seen as an existential threat, an obstacle to the ideological Zionist imperative of "blooming in the desert," an aim to be pursued either by subjecting Palestinians to a slow genocide in the Occupied Territories, or by counting 1948 Palestinians (the Nakba survivors) and their offspring in Israel, as "Arab Israelis," thus rhetorically effacing the very "Palestinianness" of its second- or third-class citizens; to become an Arab Israeli is therefore to symbolically die and disappear as a Palestinian. The first pursuit seeks to eliminate Indigenous Palestinians by incrementally dispossessing them of their land, killing or crippling them, making it so intolerable that they "self-transfer" to neighboring Arab states;[2] the latter proceeds by assimilating them to the Israeli nation-state, turning them into Israeli (de-Palestinized, de-nativized) citizens,[3] while simultaneously keeping them "separate and unequal," that is, not-quite-humans. In the Zionist order of things, Palestinians thus only scarcely count by not counting as Indigenous.

"Look, a Palestinian!" rhetorically captures the paradoxical gesture that the Zionist gaze performs: it names and recognizes the Other as Palestinian, thus de facto acknowledging Palestinians as Indigenous to the land, while simultaneously racializing and demonizing this menacing Other, depriving them of any resemblance to full-fledged humans. This move has much in common with the French/white gaze so powerfully analyzed by Fanon in the opening pages of "The Lived Experience of the Black Man," chapter 5 of *Black Skin, White Masks*. Commonality does not equal sameness, however. The lived experiences of racialized Palestinians in Occupied Palestine and Israel are *not* identical to those of Black Martinicans, like Fanon, living in the French Hexagon. At the same time, the lessons Fanon takes from his racist/racial interpellation can and do speak to global processes of racial differentiation and subject formation impacting other marginalized and colonized peoples.

Fanon's meditation focuses on a white child's utterance, "Look, a Negro!" (*Tiens, un nègre!*), at the sight of a Black man in the streets of Lyon, France—the phantasmatic scene of optical terror. Fanon recalls his ontological deflation in this moment. This utterance discloses a white world that bars Fanon from the category of the human—a category to which he affectively felt he belonged—and reduces him to an inert object, a being-in-the-midst-of-the-world. Fanon elaborates on what follows from his interpellation as a "Negro":

> The Negro is an animal, the Negro is bad, the Negro is wicked, the Negro is ugly; look, a Negro; the Negro is trembling, the Negro is trembling because he's cold, the small boy is trembling because he's afraid of the Negro, the Negro is trembling with cold, the cold that chills the bones, the lovely little boy is trembling because he thinks the Negro is trembling with rage, the little white boy runs to his mother's arms: "*Maman*, the Negro's going to eat me."[4]

Overdetermined by his surroundings, Fanon metamorphosizes into some*thing*, a threatening nonhuman being, an animality imputed with ill-intent and viciousness. A world separates what the child *thinks* Fanon is doing and what he *is* doing. What Fanon does in fact doesn't matter; his being is always already translated and defined. The "Negro" is a "nigger": "'Dirty nigger!' or simply, 'Look! A Negro!'"[5] Fanon finds no reprieve from this penetrating and devasting white gaze. As George Yancy observes, "it is a Sisyphean mode of existence."[6] The Black subject is condemned to dwell in a "zone of nonbeing,"[7] in what Lewis Gordon describes as a condition of "below-Otherness"[8]—a state in which recognition as remedy (election into subjectivity/humanity) is unavailable. All that is available is an intractable existence, a life of pure alienation.

"Look, a Palestinian!" names Palestinian interpellation. In using this phrase, I borrow and build on the Fanonian example. The utterance embodies and verbalizes the Zionist gaze: what Palestinians encounter daily at checkpoints; what Palestinian Israelis confront every day in their experience of institutionalized discrimination. "Look, a Palestinian!" confines the Palestinian to her otherness, her exclusion, confirming that she is out of place. Yet, unlike Fanon's "Look, a Negro!," "Look, a Palestinian!" does not shatter the originary illusion that she belongs.[9] Why? Palestinians in Israel and the Occupied Territories are all living under an apartheid regime. Unlike France, which endorses the abstract (= ideological) principle of universal equality but in practice privileges the rights of its white citizens, Israel segregates its citizens and is explicit in its elevation of Jewish lives above Palestinian/Arab lives. As Israeli human rights group B'Tselem observes, "One organizing principle lies at the base of a wide array of Israeli policies: advancing and perpetuating the supremacy of one group—Jews—over another—Palestinians."[10]

Palestinian citizens of Israel do not expect to be hailed differently; they hardly see themselves as full citizens. Rather, they understand themselves as always already disprivileged. And while the Israeli government never misses an opportunity to remind the West that it is the only democracy in the Middle East (and that it thus upholds the values of the universal), its message at home is quite different, increasingly placating the identitarian desires of its far-right religious extremists. Indeed, the Israeli state has no problem brutishly flaunting its Jewishness, with Jewish chauvinism reaching its apogee in the Knesset's passing of the 2018 Nation-State Law, whose basic principles are:

- The land of Israel is the historical homeland of the Jewish people, in which the state of Israel was established.
- The state of Israel is the national home of the Jewish people, in which it fulfills its natural, cultural, religious, and historical right to self-determination.
- The right to exercise national self-determination in the state of Israel is unique to the Jewish people.[11]

While Palestinian citizens of Israel can vote and some are even members of Israel's legislative body, the Knesset—a minimal requirement for maintaining at least the appearance that a state is democratic—these rights are strongly curtailed by the fact that Israel is defined by its Jewishness and its exclusion of Palestinians. Adalah (the Legal Center for Arab Minority Rights in Israel) puts it succinctly:

> Israel never sought to assimilate or integrate the Palestinian population, treating them as second-class citizens and excluding them from public life and the public sphere. The state practiced systematic and institutionalized discrimination in all

areas, such as land dispossession and allocation, education, language, economics, culture, and political participation.[12]

Political representation from racialized minority communities does not in itself dismantle systematic racism. Let us not forget, as Cornel West reminds us, that the Black Lives Matter movement emerged "under a Black president, Black attorney general and Black homeland security cabinet member" in the United States.[13] The American phantasm of upward mobility does not really have an analog in Israel. Palestinians serving in the Knesset are first and foremost Nakba *survivors*, not Palestinians living the Israeli dream!

"Look, a Palestinian!" puts Palestinian Israelis back in their place;[14] it designates and secures their position as outsiders on their own land (and, of course, for the far-right settlers and Zionists committed to a "Greater Israel," these settler-colonial principles also cover the biblical land of *Judea and Samaria*). Yancy rightly draws attention to "perlocutionary power" of "Look, a Negro!" to "incite violence, violence filled with white desire and bloodlust";[15] the utterance solicits or even provokes a sadistic call and response: "Call: 'Look, a Negro!' Response: 'Rape the black bitch!' Call: 'Look, a Negro!' Response: 'Get a rope!' Call: 'Rape!' Response: 'Castrate the nigger!'"[16] Zionist interpellation is motivated by a similar sadistic hunger to crush the Native's will. Call: "Look, a Palestinian!" Response: "Humiliate her!"[17] Call "Look, a Palestinian!" Response: "Go to Gaza!" Call: "Look, a Palestinian!" Response: "Holocaust denier!" Call: "Look, a Palestinian!" Response: "Dirty terrorist!" Call: "Look, a Palestinian!" Response: "This is our home." Call: "Look, a Palestinian!" Response: "Death to Arabs!" Call: "Look, a Palestinian!" Response: "May your village burn!"[18]

If Blacks are fantasized as "cannibals" hungry for white meat, Palestinians are conceived of as "terrorists"; they can't help themselves, because they are driven by an "intrinsic tendency for terrorism," as Haidar Eid puts it. Interpellated as bloodthirsty killers, Palestinians are imagined as lying-in wait for the opportunity to massacre Israeli Jews—*because* they are Jews, which is to say that Palestinian violence is (mis)construed as being primarily an expression of anti-Semitism (resistance to neocolonial domination and dispossession does not enter the picture). "Look, a Palestinian!" serves a pedagogical function: it is part and parcel of Zionist inculcation, learning about Jewish privilege (nurturing the phantasm of an exclusive sovereignty) and the "Palestinian peril" (cultivating a "visceral racial imaginary" of Palestinians as a "collective enemy"[19]). It casts Jews as the site of normality (they are the measure of all things, the world refers back to them and what matters is their comfort within it) and Palestinians as an intractable problem (a demographic problem, a legitimation problem, an existential problem, etc.). So that when the "Palestinianness" of the Palestinians is acknowledged (when they are not subsumed under the abstract headings of "Arabs" or "Arab Israelis"), their Indigenous recognition is quickly neutralized (the Palestinians are not an equal, a genuine, civilized peace partner) by converting Palestinianness into a sufficient and inherent form of anti-Semitism/terrorism. *Dirty terrorist!* or simply, *Look! A Palestinian!*

What Palestinians and Black people have in common, then, is their subjection to perpetual surveillance, the experience of being despised and perceived as savage, as allegedly possessing a phobia-inducing character that disqualifies them as fully human. *Look, a Palestinian and a Negro!* Yet, while both are denied their humanity, and the protections that come with being human, the paths of redress for Palestinians and Blacks have converged and diverged in crucial ways. This chapter considers and assesses the recourse to Indigeneity as a strategy for cancelling the effects of the Zionist gaze, the production and determination of Native identity/subjectivity, as a strategy for rehumanizing Palestinians and restoring their status as human, worthy of dignity and care. Claiming Indigeneity is a way for Palestinians to shift attention to the settler-colonial context, to reframe their plight for the international community: it is their humanity that is under attack; they are the ones on the receiving end of Israel's ethnic cleansing and state-sanctioned violence.

At the same time, the appeal to the human and a humanist grammar is not without its limitations and pitfalls. Scholars in Critical Black Studies, namely those associated with the movement of Afropessimism, have powerfully demonstrated that the idea/l of the human is ideologically loaded and deeply inscribed in a racializing and anti-Black discourse. In this light, what does it mean to claim Palestinian Indigeneity? Is it an act of revival? Does it necessarily point to a time prior to the genocidal colonial encounter? Is the claim of Indigeneity—the political struggle for Palestinian self-determination, more generally—too invested in the figure of the human (with its rewards of individual and collective sovereignty), neglectful of its racist and imperialist origins, and thus irremediably predicated on anti-Blackness? Does the rehumanizing of Palestinians have to come at the expense of the Black cause? Or can we imagine Palestinian Indigeneity and its relation to Blackness otherwise, and challenge the ideological coordinates of the human itself? Simply put, is Black-Palestinian solidarity possible? And if it is, which we believe it is, what does it look like? What kind of invention does it call for?

The Ruse of Analogy, or Black Exceptionalism

Afropessimism is best understood as an "ensemble of questions"[20] oriented toward "Black positionality," emanating from theorists who "share Fanon's insistence, that though Blacks are sentient, the structure of the entire world's semantic field . . . is sutured by anti-black solidarity."[21] Today's anti-Blackness is not an unfortunate residue of prior days that only occasionally manifests itself in hate crimes and excessive police brutality. Rather, anti-Black racism is constitutive of white civil society. Without anti-Blackness there is no ontology as such; "ontology is made possible by the death of blackness—onticide," writes Calvin Warren.[22]

Afropessimists set themselves apart from Marxist, postcolonial, and Indigenous theorists. They flatly reject the view that anti-Blackness is the by-product of capitalism or colonialism. "Anti-Blackness is its own beast—a conceptual framework that cannot be analogized to capitalism, or any other ism," writes Frank Wilderson.[23] A Marxist focus on political economy seeks to expose the exploitation of the many by the few. Whereas domination is a visible problem, exploitation is seen as a necessary feature of the capitalist system—and since capitalism is assumed to be the only game in town, exploitation as such is rarely seen as the genuine object of the struggle. This explains why it is imaginable to conceive of a world without domination (without racism, without misogyny) that is still a world largely conditioned or structured by capitalism. As Fredric Jameson conjectures, the struggle against domination is "an essentially moral or ethical one which leads to punctual revolts and acts of resistance rather than to the transformation of the mode of production as such."[24] Slavoj Žižek dismisses this fantasy of capitalism as "global capitalism with a human face."[25] Afropessimists, by contrast, separate anti-Black racism from class oppression, and are keen to displace political economy with libidinal economy, underscoring the extent to which anti-Blackness "naturally" springs from society's collective unconscious. Explaining further the mechanisms and logic of anti-Blackness, Afropessimists define the notion of libidinal economy as

> the economy, or distribution and arrangement, of desire and identification, of energies, concerns, points of attention, anxieties, pleasures, appetites, revulsions, and phobias—the whole structure of psychic and emotional life—that are unconscious and invisible but that have a visible effect on the world, including the money economy.[26]

Simply put, libidinal economy regulates desires and fears, the production and circulation of anti-Blackness in white civil society. It governs our sense of who affectively matters, belongs, counts—and who doesn't.

What are the political implications of Afropessimism? Cross-racial solidarity is at best precarious and short-lived, at worst, instrumental and ripe for betrayal. Wilderson repeatedly juxtaposes Blacks and Indigenous Palestinians, only to show the fundamental incommensurability of the two. Wilderson is suspicious of any movement that aligns Black activists with the plight of Palestinians. The Black Lives Matter movement is a case in point. BLM puts the Palestinian cause front and center in the struggle for racial and economic justice. They actively promoted an atmosphere of critical collaboration, soliciting activists to cast their resistance to domination and exploitation in global terms. Black-Palestinian solidarity was renewed:

> We know Israel's violence toward Palestinians would be impossible without the US defending Israel on the world stage and funding its violence with over $3 billion annually. We call on the US government to end economic and diplomatic aid to Israel. . . . We urge people of conscience to recognize the struggle for Palestinian liberation as a key matter of our time. . . . We reject notions of "security" that make any of our groups unsafe and insist no one is free until all of us are.[27]

BLM reiterated the solidarity with the Palestinian cause after 2021 Gaza war, *Operation Guardian of the Walls*: "Black Lives Matter stands in solidarity with Palestinians. We are a movement committed to ending settler colonialism in all forms and will continue to advocate for Palestinian liberation. (always have. And always will be)."[28] Wilderson cautions against this tendency to see a common struggle between Blacks and Palestinians, as if they are objecting to the same thing:

> Comparisons such as these are based on an empirical comparison of cops killing a Black youth in Ferguson and IDF forces killing Palestinian youths in the West Bank and in Gaza. If we use our eyes the two phenomena have a lot in common. It stands to reason, by extension, revolutionaries in Palestine . . . and revolutionaries in the U.S. . . . could be seen as fighting different factions of the same enemy (capitalism and colonialism), in different countries. But this is not the case.[29]

Wilderson laments the instrumentalization of Black flesh and energies for causes that are unwilling and unable to speak to "Black ethical dilemmas."[30] Against what he calls "the ruse of analogy,"[31] Wilderson stresses the importance of preserving the difference between Blacks and Palestinians not only because it is inaccurate to collapse the two (different histories, different enemies) but also because it prevents Blacks from registering and addressing the conscious or unconscious anti-Blackness of Palestinians:

> So right now, pro-Palestinian people are saying, "Ferguson is an example of what is happening in Palestine, and y'all are getting what we're getting." That's just bullshit. First, there's no time period in which black police and slave domination have ever ended. Second, the Arabs and the Jews are as much a part of the black slave trade—the creation of blackness as social death—as anyone else. As I told a friend of mine, "yeah we're going to help you get rid of Israel, but the moment that you set up your shit we're going to be right there to jack you up, because anti-blackness is as important and necessary to the formation of *Arab psychic life* as it is to the formation of Jewish psychic life."[32]

Again, Wilderson draws a sharp contrast between Blacks and Palestinians: "Ferguson is not Palestine. Ferguson is a threat to Palestine, a threat far greater than that of Israel's occupying army."[33] This is a startling observation, which if true, invalidates the dream of a Black-Palestinian solidarity.

What compels Afropessimism's suspicion is the underlying anti-Blackness informing any attachment to the "human." Afropessimists foreground the role of anti-Blackness in modernity's definition of human subjectivity. The birth of the human, understood as a subject, a sovereign being, coincides with the negation of Blackness, embodied in the image of the slave. There is no human without a negated Black subjectivity, which Wilderson renders as "'Black subjectivity' (subjectivity under erasure)";[34] the negation of Blackness is the *condition of possibility* for the human.[35] The very movement of Black people is a threat—requiring white surveillance and aggression if/when necessary. A Black person is by definition a danger, standing for criminality, always already in violation of humanity's normative ideals. "We are a species of sentient beings that cannot be injured or murdered, for that matter, because we are dead to the world," argues Wilderson.[36] For Afropessimists, the human comes into being through the constitutive exclusion of Blacks: being human means that I am not a slave (Black). Anti-Blackness engenders a hierarchy of races, with whites at the top and Blacks at the bottom. Its reach yields no escape or reprieve for Black bodies. Anti-Blackness is an all-engulfing and stifling horizon, "as pervasive as climate," writes Christina Sharpe.[37] To be invested in humanity is by definition to be anti-Black; it is to align oneself with the empire of the "human" at the expense of Black people who are *a priori* denied the possibility and privileges of humanity: "Whereas Humans exist on some plane of being and thus can become existentially present through some struggle for, of, or through recognition, Blacks cannot reach this plane."[38]

Prior critical frameworks fail to attest to the historico-ontological specificity of anti-Blackness. With a Marxist focus on political economy, there is a visible remedy to the worker's exploitation and alienation (better working condition, the destruction of capitalism). With a postcolonial focus, the Indigenous population can pursue a politics of recognition (the path of identity politics) or dream of a return to primordial origins, a *"time before the settler."*[39] But in the case of anti-Blackness no such relief is available. Within white civil society, the non-alienation of Black people is not within the realm of possibilities; there is no other side to their existence, to dwelling in the "zone of nonbeing." Living under constant scrutiny (the object of endless policing), Blacks are locked in a state of permanent alienation.

Needless to say, Wilderson, in establishing and upholding the singularity of the Black condition, simplifies a great deal here:

- there is an imputation of Palestinian motives that veers on Orientalism; Palestinians are abstractly represented as the embodiment of "Arab psychic life."
- there is pure speculation: he assumes an impending Palestinian betrayal whereas the long history of Black-Palestinian solidarity belies that belief.[40]
- there is the unwarranted assumption that what *all* Palestinians want is a return to the same by way of the ideological path of the nation-state. With Edward Said's vision of binationalism, for example, there isn't a "time before the settler" that he is seeking to resurrect. Binationalism is not about a Palestine *restored*, but about a future mode of coexistence (this will be discussed in Chapter 4).

For Wilderson, the problem of Blackness lies in the communal psyche of Palestinians (and other non-Black people). What makes Blacks "the core anxiety in the collective unconscious"[41] of Palestinians—a threat greater than the Zionist regime—is that the presence of Blackness terrifies Palestinians at the core ontological level. As a project of Black resistance, Ferguson is fundamentally at odds with the Palestinian cause—with the pursuit of saving their world. Ferguson is a call to "Black insurrection,"[42] and it terrifies Palestinians. Ferguson challenges the reliance on the human, the Black struggle against civil society—it calls for nothing short of its destruction—being irreconcilable with the Palestinian struggle for *human* recognition, because the latter (its integrity and coherence) is predicated on anti-Blackness. Again, there is no recognition for Black people, but they are needed for others to be recognized, to be redeemed and folded back into the plenitude of humanity.

For the Afropessimists, Blacks stand alone in their struggle. Achille Mbembe critically describes their struggle as "a war that would be waged against the very concept of humanity since this concept is indeed the Trojan horse that has trapped the Negro in a permanent state of death, social or otherwise."[43] Anyone or group invested in humanity is *a priori* tainted by the specter of anti-Blackness. Wilderson disparagingly labels non-Black people of color and other marginalized groups (white women and LGBTQ communities, for example) "junior partners of civil society."[44] They may not occupy the dominant position in the symbolic order, that of the white, male subject, but they still benefit from their proximity to power, to society's narrative of redemption. Unless you're Black, hope is still possible. In white civil society, Black people are beyond redemption. Their Blackness is unassimilable; it is an ontological problem. That is to say, Black is not "a subaltern category"[45] that could be *ontically* remedied (via more civil rights and more white empathy, for instance). The Left and the state have more in common than one might think: "The state kills and contains Black bodies. The left kills and contains Black desire, erases Black cognitive maps that explain the singularity of Black suffering, and, most of all, fatally constricts the horizon of Black liberation."[46] What the Left and the state have in common is "the need to disavow the singularity of anti-Black violence."[47] Black people are treated as if they were "subjects of rights, claims, and consent,"[48] subjects like everybody else. This humanist vision distorts their positionality as a permanent "phobic object," the "antithesis of humanity."[49] The call for solidarity misrecognizes the Black condition when it adopts a politics of recognition as the remedy for anti-Blackness.[50] This leftist remedy is lethal for Black folks, compounding the problem rather than resolving it.

Inclusivity for Black people remains an ideological mirage and a dangerous one at that. Indeed, the Left's grammar of suffering does not alleviate but instead perpetuates anti-Black violence, since human suffering relies on a definition of the *human as not Black*. Afropessimists rail against this racist definition and engage in "an immanent critique of . . . the paradigm of Humanity."[51] For the Afropessimist, human redemption—realizing one's potential as a subject/human—remains a possibility, however remote, for Palestinians regardless of Israeli dispossession and subjugation. This is why the kind of uncompromising Black activism favored by Afropessimists represents a bigger problem for Palestinians (and the Left, in general) than political Zionists eager to annex more Palestinian land.

Anti-Blackness Meets Settler Colonialism

Wilderson shares a formative anecdote about his disillusionment with Black-Palestinian solidarity. He was living in Minneapolis, working as a guard at the Walker Art Center where he met and befriended another guard, a fellow revolutionary, a Palestinian named "Sameer Bishara."[52] Engaged then in the Palestinian cause, Wilderson was consoling his friend who had learned of his cousin's death during the First Intifada:

> At one point Sameer spoke of being stopped and searched at Israeli checkpoints. He spoke in a manner that seemed not to require my presence. I hadn't seen this level of concentration and detachment in him before. That was fine. He was grieving.
> "The shameful and humiliating way the soldiers run their hands up and down your body," he said. Then he added, "But the shame and humiliation runs even deeper if the Israeli soldier is an Ethiopian Jew." The earth gave way. The thought that my place in the unconscious of Palestinians fighting for their freedom was the same *dishonorable* place I occupied in the minds of Whites in America and Israel chilled me. I gathered enough wits about me to tell him that his feelings were odd, seeing how Palestinians were at war with Israelis, and White Israelis at that. How was it that the people who stole his land and slaughtered his relatives were somehow *less* of a threat in his imagination than Black Jews, often implements of Israeli madness, who sometimes do their dirty work? What, I wondered silently, was it about Black people (about *me*) that made us so fungible we could be tossed like a salad in the minds of oppressors and the oppressed?[53]

This was a transformative if not epiphanic exchange, the moment when Wilderson lost faith in non-Black people of color. It is an "origin story"[54] announcing the birth of Wilderson the Afropessimist, the ceaseless and uncompromising skeptic of coalition politics. Or to put it slightly differently, this event functions as a kind of primal scene narrating Wilderson's bewildering discovery that the Palestinian uprising—and any anti-imperialist or leftist cause in general—was anti-Black and thus was no longer his.

To be sure, the Palestinian friend's comment can reasonably be understood as a spontaneous expression of anti-Blackness exemplifying a broader Palestinian unconscious. Wilderson expresses here legitimate concerns about who belongs to Palestine, who has a right to the contested land: Ethiopian Jews—or any Jews—should not be *a priori* excluded. After all, it is the exclusionary claims of political Zionism that are most objectionable, not the Jewish desire to belong. And the same holds for Palestinians: Palestinian Indigeneity is not to be exoticized or fetishized (by crudely naturalizing Palestinianness and borders, and equating territory with sovereignty, arrogating to Palestinians the right of national sovereignty). At the same time, there are additional elements that are worth considering. What might be provoking his friend's outrage is the Ethiopian Jew's status as a newcomer, an outsider, who—as a settler—is in a position of absolute control over the land's Indigenous population. Ethiopian Jews who come to Israel are fulfilling, intentionally or not, the eliminative project of settler colonialism and political Zionism: the dream of *a land without Palestinians*. Surprisingly, Wilderson registers no concern about the complicity of Ethiopian Jews with the ongoing Nakba. It is as if the theft of land was a thing of the past, as if settler colonialism was only an *event* and not a *structure*.[55] Of course, it is not a question of choosing between competing victims, between a settler-colonial framework or one that highlights the workings of anti-Blackness in the Palestinian collective unconscious. A choice that distorts the entanglement of the two paradigms is prone to promoting an unhelpful "Oppression Olympics" approach to the struggle against racial injustice.[56] Paradigms are surely incommensurable; but I don't believe that an inventive response to this dilemma lies in championing or prioritizing one analytic framework over the other. The task, rather, is to imagine solidarity and social justice otherwise[57]—to think settler colonialism with anti-Blackness (and vice versa).

"Look, a Negro!" is what Wilderson implicitly registers from his Palestinian friend. The Palestinian is really no different than the white child Fanon confronted in Lyon. They both participate in a libidinal economy that deprives Blackness of any value. But to get to this damning verdict, Wilderson must omit the relevance of the settler context in his account. There is no reckoning with the interpellative "Look, a Palestinian!" at the checkpoint. Unlike Fanon, Wilderson is insufficiently attentive to the position of the colonized. Ignoring or papering over the colonial situation in what his friend is describing, he can only hear Palestinian anti-Blackness. Wilderson draws a straight line from the Arab Slave Trade in Eastern Africa, which began in 600 CE, to the present. To be clear: Wilderson is not wrong in alerting us to the long and continuous history of Arab anti-Blackness. Palestinians, as a people, are by no means immune to the pervasive corrosiveness of anti-Blackness. The problem lies in Wilderson's overdetermination of the situation, in his failure to give appropriate weight to the logic of native elimination facing Palestinians in the Occupied Territories and in Israel proper.

Wilderson frames the Ethiopian Jew as a passive subject, transmuting this "state soldier into a slave."[58] White Israelis, we're told, enticed Ethiopian Jews to come to Israel to do their "dirty work." It is *as if* the Ethiopian Jew is a victim who just happens to be an IDF soldier. We might even describe these Black Jewish immigrants as "junior settlers" (along the lines of Wilderson's "junior partners") or "subordinate settlers,"[59] or, even better, "accidental settlers"—*accidental* because they were seduced by the promise of better economic life, and *settlers* because they are in practice contributing to Indigenous dispossession and eradication. Without minimizing the economic coercion that may have brought them to Israel, Ethiopian Jews—who willingly serve in the IDF—are not thereby beyond reproach, beyond critical assessment. Indeed, we might ask: is Blackness in the service of Occupation any less deplorable than whiteness in the service of Occupation? Would Wilderson give a pass to Black police brutality of Black people in the United States?

More generally, Wilderson paints a Manichean racial scene: Black versus non-Black is the fundamental opposition that fuels the same anti-Blackness in the United States and in Palestine (and the rest of the world). But the racial reality in Israel and in the Occupied Territories is far more complicated than the picture painted by Wilderson. Overreading Sameer's words, he (mis)translates his friend's "expression of grief into one not only about Blackness, but about a Blackness that Wilderson, in spite of his geopolitical location, has an obvious and transparent claim to immediate understanding."[60] Wilderson decontextualizes and claims Ethiopian Blackness in Israel as *his*. An eye for historical specificity would point out that Ethiopian Jews, not unlike Sephardi or Mizrahi Jews (Arab Jews, that is, Jews of Middle Eastern or North African origin), are repeatedly mistreated by Israel's Ashkenazi or European-born Jews but this is a point that must be nevertheless significantly qualified given the reality that for many Ethiopian Jews things could be much worse: they could be treated like Palestinians (the less-than Ethiopian Jews); they could be deprived of their *Jewish* privilege.[61]

Wilderson neatly decouples Blackness from the Ethiopian IDF's Jewishness in order to highlight the humanity shared by Palestinians and Ashkenazi Jews, while isolating the nonhumanity of the former: "Degraded humanity (Palestinians) can be frisked by exalted humanity (Ashkenazi Jews) and the walls of reason remain standing (notwithstanding the universal indignity of stop-and-frisk). But if the soldier is an Ethiopian Jew."[62] Jewishness is given short shrift. Wilderson treats the Ethiopian Israeli's Jewish privilege as a mere ontical upgrade, which is no upgrade at all if you are Black. What is missing in Wilderson's analysis is a deeper dive into Israel's libidinal economy, a recognition of the ways Zionism bribes non-Ashkenazi Jews with the privileges of Jewishness: you may not enjoy the same level of power and wealth as Ashkenazi Jews, but you will always be better off than Palestinians. Non-Ashkenazi Jews are compensated by a libidinal wage. But Wilderson's Black exceptionalism obscures a real engagement with the settler-colonial context/structure. In Afropessimism, only one positionality ultimately counts. And after "applying" Afropessimism to Occupied Palestine, soldiers become slaves, the oppressed become the masters.[63]

Israel's Libidinal Economy: What Is a Zionist without a Palestinian?

In Israel's racial matrix, the signifiers "Palestinianness" and "Blackness" stand for the other side of modernity: primitivism, savagery, lawlessness. The identities associated with the signifiers are tolerated only when they are neutralized and subjugated: when Palestinians are transformed into "Arab" Israelis and Blacks are identified as *Jewish*. These symbolic transformations, however, never entail equality. Israel is not only a *Jewish* state (sidelining Palestinians/"Arab" Israelis and non-Jews), it is first and foremost a *white* Jewish state (additionally sidelining Black Jews, Mizrahi Jews, and non-Jewish Blacks).

Deep-seated structures of anti-Blackness abound in Israel.[64] After tens of thousands of Jews from Ethiopia who had experienced religious persecution, famine, and civil wars immigrated to Israel in the 1980s and 1990s—fulfilling the Zionist dream of Israel as a nation for all Jews—their rescue and arrival in Israel were difficult right from the start. "When they arrived in Israel," Yossi Mekelberg writes, "these distinctive people faced appalling discrimination, racism and a lack of empathy for their hardships in Ethiopia and during their journey to Israel."[65] Things have not really changed: "Ethiopian Jews suffer from the highest poverty rate among the Jews in Israel, and suffer much higher levels of police stop-search, arrests and incarceration."[66] David Theo Goldberg comments on a report published in 2010 by Isha le'Isha, a women's rights organization, about the practice of forced contraception: "Ethiopian Jewish women in Israel were unknowingly injected with a contraceptive drug to prevent them eugenically from diluting Israel's Jewish—which here can only be read as white, European—character."[67] This policy of limiting Jewish births seems counterintuitive, because Israel perceives Palestinians as an immanent demographic threat; so more Israeli Jews should, in principle, be welcomed. But in terms of Israel's libidinal economy, the question of Black Jews takes a more ambivalent form. The controversial policy discloses Israeli aversion to Blackness; what is politically beneficial for the Jewish state—demographic domination over the "Holy Land"—clashes with Israel's phantasmatic self-image as white and Western. Ethiopian Jews thus experience both privilege and penalty. The affective logic of anti-Blackness perversely trumps Israel's political calculus, sabotaging what is in the state's strategic or basic self-interest: maintaining the demographic advantage. Too many Ethiopian Jews—uncontained Blackness, uncontained poverty[68]—risk contaminating the "purity" of Ashkenazi Jewishness, the Zionist phantasm of an economically thriving white/European/capitalism Israel. *Call:* "Look, a Negro!" *Response:* "Sterilize her!"

Non-Jewish African migrants are a favorite target of Israeli right-wing politicians. Not being beneficiaries of Jewish privilege, they face a vilification even more extreme. At the time he was interior minister, Eli Yishai stated, for example, "the migrants are giving birth to hundreds of thousands, and the Zionist dream is dying"[69] and "this country belongs to us, to the white man."[70] Likud MK Miri Regev called them a "cancer in our body."[71] Fanning the flames of racial division, Netanyahu repeatedly demonized African migrants as "illegal infiltrators flooding the country,"[72] threatening Israel's security and identity, its existence as a Jewish and democratic state (reminiscent of anti-Palestinian rhetoric). He also boasted of having protected Israel from an African invasion: "I prevented the overrunning of Israel, which is the only first-world country that you can walk to from Africa. We would have had here already a million illegal migrants from Africa, and the Jewish state would have collapsed. The Jewish State, Conservative, Reform, Orthodox, would have collapsed."[73] *Call:* "Look, a Negro!" *Response:* "Build a fence!"

In an interview with the al-Arab website, Netanyahu, trying to court the "Arab" vote, tried to convince "Arab" Israelis that the 2018 Nation-State Law didn't really target them but rather illegal African migrants; the idea of the Nation-State Law, we're told, emerged

> in connection to the danger of a flooding of illegal immigrants from Africa that flooded Israel. I built a fence that *saved us all*—and then I was told, if someone climbs the fence, he has an automatic right to be a refugee. So I decided to pass the Nation-State Law . . . It was not meant to be against *any citizen within the [borders]*,

Netanyahu explained.[74] Netanyahu—the "heroic savior" of Israel's vulnerable non-Black population—tried to interpellate "Arab" citizens in his scapegoating of the African migrants, cynically playing one racialized community against the other. It is safe to say that this strategy didn't work; the "Arab" population of Israel and their political leaders did not mobilize behind him. But Netanyahu's efforts are still telling. Netanyahu is a symptom; his appeal to "Arabs" is not only a shameless political tactic but it tells us something crucial about Israel's (and Palestinians') cultural unconscious. His remarks confirm once again the Afropessimist insight about the global currency of anti-Blackness, the universal appeal to subjugate Black bodies (and thus to phantasmatically assimilate to whiteness/humanity/power as a way to transcend their own dehumanization by the same necropolitical state), tapping into a *shared* affective disposition to fear and/or hate Black people.

We should also add that anti-Blackness in relation to Africa often takes the form of indifference. In their supposedly "undeveloped" continent, Africans are imagined as always already lost; they are typically framed as bestial and monstrous, lawless and ahistorical beings, objects of pure abjection, disposability incarnate, intrinsically susceptible to destruction and unable to break free from the senseless and repetitive cycles of violence: necessitating, in turn, only military and/or humanitarian interventions.[75] As Wilderson observes, "Africa, in the collective unconscious of the world, is a place of crisis and catastrophe.... Africa becomes a kind of automatic metaphor for disasters beyond what can be thought of."[76] And when Africans enter Israeli space, neocolonial indifference can quickly mutate into the more aggressive affects of hate or fear, culminating in anti-Black state violence.

But are Black people and their cause—a Black insurrection in Israel modeled after that of BLM[77]—really a bigger threat to Ashkenazi supremacy than Palestinians and Palestinian Israelis? Wilderson would answer in the affirmative. For the Afropessimist, it is clear that the operative antagonism in Israel's white civil society is not:

Jew versus Palestinian
Jew versus non-Jew
Ashkenazi Jew versus Jews of color

but (always) between:

Black versus non-Black.

The former set of oppositions refers to reconcilable conflicts among subjects/humans (with various chances of success: recognition of Indigenous sovereignties, more cultural tolerance of non-Jews, of Arab or non-European Jews, etc.), the latter opposition is unresolvable—undialectizable, we might say—sealing Blacks (Jewish or not) in an antagonistic relation with old and new avatars of humanity (Ashkenazi Jews, Mizrahi Jews, Palestinians, etc.).

This Afropessimist reading, however, overdetermines the framing of the struggle against anti-Black racism in hierarchical terms, with the Black and non-Black opposition standing alone at the top of the ladder of oppression. This form of reasoning oversimplifies Israel's libidinal economy, failing to account for the complexity of the state's racial regime. Race in Israel is an "assemblage of forces that must continuously articulate nonwhite [and non-Jewish] subjects as not-quite-human."⁷⁸ While anti-Blackness does play a crucial role in upholding the belief that the human (emblematized by the Ashkenazi Jew, but also phantasmatically, if temporarily, extended to non-Black Jews of color and *some* Palestinians, rebranded Arab Israelis) is premised on the negation of Blackness, Israel's libidinal economy cannot be divorced from its historical context— the state's settler-colonial status. Anti-Blackness does not so much override Palestinophobia (or vice versa) as it is inextricably entangled with it.

Israel's libidinal economy traffics in complex cultural fantasies that aim to fix the ontology of the Native and align its citizens' desires with those of the (white) Jewish state. Psychoanalytically speaking, cultural/ideological fantasies reduce anxiety. As Bruce Fink avers: "The unknown nature of the Other's desire is unbearable here; you prefer to assign it an attribute, any attribute, rather than let it remain an enigma."⁷⁹ Any knowledge of the Other lessens the anxiety triggered by the Other, "once it is named, once you conclude that this is what the Other wants of you ... the angst abates."⁸⁰ Fantasy answers the fundamental question, *Che vuoi?* (What does the Other want from me?).⁸¹ A case in point is the well-known ideological fantasy of the Jewish plot. The Nazi social fantasy narrates a story, telling German citizens what the nation wants from them: "to unearth the meaning of the murky events in which [they are] forced to participate."⁸² The German people here tragically failed to acknowledge and identify their true antagonism: capitalist relations, the problem of economic exploitation. As a result, "class struggle is displaced onto the struggle against the Jews, so that the popular rage at being exploited is redirected from capitalist relations as such to the 'Jewish plot.'"⁸³ The real antagonism—society's internal contradictions— is externalized as a fake struggle between Aryans and Jews, where the latter is imagined as stealing the social *jouissance* or enjoyment of the former. The Nazis phantasmatically identified the figure of the Jew as the fundamental cause of the nation's dire socioeconomic predicament, construed as the secret puppet master of German society. The Jews functioned as the Nazis' *objet petit a* (the object-cause of desire). They were not an object of Nazi desire but the ultimate obstacle that strictly speaking *sustained* Nazi desire/identity.⁸⁴ The figure of the Jew explained German suffering/alienation/trauma, historicized it as an episode while simultaneously pointing to a way out. Jews were essential for the Nazi narrative of national overcoming. Indeed, "What is a Nazi without a Jew?"[85] perspicaciously asks Žižek.

Today in Israel, we might ask, "What is a Zionist without a Palestinian?" Palestinians are of course not hated for their secrecy nor accused of controlling Israeli economy and politics. Zionism is not peddling these sorts of conspiracy theories about Palestinians. Rather, it operates through its framing of the Jewish attitude toward both Jews/Israel and Palestinians. Zionism at once nourishes and feeds off Israel's libidinal economy. Zionism answers, for its Jewish audience, the primordial question, "What do Palestinians really want from me?" "What does the big Other—the order of laws and rules of Jewish society—want from me?" Zionism's racialized assemblages fix the ontology of both Palestinians and Jews, making their desires seem all too knowable and decipherable. The former are read through the lenses of 9/11 and the War on Terror: Palestinians hate Jewish freedom, their anger and *ressentiment* is rooted in their anti-Western and anti-Semitic character. The latter are claimed as belonging to the Promised Land, urged to cultivate an ethos of exclusive sovereignty and to identify with (Greater) Israel, which is itself premised on the negation or disappearance of Palestinians. The elimination of Palestinians sustains Zionist desire/identity. Zionism teaches Jews (including Ethiopian Jews) to desire Israel, and interpellates them as would-be loyal citizens of the Jewish state. It also appoints itself as the ultimate authority over Jewish matters, determining not only Jewish self-worth but also what constitutes anti-Semitism. Jews themselves are not exempt from Zionism's self-serving verdict; if Jews decline their hailing by the Jewish state—if they disidentify with Israel, divest in Zionism's authorized symbolic identity—they are viciously judged "self-hating."

Israel's Zionist self-narrative is rooted in fantasy. Zionism, born in the late nineteenth century, adopts a separatist ideology; it posits a curative world *for* Jews, a world without social antagonisms, a polity of Jews (a society of equals), governed by Jews for the good of all Jews. In such a state, Jews would be able to overcome their "psychopathology" and regain their dignity; to recall, according to the founders of Zionism only a Jewish homeland could counteract the "degeneration"—the ontological effects of alienated existence in Europe, of living with non-Jews—that diasporic Jews were experiencing.[86] The settlement of European Jews in Palestine took the form of a "collective passion,"[87] an urgent ethico-political imperative: only a properly Jewish state can redeem Jews. In contradistinction to the diasporic Jew, who struggles with anti-Jewish bigotry and the vicissitudes of assimilation, Zionism envisioned the birth of a strong, healthy "New Jew" who finds ontological nourishment in the Promised Land, where a divinely sanctioned identity awaits. But as Žižek notes, "the greatest mass murders and holocausts have always been perpetrated in the name of man as harmonious being, of a New Man without antagonistic tension."[88] The "New Jew"—the "Jew" whose harmony has been restored, whose Jewishness returns to itself from Western-induced alienation—is premised on the elimination of the Native.

Consistent with a settler-colonial ethos, this polity of Jews is imagined as an "organic Whole"[89] and/as Palestinian-free. A critique of Zionism can without difficulty debunk settler fabulations and counter the early Jewish narratives of *terra nullius* by documenting the existence of Indigenous people (the Palestinians) prior to the Zionist movement and the migration of Jews (*aliyah*) to historic Palestine.[90] This critique of Zionist myths is indispensable but a psychoanalytic approach, with an eye for the working of fantasy, pushes further. For instance, *terra nullius*, within the frame of Zionism's fundamental fantasy, possessed an affective and ideological appeal for the early Jewish settlers. It fortified their libidinal bond with the land, legitimized their maddening desire for a home.[91] As Jacqueline Rose points out, the Zionist claim that "Palestine was a land without a people" is not merely a "blatant lie" but also a "cover."[92] Its pull was such that even if these settlers "knew" about the Indigenous population, their encounter with the Native inhabitants involved a kind of "fetishist disavowal." The structure of a fetishist disavowal is, "*I know very well, but still . . .*" As Žižek explains, "fetishist disavowal" is an attempt to deal with anxiety; it splits the ego between knowing and not knowing; new information has been admitted into consciousness but its symbolic impact has been minimized and "not really integrated into the subject's symbolic universe."[93] There is a willful blindness in fetishist disavowal: "'I know, but I don't want to know that I know, so I don't know.' I know it, but I refuse to fully assume the consequences of this knowledge, so that I can continue acting as if I don't know."[94]

By putting Israel's libidinal economy front and center, we are in a better position to account for Zionism as a frame of reference, a fantasy that manipulates and governs its citizens' sense of who affectively matters, belongs, counts, and who doesn't. We know that Israel prides itself as "the most moral army in the world,"[95] but we also know that this is sounding more and more hollow for a global audience after Israel's well-documented war criminality in Gaza and its ceaseless ethnic cleansing campaign. The historical suffering of the Jewish people does not guarantee the state's claim of its army's moral superiority. Victimhood, in and of itself, does not "necessarily enable an enhanced sense of humanity," writes Edward Said.⁹⁶ The Israeli police is experiencing a similar downgrade in global opinion, though we should make clear that Palestinians—not unlike Black communities in the United States—felt and understood police brutality long before it was comfortable for white liberals to advocate defunding the police in the United States or adding modest conditions to the $3.8 billion in military aid the country provides to Israel. Coverage of the latest Gaza war was extensive, and even after the cease-fire was secured, media coverage returned to the illegal eviction of Palestinians from the neighborhoods of Sheikh Jarrah and Silwan, finally raising questions about what Sari Hanafi dubs Israel's "spacio-cide,"⁹⁷ its ethnic cleansing and the Judaization of East Jerusalem. The pro-Zionist interpretive frame, that typically dominates mainstream media, was (temporarily) unsettled, enabling Palestinians to *narrate* their displacement.

At the same time, Nadia Abu El-Haj points out that "counter-narrative," or narrating one's story, may prove insufficient in igniting a seismic shift in the Palestinian struggle. Why? A vocal and growing segment of Israeli Jews is no longer disavowing the Nakba; quite the contrary, they want to repeat it, to complete the Palestinian removal started in 1948, and thus perfect Zionism's eliminative project: "Palestinians were expelled in '48 and they might need to be expelled again. . . . Yes, the Nakba and . . . we Israelis don't care."⁹⁸ Rather than provoking soul-searching in Israel, knowledge of the Nakba has thus only hardened the will of today's committed Zionists. If Palestinians didn't exist, if they didn't viciously oppose the noble idea/l of Israel and make a counterclaim on the land, their *objet petit a* (the cathexis that magically turns ordinary land into a desirable object—the Promised Land), Jews would be *whole*, able to fully enjoy their nation-state, and delight in the utopian "land of milk and honey." Zionism explains the nation-state's failure to overcome alienation and achieve harmony by framing Palestinians as "foreign and unwelcome," the *external* cause of its troubles, a "pathogenic idea,"⁹⁹ endangering its health and national integrity, its socioeconomic well-being. Consequently, Palestinians outside and inside the Green Line are to be cruelly managed, cast as an unending source of anxiety, the ultimate menace to Israelis' enjoyment and global image.

Forget calling out and shaming Zionists on the cultural fantasy of *terra nullius*. There is no longer any need for colonial erasure, denying that Palestinians were their *aborigine*. *Yes, there were Palestinians on the Promised Land. Too bad we didn't liquidate all of them!* With the normalization of chants that incite violence and elicit genocide, the hard-fought Palestinian right to narrate may prove insufficient.¹⁰⁰ And yet, Israel's hard turn to ethnonationalism has symbolic consequences. It casts "Look, a Palestinian!" in a different light. It shatters the distinction between liberal Zionists and political/religious Zionists. The former gentrifies the anti-Palestinian Zionist gaze, whereas the latter celebrates its rawness. Liberal Zionists purporting to care speak of forgiveness and reconciliation with their historical enemy. They say, "We need to deal with the trauma of the Nakba, own up to our founding violence, make life easier for our Arab neighbors, etc."—but this does not enjoin anyone to seriously confront their Zionist privilege. Why? Denouncing privilege would necessitate an act of self-violence, an undoing of a self whose identity is predicated on the devalorization/racialization of others.[101] But liberalism, in its various shades, displays an aversion to such radical change, preferring "Occupation on cruise control." Liberals can preach and enjoy their moderation, favoring a "centrist" position (while the very meaning of centrism has been radically shifted by the rise of right-wing Jewish nationalism[102]). Commenting on the anti-Palestinian slurs heard during the right-wing *Flag March* through East Jerusalem, June 15, 2021, Yair Lapid, the alternate prime minister of Israel, said: "The fact that there are extremists for whom the Israeli flag represents hate and racism is abominable and intolerable."[103] This is Israeli liberalism's "move to innocence" at its best. It tells the world that liberal Zionism is on the side of tolerance and anti-racism. Lapid adds: "It is incomprehensible how one can hold an Israeli flag in one's hand and shout 'death to Arabs' at the same time. This isn't Judaism, it isn't Israeli, and it definitely isn't what our flag represents. These people are a disgrace to Israel."[104] Really? Is it so "incomprehensible"? Zionist excess stems quite predictably from an idea of Israel that stands for Jewish exclusivism, illegal settlements, and the indefinite Occupation of the land's Indigenous population. What liberal Zionists and centrist politicians are after is nothing short of an ideological fantasy, an Occupation with a human face, Jewish supremacy without (explicit) Palestinophobia.[105] They disavow that Zionism's excess is constitutive of Zionism. But the genocidal chants, disseminated on social media for the world to witness, placed a strain on Israel's PR machine, embarrassed Zionism's self-image, and put the state's "moderate" leaders on the defensive: *this is not who we are.*

In contrast, political/religious Zionists see no real need to reign in extremists. Quite the contrary, they are happy to flaunt Israeli might, eager to escalate the dispossession of Palestinians. "Shoots and weeps,"[106] the condition of the morally sensitive occupier, vanishes and is substituted with "shoots and cheers." Ethnonationalist Israeli politicians unleash the truth of Israel's libidinal economy, an ungentrified Zionism for the world to see. If "Occupation on cruise control" describes the liberal Zionist stance, "Occupation on steroids" is the more apt metaphor for the political/religious Zionist side. But let's not be mistaken: Occupation thrives among both camps. Political/religious Zionists openly welcome right-wing Jewish nationalists and proudly identify with Israel's brutal colonial origins. While the political/religious attitude is utterly terrifying—for it takes a fascist approach to the Palestinian question, laying bare the murderous underpinnings of "Look, a Palestinian!"—the liberal attitude toward the Nakba is, I believe, more dangerous in the long term, because it still projects the ideological fantasy of Israel as a democratic and Jewish state. For the latter, ethnonational outbursts are democratic "hiccups," something containable and ultimately eradicable, not a permanent feature of the Jewish state. But can Zionism keep projecting a palatable image of Israel to the rest of the world? Or is its racial supremacist underpinning—Israel as a "*Herrenvolk* republic"[107]— becoming harder and harder to deny?

The least we can say is that Zionism's master narrative is faltering. The world is taking stock of Israel's internal contradictions, witnessing the disintegration of its "rule of law."[108] Mainstream media outlets displayed dismay and surprise at the ways armed Israeli mobs attacked other Israeli citizens, during *Operation Guardian of the Walls*, chanting "Death to Arabs!" and seeking to purge the nation's "mixed" cities of any Arab presence (these so-called mixed cities are not harmonious spaces where coexistence flourishes; rather, they are segregated cities made up of "Arab ghettos suffering from poverty and crime and ... wealthy Jewish neighborhoods"[109]). The Western media's surprise comes from the fact that this violence is originating from inside the Green Line, in Israel proper, not in the Occupied Territories. "Arab" Israelis transmuted into *Palestinian* citizens of Israel, standing unified in solidarity with their brethren in Occupied Palestine, equally engaged in the struggle against the settler-colonial state of Israel. Their Palestinianness was reclaimed, resurrected from the assimilative settler's logic: *Kill the Palestinian, save the democracy.*

The Western belief in Israel as a liberal democratic state is waning. Israel is no longer capable of maintaining the rule of law as an "appearance" (as it had succeeded in doing for decades with "Occupation on cruise control"). The implications of this demystification are ideologically significant. It is not simply that the world can now see what Palestinians had been reporting all along. As Žižek argues, "appearances are essential; they oblige us to act in a certain way—so without the appearance, the way we act also changes."[110] By acting even more cruelly, Israel is having more and more difficulty *passing* as a democratic state (this fantasy is rapidly losing currency in the West; under pressure from its citizens, Western powers can no longer—if they are still attached to the "appearance" of fairness—willfully ignore Israel's egregious rhetoric and actions, its "Occupation on steroids").

The world is starting to see Israel as an apartheid regime, its police as agents of injustice rather that the protectors of (just) laws. Even Israel's historically strongest foreign base is shifting. A 2021 poll reveals that a quarter of US Jews consider Israel an "apartheid state" and 22 percent also believe that it is committing genocide against the Palestinians.[111] The *becoming* fascist of Israel is on full display. For Palestinians, there is no real separation between the police and the murderous mobs of Israeli Jews. The former does not control or impede the latter's violent actions, but collaborates with them. Mixed cities are "policed like occupied territory," as James Baldwin says about Harlem in the 1960s.[112] In Israel, Palestinophobia structures Jewish civil society's libidinal economy. To paraphrase Wilderson: Jews are not simply "protected" by the police, they are the police.[113] Call: *"Look, a Palestinian!"* Response: *"Lynch him!"*

Let us return to the primal scene of the checkpoint. The Afropessimist lens importantly discloses the unconscious biases potentially informing Wilderson's Palestinian friend's singling out the Ethiopian Jew as the worst form of offense, but Wilderson also obfuscates the power relation structuring the relation between the settler and the Native. Rather than attending to the ways Zionism, as a racial regime, uses and abuses Black bodies in its attempt to maintain its supremacy over Israel's racialized communities, which would align the Palestinian struggle with those of African migrants and Ethiopian Jews (and other non-white Jews), Wilderson limits his discussion to his friend's anti-Blackness, focusing on the Ethiopian Jew's nonhumanity versus the Palestinian's degraded humanity. Wilderson might counter by insisting that he is not evoking the Blackness of the Ethiopian Jew as a cultural identity to be rescued or defended (as one would in "identity politics") but as "a kind of vector of violence and rituals."[114] In other words, Wilderson's intervention is not about a struggle between competing marginalized identities: Palestinians versus Ethiopian Jews. Blackness is about positionality rather than a cultural marker. A Palestinian can dream of cultural recognition (Indigeneity = humanity); a Black individual can only expect more "gratuitous" violence, because she is "a sentient being for whom recognition and incorporation are impossible."[115] The problem with this explanation is that it ignores how Palestinianness is as much a positionality as an identity. Palestinians also endure constitutive limitations. Not unlike Fanon's staging of the (non)choice given to Blacks—*"turn white or disappear [se blanchir ou disparaître]"*[116]—Palestinian citizens of Israel hear: *de-Palestinize or get out*; give up your attachment to Palestiniannness, be grateful of your status as an Arab Israeli—that is, live with immutable constraints and accept your permanent position as a subhuman citizen—or simply "self-transfer" and join your fellow stateless Palestinians. Within Israel's libidinal economy, Palestinian Indigeneity—"Look, a Palestinian!"—also functions very much as "a kind of vector of violence and rituals." Palestinians, who are cast by Zionism as the imminent threat from within and without, give Israel's civil society its current coherence. Zionism's anti-Palestinianness is not a response to the Palestinians' anti-colonial struggle. That some Palestinians are indeed a threat to Jewish supremacy should not distract us from Zionism's pathological underpinnings, its repressed truth that it needs to hate/fear Palestinians in order to sustain its ideological position. *What is a Zionist without a Palestinian?*

Wilderson does not completely repudiate the Palestinian cause. At best, it is a just fight that does not go far enough in addressing the concerns and demands of Black folks; at worst, it is anti-Black, since what Palestinians ultimately want is premised on prolonging the social death of Black people. But if Black activists are still going to support the Palestinian cause, Wilderson urges them to keep an ironic distance with the Global Left and its anti-imperialist projects, of which Free Palestine is one:

> I believe that looking at it from an anti-capitalist perspective, from an anti-White supremacist perspective, the Palestinians are right—*provisionally*—until they get their shit, then they're wrong. So this is a historical thing: what we have to do is remind each other, to know our history in terms of slavery and our resistance to it, but also to be able to have X-ray vision, and say that just because we're walking around in suits and ties and are professors and journalists doesn't mean we're not slaves. [. . .] And that will allow us to be in a coalition with people of color, moving on the system with them, but ridiculing them at the same time for the paucity—the *lameness*—of their desire and demand. And for the fact that we know, once they get over [their own hurdles], the anti-blackness that sustains them will rear its ugly head again against us.[117]

Wilderson's "knowledge" that Palestinians will betray Black people is more than pessimistic; it is fatalistic in its outlook. For Wilderson, the divide between Blacks and Palestinians is insurmountable, quasi-metaphysical; there is in Wilderson's analytic framework "a kind of absolutism at work," as David Marriott puts it.[118] Weakening the hold of anti-Blackness on the collective psyche of Palestinians is not an option. The counter to anti-Blackness ends up reifying it as a permanent condition of non-Blacks. Wilderson overcorrects: it is one thing to question the necessity and naturalization of the link between the Black cause and the

Palestinian cause, as if both groups are saying the same things, demanding the same changes. But Wilderson goes much further, cynically dismissing as inauthentic any attempt on the Palestinian side to understand the plight of Blacks, and therefore ruling out in principle any rapprochement between the two communities.

Il Faut Bien Détruire Ensemble

Can there be a form of solidarity that responds dialectically to the challenges of Afropessimism? The expression, *Il faut bien détruire ensemble*, explores such a possibility. This expression is itself inspired by Jacques Derrida's two formulations, *Il faut bien manger* and *Il faut bien vivre ensemble* (the latter is itself a kind of rewriting of the former). Derrida's earlier phrase can be translated into English in two ways: "it really is necessary to eat" (we have no choice) and "it is necessary to eat well." With this formulation, Derrida seeks to move beyond the stale and predictable debate over sameness and difference, pointing out that relating ethically to the Other is not a matter of opting for either a cannibalistic or a non-cannibalistic mode of contact. There is no avoiding symbolic assimilation; interpreting Others will happen; the question is *how* to do it: "The moral question is . . . not, nor has it ever been: should one eat or not eat . . . but since *one must* eat in any case . . . *how* for goodness sake should one *eat well* [*bien manger*]?"[119] Like *Il faut bien manger*, the imperative *Il faut bien vivre ensemble* can be translated as: (1) It really is necessary to live together (again, we have no choice in the matter); (2) It is necessary to live together well (coexistence takes on an ethico-political dimension).

Accordingly, *Il faut bien détruire ensemble* can be translated as: (1) It really is necessary to destroy together (meaning: destruction is not an individual project; no one group can do it on its own; it takes a village to destroy); (2) It is necessary to destroy well (destruction is not an end in itself; it is destruction infused with an ethico-political purpose). We may, however, also add a third translation: It really is necessary to destroy the idea of togetherness. It is helpful here to return to Derrida's own gloss of *il faut bien vivre ensemble*. Derrida draws attention to the adverbial function of "ensemble" in his formulation. As an adverb, "together" (*ensemble*) makes living something never full nor complete but always already open to the stranger, to the neighbor as stranger: "There is 'living together' only there where the whole [*ensemble*] is neither formed nor closed [*ne se forme pas et ne se ferme pas*], there where the living together [*ensemble*] (the adverb) contests the completion, the closure, and the cohesiveness of an 'ensemble' (the noun, the substantive), of a substantial, closed ensemble identical to itself."[120] As a noun, "ensemble" stands for what Derrida describes as the fantasy of an "organic symbiosis."[121]

In this light, what is being destroyed—the object of the destruction—is the phantasmatic idea that we all belong to some organic whole—let's call it humanity or world, or simply humanist world. I want to purse the implications of this last translation of *Il faut bien détruire ensemble* in connection with Afropessimism. Wilderson would most likely welcome the destruction of the idea of "togetherness," which for him relies on the exclusion and negation of Blackness. The destruction of "togetherness" goes hand in hand with his dismissal of cross-racial solidarity—read as "anti-black solidarity"[122]—along with any emancipatory leftist project. For the Afropessimists, saving the world—which always meant saving the human—feeds rather than halts the global spread of anti-Blackness (killing the slave). Wilderson stresses that Afropessimism is not after reforming the world, since it would leave untouched the metaphysics of the human that underpins it; what it wants is its utter destruction: "True Afropessimism is not animated by reformist desire to end discriminatory practices in the world; it is animated by an understanding that world itself is unethical and needs be undone."[123] Wilderson repeats and embraces Fanon's quoting of Césaire's revolutionary claim that "the end of the world" is the "only thing . . . worth the effort of starting."[124]

To stop the gratuitous violence that is visited on Black people, the world as such must be seen as unworkable. The next step is crucial. Merging the Palestinian cause with the Black cause (under the heading of Black-Palestinian solidarity) can only do conceptual and psychic damage to the latter, weakening its demands, containing its rage, and defanging its radical bite. Again, Wilderson forecloses the very idea that the Palestinian cause can in any way speak to the Black cause. Affirming the former betrays the latter. Against this type of reasoning, we can look at two recent examples that complicate Wilderson's swift dismissal of Black-Palestinian solidarity. The first is the initiative founded by "the Arabs for Black Lives Collective," a collective which foregrounds the question of anti-Blackness in its struggle for global justice. Against "the systemic and cultural devaluing of Black life globally," they urge, on their website, that non-Black Arabs scrutinize their contribution to and complicity with the production and dissemination of anti-Blackness:

> We must collectively work to eradicate anti-Blackness and racism from anywhere it persists within the community. We must have the vital

conversations within our own families and with our loved ones about things we can do to ensure we actively do anti-racism work. We continue to fight against both racism and anti-Blackness against Black Americans and Afro Arabs within our own community. It is our responsibility to confront our households, neighborhoods, and places of worship when they perpetuate anti-Blackness as well as take necessary action to divest from the carceral system and the policing of Black people that destroys lives. It is our responsibility to fight for a future that invests in education, healthcare, reparations, as well as healthy communities—safe from toxic food, water, dumping and profit-driven pollution—where families can flourish and thrive.[125]

For this collective, the futurity of Blacks is constitutive of their own futurity. There is no Palestinian liberation without Black liberation. The Arabs for Black Lives Collective avoids reducing political solidarity to *"a market exchange,"* premised on a crude vision of symmetry and self-interest: "It's not, you need to give us your love and we'll give you ours."[126] This is part of a trend among principled Palestinians to keep and sustain "a focus on the specificity of anti-Black racism in the United States, both as a mode of oppression in which Palestinians in the United States like other immigrant communities, even those from the third world, participate, and as an experience historically distinct from that of Palestinians living under Israeli colonialism and occupation."[127] Actively combatting anti-Blackness sets the tone for an anti-racist and anti-neoliberal global project. The collective understands that there is no serious redress to "Look, a Palestinian!" (the devaluing of Palestinian life) unless Palestinians and their supporters actively deal with "Look, a Negro!" (the devaluing of Black life), starting in their own communities. Contra Wilderson, the Palestinian cause is not threatened by the Black insurrection of Ferguson or Minneapolis but invigorated and strengthened in its eternal fight for egalitarian justice.

The second example comes from Palestinian artist Lina Abojaradeh. Marked by the brutal murder of George Floyd in summer 2020, Abojaradeh's artwork invites us, even compels us, to draw analogies between the racial injustice of Blacks in the Unites States and Indigenous populations—namely Native Americans and Palestinians (see Figure 1.1).

In her drawing, Abojaradeh highlights the agent of racist violence: the white male colonial subject. Incarnated in US police officers and IDF soldiers, this subject exercises his domination over Black, Palestinian, and American native women, with impunity. This domination, however, is not complete. The abjection condition of Blacks, Palestinians, and Native Americans does not reduce them to docile victims. By depicting their "fist clenched," Abojaradeh gestures to their

Figure 1.1 [Black Lives Matter], by permission of the artist, Lina Abojaradeh(@ linaabart), www.facebook.com/linaabojaradehart.

collective resistance to white supremacy, to their refusal to submit to the racial order of things.[128]

An Afropessimist reader would argue that Abojaradeh romanticizes antiracist struggle and misrecognizes the fundamental problem of civil society as white (Ashkenazy) supremacy. Jared Sexton, for instance, objects to the ways non-Black people of color mistakenly assume "the monolithic character of victimization under white supremacy—thinking (the afterlife of) slavery as a form of exploitation or colonization or a species of racial oppression among others."[129] For the Afropessimist, despite being motivated by the murder of George Floyd, the depiction of anti-Blackness in this artwork is flattened, *as if* Black folks are precisely fighting the same fight under the banner of Black Lives Matter. On this interpretation, Abojaradeh does not see that the true antagonism (as opposed to resolvable conflict) is not between whites and non-whites but between Blacks (nonhumans) and non-Blacks (humans). Black suffering permits no analogy. BLM, in its Afropessimist inflection, is not a humanist project. Abojaradeh's perceived failure to make this distinction makes her, in the eyes of Afropessimists, unconsciously anti-Black.[130]

Indigenous struggles, like that of the Palestinians, will always fall short of destroying the world as long as the category of the human is left untheorized, its constitutive anti-Blackness unaddressed. But to stop the discussion here is to neglect the importance of imaginative world-making. It is to decline Abojaradeh's intervention and invitation for political solidarity, ignoring the ways her artwork struggles with anti-Black violence, foregrounding it as civil society's current horizon of violence. Her artwork does *not* leave anti-Blackness in "the position of the unthought."[131] Rather, it implores non-Blacks to take up "the vantage of black existence."[132] Such artwork short-circuits the impulse to rank the suffering of racialized others. To the question "Blackness or Indigeneity?," it implicitly answers—as we should as well—"Yes, please!"[133]

In a roundtable on anti-Blackness and the prospects of Black-Palestinian solidarity moderated by Noura Erakat, Nadera Shalhoub-Kevorkian expresses the political stakes in thinking solidarity among these two communities. Palestinians and Blacks confront a global socioeconomic system that is hell-bent on silencing them, on denying them the rights that the ruling elites of the world hoard and enjoy for themselves:

> We are talking about two groups that are globally perceived as living dead. As a Palestinian, I see clearly, that on a global level, Palestinians do not have a right to exist. Israelis have a right to exist because of a Biblical right and in that narrative we are invaders and are disturbing a world order. This is where I see solidarity between Blacks and Palestinians because the political economy of Blackness is the political economy of Palestinianness whereby there is other-ization and being perceived in zoological terms, in the Fanon sense. Consider the Balfour Declaration—therein we are not even people to be consulted. And the same can be said of Blacks—who are slaves and should not be consulted. They are not there to be consulted, we are not even people.[134]

If social death, living without basic rights, reduced to flesh, a being devoid of agency and worth, characterizes the paradoxical existence of Blacks and Palestinians, their common exclusion—both deemed "a non-people," nonhumans and uncivilized, ~~subjectivities~~ with whom no consultation is required—inspires and enables a transnational project, tying their causes together. This Black-Palestinian solidarity is always in the making, *à venir*. This is a solidarity that is not based on a shared positive humanity (which would foreclose the birth of new identities, new realities, new humanisms), a narcissistic reduction of the Other's trauma to one's own (which would iron out differences and frictions),[135] nor a "shared analogy of oppression," but on a common struggle for emancipation or "shared principles of liberation," as Robin D. G. Kelley puts it.[136]

Affective belonging, a recognition of shared victimization, though necessary, is never sufficient for political emancipation. Indeed, an effortless claim of shared victimization might in fact hide an appropriation or a neglect of the plight of other oppressed and racialized communities, so that the liberation of one might come at the expense of another. Declining a "politics of equivalence," however, does not mean embracing "political or intellectual isolation" nor indulging in separatist fancies.[137] Identity-based interventions are anathema to the Palestinian cause. The struggle against Ashkenazi supremacy and its overrepresentation of the human as white/European does not only implicate Palestinians but touches all of us. This is why the racial and economic justice sought by Palestinians and their Black comrades in the United States is part and parcel of a universal project.

"Destroying this world together" makes a libidinal *divestment* from the "human" axiomatic, a key precondition for cross-racial solidarity. "Look, a Negro!"—the denial of Black people's humanity, the racialized assemblage par excellence—haunts the Palestinian cause. It serves as a reminder and remainder of who was/is barred from and left out of the liberal humanist project. The grammar of humanity/humanism is no doubt all too tempting, but it comes at a price; its grammar's intrinsic relation to anti-Blackness can no longer be denied or ignored.[138] Palestinian proximity to the human may elicit humanist dreams and fantasies. Claiming Indigeneity might result in the liberal award of more rights, more recognition, more inclusion. But Palestinian abjection will not truly end until the racial matrix is itself abolished and a *collective* redefinition of the human—the invention of a "new man," as Fanon puts it[139]—is initiated and carried through. For this reason, the vitality and fate of the Palestinian cause depends on its prioritization of and engagement with the Black cause. Exceptionalizing one's plight, adopting a Manichean view of the social world, is ultimately of minimal political value. No matter how you spin it, you end up fostering a zero-sum approach to the fight against racial injustice; this is an "Oppression Olympics," paradigms of subjugation outrivaling one another, that can only serve to perpetuate the status quo. The immediate challenge is to see how Indigeneity *and* Blackness are both entangled in the shifting dynamics of racialization and neocolonialism. Dismantling the settler/master's house must pass through the undoing of the category of the human and/as a recasting of its underside: Blacks and Indigenous peoples.

2

Thinking under Occupation

Being where one thinks . . . becomes a fundamental concern of those who have been relegated to a second or third place in the global epistemic order. "I am where I think" sets the stage for epistemic affirmations that have been disavowed. At the same time, it creates a shift in the geography of reasoning.
—Walter Mignolo[1]

Although some people claim there are fundamental differences between the disposition of the territories Israel captured in 1967 and the territories it captured during its creation in 1948—or even that there are important moral and political differences between Israel pre- and post-1967—such sentiments of entitlement, and the use of force that necessarily accompanies them, reveal the seamless continuity of the Zionist project in Palestine from 1948 to our own time.
—Saree Makdisi[2]

Imprisoned in Israel's colonial matrix of power, Palestinians inside and outside the Green Line are systematically discriminated against, deprived of dignity and equality. The Israeli state casts Palestinians in the Occupied Territories as a permanent external enemy, bloodthirsty brutes whose lands lie in wait for annexation and the realization of a "Greater Israel." As for the Palestinians at home, over one-fifth of the Israeli population, the Jewish state considers them something of a burden, the price of democracy, or what Israel had to do (keep and assimilate its Arab minority rather than genocide them) to display its "democratic" bona fides to Western powers. But to be clear: it is not that the former are despised, while the latter are tolerated. No, as we saw in Chapter 1, the Palestinian Other remains an alien at home and abroad, a phobic object wherever she is encountered. "Our interior is always to some extent occupied and interrupted by others—Israelis and Arabs," writes Edward Said.[3] Occupation is constitutive of the Palestinian condition, not just a post-1967 phenomenon affecting only the inhabitants in the Occupied Territories. Indeed, as Saree Makdisi notes, there is a "seamless continuity of the Zionist project in Palestine from 1948 to our own time."[4]

Thinking under Occupation—thinking in the face of an occupier whose logic aims to fragment Palestinians as a people so as to better contain and subjugate them—becomes both vital and dangerous, not a luxury but a necessity. In this chapter, I turn to Walter Mignolo's alluring decolonial dictum, "I am where I think,"[5] and explore its appeal, relevance, and ultimately its limits for understanding Palestinian identity under Occupation. Mignolo's "I am where I think" radically reworks Descartes's original formulation, "I think therefore I am" (a synecdoche for European modernity). From the vantage point of decolonial thinking, the latter formulation can only invite abstraction, promoting an imperial epistemology (we are all *cogitos*) and the devaluation of non-Europeans. Avoiding the abstract universalism of the Cartesian tradition, the decolonial critic makes the question of geography central to any questions of knowledge and biography. In the decolonial statement "I am where I think," the word "where" pluralizes—that is, democratizes—meaning and the experiences of the world, affirming a planetary sensibility in place of a reified Eurocentric global vision.

Decoloniality points to a way out of Zionist enclosures. Indigenous Palestinians are urged to delink from coloniality and relink to precolonial ways of thinking and learning. And yet decoloniality's solution to settler colonialism—"epistemic reconstitution"[6] as its vision of the Palestinian cause—is prone to mystification: it fetishizes origins or local culture, homogenizing and romanticizing Palestinian precolonial roots. In the decolonial imaginary, the spaces of Indigeneity are uncontaminated by coloniality, Palestinian wholeness is regained, freed from Zionist epistemic constrains. Moreover, this redemptive approach to Indigeneity crowds out less insular models of Palestinian identity emphasizing an exilic mode of Palestinianness, as one finds in Edward Said and Mourid Barghouti. For Said, exile is "the fundamental condition of Palestinian life," a condition that unites all Palestinians.[7] In his work and Barghouti's, exile becomes a paradoxical gift, bestowing a mode of perception akin to the second sight of "double-consciousness" W. E. B. Du Bois detailed so well in his study of Black experience in the United States.[8] In *I Saw Ramallah*, Barghouti muses on the vantage of diasporic experience as he observes and interacts with Palestinians living under Occupation. His memoir stages a fascinating encounter between exile and Indigeneity. This encounter does not lead, however, to a simple choice between exile and Indigeneity as mutually exclusive options. Such a move would serve the Zionist project of fragmenting and dividing Palestinians. Instead, I explore what a contrapuntal reading of exilic identity—what a diasporic inflection of Mignolo's "I am where I think"—opens up for the Palestinian subject (what kind of shared identity is exile?) and the Palestinian cause (what constitutes solidarity among Palestinians?).

Zionist/Colonial Enclosures

From the vantage point of decoloniality, Western modernity exerts its hegemonic control over non-Europeans by determining their identity or being through a process of racialization.[9] Whiteness is aligned with modernity and humanity (the site of civilization), while non-whiteness is aligned with non-Europeans—modernity's underside—the less than human (the site of savagery). The decolonial task is to destabilize this imputed identity by challenging the self-imposed authority of the West and reimagining modernity more expansively, more generously, as touching the whole planet. Toward that end, Mignolo prefers the formulation "identity in politics" over "identity politics,"[10] because, unlike the latter, the former is always already denaturalized, lacking any intrinsic properties or force. Identity in politics acknowledges from the start that one's identity has been constructed and allocated by European colonial powers. Rather than playing within the rules of modernity, decolonial theorists seek to forge an identity free from the prison house of coloniality.

Indigenous reason—as the Western/Zionist consciousness of Palestinian Indigeneity—classifies the Native as the known rather than the knower. In this classification, the known is deemed backward and rendered racially inferior while the knower is elevated and universalized as the (overrepresented) symbol of humanity. Mignolo describes the alchemic process by which a racist Western epistemology, driven by an unshakable will to classify, produces a set of divisions, a hierarchical ontology that places the non-Europeans squarely at the bottom and Europeans at the top:

> Racism consists in devaluing the humanity of certain people by dismissing it or playing it down (even when not intentional) at the same time as highlighting and playing up European philosophy, assuming it to be universal. It may be global, because it piggybacks on imperial expansion, but it certainly cannot be universal. Racism is a classification, and classification is an epistemic maneuver rather than an ontological entity that carries with it the essence of the classification.[11]

As Ta-Nehisi Coates poetically put it, "race is the child of racism, not the father."[12] Race is to be aligned with the imagination rather than perception.[13] The phobic Native does not precede settler colonialism but rather results from it.[14] Coloniality, the afterlife of colonialism, makes the inequality of racial lives axiomatic: Jewish lives matter, Palestinian lives don't. The former are protected, the latter exposed; the former dominate, the latter are dominated.

The birth of Western modernity coincides with (settler) colonial domination. As Mignolo asserts, "there is no modernity without coloniality."[15] Modernity without racial difference, without its imperial agenda, is not just an incomplete definition: it is a complete distortion of its matrix and legacy. "Modernity and progress in Europe meant stagnation and misery (coloniality) in the rest of the world."[16] For the past five centuries, the West has assumed and asserted its epistemic superiority, its authority (emanating from Christianity or Reason itself) to rule over non-Europeans: "Decolonial options have one aspect in common with dewesternizing arguments: The definitive rejection of 'being told' from the epistemic privileges of the zero point what 'we' are, what our ranking is in relation to the ideal of the humanitas and what we have to do to be recognized as such."[17] It is in this light that we must see the Zionist project. Inspired by nineteenth-century European nationalism, Zionism enthusiastically accepted its logic: "one state, one nation."[18] Settler colonialism eagerly exported the idea of the nation-state, this "universal form of governance,"[19] to historic Palestine. Driven by a nationalist desire for a Jewish homeland, Zionist settlers dispossessed the Indigenous population, claiming "Manifest Destiny" as the justification for their ethnic cleansing of the non-Europeans.[20]

After the creation of Israel (1948) and its subsequent Occupation of Palestinian territories (1967), the Israeli state was confronted with the modern challenges of governance: "to look after the well-being of its citizens and to deem everyone else as suspicious or as a lesser human and dispensable in relation to a given nation-state."[21] Of course, in Israel, citizenship is itself an institution of domination, part and parcel of its apartheid regime. Its citizens are not all created alike. The Israeli state distinguishes between Jewish citizens and non-Jewish citizens: the former are nationals and the latter nonnationals.[22] Nationality entitles Jewish people to preferential treatment (= Jewish supremacy[23]), shielding them from discriminatory practices (though, as we saw in Chapter 1, Black and Brown Jews are never fully immune or protected from such racialized assemblages). Consequently, this foundational distinction between Jew and non-Jew makes Palestinian citizens of Israel closer to their noncitizen brethren in Occupied Palestine than to Jewish Israelis.

Is Israel, then, really justified in describing itself as both Jewish *and democratic*? A democracy worthy of the name is not simply unable to flourish in Israel—it is dead on arrival! Coloniality rules out equality between (European) Jews and non-Jews. The non-European, the Palestinian, is, *aborigine*, disprivileged and defiled, not a fellow subject, occupying the paradoxical status of an internal outsider on her own generational land. Palestinians inside and outside Israel are an intrinsic threat to Zionism, to the "homogeneity of the nation-state."[24] In this age of security, Palestinians must be (kept) separated from Israeli Jews. Enclosure characterizes the condition of the Indigenous. They are subjected to what Mbembe calls the *matrix of rules*, a matrix "mostly designed for those human bodies deemed either in excess, unwanted, illegal, dispensable, or superfluous."[25] From the settler/Zionist perspective, Palestinian presence indexes danger and provokes fear to Jewish life. Mbembe singles out Gaza as particularly exemplary of this matrix, underscoring both its link to prior modes of "enclosure, contraction, and containment" (such as Native American reservations in the United States, Bantustans in South Africa, island prisons, and penal colonies, among others) and its novelty in combining "spatial violence, humanitarian strategies, and a peculiar biopolitics of punishment,"[26] in order to generate "a peculiar carceral space in which people deemed surplus, unwanted, or illegal are governed through abdication of any responsibility for their lives and their welfare."[27] Israel manages to exert its sovereignty over the Indigenous population without assuming any of its responsibility or obligations toward the occupied Palestinians.[28] Mbembe warns of a certain Gazafication of the world, casting Gaza as a prefiguration of "what is yet to come."[29]

This Gazafication is already taking place in the other regions of the Occupation. If Gazans live in the largest open-air prison, West Bankers and East Jerusalemites are immobilized, precariously dwelling on forbidden and annexable lands; refugees are excluded from the land, denied their internationally recognized right of return; and the citizens of Israel are separate and unequal. The latter are in some ways a greater danger to Israel's global image. The status of the Occupied Territories is in principle resolvable if the peace process is reignited (as witnessed in the West's attachment to the Oslo Accords); the denial of the right of return can be rationalized away as the price of compromise (in an eventual resolution to the "conflict"). With "Arab" Israelis, matters appear more complicated. Israeli politicians purport to care for *all* citizens—including the "Arab" minority. For example, when called on to defend its disproportionate use of force during *Operation Guardian of the Walls* at the United Nations Security Council virtual session on May 16, 2021, Gilad Erdan, then Israel's ambassador to the United States and the United Nations, repeated the standard Israeli script, which always locates the start of conflict not with the Occupation, the colonial situation, but with Hamas missiles falling indiscriminately on Israeli civilians in unprovoked terrorist attacks, against which Israel can only defend itself heroically. This time, however, Erdan added a twist to this narrative. He held up a picture of an "Arab" Israeli girl who was "murdered" (Erdan's language) by a Hamas rocket: "Nadine Awad, a 16-year-old girl, an Arab citizen of Israel."[30]

And yet this ostentatious profession of outrage over an "Arab" Israeli death, this shameless "Browning" of the Israeli victim and instrumentalization of de-Palestinized suffering for PR reasons (Israeli *hasbara*: "Look, we also care about Arab Israeli lives"), can appear only as a tasteless instance of "Arabwashing" meant to distract from Israel's systemic neglect and mistreatment of its national minority, its cruel policies of keeping the *Palestinian* citizens of Israel docile, in check.[31] True to its colonial roots—to its dual ethnocracy and racial matrix—Israel prioritizes the well-being of its "true" people, its (Ashkenazi) nationals. But the rhetoric of priority fails to address fully what is taking place. The well-being of nationals not only takes precedence over that of nonnationals, but the former is predicated on the negation or degradation of the latter. As I have been arguing in this book, for Jewish life to matter, Palestinian/"Arab" life must be made to un-matter. Under "one state, one nation" the two can never both matter. The former stands for humanity, the latter not-quite-humanity/nonhumanity. Indeed, Israel consistently restricts the range of its democracy, targeting its non-Jewish citizens, singling out its "Arab" minority for diminished rights. In this light, parading a Palestinian-Israeli victim of rockets before the international community also functions to confirm the savagery of Arabs generally ("Look, they kill their own people").

The Nakba Law and the Citizenship Law are two examples that showcase Israel's ongoing coloniality. They illustrate and enact Israel's "legalized violence,"[32] embodying the ethnic state's indefatigable will to enclose and racialize the "Arab" threat from within, the internal outsider. National security naturally opens to Jewish supremacy. The Israeli Knesset passed what has been dubbed the "Nakba Law" on March 22, 2011; this legislation instructs the government to deny state funding to any organization, institution, or municipality that commemorates the birth of Israel as a day of mourning. Thus, when it comes to learning about your heritage as a Palestinian-Israeli child, this formative act of dispossession will *not* be covered in your public education. The basic "right to remember" is denied.[33] Palestinians are deprived of the right to learn about *their* own past. Now, it is crucial to juxtapose the Nakba Law with

Israel's evolving educational policies toward its minority population. Needless to say, education is a contentious site for the prospect of thinking critically under the Occupation. In Israel, the government controls all of the branches of the educational apparatus involving both its Jewish and Palestinian students; "the Israeli secret service . . . vets teachers and headmasters alike, as well as any changes in the curriculum."[34] Palestinians are cast exclusively as consumers rather than producers of knowledge. According to Adalah, "the policies which determine educational content and syllabi are set without the participation of Arab citizens or teachers."[35] As Mahmood Jrere, cofounder of the Palestinian hip-hop group DAM, put it: "We can't learn about Mahmoud Darwish, for example, who is the most important poet in Palestine. We can learn about Herzl. We can learn about our occupiers, but we cannot learn about our own poets and leaders."[36] Learning about the occupier's culture at the expense of your own involves what José Medina calls "epistemic death," cultural genocide, the silencing and starving of Palestinian minds, denying Indigenous agency and barring their involvement in official knowledge production.[37] The purpose of Israeli education is "to 'Israelize' Palestinian citizens of Israel,"[38] to normalize and depoliticize Indigenous children, fulfilling, in turn, the objectives of a "nationalizing state," which is "conceived as complex institutional entities composed of legal, economic and cultural components, design and render the citizenship of indigenous national minorities into a 'hollow citizenship' that is devoid of substantive cultural, economic and political meaning, since these minorities, often by their mere existence, tend to challenge the basic vision of the state."[39] Moreover, Israel's pedagogical model breeds horizontal hostility among Palestinians; it teaches Arab Israelis to identify with the state of Israel and the Zionist cultural script, not with their brethren in the Occupied Territories and the Palestinian cause.

Autonomy over Indigenous education, for example, becomes fertile grounds for decolonial struggle, for Palestinian cultural resistance—the remedy to culturecide and the making of "hollow citizenship." Pappé delineates the stakes of a would-be decolonial teacher:

> The struggle is consciously one for educational autonomy, within the present regime. In the past, teachers who challenged the curriculum by teaching the Palestinian narrative paid a high price of exile and imprisonment. Today they need to navigate between the regime's refusal to recognize the Palestinians in Israel as a national minority and the latter's own refusal to accept the imposed Zionist narrative of the Israeli educational system.[40]

"Indigenous cultural resistance," for Pappé, is the only option available that enables Palestinians to fight for educational autonomy while still working within the present regime.[41] More generally, the term "Indigenous" denotes "an evolving position of empowerment and resilience against the discrimination and oppression of the natives."[42] Drawing on the discourse of Indigenous rights, Palestinian educational reformers have put forward demands centering on history and cultural heritage:

- Raise the level of knowledge of the cultural icons, symbols, and institutions of the Palestinian people.
- Deepen and reinforce the link between our children and the Palestinian people's history and struggle.
- Create a dialogue with the Israeli authorities over the importance of our cultural characteristics and collective identity.
- Expose the approach of Israel's educational system, which endeavors to emphasize the "Jewishness" of the state, to the exclusion of 20 percent of the citizens of the state.[43]

In de Certeauian terms, Palestinians are in the position of the weak. Deprived of a "proper" space of their own, the weak "must continually turn to their own end forces alien to them."[44] Palestinians cannot generate alternative educational "strategies"; their only options are "tactics," which effectively "belong to the other."[45] To effect change, Palestinians must operate "within enemy territory."[46] If a frontal attack—teaching about national struggle—is not an option, rusing might be.[47] We may consider cultural resistance a form of "rusing"; it does not violate the laws of the state but rusing can potentially "smuggle new values and meanings" into that state, as Nicole Simek puts it; it can introduce dissident ideas into the authorized curriculum.[48] Rusing with the Israeli curriculum might start with exploiting Israel's democratic aspirations in order to render democracy concrete and unsettling (the idea of a state *open to all*), frustrating what the state currently envisions and enjoys only as an ideological abstraction.

On the Israeli side, the government has signaled a willingness to change its procedures and allow for more "Arab" input. Since the "Arab problem" in Israel is often framed as a problem of integration—though the 2021 Gaza war and the unrest in Israel's "mixed" cities reframed Palestinian Israelis as a problem of security, constituting what Netanyahu called a "second front"[49]—the government has focused on "non-formal education" (hours spent in extracurricular activities) to supplement the "Arab" curriculum. In 2015, it passed Resolution 922, a five-year economic development plan for Arab communities, earmarking

$182 million to increase non-formal education programs in "Arab" society. The programs are meant to address the question of belonging and identity: "What does it mean to be an Arab in a predominantly Jewish society and how can you create social solidarity with the state? What does it mean to be an Arab citizen in Israel?"[50] Whereas the Palestinian demands can be seen as incremental steps toward the task of *decolonizing* the Israeli curriculum, the government's sanctioned remedy, which determines the parameters of educational reform, is really not a remedy at all, but a softer version of the imperative to "Israelize" Palestinian children, to naturalize the settler way of life, which goes hand in hand with the colonization of the minds of the "Arab" minority. There is no interest in developing alternative *strategies*. Learning about the unfolding of Zionist destiny remains the pedagogical doxa. There is no reckoning with the exclusionary practices that have silenced Palestinian voices and reduced the Palestinian question (of which sovereignty/land repatriation is central) to the "Arab" problem of inclusion/integration. The Israeli message to its minority is clear enough: we will continue with our civilizational development, but we will also invest economically in your communities, enabling you to learn more about your cultural heritage (and thus reduce your alienation), so that you can "fit" better in society and become productive economic subjects. Educational reform as part of a multiculturalist project really only serves an ideological function: it is meant to squelch national aspirations and reorient the Arab minority to the fact of Zionist reality.

Colonial difference never factors in. Abstractly, the government treats Palestinian children as if they were Jewish children; their pedagogical needs are the *same*. The question of power—anti-Palestinian formation, the settler/Native structure that generated and continues to generate colonial difference[51]—is bracketed from the project of integration (so that integration is never predicated on decolonizing the curriculum, let alone the nation-state). The government's Resolution 922 can be seen simultaneously as an attempt to placate Palestinian demands for more cultural rights (reduce the call for justice underpinning the Palestinian cause to a depoliticized politics of recognition) and as another liberal "move to innocence" (change without real change, that is, change without the undoing of Jewish privilege). Israel's education reform reenforces rather than deviates from its long-standing colonial management of its "Arab" minority:

> The aspiration was to reshape Arab consciousness and identity in accordance with the hegemonic Israeli worldview by controlling the society's political discourse. Israel's leadership understood that consciousness guides the

behavior of individuals. The state's goal was to detach the Palestinian Arabs in Israel from the Palestinian Arab identity that was central for many of them and to create something new—the Israeli Arab. The consolidation of such an identity may well have been inevitable in light of the peculiar circumstances that prevailed after the 1948 war—principally, these Arabs' new status as a minority in a Jewish state—but the regime wanted to sever their ties to the Arab national movement. Through its loyalists, the state sought to indoctrinate *Arab schoolchildren with the Zionist narrative*, to widen the fissures between and within religious communities (Muslims, Christians, and Druze), to promote obedience to the authorities, and to challenge non-Israeli national identities (Palestinian or pan-Arab). No less important, by reporting on the day-to-day speech of Arabs and by summoning and interrogating those Arabs who spoke against the state, the security authorities "taught" the minority what was fit to be said and what was unacceptable, thus shaping the contours of Arab political discourse in Israel.[52]

Learning about one's culture is a relative good; learning about one's national struggle is an absolute evil (unlike the former, the latter poses a more significant risk of traversing the artificial boundaries and healing the divisions among Palestinians instilled in "Arab" Israeli children). Teaching the Nakba—what does it mean to be a colonized body in a Zionist settler regime? What does it mean to be the child of Nakba survivors in Israel?—clearly falls in the latter category.[53]

As with the Nakba Law, the Citizenship Law was born out of the fear of a politicized Palestinian body: "Arab" Israelis disidentifying with the state of Israel, joining the Palestinian national struggle. The law "bars granting citizenship or residency to Palestinians from the occupied West Bank or Gaza who are married to Israeli citizens."[54] Israel first passed its infamous amendment to the Citizenship Law in 2003 during the Second Intifada. Shin Bet, the Israeli Internal Security Service, strongly supports the law as a means to protect its citizens, while the ethnonationalists back it for demographic reasons. Keeping undesirable Palestinians out (undesirable *because* they are Palestinians) is the goal of the law. This apartheid legislation had been extended annually till its defeat on July 5, 2021 (to be sure, the defeat was not so much a recognition of the law's immorality than a result of the power struggle between prime minister Naftali Bennett and his rival, former prime minister Netanyahu). On March 10, 2022, Israeli lawmakers, spurred by Minister of Interior Ayelet Shaked, who managed to gather support from the Right and Center-Left, reinstated the racist Citizenship Law.⁵⁵ But what kind of a democratic state erects a law that bars a group of its Indigenous citizens from the privileges clearly afforded to its others? Two explanations are given: the need for security (Palestinian interdiction for the well-being of the Jewish *state*) and the preservation of Jewish majority (= Jewish supremacy). For Bennett, the failure to renew the law amounts to a "direct blow to national security." And for the "centrist" Foreign Minister Yair Lapid, "It is one of the tools designed to ensure a Jewish majority in the State of Israel." It is a "legal" means to block the pursuit of a backdoor right of return. And without the Citizenship Law "there would be an increase in Palestinian terrorism," adds Lapid, tying Jewish/white supremacy back to security (its preservation). Israeli leaders implicitly cast true democracy (all its citizens possessing the same rights) as a threat to the state of Israel. Religion trumps citizenship. Without the Citizenship Law to safeguard the Jewish state from Palestinian encroachment, the "Arab" Israelis petitioning for their spouses will be either deceived by the ill-intending Palestinians on the other side Green Line (who are assumed to be guilty infiltrators or would-be terrorists—a risk too great for Israel to take) or they will be emboldened by the increase of Palestinians in Israel and seduced into joining the "enemy" in rebelling against the Jewish state. Palestinian Israelis are always already virtual enemies, "even if Palestinians have Israeli identity cards and passports," writes Michael Warschwaski, "they are not citizens, not even second-class citizens, but enemies."⁵⁶ Not unlike Netanyahu's alarming rhetoric about a "second front" opening on Israeli soil, Lapid's commentary about Palestinian infiltration is shaped by anxieties about the loss of both demographic and racial dominance. *Meet the new boss, same as the old boss . . .*

But to be clear: to oppose Lapid and Bennett is not to reject the idea that this Palestinian rebellion can or should happen. Rather, it is to flatly reject the Zionist narrative about Palestinian terrorism, where the Palestinian terrorist stands for a general, highly Orientalized Arab: "the mad Islamic zealot, the gratuitously violent killer of innocents, the desperately irrational and savage primitive."⁵⁷ Unlike Israel's "Arab" minority, who have been somewhat tamed by Israel's civic institutions, Palestinians outside of the Green Line are "raw" Arabs—uncivilizable, un-Europeanizable, if you will—whose savagery is intrinsic and immanent to their being. To reject this mendacious narrative is to challenge Israel's belligerent right to exist *as a supremacist regime*. For Zionism, Palestinian terrorism is always divorced from the colonial situation—armed struggle against the invisible *terror* of the settler colonizer who is robbing the Native of her land and dignity—pathologized as irrational, as the by-product of a despicable and irrepressible anti-Semitism.[58] What Israel really fears is that allowing more Palestinians into Israel might intensify the demands for equality and Indigenous self-determination. Increased collective will might strengthen the push to decolonize Israel and make it more difficult for the Zionist regime to normalize the habitual violence of settler colonialism. Israel's political leaders know that the settler project is not yet a fait accompli—whence the proliferation of racist, nationalist laws aimed at "saving" the colonial Zionist state.[59] Israel serves as a reminder of decolonization's "unfinished project." While all settler nations are tainted by what Walter Benjamin calls "state-founding violence,"[60] Žižek rightly notes that Israel's infrastructure of violence still hasn't been fully accepted or naturalized as a feature of everyday existence. The Israeli state "hasn't yet obliterated the 'founding violence' of its 'illegitimate' origins, repressing them into a timeless past. In this sense, what the state of Israel confronts us with is merely the obliterated past of every state power."[61] The Israeli state's PR machine actively promotes collective "amnesia" about its horrific, settler beginnings.[62] The Nakba survivors, in particular, are a bone in the throat of the Zionist regime; in their refusal to be subjugated, they are an unshakable irritant, physical evidence of the Israeli state's original and ongoing criminality.[63] In this respect, it is not surprising that Zionist politicians fear that more Palestinians in Israel might provoke a tipping point within its minority community. Israel as a Jewish state is not destiny. The structures of Jewish privilege/Palestinian disprivilege are not immovable or unalterable. *Palestine/Israel can still be imagined otherwise.*

Thinking—rather than merely subsisting—under Occupation keeps open the "wounds" of coloniality.[64] There is no suturing of the wound, no healing under Occupation (a return to normalcy as a shared condition of Jews and Palestinians), only brutality (exile and imprisonment) or pacification (becoming a "good Arab"[65]). From the Zionist perspective, then, the (temporary) defeat of the Citizenship Law jeopardizes the immanent "triumph"[66] of Israel's settler-colonial project, endangering the sanctity of "one state, one nation." The Nakba Law and the Citizenship Law bear witness to Israel's endless ambitions to enclose Palestinians, to make them disappear as Palestinians. The former does it by disavowing Israel's facticity, its original sin, and repressing knowledge of this foundational trauma for the Palestinian people, by erasing its trace and content from the curriculum, seeking, in turn, to isolate its "Arab" minority from the larger national struggle; the latter by maintaining demographic control and consolidating territorial control. Whereas Zionism masks the colonial difference at home by separating the hostile Palestinians of the Occupied Territories from the "good Arabs" (if formed properly by Israel's civic institutions) inside the Green Line, decoloniality underscores the unity of the Palestinian people, their Indigeneity in the face of Israel's coloniality. The saying "I am where I think" is at once an act of world-salvaging and world-making. It renders visible and legitimizes the subaltern voices of Palestinians, and thus declines "the universality to which everyone has to submit"[67] (e.g., Palestinian children submitting to the Zionist settler narrative), shifting back to history and locality, to non-Europeans' positionality in relation to "the epistemic and ontological racism of imperial knowledge."[68]

The Palestinian cause is clearly not a regional struggle, but a struggle against the West's "coloniality of power."[69] Decoloniality in Palestine/Israel revolves around empowering native cultures and making Indigenous knowledges visible, relevant, and comprehensible, counteracting what the Israeli government has constituted as false, insignificant, or dangerous, falling outside what it considers legitimate knowledge. Decoloniality preaches Indigenous/Palestinian "epistemic disobedience."[70] More generally, in provincializing Western discourse and moving beyond "macronarratives from the perspective of coloniality,"[71] decoloniality substitutes transmodernity for modernity. Whereas the old model takes a teleological and linear view of progress, starting with Greece then moving to Rome, the Renaissance, and the modern world (with Israel "bringing" modernity to the Middle East), transmodernity makes the colonial encounters constitutive of modernity, spatializing modernity by making it encompass the entire planet. As Linda Martín Alcoff aptly puts it, "if modernity is imagined to be European, transmodernity is planetary, with principal players from all parts of the globe."[72] We might add, if modernity adopts Descartes's "I think therefore I am" as inaugurating Europe's modern ethos, transmodernity adopts Mignolo's decolonial thesis, "I am where I think."

The shift from modernity to transmodernity casts colonial difference in a new light, as a "critical source of knowledge."[73] It is a difference unshackled by the "myth of modernity":[74] a view of modernity that authorizes the West (including the Occidentalized Israel) to outline the parameters of the universal, to define identity, positioning it in the role of the definer while positioning the rest of the world, the non-Europeans (e.g., the Orientalized Palestinians) in the place of the defined.[75] Decolonial thought, then, is as much about unlearning as it is about relearning: undoing the colonization of the mind via a recovery, restoration, and appreciation of subalternized knowledges, formerly discredited Indigenous modes of knowing and life-forms that sprung from it. By delinking from Zionist narratives and relinking to their cultural heritage, Palestinians can, in principle, retrieve a far more valuable, pre-settler past prior to their excision from the realm of the human and the universal.

Tarrying with the Exilic

This critique of Zionism/coloniality sounds promising and hopeful, but what happens to the Palestinian diaspora in the decolonial narrative? What role, if any, does it play in combatting Israeli dominion and in overcoming colonial difference? Are Palestinians living in the West, for instance, operating unwittingly within a "modern/colonial epistemology,"[76] subservient to a Eurocentric ethos? Or to put it slightly differently, what does "I am where I think" mean for the exilic or cosmopolitan Palestinian? And without disputing the merits of reclaiming and taking pride in modes of existence and relationality that had been systematically denigrated under the Occupation, a decolonial vision tends to assume an insular model of identity that is ripe for nostalgia. But as Mbembe states, "decolonization never meant the return to some egosphere or to some elective self-image that would procure a stable identity, protection, safety and security and eventually immunity to an embattled self."[77] The idea/l of a pristine Palestine untainted by coloniality, the purity and authenticity of a Palestinian identity regained, freed from the logic of the nation-state, reinscribes Palestinian Indigeneity/identity in some dubious "idyllic and mythical past."[78]

Mignolo's decoloniality subscribes to the tripartite structure of emancipatory projects identified by Frank Wilderson:

> The arc of an emancipatory progression which ends in either equality, liberation, or redress, in other words, a narrative of liberation, is marked by the three generic moments that one finds in any narrative: a progression from equilibrium (the spatial-temporal point prior to oppression), disequilibrium (capitalist political economy or the arrival and residence taking of the settler), and equilibrium restored/reorganized/or reimagined (the dictatorship of the proletariat or the settler's removal from one's land).[79]

Turning to Said and Barghouti's musings on exile, I take up a different response to Zionist coloniality, one that contravenes the decolonial narrative arc: equilibrium (Palestine$_1$), disequilibrium (the creation of the settler state of Israel/Occupation), equilibrium (Palestine$_2$). Exile blocks the impulse for rootedness but does not give up on Palestinianness and (the desire for) national belonging. Said and Barghouti, in their own distinct ways, tarry with the exilic, linger in uncertainty, and prolong the experience of this disequilibrium otherwise.[80] There is no "cultification of the Indigenous."[81] They decline a return to an imaginary sameness. Dreaming of a *time before the settler* (the resurrection of Palestine, Palestine$_2$, from the ruins of the past) is antithetical to their projects.

The implications for internal solidarity are both sobering and disquieting. Solidarity with one's kin, suturing Palestinian fragmentation, is not a given. What Palestinians share is an open question.

Saidian exile constitutes first and foremost a melancholic disposition, "the unhealable rift forced between a human being and a native place, between the self and its true home: its essential sadness can never be surmounted."[82] And if this sadness is insurmountable, the exile must also avoid fetishizing what has been *historically* lost, transforming the lost "true home" into a *mythical* or metaphysical object (the stuff of redemptive narratives).[83] Said ties his reflections on exile to the worldly hermeneutic of the contrapuntal, the "core quality of the exilic intellectual practice,"[84] which foregrounds internal dividedness and multiplicity: "Most people are principally aware of one culture, one setting, one home; exiles are aware of at least two, and this plurality of vision gives rise to an awareness of simultaneous dimensions, an awareness that—to borrow a phrase from music—is *contrapuntal*."[85]

As a condition (of the intellectual), exile frustrates the temporal stability of any interpretative stance. Exile yields no ontological comfort or satisfaction. For Said, the exiled person not only learns to live in discomfort, but derives a certain *jouissance* (the experience of pleasure with pain) from it: "Exile is never the state of being satisfied, placid, or secure . . . Exile is life led outside habitual order. It is nomadic, decentered, contrapuntal; but no sooner does one get accustomed to it than its unsettling force erupts anew."[86] If exile is contrapuntal, since it is prone to split and double the self, to read contrapuntally is to embrace exile's irruptive becoming; it is to tarry with the exilic and sustain the irreducibility of the self to her environment. Exilic subjectivity is a locus of negativity. Tarrying with the exilic holds on to negation—the gap between the subject and her organic community—as the condition of Palestinian identity.

To read contrapuntally is to adopt a "double-consciousness," a parallax perspective: to testify to the entanglement of visions or voices. As "a form of illicit seeing,"[87] a contrapuntal reading unsubscribes from the cultural script, destabilizing the script's hermeneutic norms, breaking with any logic invested in the reproduction of the status quo. The contrapuntal mode also hinders the self's narcissistic propensities; it considers the culture's affective attachment to the self, to the "the idea of a solid self,"[88] not only illusory but wholly undesirable. Contrapuntal consciousness propels the self beyond the confines of her ego, exposing the self to different positions and views, with no dialectical synthesis in sight. But hermeneutic generosity does not come at the expense of critique (and vice versa). This is not another version of toothless cultural relativism, in which each vision or difference is reified or essentialized as a condition of its readability and valorization. Rather, the contrapuntal nurtures a taste for the provisional and is a perpetual check on absolute authority, emanating either from the self or the symbolic order; it is an initiation into a nonhierarchical and illegitimate mode of thinking, a lesson in overcoming the primacy of the self and biological filiation. Said touts the values of contrapuntal thinking: "it is more rewarding—and more difficult—to think concretely and sympathetically, contrapuntally, about others than only about 'us.'"[89] "Seeing the self through the eyes of hostile others"[90] can be, and often is, unbearable—"Look, a Palestinian!"—but despite, or because of, this pain, the self gains a "second-sight";[91] the Palestinian subject develops a sharper vision and understanding of the colonial situation.

Saidian exile does not take place in abstraction. A certain degree of privilege must be secured: the act of declining belonging and the comforts of rootedness assumes, first, that these are actual options and, second, that you have the *capacity* to decline what is offered to you (i.e., your survival does not depend on your compliance with the status quo). Said is by no means oblivious to this concern; he is quite wary of romanticizing and personalizing (and thus depoliticizing) exile, robbing it of its (collective) traumatic quality: "Exile is strangely compelling to think about but terrible to experience."[92] Exile is "horrendous"; it has "torn millions of people from the nourishment of tradition, family, and geography."[93] Said's exile—the intellectual's metaphorical exile—is not the refugee's exile, nor is his modernist alienation—the feeling of being "out of place" (the title of Said's memoir and last substantial work)—that of the alienation of the Palestinian living under the Occupation. At the same time, a contrapuntal interpretive sensibility enables a rapprochement between Said and his Palestinian brethren, between exile and Indigeneity.[94] Said's own coming to terms with his Palestinianness is noteworthy. He connects it to his commitment to the Palestinian cause in the aftermath of the devastating and humiliating defeat of the Six-Day War in 1967: "I was no longer the same person after 1967; the shock of that war drove me back to where it had all started, the struggle over Palestine."[95] Though it is tempting to see Said's Palestinianness as *"chosen*, as a matter of belief instead of being,"[96] it does simplify Said's quasi-epiphanic scene. Rather than *choosing* the Palestinian cause—that is, willfully deciding to politicize his Palestinianness—Said describes the process as a kind of (non-Althusserian) interpellation. The events of 1967 interpellated him into Middle Eastern politics. Palestine was now his calling.

Exile, along with the contrapuntal hermeneutic that reflect and sustain it, guides Said's meditations on (his) Palestinianness and engagement with the

Palestinian cause. Understood as the historico-ontological condition of *all* Palestinians, exile not only blocks Palestinian fragmentation by the Zionist regime but also serves as a check on their own identitarian desires and Manichean tendencies (us versus them, Nakba versus Shoah, autochthonous nationalism versus the enemy's nationalism, etc.).[97] Said takes his inspiration here from Fanon and his own "contrapuntal" gesture of refusing to fetishize the suffering of one particular people, opting, instead, to reorient his/our intellectual energy toward the universalist plight of the dispossessed, the *other* wretched of the earth:

> It is inadequate only to affirm that a people was dispossessed, oppressed or slaughtered, denied its rights and its political existence, without at the same time doing what Fanon did during the Algerian war, affiliating those horrors with the similar afflictions of other people. This does not at all mean a loss in historical specificity, but rather it guards against the possibility that a lesson learnt about oppression in one place will be forgotten or violated in another place or time.[98]

What Said appreciates in Fanon is his willingness to counteract his over-identification with any one oppressed minority. Fanon's guardedness against intellectual myopia and the exclusive concern for one's own people (against identity politics as the remedy for racial consciousness) protected him from the kind of insular gaze that breeds thoughts of exceptionalism and separatism. Fanonian liberation entailed "a transformation of social consciousness beyond national consciousness."[99] Likewise, "exclusivism and a return to some idyllic and mythical past"[100] were resolutely not Said's answers to the disequilibrium that plagued the Palestinian people. Exile—the desirability of not being "at home"—allowed Said to recast the problem of Occupation in a new light: the refusal to acquiesce to a Western/Zionist vision did not have to take the form of nativism. The question of Palestine demanded a new set of responses. Tarrying with the exilic set the ontological mood for such ethico-political explorations.

In his memoir *I Saw Ramallah*, the poet Mourid Barghouti illustrates and enacts the exilic mode in his return home, his first return trip to Palestine after thirty years of imposed exile due to the Six-Day War and the subsequent occupation of the West Bank in 1967. When the war broke out, Barghouti was a student at Cairo University. The Israeli victory kept him out, made him an exile, but after the signing of the Oslo Accords in 1993, Barghouti was allowed to reenter his homeland by the land's new masters. In *I Saw Ramallah*, a mixture of memoir, essay, and prose poetry, Barghouti chronicles his experiences, giving us penetrating insights into Palestinian life under Occupation. Barghouti's position is paradoxical to the extent that he is both an outsider and an insider to Palestine. Barghouti's exilic positionality stretches Mignolo's decolonial dictum "I am where I think," exerting hermeneutic pressure on the significance of the *where*. The memoir stages a dialectical encounter between Barghouti, the exile, and the Indigenous people of Ramallah.

In his highly influential forward to the English translation of Barghouti's memoir, Said claims *I Saw Ramallah* as distinctively a work of exile, powerfully displaying and humanizing the Palestinian experience: "Despite its joy and moments of exuberance this narrative return reenacts exile rather than repatriation. This is what gives it both its tragic dimension and *its appealing precariousness*. . . . The Palestinian experience is therefore humanized and given substance in a new way."[101] Here we might draw on Judith Butler's key distinction between precariousness and precarity:

> Lives are by definition precarious: they can be expunged at will or by accident; their persistence is in no sense guaranteed. In some sense, this is a feature of all life, and there is no thinking of life which is not precarious. . . . Precarity designates the politically induced condition in which certain populations suffer from failing social and economic networks of support and become differentially exposed to injury, violence and death.[102]

In *Rhetorics of Belonging*, Anna Bernard appreciates Barghouti's sensitivity to Palestinian precarity, but faults Said for falling prey to abstraction because of his gravitation toward precariousness. The precarious aligns with abstract uprootedness, an endless resource for the intellectual's self-discovery and self-fashioning: "Barghouti the exile and dispossessed writer finds himself anew—only to find himself again and again in the new forms of his displacement."[103] For Bernard, the politics that emerge from these two thinkers are quite distinct. Said's *parti pris* for exile opens to an "identitarian" politics and Barghouti's investment in a fragile and multiple Palestinian "we" aligns with a preferable "coalitional" politics.[104] By transforming *I Saw Ramallah* into a "voyage of self-discovery"—and not a "document of 'repatriation'"—Said isolates "Barghouti's experience from that of other Palestinians."[105] He praises the exemplarity of Barghouti's story, the latter's "personal experience becomes a metonymic figure for the experience of all Palestinians."[106] The exilic optic translates/distorts Barghouti's staging of the vicissitudes of repatriation into a hermetic story of self-discovery.

If Said has been accused of "collaps[ing] the different experiences of displacement and dispossession into one another,"[107] Barghouti is credited for keeping separate the violence of displacement from that of occupation. Bernard contests Said's assertion that exile serves as an ontological condition that *all* Palestinians share. What presumably gets eclipsed are diversity and disparity among the Palestinian population:

> Against a national narrative which defines the Palestinian collective through its members' sense of a shared identity . . . *I Saw Ramallah* employs a materialist aesthetic which emphasizes both the circumstantial diversity of Palestinian lives and Barghouti's sense of his own responsibility, as a poet, to resist the temptation to reify the dynamic materiality of that diversity.
>
> For Barghouti . . . the "pleasures of exile" . . . signify not the privileged understanding of more than one culture, but the material disparity between most of the Palestinians living in the occupied West Bank and those in the bourgeois diaspora.[108]

Said's focus on a *shared* exile (displacement) crowds out the Indigenous population, the experiences of Palestinians living under Occupation.

On Bernard's account, Said moves too quickly in his appropriation of Barghouti's story, focusing too narrowly on Barghouti's claim, "It is enough for a person to go through the first experience of uprooting, to become uprooted forever" (which Said quotes in his forward).[109] There is no real cure ("displacements . . . cannot be cured by anything, not even the homeland"[110]), no recovery from being uprooted, no return to the same—the disequilibrium stays with you. This line thus echoes Said's understanding of exile as "a catastrophic and irreversible condition."[111] However, as Bernard observes, Barghouti does not stop here; he continues his meditation on exile by adding, "But the paradox is that strange cities are then never completely strange. Life dictates that the stranger acclimatize every day. This might be difficult at the beginning, but it becomes less difficult with the passage of days and years. Life does not like the grumbling of the living."[112] Barghouti situates the figure of the exile/the stranger in the numbing reality of the Occupation, and in doing so qualifies its subversiveness and defetishizes its virtues. Once the tyrannical face of normalcy sets in, the imperative to tarry with the exilic will fall on deaf ears. The "idealized exilic perspective"[113] meets the reality principle: the stranger cannot indefinitely dwell in the exilic mode; the exile's modernist penchant to defamiliarize has its limits. Like it or not, the exile's symbolic identity will retake root under the Occupation (the question for Barghouti is what comes next, how to go on living without the nostalgia for an unretrievable past). Exilic thinking is thus short-lived and cannot serve as a touchstone for all Palestinians. The collective experience of Palestinians under Occupation has less to do with exilic feelings than economic pangs.

This reading of Said, however, is not without its shortcomings. Said would contest exile's complete eclipsing, the complete halting of its interruptive becoming, its "unsettling force." But perhaps, more important, Bernard erroneously treats Saidian exile as if it were a positive or substantial identity rather than seeing it as a limit on identity, a negativity at the heart of being. True, exile avows the precariousness of lives (the ontological fact of vulnerability) but given Said's insistence on the worldly quality of all things that matter (their historically contingent character, the way they are always already entangled in the dynamics of power), he is not keen on staying or operating exclusively at the ontological/ahistorical level. Precarity remains a fundamental concern for Said; precarity gives the lie to the fantasies of wholeness and sameness. So rather than oppose precarity to exile, I read them contrapuntally. As a member of the bourgeois diaspora, the Palestinian intellectual exile (e.g., Said and Barghouti) may come to fetishize his position as an outsider, enjoying his freedom from all forms of attachments, and come to ignore the material socioeconomic conditions that negatively impact the lives of so many of his kin. But this possibility—a kind of apolitical cosmopolitanism—is only *a* possibility. When Said distinguishes between exile as a reasoned choice and a brutal imposition, he is implicitly acknowledging the difference between precariousness and precarity. There is a differential allocation of vulnerability among Palestinians (in the refugee camps, in the West Bank, Gaza, Israel, and the diaspora). Contrary to what some critics have argued, taking up the position of exile can heighten rather than diminish the self's attentiveness to the possible modes of resistance that are available, or blocked and foreclosed, by such a positionality.

Said can, on one hand, praise the virtues of metaphoric exile, and, on the other, display no patience for lofty language about "visions" of Palestinian statehood that ignores the material realities of the Palestinian people. Divorcing the Palestinian question from their legitimate claims to the land plays into the Israeli narrative:

> No Israeli leader . . . has either officially recognized the occupied territories as occupied or gone on to recognize that Palestinians could or might theoretically have sovereign rights—that is, without Israeli control over borders, water, air or security—to what most of the world considers Palestinian land. *So to speak about the vision of a Palestinian state, as has become fashionable, is a mere vision unless the question of land ownership and sovereignty is openly and officially conceded by the Israeli government.* None ever has and, if I am right, none will in the near

future. It should be remembered that Israel is the only state in the world today that has never had internationally declared borders; the only state not the state of its citizens but of the whole Jewish people; the only state where more than 90 percent of the land is held in trust for the use only of the Jewish people.[114]

Said can be heard saying, well before Tuck and Yang, "decolonization is not a metaphor." Maintaining a vision of Palestine that does not take into consideration land seizure and native expulsion is ideological obfuscation at its best, another instance of the liberal move to innocence: *Yes, I support a vision of a Palestine state, but let's not impose any pressure on the Israeli government—their security, after all, comes first.* To be clear: Said invested a lot of his intellectual energy into thinking Palestine otherwise; he produced his own powerful "vision" or "idea"[115] of Palestine—and what allowed it to be inventive was in no small part his *parti pris* for exile, his refusal to be overdetermined by existing nationalist narratives and modes of belonging. Still, Said did not regard this labor as sufficient for fully addressing the Palestinian condition.[116]

A contrapuntal consciousness may start with an intellectual embrace of the exile's will to transcendence—the capacity to separate the self from its environment, to unplug from one's organic community—but this position, if it is to avoid ideological abstraction (turning exile into a homogenized and homogenizing identity), must relate to Others, especially to those whose lives are deemed not to count. In keeping with Said's stated goal in *Culture and Imperialism*—"my principal aim is not to separate but to connect"[117]—a contrapuntal consciousness is wary of the false opposition that reifies and separates the universal (the exile) from the particular (the Indigenous population). In thinking the universal/particular opposition otherwise, Said condemns both Europe's "blithe universalism,"[118] registering its appalling record when it came to race and representation, along with the retreat into particular difference, into the ideological comfort of rootedness (what Zionism mastered in rooting Jewishness in the soil of historic Palestine). The Saidian exile is not interested in perpetuating the West's "blithe universalism," but hungers for otherness and contact: What do my kin in Occupied Palestine want? At the same time, exile prompts a skeptical riposte to programmatic solutions or nostalgic narratives of returns and belongings (Palestine$_2$). As Said used to say, "never solidarity before criticism."[119] Palestinian solidarity, as with cross-racial solidarity, is not held together via hegemonic consensus (that hides the antagonisms in one's culture) and a shared identity (agreement on a substantial account of some authentic Palestinianness), or even a shared trauma (the Nakba), but a common vision of a more just future. Tarrying with the exilic concerns the latter rather the former, Palestinian futurity rather than an identity-based sameness.

Nivedita Majumdar repeats Bernard's objections about Said's alleged neglect of Palestinian voices, which Barghouti rectifies, but she also offers a middle ground position between the two. Majumdar stresses how Said and Barghouti both converge in their elevation of the poet/intellectual's "detached stance" but diverge on exile's relevance. Whereas Said argues for the self-imposed exile of the intellectual as a precondition for genuine thinking, Barghouti bypasses the virtues of exile, focusing on the singularity of the artist/intellectual: "Barghouti, too, upholds the detached stance of the poet and the intellectual—except that, in his case, the stance in not a by-product of exile but rather a more clearly connected feature of the older idea of positing the artist/intellectual as separate from and superior to the collective."[120] On Majumdar's reading, exile is not a precondition for thinking inventively. The poet enacts his freedom and preserves his intellectual integrity and singularity by distancing himself from group-think in all its forms:

> I cannot, if I march in a demonstration, shout slogans. I may join a demonstration to advertise my position but I cannot raise my voice to cry out slogans or demands, however convinced of them I may be.... As for the waving of arms and the raised fists, hitting the air above the demonstration, there have been times when they have made me laugh despite my embarrassment and my fear that my laughter would be taken amiss by those around me.[121]

An indocility of the will thus characterizes Barghouti's principled defiance:

> I ... do not find it easy to fit in with any grouping. I was never convinced enough to join any political party and I have never joined any faction of the Palestine Liberation Organization. Perhaps, for someone who has lost his country, that is a vice rather than a virtue. Not only that I have resisted open and implicit invitations from those factions and parties. And I have paid varying prices for my abstention.
>
> I cannot condone every decision of the "tribe." I do not measure behavior by right and wrong, nor by what is "permitted" and what is "sinful." My measure is aesthetic. There are things that are right and ugly and that I will not do and will not follow even though I have the right. And there are beautiful mistakes I do not hesitate to make impulsively and contentedly.[122]

Barghouti the poet/intellectual seems, then, to view all calls to conformity and homogeneity with an unmistakable disdain. If Barghouti does not mystify exilic thinking and is allergic to Indigenous group-think, does he—as an elitist of culture—exempt himself from critique? No. He quickly nuances his position. While decrying politics' pernicious ways, he also acknowledges its inescapability, his own implication in it. There is no outside politics:

> Can the defeated be let off politics? Can they be distanced from it? . . . . Politics is the family at breakfast. Who is there and who is absent and why. Who misses whom when the coffee is poured into the waiting cups. Can you, for example, afford your breakfast? Where are your children who have gone forever from these their usual chairs? Whom do you long for this morning? . . . . Staying away from politics is also politics. Politics is nothing and it is everything.[123]

An aversion to politics does not liberate you from politics. Absolute independence from politics is as ideologically dubious as complete losing yourself in it. To put it slightly differently, Barghouti does not join the ranks of the "Beautiful Souls"; he does not pretend to be a pure and uncompromised soul, an individual who refuses to get his hands dirty, a stance that makes the individual "an accomplice in the disorder of the world it bemoans."[124] Palestine does not need "Beautiful Souls," and a refusal to be interpellated can only get you so far.

Barghouti pushes through by diagnosing the evils of the Occupation. He emphatically decries Palestinian injustice: "We sing for it only so that we may remember the humiliation of having it taken from us. Our song is not about some sacred thing of the past but about our current self-respect that is violated anew every day by the Occupation."[125] The Occupation is a monster; it devours the self-respect of Palestinians. The Oslo Accords failed to deliver Palestinians from bondage: "others are still masters of the place."[126] Worse, the Occupation perverts and abstracts the lives of Palestinians:

> The long Occupation has succeeded in changing us from the children of Palestine to the children of the idea of Palestine.
> I have always believed that it is in the interests of an occupation, any occupation, that the homeland should be transformed in the memory of its people into a bouquet of "symbols." Merely symbols. . . . The Occupation forced us to remain with the old. That is its crime. It did not deprive us of the clay ovens of yesterday, but of the mystery of what we would invent tomorrow.[127]

Zionism sought to eject Palestinians from history, the space of worldliness and change; it locked them in the past (the settlers "moved forward as fast as they could and made sure that we keep moving backward"[128]), in a place devoid of invention. Indeed, the Occupation is an invention killer. It impoverishes the lived experience of the Palestinians, rendering it a "bouquet of 'symbols,'" divorced from the affective richness of life. And yet Barghouti also suggests that Palestinians might be unwittingly contributing to their own reification when they imagine the *time before the settler* as a romanticized pastoral scene. Barghouti reminds his brethren: "Let us be frank: when we lived in the village, did we not long for the city? Did we not long to leave small, limited, simple Deir Ghassanah for Ramallah, Jerusalem, and Nablus? Did we not wish that those cities become like Cairo, Damascus, Baghdad, and Beirut?"[129]

As an outsider/insider, Barghouti grapples with question of Palestine. Upon his return, he is utterly disoriented by the land. His positionality is a question. Does the exile become Indigenous anew? He especially struggles with the idea of being a suspicious guest in his own homeland:

> And now I pass from my exile to their ... homeland? My homeland? The West Bank and Gaza? The Occupied Territories? The Areas? Judea and Samaria? The Autonomous Government? Israel? Palestine? Is there any other country in the world that so perplexes you with its names? Last time I was clear and things were clear. Now I am ambiguous and vague. Everything is ambiguous and vague.[130]

Is a Palestinian nation the solution? True, partition and new borders would remove ambiguity and vagueness. But at what existential cost? He continues:

> Am I hungry for my own borders? I hate borders, boundaries, limits. The boundaries of the body, of writing, of behavior, of states. Do I really want boundaries for Palestine? Will they necessarily be better boundaries? It is not only the stranger who suffers at the border. Citizens too can have a bad time of it. There are no limits to the questions. No boundaries for the homeland. Now I want borders that later I will come to hate.[131]

National belonging cannot be ignored but it does come with potential costs and losses. Borders can signify both liberation and oppression. The poet/intellectual records his skepticism; he maintains his distance from the euphoria of the nation.

This skepticism is also aimed at the global community. What script is the Western world going to impose on the Palestinians? The "peace process" that was set in motion by the Oslo Accords solidified and normalized the Occupation. Said and Barghouti foretold its demise by alerting us to the imbalance of power, to the fact that the narrated, the wretched of the earth, cannot get a fair hearing.[132] Who is going to take the Palestinians seriously when they enter the world stage always already narrated, cast as terrorists, the ugly agents of brutal violence?

> It is easy to blur the truth with a simple linguistic trick: start your story from "Secondly." Yes, that is what Rabin did. He simply neglected to speak of what

happened first. Start your story from "Secondly," and the world will turn upside-down. Start your story with "Secondly," and the arrows of the Red Indian are the original criminals and the guns of the white men are entirely the victim. It is enough to start with "Secondly" for the anger of the black man against the white to be barbarous. Start with "Secondly," and Gandhi becomes responsible for the tragedies of the British. . . . It is enough to start with "Secondly," for my grandmother, Umm 'Ata, to become the criminal and Ariel Sharon her victim.[133]

In this brilliant move, Barghouti is not only undoing the Zionist narrative, exposing its rhetorical trickeries, he is also universalizing the crisis of the Palestinian people, aligning their cause with that of the oppressed across the world.[134] Similarly, Ghassan Kanafani casts the Palestinian cause in squarely universalist terms: "The Palestinian cause is not a cause for Palestinians only, but a cause for every revolutionary, wherever he is, as a cause for the exploited and oppressed masses in our era."[135] The struggle for Palestine is framed as part of a global struggle, an anti-imperial struggle against the grammar and narrative of the oppressors. Said reiterates this points: "To testify to a history of oppression is necessary, but it is not sufficient unless that history is redirected into intellectual process and universalized to include all sufferers."[136] The wager is that the "explosive combination" of these different sufferers will constitute a "new emancipatory politics."[137] Systematically deprived of their substance, violently targeted by the IDF, police, and vigilante settlers with impunity, Palestinians embody a "proletarian position,"[138] casting (Occupied) Palestine as an evental site for forging a reinvigorated transnational solidarity movement. In seeking to remedy their wrongs (demolition and expropriation, racialization and ghettoization, the commodification of their lives, etc.), Palestinians are speaking to universal concerns, to the urgent need of imagining a new humanity. This humanity *à venir* jams the colonial matrix of power; it refuses to replicate or subscribe to modernity's hierarchical ontology. The implications are immediately visible. Palestinian activists working in this vein refuse to exchange one racist horizon (Ashkenazi supremacy) for another (Palestinian hegemony). Unlike that of their Zionist counterparts, their struggle to make Palestinian Lives Matter is not preconditioned on making Jewish lives un-matter. In universalizing their plight, Palestinians are helping to reimagine the ethico-political landscape of resistance; they are not claiming special status as if they were the chosen people of the Left. Nor are their demands couched in the familiar language of identity politics, tying their interests to their potentially upgraded social status (which, as we know, always comes at the expense of another minority, or excluded group, when the system itself is not significantly altered). Affirming Palestinian Lives

Matter is a universalist chant for racial and economic justice, one that boldly repeats, in solidarity, the revolutionary call of Black Lives Matter.[139]

Barghouti reminds us that there is nothing exceptional about Palestine ("it is a land, like any land"[140]) or the Palestinian people, for that matter. They are "a people like any other people," as Gilles Deleuze reminds us.[141] The rhetoric of exceptionalism—such as the figure of the Jew as the "eternal Victim"[142] promulgated by Zionism and the Holocaust industry[143]—belongs to the oppressors of the world, who are deeply obsessed with monopolizing victimhood (by precisely and consistently beginning at "Secondly"). And yet, as Elias Sanbar stresses, "no people, no community can claim to occupy this position of the marginalized, the cursed 'Other' in a way that is permanent and inalterable."[144] The oppressed of the world must forge a new counter-grammar of global solidarity, one that universalizes equality and freedom, making them axiomatic, concretely available to all peoples.[145] They must thwart and rewrite their oppressor's malignant narrative. First, white Europeans dispossessed the Natives of Turtle Island; first, white men uprooted and enslaved Africans, turning them into Blacks; first, the British colonized India and subjugated its people, and so forth. To paraphrase an old saying, it takes a village to decolonize an oppressor.[146]

Is Barghouti, then, enacting the decolonial dictum, "I am where I think"? Is his critique stemming from his geographical position? Not so much. The "where" is a far more ambivalent space for Barghouti. His vision of the artist/intellectual might even strike a decolonial critique as too Eurocentric, too Cartesian or universalist in its orientation, leaving behind the particularity of Palestinian voices, and thus repeating the error of Edward Said, as his critics see it. But, as we have seen, the charge against Said is premised on a fundamental misreading of the intellectual exile as *a priori* substantive and abstract. The exilic is a limit on substance and is only conceived as abstract when the contrapuntal supplement is ignored or downplayed. There is, strictly speaking, no tarrying with the exilic without the contrapuntal.

In *I Saw Ramallah*, Barghouti entertains the perspective of the settler, displaying contrapuntal sensibility for the Palestinian's enemy:

> I wonder what their lives look like on the inside? Who lives in this settlement? Where were they before they were brought here? Do their kids play football behind those walls? Do their men and women make love behind those windows? Do they make love with guns strapped to their sides? Do they hang loaded machine guns ready on their bedroom walls? On television we only ever see them armed. Are they really afraid of us, or is it we who are afraid?[147]

If Palestinians have been reduced to one-dimensionality by their oppressors, Barghouti endeavors, à la Said, "to think concretely and sympathetically, contrapuntally," about these Jewish settlers. He marks the vexed interdependence of the two peoples on this stolen land, but he also declines to dwell on their overlapping histories (perhaps out of fear of eclipsing the fundamental antagonism that defines their mutual realities). Barghouti then follows this passage with another counterpoint:

> If you hear a speaker on some platform use the phrase "dismantling the settlements," then laugh to your heart's content. These are not children's fortresses of Lego or Meccano. These are Israel itself; Israel the idea and the ideology and the geography and the trick and the excuse. It is the place that is ours and that they have made theirs. The settlements are their book, their first form. They are our absence. The settlements are the Palestinian Diaspora itself.[148]

Recalling the humanity of the enemy does not mean forfeiting blistering critique. The diaspora is (in) the Occupied Territories. Displacement and Occupation poetically and materially coincide. What is happening in East Jerusalem—the merciless eviction of Palestinians from the ancestral neighborhoods of Sheikh Jarrah and Silwan—is a dress rehearsal for the official Israeli annexation of the West Bank. These tragic scenes of ongoing ethnic cleansing touch all Palestinians; there are no settlements without geographic fragmentation and ontological erasure. Stopping the "settlement-industrial complex"[149] entails the dual Herculean task of cancelling the reign of Zionism in Israeli politics and diminishing its sway over European and American governments. As it stands, "Occupation on steroids" and "Occupation on cruise control" both lead to the same end: the end of Palestinians. Zionist enclosures and/as settlements are not to be managed but abolished; they mediate, generate, and perpetuate Palestinian death-worlds. Under Occupation, Indigenous thinking is an endangered species.

3

Ressentiment/Paranoia

> *Not only is anti-colonial struggle branded anti-Semitic, but so, apparently, is feeling occupied.*
>
> —Jasbir Puar[1]

Evoking Palestinian resentment and paranoia comes with a risk. It could easily resonate with right-wing Zionists, confirming their racist depictions of Palestinians as pathological bodies, psychically and morally deficient, and thus unfit to join the community of civilized human beings. But resentment and paranoia do seem to mark the Palestinian condition. Resentment is often tied to feelings of anger and helplessness. Israel's brutal Occupation all but guarantees "years and years of resentment and hatred," for its "divisiveness and factionalism have compounded the situation of helplessness and resentment in which most Palestinians find themselves," writes Edward Said.[2] Palestinian resentment, or *ressentiment*, to evoke the Nietzschean register to which I will return to shortly in the chapter, casts the dispossessed Native as a vulnerable and pitiful subject, locked in her permanent anger. Paranoia shares much with *ressentiment*; it equally indexes a frustrated, compromised, and potentially vengeful subject. But Said also associates paranoia with uprooting. The experience of collective displacement plunges the exilic Palestinian into a zone of precarity and hypervigilance, "where everyone not a blood-brother or sister is an enemy, where every sympathizer is an agent of some unfriendly power, and where the slightest deviation from the accepted group line is an act of the rankest treachery and disloyalty."[3] For Palestinians, non-Palestinians are *a priori* an object of suspicion. As "paranoid subjects," Palestinians anticipate betrayal from others, that is, complicity with Israel. But not unlike "Black paranoia"—or "Black anger," for that matter—Palestinian paranoia resists easy pathologization and rash dismissal. In fact, Palestinian obsession about a looming betrayal sounds more like reasoned extrapolation than irrational speculation.

If we examine the relation between the two affects, we might say that paranoia gives voice to the *ressentiment* of Palestinians living under a psychically suffocating Zionist regime. While some older settler-colonial nations have begun to come to terms with their "past" wrongs through land acknowledgment statements (a recognition of, and a desire to atone for, violence done to the land's Indigenous inhabitants—though one that can fall short of addressing ongoing injustice[4]), Israel, as we saw in Chapter 2, criminalizes any such decolonizing/reparative practice (as it did, for example, through the Nakba Law). It is in this context that Palestinian paranoia must be understood; it sends us back to Israel's settler-Indigenous relations. Their *ressentiment*-infused paranoia leads them to expose and denounce liberal Zionism as a fetish that allows, or even excuses, the West's indifference and inaction on behalf of Palestinians. Western powers know that Zionism has excessive or fanatic supporters, with genocidal intentions toward the Indigenous population, but they still believe in Zionism, in *liberal* Zionism's commitment to peace and justice. Without the ideological fantasy of liberal Zionism, the idea of Israel as a Jewish and democratic state would lose any remaining veneer of credibility. Hardly delusional in any straightforward sense, Palestinian *ressentiment*/paranoia expresses an anti-colonial refusal to accept a peace process that perversely interpellates them in their own demise.

Palestinian paranoia thus promotes an anti-Zionist hermeneutic; it critiques the Zionist framing of the Palestinian and her struggle. At the same time, an anti-Zionist hermeneutic can reinforce a static Manichean logic. As it denaturalizes the world, making Zionism a worldly matter, it simultaneously renaturalizes it and positivizes both sides of the struggle, locking Israeli Jews into their identities as oppressors, and Palestinians as oppressed. Basically, a Zionist identity exists solely to subjugate a Palestinian identity. True, such a hermeneutic strikes back against the occupiers, refusing to submit to their brutal ideology, but it also remains in its core a *reactive* hermeneutic; it defines itself in opposition to the Zionist vantage point. Stuck in the very Zionist structure it desperately seeks to dismantle, this hermeneutic is incapable of change, and can only authorize and foster what Said calls an unenviable "rhetoric and politics of blame."[5]

An alternative anti-Zionist hermeneutic is possible if we think of Palestinian paranoia as akin to Holocaust survivor Jean Améry's life-affirming form of *ressentiment*. Unwilling to go along with his culture's investment in putting the atrocities of the past behind, Améry, fueled by *ressentiment*, broke with the German consensus of the day by refusing to normalize injustice, to betray his desire for justice, for "nailing the criminal to his deed."[6] Similarly, today's Palestinians, who reject the possibility of a "Zionism with a human face," exhibit a *ressentiment* like Améry's.⁷ Paranoia still nourishes this anti-Zionist hermeneutic, but it isn't driven by a hatred that invariably manifests itself in the will to simplify. Its hyperbolic suspicion cedes the way to a skepticism accompanied by *ressentiment*.

In this chapter, I anchor *ressentiment* and paranoia in the material reality of the Occupation. The reason is simple: to dislodge Zionism's ideological pairing of *ressentiment* and paranoia with anti-Semitism, and to recast the two as by-products of an oppressive environment, not some quasi-ontological feature of the Palestinian mind. Read through a Zionist lens, *ressentiment* and paranoia are always framed as bad not only for Israel but for all Jews. The former posits a spiteful and self-loathing Palestinian, bent on the vengeful destruction of innocent Jewish life; the latter fuels a slanderous discourse, demonizing Jews as the nefarious orchestrators of Palestinian misery. In engaging Palestinian *ressentiment*, I first turn to Elia Suleiman's irreverent, dystopic, and parodic film *Divine Intervention* (2002). The Palestinian communities of *Divine Intervention* are precisely not the object of cultification, "convivial, dialogical, or plurilogical,"⁸ as Mignolo imagined, but replete with tension and *ressentiment*—brought about not only from without (living under Zionist Occupation) but from within (living with fellow Palestinians). Suleiman's film displays *ressentiment* as an ontological fact of the Occupation. At the same time, this vision of *ressentiment* is not destiny. A magical mutation takes place when Palestinians come to harness *ressentiment*'s negativity, when the latter triggers a disruption in the Zionist order of beings. *Ressentiment* here no longer operates as a purely corrosive and self-destructive affect, but becomes the basis for what I call the "public use of *ressentiment*," modeled after Kant's "public use of reason." The "public use of *ressentiment*" transforms and elevates the existential pain of Palestinians, making it a collective moral feeling grounded in the shared but intolerable condition of exclusion. The alternative use of *ressentiment* shifts the affect from the personal realm of blame and hatred into the public sphere of anger and politics, or what Glen Coulthard calls "politicized anger."⁹

Next, I explore the possibility of an "anti-Zionist hermeneutic" that counters the Zionist designation of Palestinian paranoia as anti-Semitic without simultaneously reproducing a Manichean scheme that locks the Native's subjectivity in terms shaped, if not dictated, by the settler-colonial regime. To that end, I turn to the "controversy" surrounding a 2016 talk given at Vassar College by Jasbir Puar on her ethnographic research from a recent trip to the West Bank. Puar relayed to her audience the ethnographic observation that some West Bankers believed that the Israeli government harvested Palestinian organs. While Puar, through her example, clearly meant to convey the terrorized state of mind of the Palestinian people and to shed light on the ways living with the petrifying "fear for their bodily integrity"[10] seems to overdetermine every contact with the Israeli state, her detractors quickly seized on the opportunity to accuse her of anti-Semitism, of viciously updating, recycling, and disseminating "blood libel,"[11] the mendacious accusation from the Middle Ages that Jews ritually murdered Christian children and consumed their blood during Passover. This fabricated controversy, which shamelessly caricaturizes Israel's critics as anti-Semitic, will serve as a case study for thinking the politics of paranoia, for accounting for the stakes of critique, and the fault lines separating an anti-colonial reading of paranoia from a depoliticized, moralizing hermeneutic of Israeli policies and actions.

The Occupation's *Monde à l'Envers*

A fully naturalized occupation normalizes the abnormal condition of the Indigenous population. The least we can say about the Occupation is that it causes *ressentiment* to fester among the vilified Natives. *Ressentiment* is itself a complex affect. After Nietzsche, *ressentiment* denotes everything that is undesirable in "slave morality." Briefly, to recall, the men of *ressentiment* are "these cellar rodents full of vengefulness and hatred"[12] as Nietzsche cruelly describes them in *On the Genealogy of Morals*. They incarnate the reactive and vindictive morality of the weak. In Elia Suleiman's *Divine Intervention*, the bitter feeling of *ressentiment* frames the spectator's exposure to Palestinian life in the post-Oslo era. Filmed after the eruption of the Second Intifada in 2000, *Divine Intervention* is a series of short, disconnected vignettes portraying Palestinian lives under occupation. Its silent protagonist is named E.S. (played by Elia Suleiman) who is caring for his sick father in Jerusalem; he meets up with his Palestinian girlfriend (Manal Khader) who is living in Ramallah at the checkpoint between Jerusalem and Ramallah.

The Palestinians depicted in the film come from both inside and outside the Green Line. *Ressentiment* is the collective feeling that binds them. Consistent with its Nietzschean undertones, this shared affective mode proves destructive and detrimental to the already precarious Palestinian communities. *Divine Intervention*'s opening scene jolts the audience with this *ressentiment*. We witness a stabbed Santa Claus fleeing a group of rock-throwing Palestinian kids who are literally hunting him through the hills of Nazareth, an Arab majority city in northern Israel. This is indeed a *monde à l'envers*, the upside-down world of the Occupation (which penetrates Israel proper). The children chasing Santa Claus have clearly "lost their innocence" and St. Nick has been degraded in the imaginary of the Palestinian civil society. *What kind of catastrophe could have brought about this miserable state of affairs?* a naïve spectator may ask. The Palestinians call it the Nakba.

The French Renaissance author Michel de Montaigne once said that "friendship feeds on communication."[13] Suleiman gives us its converse, a *ressentiment* that feeds on the "breakdown of communication."[14] If Suleiman's earlier film, *Chronicles of a Disappearance*, produced during the optimistic days following the Oslo Accords, was "the silence before the storm," gesturing to Palestinian Israelis' discontent with their neglect and invisibility in the so-called peace process, *Divine Intervention*—which is subtitled *A Chronicle of Love and Pain*—displays social disarray itself, "all hell breaking loose."[15] In *Divine Intervention*, full-blown *ressentiment* eclipses anxiety about Palestinian futurity. *Ressentiment* does not attach itself exclusively to Palestinians in the Occupied Territories, but thrives among Palestinian Israelis as well. Everydayness is a mess. The everydayness of the Occupation—what it is doing to Palestinians in Palestine/Israel—is the problem.

The second scene—following the unsettling takedown of Santa Claus and all the ideals that he symbolizes (the two-state solution?)—focuses on an older, angry man driving his car in Nazareth, E.S.'s father (Nayef Fahoum Daher), who, from a distance, seems to perform the appropriate gestures of greeting toward those he encounters on his morning drive. The audience however is placed in privileged position of actually hearing what he is saying to them: a colorful list of insults. Mere social pleasantries—the stuff of idle chat—are perverted. The basic, minimum form of social glue is no longer taken as a given. Neighborly relations are in crisis. If there is any reciprocity, it is reciprocal disrespect. Witness this absurd exchange between two neighbors who have been tossing garbage bags into each other's yards:

"Neighbor, why do you throw your garbage into my yard? Aren't you ashamed?"
"But neighbor, the garbage we throw in your yard is the same garbage you throw in our garden."
"But it's still shameful. You should have spoken to me about it. Neighbors should respect each other."[16]

The lack of sanitation services generates the suspension of basic laws of civility. Palestinians mostly strike at themselves. In another example, a neighbor irritated that a child's soccer ball has landed on his roof, angrily punctures and deflates it; two neighbors simply observe the man's small act of cruelty in silence. Does the corrosion of communal existence make Palestinians faceless to each other, turning them into spiteful victims? Are they subjects of *ressentiment* who enjoy victimizing each other? To answer in the affirmative would overlook two features of the film: (1) the function of humor in undoing the stock images of Indigenous Palestinians as either bloodthirsty terrorists or abject victims, the two dominant ways the West imagines the Palestinian body; (2) the times that Palestinians do strike at their actual enemies, the occupiers, in the magic realist/revenge-fantasy scenes.

The force of pathos is at some level unavoidable when dealing with the Occupation and the suffering of the Palestinians. Any intervention—cinematic or otherwise—has to confront the problem of representation: How do you visualize Palestinianness? The "you" here is intentionally vague; it is meant to cover a wide range, from Western media to Palestinian artists themselves. The latter are often forced to react to the former's misrepresentations, to contest their one-dimensional account of Palestinian identity but also jam an Orientalist interpretive machinery that dehistoricizes and fixes Palestinians in undesirable positions. Of these challenges Edward Said comments:

> Palestinian cinema must be understood in this context. That is to say, on the one hand, Palestinians stand against invisibility, which is the fate they have resisted since the beginning; and on the other hand, they stand against the stereotype in the media: the masked Arab, the *kufiyya*, the stone-throwing Palestinian—a visual identity associated with terrorism and violence.[17]

If visibility is a fundamental concern of Palestinian cinema, so is an overdetermined visibility, a stereotyped existence, buried deep in the Western imaginary.

In a slightly different vein, Jacques Rancière raises the problem of visibility at the level of genres, taking up Godard's distinction between the epic and the documentary as it relates to Palestine/Israel:

> The main enemy of artistic creativity as well as of political creativity is consensus—that is, inscription within given roles, possibilities, and competences. Godard said ironically that the epic was for Israelis and the documentary for Palestinians. Which is to say that the distribution of genres—for example, the division between the freedom of fiction and the reality of the news—is always already a distribution of possibilities and capacities: To say that, in the dominant regime of representation, documentary is for the Palestinians is to say that they

can only offer the bodies of their victims to the gaze of news cameras or to the compassionate gaze at their suffering. That is, the world is divided between those who can and those who cannot afford the luxury of playing with words and images. Subversion begins when this division is contested, as when a Palestinian filmmaker like Elia Suleiman makes a comedy about the daily repression and humiliation that Israeli checkpoints represent and transforms a young Palestinian resistance fighter into a manga character.[18]

What I find helpful in Rancière is his insistence on expanding the "distribution of possibilities and capacities" when it comes to the figuration of Palestinians. Those whose lives matter are granted "the luxury of playing with words and images," and those lives that don't matter are precluded from that artistic privilege (which, moreover, then works to compound the inequality between the two). Conversely, we could say that democratizing artistic freedom will be an indispensable step in that process of making Palestinian Lives Matter. This is *Divine Intervention*'s political contribution: it performs dissensus by unsettling "the coordinates of the sensible."[19]

By staging *ressentiment* within a comedy about the Occupation, *Divine Intervention* discourages us from taking it at face value. Just like the daily repression and chronic humiliation that gave rise to it, *ressentiment* is not exempt from Suleiman's alchemical art. But Suleiman's humor does not simply negate the *ressentiment* of his Palestinian characters. They are still spiteful beings, but their spitefulness takes on additional meanings when they are seen as exaggerated, transformed into a comical image. In other words, the ludic counterbalances the force of pathos, short-circuiting the emergence of compassion at the sight of the abject.

To be sure, Suleiman does not exclude all mimetic accounts of Palestinian suffering. The Al-Ram checkpoint between East Jerusalem and Ramallah is a site/sight of Israeli belligerence and Palestinian humiliation. Suleiman frames the checkpoint as the place of the rendezvous of E.S. and his lover. The former comes from Jerusalem, the latter from Ramallah. They sit together in silence, tenderly holding hands, while observing the sadistic violence of the checkpoint as if they were at a drive-in theater. In one egregious episode, an IDF soldier abuses his powers with impunity; he chaotically orders drivers to switch cars, robs a driver of his jacket, ridicules the Palestinians anxiously waiting for being bad Muslims in wanting to go Jerusalem to break their fast during Ramadan, and obnoxiously uses his megaphone to sing "Long live the people of Israel!" All that E.S. and his lover can do is watch the obscene display of Zionist machoism. Except that, in an earlier occasion at the checkpoint, his lover metamorphosized into a femme fatale, and did manage to strike at the enemy.[20] Refusing to be disciplined by the soldiers, she disregards their commands to stop; utterly ravished and bewildered by her looks, they are unable to stop her, and as she crosses the checkpoint, the watchtower crumbles behind her. Toward the end of the film, the same Palestinian woman transforms into a superpowered ninja who single-handedly strikes at and demolishes an Israeli commando unit. She emerges, dreamlike, from behind a cardboard copy of her silhouette that the commando team was using for target practice, suggesting that they see this mysterious Palestinian freedom fighter as a wanted terrorist. These are "moments of self-flauntingly magical solutions for the intractable challenges set up by the occupation," writes Robert Stam.[21]

John Menick sees in the film what we might call a pedagogy of the occupied: "*Divine Intervention* is a lesson in the occupied imagination, of what might be running through the minds of millions facing second-class citizenship, non-citizenship, random detention, constant curfew, interminable waiting, and random execution."[22] The film thematizes "the fantasies of a society, and in this case, a people whose desires seem to mean little to the world at large." And yet these revenge-fantasy scenes are surely prone to offend many liberal sensibilities.[23] Dennis Grunes, for example, praises the film's many qualities, including its anti-naturalist bent, but faults Suleiman for its "one-sidedness," for failing to acknowledge that "his spectacular scene of Jewish slaughter" contributes to the world's anti-Semitism, to "the relentless Palestinian killing of innocent Jews."[24] But here again we might adapt Horkheimer to this situation: *Whoever is not willing to talk about the Occupation should also keep quiet about Palestinian revenge-fantasies.* Sure, Grunes "talks" about the Occupation, but he does so in a way that flattens the horror of the Palestinian condition. The film's *monde à l'envers* impacts Palestinians and Israelis equally on this reading:

> Suleiman's decision not always to identify which are Israelis, which are Palestinians, thus blossoms into a gracious satirical vision of losers all around. Such small things as Suleiman lights on, one after the other, and each thing, and all of them cumulatively, moreover, thus contribute to a funny, sometimes hilarious, portrait of an agitated and endlessly unpleasant situation. This is the best part of Suleiman's film.[25]

This is another instance of a "move to innocence." Everyone is a victim (loser) of the Occupation. But is what they lose really the same? Western liberals "support" the Palestinian cause *as long as* it is nonviolent, as long as Palestinians abandon their armed struggle and disidentify with the likes of Hamas or Islamic

Jihad. But here again they ignore the fact that the violence that they fear is not the originary violence. They start with "Secondly," to recall Mourid Barghouti's formulation; their objection to Palestinian violence is predicated on the willful forgetting of the nonspectacular violence of the Occupation.[26] And if Grunes is sensitive enough to note the "anger and resentment simmer[ing]"[27] among the Indigenous population (he even describes "the Israeli Occupation" as "ten times worse than Suleiman shows"), he still cannot take the next step. Grunes, like many Western liberals, cannot entertain or begin to grasp the relevance of Fanon's anti-colonial insight that "at the individual level, violence is a cleansing force. It rids the colonized of their inferiority complex, of their passive and despairing attitude. It emboldens them, and restores their self-confidence."[28] Anything that symbolizes violence against those who count provokes alarm. Violence here only needs to be associated with a name to evoke terror and outrage. Grunes turns his focus on one of the most iconic scenes of *Divine Intervention*, E.S.'s release at a checkpoint of a balloon bearing Arafat's portrait. The balloon flies out as a distraction maneuver, provoking absolute bewilderment among the Israeli soldiers, which enables the two lovers to pass through the checkpoint and sneak into Jerusalem. The balloon passes over the Old City and the Western Wall, and ultimately lands symbolically on the dome of Al Aqsa Mosque, the site that triggered the Second Intifada in 2000 and the third Gaza war over two decades later. In response to the scene, which he acknowledges is "humorous," Grunes discloses his old-fashioned Eurocentrism: "For many Palestinians, Arafat may be some sort of tribal hero or symbol of the Palestinian nation that their hopes pursue; to most civilized people, though, he is a mass murderer of Jews, one of the most evil men now in *two* centuries."[29] Matters escalate. Grunes doubles down on the "Secondly" narrative:

> Israeli actions against Palestinians are reactive and self-defensive, while Palestinian actions against Israelis are fueled by their historic hatred of Jews and by other-Arab (and their own) incitement of their feelings of having gotten the short end of the stick when modern Israel was created to maintain the historic habitation of Jews and to provide also a home for displaced European Jews, survivors of the Holocaust. . . . Palestinian violence against Israelis is responsible for the Israeli election of hardliner Ariel Sharon.[30]

Palestinians are blamed for Sharon. "Civilized" Zionists find Sharon (and Netanyahu and Bennett) an embarrassment, but what's the alternative, blaming Jewish supremacy?

Equating Palestinian violence with terrorism eclipses the Palestinian national struggle by depicting it as "violence for its own sake, devoid of any politics and meant to solely inflict suffering on Israeli citizens."[31] Liberals in Israel and the West treat violence as if it were a character flaw, by which Palestinians—in conformity with Orientalist tropes—are said to be indelibly marked. What liberals of all shades really want are "decaffeinated" Palestinians, Palestinians whose aspirations (for equality, collective freedom, etc.) are manageable and amenable to the Zionist order of things.[32] But to the chagrin of liberal reviewers, *Divine Intervention* gives us hyper-caffeinated Palestinians! Or at least what can only appear as hyper-caffeinated characters from a Western/Zionist perspective, since a recalcitrant Palestinian is always already an excessive, militant Palestinian, as if wanting respect or asserting self-determination were itself an abnormal behavior, a kind of pathology.

The Public Use of *Ressentiment*

To paraphrase Audre Lorde's comments on the uses of anger, Palestinian *ressentiment* is a response to Zionist racism.[33] Reading Suleiman's Palestinian ninja as a manifestation of spiteful *ressentiment* misses its mark. This figuration of resistance poetically speaks to a collective feeling, registering the stubborn refusal to forget about Israel's historical crime, the refusal to play nice, to conform to a politics of respectability where a grievance is legible only if it steers clear of violence and any whiff of critique of Israel (meaning: no attack on the idea of Israel or its commando units, please). Here, Palestinian *ressentiment* is not that of Nietzsche's slave moralist, which invariably locks the individual in her bitter particularity. Rather, it is a collective feeling that binds the wretched of earth. The defiant Palestinian ninja incarnates a life-affirming manifestation of *ressentiment*. The basis for this recalcitrance is *open to all*, to whoever refuses to cover over colonialism's "fracture or wound."[34] These subjects of *ressentiment* are not interested in ideological healing nor are they looking to capitalize on their victimhood and privatize their suffering. Their demands cut much deeper. Anti-settler *ressentiment* alerts us to the inadequacies of thinking of the Palestinian struggle as a conflict "between different parts of society," which would suggest that the Israeli government can fix the "conflict" by giving their Arab minority/PA more rights. *Ressentiment* in its life-affirming mode recasts the conflict as a fundamental antagonism "between non-society and society, between those who have nothing to lose and those who have everything to lose, between those without a stake in their community and those whose stakes are the greatest."[35]

Ressentiment's negativity, the subject's refusal to let go of her anger, to be domesticated and pacified, opens to a universalist project. It gathers strength from the participation of others, from "those who have nothing to lose." It is this shift from *ressentiment* as a personal, impotent expression of frustration to *ressentiment* as a collective response to the evils of settler colonialism that terrifies the liberal gatekeepers of the status quo. We might explain this fear by drawing on Kant's notion of the "public use of reason." In "What Is Enlightenment?," Kant argues that while individuals in an official capacity (in the domain of the "private use of reason") have to obey orders, individuals (as would-be philosophers) must not compromise on their "public use of reason," that is, they must not censure themselves and give up their right to address their views, to speak as "*a scholar . . . before the entire public of the reading world.*"[36] As Žižek elaborates, the public use of reason, "in a kind of short-circuit, by-passing the mediation of the particular, directly participates in the universal."[37] This public use of reason empowers the individual, allowing her to be modern and cosmopolitan—a universal subject—breaking with the "communal-institutional order of one's particular identification."[38] A "public use of *ressentiment*" characterizes the unsettling shift above. The "private use of *ressentiment*" urges you to privatize your grievance and continue to support the state in deed. *Ressentiment* reproduces Manichean racism in an inverted form, reifying the colonized in her rage.[39] Unable to overcome the internalized logic of good/evil, which, in the colonial situation, aligns ideologically with the white/Black binary,[40] the racially oppressed is condemned to a bitter life of reactivity. As Fanon puts it, "there is always *ressentiment* in reaction."[41] In contrast, the "public use of *ressentiment*" both negates the imperative to accommodate (as with Améry, who declares, "my resentments are there in order that the crime become a moral reality for the criminal, in order that he be swept into the truth of his atrocity"[42]) and enjoins you to connect and universalize your grievances, to see your antagonism as cutting across societies.[43]

The first form of *ressentiment* fuels a politics of blame, generating a murderous hatred for the enemy. As Said warns, this form of *ressentiment* "abandon[s] history for essentializations that have the power to turn beings against each other."[44] This "tremendous *ressentiment*," as Said calls it, indulges nativist desires; it is prone to the fetishization of *your* victimhood, or your *group*'s, but poses no real threat to society.[45] Moreover, this *ressentiment* as would-be victim is tolerated by power, even encouraged (the state's qualified recognition of your victimhood can serve to legitimize the dominant regime: *look, we listen to our less fortunate*).[46] The second form enacts a form of counterviolence;[47] it historicizes and politicizes anger, turning personal trauma or loss (or that of a people) into a "common loss,"[48] a common cause. And though this *ressentiment*-filled subject is *reacting* to the world, her reaction also gestures toward alternative modes of being and being-with; her reaction is not life-denying insofar as its aim is to liberate and stretch the colonial realm of the possible rather than ensnare and keep us in our place. Put slightly differently, *ressentiment*, in its public use, hungers for transformative solidarity, finding no satisfaction in the rewards of identity politics.

It is not an overstatement to say that emancipatory politics begins with the public use of *ressentiment*. I submit that Black Livers Matter illustrates and enacts this vision of *ressentiment*. Right from the movement's inception, BLM activists did not compromise on their *ressentiment*; they refused to forget about the democrats' dismal record when it came to racial and economic justice and play the game of pragmatic politics. We should recall how BLM emphatically refused to endorse Hillary Clinton in her 2016 presidential bid. Would you endorse someone who willfully capitalized on America's long history of anti-Blackness by championing the notorious 1994 crime bill and characterizing "gangs of kids"—implying Black youth—as "superpredators"? As we know, BLM also ruffled liberal feathers, especially those of the Democratic National Committee, with its bold endorsement of the Palestinian cause. BLM both reflected and set the intellectual tone for Black-Palestinian solidarity, for connecting the hidden antagonism in American culture to the antagonism of Palestine/Israel. A short video titled "When I See Them, I See Us" (Black-Palestinian Solidarity), released October 14, 2015, highlights what a collective labor of *ressentiment* might look like: "The onslaught on Black and Palestinian lives is rife with a discourse of victim-blaming that softens the edge of systematic violence and illuminates the dehumanization process. [It] is a message to the world as much as it is a commitment among ourselves that we will struggle with and for one another. No one is free until we all are free."[49] Each participant in the video visually performs her *ressentiment*, the refusal to forget the injustice done to her *and* her comrades, with protest signs including "Gaza stands with Baltimore," "I remember: Deir Yassin, Greensboro, Gaza, Charleston," and "solidarity from Ferguson to Palestine." The political response to victim-blaming is thus not simply to decouple "victim" and "blaming," and cancel the latter as an illegitimate treatment of the former. No, it uses *ressentiment* as a means to expand the category of the victim (who counts as a wronged body?), to globalize it and universalize Black struggle. This version of *ressentiment* can "nurture a war of liberation."⁵⁰

BLM's message is thus through and through universalist. There is no reactionary *ressentiment*, no victim-envy (of the sort "Blacks are the new Jews"). Its call for redress is not exclusive to Black folks (the private use of *ressentiment*). This critical orientation is a problem for moderates and reformists—the most ardent defenders of the status quo. BLM's activists don't want to be recognized *within* the system, assuming their allocated place within the symbolic order. They are not seeking inclusion into the privileges of white society. They aren't looking for appeasement or accommodation. Their goal is clear: to affirm what Étienne Balibar calls *égaliberté*, equality-freedom, as an unconditional demand, to bring the unjust system down in the name of a more just state *à venir*.⁵¹ In a similar vein, Stefano Harney and Fred Moten's work on the undercommons is refreshing. As BLM does, they proceed by complicating liberal assumptions and formulations of problems—indeed, bad questions often engender worse answers. The prison-industrial complex is a case in point. Harney and Moten seek to reconfigure the coordinates of the prison debate: for them, it is "not so much the abolition of prisons but the abolition of a society that could have prisons, that could have slavery."⁵² But if white liberals are lukewarm about defunding the police and prison abolition, they are even more hesitant about renouncing their long investment in capitalism.⁵³ They are for the most part still invested in reforming capitalism, pushing for a "woke" capitalism with more rights for Blacks and other people of color. They don't see capitalism as an enterprise that was and is racist in its operational logic. At the same time, they fail to see that white people themselves are becoming less and less immune to capitalism's voracious appetite, to what Achille Mbembe describes as the "*becoming black of the world*"⁵⁴ (I will return to this topic in the context of Palestinian sovereignty in Chapter 4). This is why BLM is so vital for the Left and the prospect of a universal politics.⁵⁵ BLM's racial justice message is intertwined with its call for economic justice, foregrounding the devastating role of racial capitalism, but here again: *Is this a message that white liberal America will hear?* We might consider the legacy of Martin Luther King Jr. a cautionary tale: MLK is now remembered in mainstream discourse and white minds as an icon of the Civil Rights Movement, preaching racial tolerance and nonviolence—but what is all but erased from this portrayal is King's profound anti-capitalist (and anti-military) message. The legend promoted by liberals and conservatives alike is an MLK of toothless identity politics: an MLK wholly compatible with capitalism's ways, deprived of his revolutionary message, of his symbolic violence/his violence to the symbolic order. Isn't a true change to the social order after all, always already, violent?[56] BLM, I believe, can avoid this sanitized fate only by maintaining and underscoring its public use of *ressentiment*, its dual but interlocking struggles against racial domination and economic exploitation, by its commitment to societies' excluded others, its solidarity with the globally dispossessed—the wretched of the earth.

BLM's message resonates strongly with many Palestinian activists. Staged as the uncompromising desire for social justice against the backdrop of Western liberalism—a refusal to reconcile with the Nakba, with chattel slavery, with the horrors of the past still informing the horizons of the present—Palestinian *ressentiment* becomes a collective moral feeling, based not on a shared identity but on the unacceptable condition of erasure and dispossession. To adopt and adapt Améry, this *ressentiment* is there in order that the crimes of Indigenous genocide and racial enslavement become a moral reality for the white supremacists, in order that they be swept into the truth of their atrocity.

Living with Paranoia

If you are a Palestinian, you've witnessed firsthand the ideological sham of the "peace process." While promised "land for peace," as per the Oslo Accords, Palestinians in the Occupied Territories have seen a massive expansion of illegal settlements, the uninterrupted ethnic cleansing of their neighborhoods, the strategic fragmentation of their people, a numbing increase in humiliating and dangerous checkpoints, devastating attacks on a besieged Gaza, Israel's flagrant defiance of international law, an uptake in serious talks of annexation of Palestinian land in Israeli political discourse, the passing of the Nation-State Law and the continuing disenfranchisement of Palestinian citizens of Israel, and the symbolic relocation of the US Embassy from Tel Aviv to Jerusalem. To the betrayal from *without*, a betrayal from *within* has also plagued Palestinians: the "Abraham Accords,"[57] the premature normalization of diplomatic ties between a number of Arab despots and Israel, who self-interestedly suspended their demand for Palestinian self-determination as a precondition for such normalization. In this light, the idea of Palestinian paranoia might seem misplaced, if not Palestinophobic. There is no paranoia—only life-affirming *ressentiment* put in practice. Palestinians remember the Nakba and the injustices visited on them (*Divine Intervention*'s ninja refuses to leave the past alone, refuses to naturalize Palestinian fragmentation and elimination); they remember the

West's unconditional support of the Zionist regime, and how their recognition of Israel was and is rewarded with native removal and dispossession.

And yet, there is something hermeneutically apt about drawing on the concept of paranoia *so long as* we locate paranoia's roots in politics rather than biology, in the violent and visceral world of what Fanon calls the "colonial situation"[58] instead of some abstract or ahistorical notion of a pathologized "Palestinian mind." The contemptuous accusation of Palestinian paranoia, prevalent among political Zionists and far-right supporters of Israel, displays the latter's (mis)understanding of this psychopathology. As Lara Sheehi and Stephen Sheehi point out, Israeli pundits repeatedly cast Palestinians as mentally confused or sick, claiming, with self-righteous authority, that "the 'Arab mind' suffers from paranoia with an inability to 'reality test,' because they allow ideology to manipulate how they perceive reality."[59] In its Palestinophobic form, the accusation naturalizes the mental disorder, obscuring its sociopolitical origins, making the paranoia of the Indigenous population an ontological or essential problem, a permanent feature of their biological or cultural DNA, discounting and disregarding, in turn, their daily humiliation and land-based grievances. If, according to Israeli propaganda, Palestinians are so delusional, intolerant of Jewish difference, and prone to irrational bursts of violence, how, then, can you make permanent and meaningful peace with them?[60] In this ideological light, the Occupation is recast as a self-protective Israeli policy (it is an existential question of survival) rather than an expression of the Jewish state's expansionist and imperialist desire.

The charge of Palestinian paranoia thus implicitly obfuscates another paranoia, a Zionist paranoia, whose origins lie in Western Orientalism. Said draws our attention to Orientalism's paranoid tendencies: "Psychologically, Orientalism is a form of paranoia, knowledge of another kind, say, from ordinary historical knowledge."[61] As a style of thinking, Orientalism is about the West's paranoid *construction* of the Orient as an object of knowledge and mastery, and in this respect, its racial stereotyping—exemplified in the figure of the bloodthirsty, irrational Palestinian—always tells us more about the anxious psyche of the Zionist/Western knower than its putative object of study. Israel traffics in paranoid knowledge, emblematized in its narrative about the imminent danger of *coming undone*, repeatedly framing the Palestinian people as an existential threat to its identity and its people. Wanting to end Israel as a Jewish state (a state *only* for Jews) means wanting to end the Jewish people—a Palestinian (and their supporters') version of the "Final Solution." Against this paranoid backdrop, the Israeli PR machine encourages an Orientalist reading of the Palestinians, a reading that underscores the "darkness and strangeness"[62] of their behavior and statements, and casts suspicion on their very being. Within the Zionist settler imaginary, what Palestinians *do* (violent terrorist acts) is inextricably linked to who they *are* (terrorists); in other words, violence, spitefulness, and hate emanate naturally or unprovokedly from Palestinian bodies, which, in turn, positions Israel as the aggrieved party, whose grossly disproportionate acts of violence are ideologically reframed as defensive and thus justified.

How are we to relate Palestinian paranoia to Zionist paranoia? How does power factor into the discussion? What kind of hermeneutic labor is the concept "paranoia" doing and soliciting? Following Lacan, Žižek expands the scope of paranoia beyond its narrow clinical scene. Paranoia is a mood or an orientation; it functions as a "transcendental-ontological category" or a "modality of the disclosure of the world."[63] Paranoia involves "a vision of reality as being dominated by a hidden manipulator who persecutes and controls us."[64] Alarmed by contingency and inconsistencies in the social order, the paranoid subject looks for certainty, yearning for a totalizing picture of reality:

> paranoia is at its most elementary, a belief into an "Other of the Other," into another Other who, hidden behind the Other of the explicit social texture, programs what appears to us as the unforeseen effects of social life and thus guarantees its consistency: beneath the chaos of market, the degradation of morals, and so on, there is the purposeful strategy of the Jewish plot.[65]

Paranoia engenders a corrosive form of suspicion, enabling its subject to regain and enjoy a sense of mastery over the external world (having succeeded in determining the elusive or hidden cause of the nation's socioeconomic ills). And the least we can say about the subject of paranoia is that it is prone to producing overreadings in its violent search to unearth or pin down the deeper meanings of events or actions.

In the colonial situation, though, paranoid overreadings are not just excessive but a matter of *actual* survival (and thus must be distinguished from Israel's self-serving rhetoric of survival against an invented Palestinian *existential* threat). Colonialism robs the colonized not only of their sovereignty (collective and personal) but scrambles their judgment, negatively impacting the ways the world discloses itself to them. For the "wretched of the earth," life without paranoia is a life ripe for disaster and trauma. We might even say that an unparanoid life—a life driven by the belief in the "good settler"—is a life doomed to early termination. In the context of Palestine/Israel, more specifically, the paranoia of the colonized often takes the form of an "anti-Zionist hermeneutic."⁶⁶ But here the Zionist settler is—at least *for the Palestinians*—a highly visible figure rather than a hidden manipulator, unlike, for example, the figure of the Jew who was phantasmatically construed in Nazi ideology as the secret puppet master of German society. As the agent of Indigenous dispossession, this settler/manipulator is habitually persecuting and controlling Palestinian lives. The question, then, is about the reach of the manipulator: what is the Zionist regime actually doing and what is it imagined doing to Palestinians? For Zionists and their supporters, Palestinian paranoia happens when "anti-Zionist hermeneutic" slides from the former to the latter, as it is alleged to do frequently. At this point, we're told, an "anti-Zionist hermeneutic" discloses its true colors: it is a spiteful anti-Semitic hermeneutic.

The "Facts" of the Case

Jasbir Puar's ethnographic research from Occupied Palestine exemplifies, in the eyes of her detractors, the Left's duplicity with Palestinian paranoia, the ease with which anti-Zionism mutates into anti-Semitism. While facts never speak for themselves, it is still important to establish facts in order to evaluate vying interpretative claims. In "Speaking of Palestine: Solidarity and Its Censors," Puar repeats her ethnographic observation from her talk: "Some speculate that their bodies were mined for organs for scientific research."⁶⁷ Puar stresses that she was reporting Palestinian views, which are typically neglected or ignored in US mainstream media, not making "empirical claims"⁶⁸ about organ mining herself. Even so, Puar pushes back against the outrage *as if* it had no basis in the social reality of the Occupation. The charge of "blood libel" imposes a ready-made horizon of interpretation, which radically recasts the roles of the parties involved. It rhetorically transmutes fearful and grieving Palestinians into the powerful anti-Semites of the Middle Ages, imposing a crushing continuity and timelessness to the hatred of Jews, ideologically flipping the contemporary positions of the persecuted and the persecutor in the West Bank.

"The specious conflation of anti-occupation expression and anti-Semitism represents," according to Puar, "an intensification of both the occupation itself and the policing of scholarship about it."⁶⁹ The consequences are grave: "not only is anti-colonial struggle branded anti-Semitic, but so, apparently, is *feeling occupied*."⁷⁰ Against such weaponizing of anti-Semitism, along with the policing and disciplining of the Other's affects, Puar reorients our attention back to the socio-psychic basis of the Palestinian belief in organ theft:

- There is a documented history of Israelis harvesting organs from both IDF soldiers and Palestinian bodies during the 1990s.
- There is a documented history of Palestinian bodies being held at the Abu Kabir Institute of Forensic Medicine, under its Director Dr. Yehuda Hiss, for organ mining during the Second Intifada (2000–5).
- Credible recent ethnographic research point to the persistence of organ mining practices in Abu Kabir until 2012, contradicting claims by the Israeli Health Ministry.

One may, of course, dispute the findings and question the evidence of the researchers, but is it shocking to believe that Israel might be continuing or reviving its prior practices? Is the Palestinian belief in an ongoing organ theft self-evidently irrational or, worse, anti-Semitic? Puar stresses the plausibility of this belief, given the state's prior actions: "This history [of organ mining] is well known among Palestinians so it should be rather unremarkable that grieving Palestinian families might wonder and fear about the fate of their loved ones' corpses. Why would they—or anyone—assume that the pervasive colonial exercise of control over the lives of an occupied population ends at death?"[71] Palestinians living under occupation are by no means unique in entertaining this belief. Anyone aware of Israel's brutal occupation and track record vis-à-vis Palestinians would *not* find their belief beyond the pale, dismissible out of hand as Israel's apologists righteously urge.

The feigning of outrage—the public performance of denouncing Palestinian paranoia—shifts the Western liberal gaze from the political horizon of occupation to the timeless moral horizon of Jewish victimhood. The former is a bitter pill that Western liberals are more comfortable disavowing or ignoring, the latter is something that aligns with what they already comfortably know: anti-Semitism is evil. And by labeling Palestinians anti-Semites, Israel solicits, and almost always receives, Western sympathies (you must stand with Israel against anti-Semitism, against Palestinians), which, in turn, muffles the Palestinian global plea for justice.[72] As a result, the hype of Palestinian paranoia works to strengthen Israel's settler-colonial regime while ostensibly weakening the Palestinian cause. Western liberals can accept or even forgive force, a strong state intervention—under the cover of Israel's right to self-defense—when (rather than if) it is initiated for the noble purposes of rooting out anti-

Semitism; likewise, anyone or anything tainted with anti-Semitism loses, in principle, liberal support: who wants to be associated with the evils of anti-Semitism?

It is noteworthy that the charge of anti-Semitism and paranoia covers both Palestinians and their leftist supporters. It is as if taking up the Palestinian cause were itself pathological; you are siding with anti-Semites, and, like them, you obsessively single out Israel and see its abuses everywhere. Jewish paranoia can be brought up but only if it emerges from a friendly Israeli camp. Seyla Benhabib, for example, faults Judith Butler's *Parting Ways: Jewishness and the Critique of Zionism* for taking a hermeneutically shortsighted view of the historical trauma of Jews in her critical assessment of Zionism and the Israeli state:

> As psychoanalytically astute as Butler is, she seems to turn a blind eye to the lingering collective psychosis of many Jews, whether in Israel or not, namely, their fear of annihilation in the hands of a hostile world as well as the post-1945 persecution of the Jews of the Middle East, such as in Iraq and Yemen. The tragedy of Israel is that the stronger Israel has become militarily, the more paranoid and bullyish it has become. The volatility of shifting political alliances in the Middle East as well as the new weapons technologies, which can easily threaten Jerusalem and Tel-Aviv in minutes, have contributed to this growing paranoia.[73]

Israeli paranoia is explained (away) as a response to past trauma (the Shoah and other instances of anti-Semitism) and security interests (the imminent threat from Israel's Arab or Muslim neighbors; some, after all, preach the destruction of Israel).[74] Consequently, the colonial situation drops out of the discussion altogether. Jewish paranoia is minimized or even excusable, an expression of timeless vulnerability and absolute victimhood, and has nothing to do with Zionism's raison d'être, managing Jewish supremacy over the Palestinians, that is, preserving Jewish/white privilege over the (stolen) land.

Whitewashing Israeli Violence

If Benhabib acknowledges anti-Palestinian paranoia, giving voice to Jewish fears in her reflections on Palestine/Israel, Cary Nelson focuses his interpretive energy on the anti-Semitism underpinning Palestinian/leftist paranoia about Israel's ways. In *Israel Denial*, Nelson positions himself as a sensible critic, wanting to find a "pragmatic" (i.e., reformist rather than revolutionary) solution to the plight of both Israelis and Palestinians. We hear the usual platitudes about how both parties will have to make compromises, how nobody will get everything they want, and so on (as if Palestinians getting more than their just share were an actual possibility).[75] Occupying the position of the liberal Zionist, Nelson reaffirms his strong support for a two-state solution and condemns the hawkish policies of Netanyahu and the Likud Party. But contrary to his leftist Western foes, Nelson doesn't believe that the problem is the Israeli state as such; Israel's birth does not constitute its "original sin." As with the IHRA's working definition of anti-Semitism, Nelson deems anti-Semitic the belief that the 1948 ethnic cleansing and land dispossession of the Indigenous Palestinian population taints Israel's existence from its beginnings. Rather, Nelson limits the scope of the Israeli and Palestinian "conflict" to its post-1967 reality, to territory conquered after the Six-Day War, assertively containing "the problem of Palestinian *subjugation* to the West Bank."[76] Israel proper and Israel as an occupying force are thus not one and the same. For Nelson, Puar and others on the Left irresponsibly conflate the two Israels and exaggerate Israel's ethnonationalism or supremacist ethos (though the accelerated normalization of racist far-right beliefs in Israel's public political debates renders this distinction strikingly naïve), making their paranoid anti-Zionist hermeneutic intrinsically anti-Semitic.

Nelson confronts Palestinian paranoia over illegal organ harvesting not by denying the practice but by rhetorically defusing the force of the critique by: (1) disputing its scope and impact ("Hiss never harvested major organs for transplantation"[77]); (2) questioning the seriousness of the violation (other places harvest organs without consent); (3) nullifying the originality and thereby necessity of the accusation (ultra-Orthodox Jews had already complained about the practice[78]), and, most important, (4) multiplying the focal points of the debate: there is nothing special about the Palestinian victims; don't be misled by the word "Orientals" used by Hiss in his 2000 interview with Nancy Scheper-Hughes:

> Hiss's reference to "Oriental" bodies in an interview suggests most of the cadavers were Near Eastern Jews, not Palestinians; at the time, Ashkenazi Jews sometimes referred to Near Eastern or Mizrahi Jews as Orientals. That is not to say that there were no Israeli or Palestinian bodies in the mortuary, especially during the Second Intifada, but it is to say that the claim that Palestinian bodies are at the center of the story is at best a colossal error and at worst a deliberate falsehood or a paranoid fantasy.[79]

Nelson's message is clear: move along, nothing to see. Hiss's biomedical overreach did not target Palestinians; there isn't a Jewish plot to plunder Palestinian organs. Reenforcing his point, Nelson adds an endnote after the word "Orientals" from the above quote: "As Sternberg points out, people of his generation would not have read Edward Said's *Orientalism*."[80] It is, however, unclear what this bizarre clarification of "Orientals" actually accomplishes. True, the focus is no longer exclusively on Palestinians, but race and racism now move to the forefront. Nelson seems ironically oblivious to his whitewashing of the organ harvesting fiasco. Nelson's apology for the Israeli authorities turns into an implicit indictment of the state's generalized white supremacy.

Nelson's reading of Hiss's "Orientals" also inadvertently confirms an important insight from Nancy Scheper-Hughes's research. While Scheper-Hughes had audiotaped the interview with Hiss in July 2000, she chose not to publish it out of a justified fear that it would be received as anti-Semitic, which would have a negative impact on her standing as an anthropologist. But after Donald Boström published his article on organ harvesting from Palestinians in the Swedish tabloid, *Aftonbladet*, in August 2009, Scheper-Hughes felt uneasy about remaining silent when the charges of "despicable blood libel by the Swedish media"[81] were being leveled by the Israeli Ministry of Health (who knew about Hiss's record—thus feigning moral outrage). Encouraged by Israeli researchers to set the record straight, she made the transcript of the interview available in order to counter the narrative of those "'crying wolf' and using blood libel accusations to bludgeon their critics into submission."[82] Nelson's bullying tone, accusing Palestinians/the Left of paranoia, demonizing them as anti-Semitic, serves the same end: *bludgeon Israel's leftist critics into submission.*

Whereas Nelson is keen to deemphasize the organ harvesting of Palestinians and downplay its injustice, Scheper-Hughes insists on bringing to light the practice's symbolic importance: "the symbolism, you know, of taking skin of the population considered to be the enemy, [is] something, just in terms of its symbolic weight, that has to be reconsidered."[83] But Scheper-Hughes's point is never to single out Israel; rather, she repeatedly situates Israel within the global traffic in human organs. Scheper-Hughes reads Israel like any other country, focusing on the ways its "hierarchy of bodies . . . produces new social groups and categories—the 'bio-assured' or 'bio-secured'—as well as expendable populations—the 'bio-available' and the 'bio-disposable.'"[84] Under Hiss's tenure, the Institute of Forensic Medicine clearly favored a particular hierarchy, which placed Palestinians squarely at the bottom. Drawing on the ethnographic work of Meira Weiss, a distinguished anthropologist and Emeritus professor at Hebrew University, Scheper-Hughes observes:

> Weiss spoke about dark science in the military, about the conflict between secular and religious modalities concerning the uses of the body, and about the hierarchy of bodies at the institute that put Israeli soldiers at the top and gave them a reprieve from the worst and most savage harvesting; ordinary Israeli citizens beneath them; non-Jewish tourists in the middle sector; Palestinians on the bottom. New immigrants to Israel, the not-quite-Jewish-enough Russians and Ukrainians, were positioned just above the Palestinians.[85]

Hiss exploited Palestinian vulnerability. Quoting Chen Kugel, the whistleblower on the forensic institute, Scheper-Hughes avers:

> Some bodies were more vulnerable to theft than others: "It was easier to take tissues and organs from the new immigrants, and needless to say, it was easiest of all to take skin, bone, cornea and solid organs from the Palestinians. *They would be sent back across the border, and if there were any complaints, coming from their families, they were the enemy and so, of course, they were lying and no one would ever believe them.*"[86]

Scheper-Hughes does not say this explicitly, but it seems that what sets Palestinians (and the other "Orientals") apart from the new immigrants from Russia and Ukraine is their racialized or infrahuman status, what effectively makes them less than equal, *a priori* "bio-available" and "bio-disposable." The new white immigrants from Eastern Europe can eventually be fully integrated into Jewish society, and shed their outsider skin, but the Palestinians or Arab Jews will always be marked as racially other, excluded from the enjoyment of universalism (hegemonic whiteness). But here, we would add that the Palestinian body also differs, in important ways, from that of fellow "Orientals." As Noura Erakat pointedly remarks,

> The State's violent practices aimed at rehabilitating Middle Eastern Jews by cleansing them of their oriental qualities so as to bring them closer to Whiteness, stems from the same logic that presupposes the dispensable nature of the Palestinian body. That body lacks material value: it does not have access to capital, its land claims are retroactively delegitimized, its standing before the law is truncated and diminished, it lacks meaningful security from the State or otherwise, and its presence is always tenuous. Proximity to Palestinian-ness thus signals social death. Conversely, proximity to North American and European Whiteness signals the condition of possibility.[87]

In Zionist discourse, Arab Jews are still available for Israel's civilizing mission. Zionist culture possesses the ideological tools to "de-Arabize" Oriental Jews. "While presenting Palestine as an empty land to be transformed by Jewish labor," Ella Shohat writes, "the Zionist 'Founding Fathers' presented Arab-Jews as passive vessels to be shaped by the revivifying spirit of Promethean Zionism."[88] Zionism undeniably produces its Jewish victims, but the Palestinian body holds a distinct position. Palestinianness denotes an irremediable marker for otherness, for what lies beyond redemption and rehabilitation, condemned to otherness, and relegated to the realm of the "living dead."[89] Rendered a permanent threat within the settler order, the Palestinian body is a problem to be dealt with, with impunity if necessary.

Not unlike Scheper-Hughes, Puar pays close attention to the terrifying psychic implications of seeing oneself as purely instrumentalizable, devoid of worth or rights. This terror-inducing reality—this living death—is not an aberration, the result of a past policy that has now been discontinued or lawfully corrected. There is no juridical remedy for the naturalized state terror inflected on Palestinians in their daily life. Their disposability is not a contingent feature of the Zionist settler regime but a permanent one. Again, Palestinians are always already guilty of *being* Palestinian. The sheer presence of Palestinians—their stubborn refusal to disappear—induces Zionist anxiety about who belongs on this contested land: who are these "Arabs" contesting Israel's biblical claim to the Promised Land? And if the land is divinely sanctioned, why are the people in Palestine and across the world rejecting Jewish hegemony and legitimacy?

Excised from the human realm of the living, Palestinians are caught "between-two-deaths,"[90] between a symbolic death (imprisoned in their territories) and a physical death (what awaits them if they resist *or not*). We might say that terrorizing Palestinian bodies is Israel's modus operandi: the default (non)relationality afforded to Palestinians. As Puar aptly contends, "the maintenance of an affective economy of fear is a pivotal modality of control in settler colonial regimes."[91] And this morbid "modality of control" is precisely what nourishes Palestinian paranoia.

It's the Colonial Situation, Stupid!

The fear of having your community's organs mined, however, is not exceptional to Palestinians. Scheper-Hughes insightfully points out that the fear of being killed for one's organs is "a fear that occurs often enough to poor and politically disfranchised people whenever mortally injured persons are carried away by officials and later returned dead and their bodies harvested. Similar fears are recounted in Brazilian shantytowns and in South African townships and squatter camps during the anti-apartheid struggle."[92] Abused peoples fear their abusers/masters/colonizers. Palestinians understandably imagine the worst from a settler-colonial state that exercises absolute power over their lives and futures. Likewise, there is nothing unique about Israel. The Jewish state is like any other apartheid or colonial regime that relentlessly divides or segregates its society into the included and the excluded, into those who belong and those who don't. Witness the opposite logic at work in Nelson: "Academics and journalists who write about organ harvesting in connection with Israel have a special ethical responsibility to avoid using tropes that echo traditional blood libels, since they will otherwise be underwriting antisemitic beliefs."[93] What does this mean? Jews are either incapable committing crimes like organ theft (which, we know, is not the case) or if they are guilty of such crime the critic's language must be understated so as not to offend (actual victims be damned!).[94] The will to exceptionalize Israel/Jews characterizes Nelson's pro-Zionist hermeneutic—a Manichean hermeneutic obsessively suspicious of the Palestinian position and naïvely trusting of the Israeli's.

The Israeli state is not only presumed innocent, it is more or less immunized from any substantial critique. "Blaming the victim," as Said put it, is a common retort from the Zionist camp.[95] With Nelson, the blame is equally placed on the victim-sympathizer, the critic who dares to report or make known the Palestinian attitude. Any piece of information is aggressively scrutinized for its misinformation, dissected for its anti-Semitism. Puar repeats Palestinian questions and concerns about their kin's dead bodies. Why were the bodies of Palestinians being stored for months at Abu Kabir forensic institute rather than returned to their relatives? She highlights "the affective distress and pain" of these families. Puar further adds that they were held for "prolonged periods without explanation."[96] Nelson pounces on this last point, parroting Israeli authorities' official statement: "In fact, they did, explaining that they wanted to prevent funerals from turning into mass demonstrations, which in the past had incited further violence."[97] But was this "explanation" clearly conveyed to the families? If so, when was it communicated to the grieving families? Is Nelson at all troubled by the fact that Israel is in strict violation of international law[98] by holding Palestinian bodies for months? Moreover, Nelson seems overly confident that the security reasons offered constitute a satisfactory explanation for Israel's callous behavior. Chris Moore-Backman paints a more complicated picture:

> If [the withholding of bodies] is meant to stem violence on the part of Palestinians . . . the policy has been an abysmal failure. Like most if not all policies designed to humiliate and degrade, the policy of withholding bodies only fans the flames of unrest and desperation among Palestinians. On November 5, Israeli Defense Minister Moshe Yaalon himself conceded as much, saying that "holding onto bodies is in itself not a deterrent." He then announced that dead bodies would be returned on a "case-by-case basis," as if that were a step toward rapprochement rather than the continuation of a cruel and arbitrary system in which Israel may deny mourners access to their loved ones' bodies at any time.[99]

Holding Palestinian bodies hostage is not an isolated event, but a ruthless form of collective abuse. Adalah finds the security narrative simply disingenuous: "The Israeli security cabinet's decision to withhold the bodies of Palestinians is extremely problematic and is driven clearly by motivations for vengeance."[100] The punishment of Palestinians has no limit, no end; "even after death they will be treated cruelly,"[101] says Noura Erakat (with reference to the suspicious death of her cousin, Ahmad Erakat, at an Israeli checkpoint).

Nelson and Yaalon, to different degrees, disavow the colonial situation. Nelson uncritically reproduces the government's stated position, never questioning its vengeful tone nor entertaining how things might look like from a Palestinian vantage point, while Yaalon, conceding the futility of the policy, tries to soften its edge and make it more humane, by allowing some future bodies to be grieved. But as Moore-Backman rightly suggests, we must denounce the latter gesture of rapprochement as fake, and insist—in solidarity with the Palestinians in the territories and Israel proper—that there is no humane occupation, no occupation or governance without Israel's necropolitical regime of control and terror.

Palestinian Paranoia Redux

Belief in the two-state solution serves as Nelson's alibi; it allows him to maintain the ideological fantasy of an innocent, non-racist Jewish state coexisting with its Palestinian neighbors inside and outside of Israel. We are repeatedly told that he and the majority of Israelis do not want a "Greater Israel," and that Zionism without its expansionist excesses is not an oxymoron. For Nelson, the anti-colonial Left is only fueling Palestinian paranoia by irresponsibly disseminating ghoulish stories of Palestinian organ plunder, and thus contributing to the production of global hostility toward the state of Israel. Nelson, for his part, wants to contain the damage to Israel's reputation, and protect the Jewish state from the Left's project of delegitimization. Why? Because, to Nelson's chagrin, Israel is actually losing what Richard Falk calls "the legitimacy war," a war most valiantly waged on the "symbolic battlefield" by the Boycott, Divestment and Sanctions (BDS) movement against Israel at colleges and universities around the world.[102] For Nelson, mistakes were surely made at the Abu Kabir Institute, but now they've been corrected. He urges Western readers not to forget that Israel is doing the best it can given that it is surrounded by hostile forces—dangerous Arab bodies—and to see Palestinian paranoia for what it is: unadulterated anti-Semitism. The Left is either willfully blind to this hateful ideology or, more likely, shares Arab vitriol for the Jewish state.

Again, a contrast between Benhabib and Nelson on paranoia proves useful. Both seek to shield Israel from a delegitimizing anti-colonial critique and blame what's wrong with Israel on the excesses of *some* of its far-right politicians and citizens (e.g., settler hooligans). These fringe groups do not define Israel, but stand instead in tension with its purported democratic character. Israel is not simply passing as democratic, it *is* democratic. But whereas Benhabib makes a plea, on behalf of those in power, for understanding or even forgiving Israeli paranoia,[103] Nelson makes a plea to Western powers and fellow academics for the purposes of condemning Palestinian paranoia as anti-Semitic *tout court*. When it comes to Israel, there is no daylight, Nelson avers, between hostile Palestinians and the anti-colonial Left. To make this assertion, Nelson must rule out the possibility of a nuanced (i.e., non-anti-Semitic) anti-colonial reception of and engagement with Palestinian paranoia. For him, either you endorse its anti-Semitic vision or you denounce it. Indeed, Nelson fails to consider, in his defensive remarks on the organ harvesting affair, a rudimentary but crucial distinction between understanding and contextualizing, on one hand, and justifying and endorsing a position, on the other. It is true that Puar maintains that she wasn't herself making empirical claim about Israeli organ theft but conveying the suspicious sentiments of Palestinians, while still insisting that what they're saying is not irrational or so easily dismissible as anti-Semitic. Nelson concludes that "the suggestion that she was only reporting popular suspicion, not indicting Israel's actual practices, was moot from the outset."[104] Whereas Nelson projects hypocrisy or rhetorical manipulation onto Puar, I see Puar both registering Palestinian pain and affective disorientation, bearing witness to a destitute people, *and* implicitly calling for an understanding of the Palestinians, an understanding of the daily terror of the Occupation and its immeasurable impact on the mind of the occupied people.

Normality in Israel proper and the Occupied Territories is a rare thing for Palestinians, a luxury of the neoliberal few. Or as Said once put it: "If, in a Jewish state, normality is defined by Jewishness, abnormality is the normal condition of the non-Jew."[105] Within and outside the Green Line, this Palestinian "abnormality," normalized by the Occupation, as Roger Cohen laments, transmutes into "invisibility," the result of a "systematic blindness" among Israeli Jews, willfully oblivious to the condition and plight of the Indigenous population.[106] Abnormal and invisible, Palestinians are plagued by a context not of their collective choosing, operating in a world in which their consciousness is "at war with the given,"[107] to borrow a poignant expression from Saidiya Hartman. Living under settler colonialism closes up the world of Palestinians; it courts insanity and deviancy. But without reducing Palestinians to a state of pure ontological passivity, I want to suggest that Palestinian paranoia should not be seen either as an intrinsic property of the stereotypic "Arab mind" (in conformity with Orientalist discourse) or as an "aberration from mental health"[108] (as an exception to normalcy), but as a prevalent mode of being Palestinian under occupation, as the onto-political consequences of living under Zionist eyes, constantly subjected to a racialized and racializing field of visibility and intelligibility.

Palestinian paranoia is, therefore, not the manifestation of some abstract or timeless Arab anti-Semitism, an indicator of a pathologized "Palestinian mind," a diseased community, incapable of coexistence and peace with its Jewish neighbors. This is the paranoia that Zionists and their supporters like to project onto Palestinians. The ongoing killing and systematic harvesting of the organs of Palestinians may very well be factually inaccurate, but this should *not* distract us from Israel's vicious control over Palestinian bodies. In rejecting what Puar's critics take to be her "empirical claims" about organ mining, we should not overlook the next ideological step taken by Nelson and other manipulators of truth, which is to dismiss all inquiries into Israeli necropolitical governance. The Israeli state is *"lying in the guise of truth."*[109] The "truth" (it is not the *current* policy of the state of Israel to harvest Palestinian organs) is deployed to obfuscate Israel's cruel occupation and racist domination from the river to the sea, invalidate all grievances against the settler regime, and authorize racist ideation in Israel and abroad, producing demonized images of Palestinians as extremists, delusional, and, of course, dangerously anti-Semitic.

Once more, the task here is not to deny Palestinian paranoia, and double-down on conspiracy theories, as it were, but to understand the phenomenon of paranoia as the socio-psychological effect of the dreadful Occupation. The situation calls for an "aggressive counterreading,"[110] asking us to read paranoia against the grain, against a racist interpretive horizon, against what we might call, after Fanon, the "Zionist collective unconscious": "The collective unconscious is quite simply the repository of prejudices, myths, and collective attitudes of a particular group... it is cultural, i.e., it is acquired."[111] Palestinophobia, not unlike anti-Semitism, is not something instinctual but the offspring of social habits. An aggressive counterreading unsettles the ways the symbolic order overdetermines the paranoia of the oppressed, questioning its self-evidentiality and ascribed/naturalized meaning. This task starts with seeing Palestinian paranoia as a reaction to the colonial situation. Palestinians adopt a suspicious mood about the settlers' nefarious plans for the Natives, cultivating a healthy dosage of *ressentiment*, an affective response to a Zionist program bent on "a systematized negation of the other, a frenzied determination to deny the other any attribute of humanity."[112] What Palestinian paranoia discloses is a ruthless settler-colonial regime. This is not a simple case of persecutory paranoia. Palestinians are not only suffering from *delusions* of persecution (Israelis are chasing and hunting them for organs); they are suffering *because* they are habitually persecuted.[113]

Occupation, in the form of an apartheid regime, touches the very being of the colonized; it disorients and scrambles the Native's "cognitive mapping," the capacity to connect Palestinian experience or action to the larger global context. As a response to the permanent assault on Palestinians, a paranoid disposition—along with *ressentiment* and anti-colonial anger—emerges not so much as a loss of sense, an eclipsing of rational subjectivity, but as a survival strategy, a refusal to naturalize and normalize the Occupation, and an attempt—albeit, at times, a desperate one—at making sense out of their predicament: *Don't tell me that Hiss/Abu Kabir Institute is an exception.* The illicit organ harvesting emblematizes the Zionist necropolitical agenda toward Palestinians. Organ theft—literally stealing Palestinian vitality—is but a manifestation of Israel's ongoing eliminative project.[114] The Palestinian cry that they are taking my kin's organs is a call for action; it speaks to the larger framework of Israel's instrumentalization and thingification of Palestinian bodies, who remain unprotected (from state violence, land theft, native removal) and denied the privileges of being human/white (dignity and self-determination). But when read exclusively via the paradigmatic frame of the Shoah[115] and anti-Semitism—which necessarily abstracts and dehistoricizes, imparting trauma exclusively to Israeli Jews, casting them as innocent victims and all Palestinians as pathological perpetrators—Palestinian paranoia is effortlessly subsumed under the subheading of "Arab anti-Semitic instinct"; their suffering is displaced and silenced once again.

So is Palestinian paranoia a thing? Yes and no. In the context of Israel's illegal organ harvesting, the belief of some Palestinians in its ongoing practice, certainty in the state's continuous intent to kill, instrumentalize, and steal Palestinian bodies, might constitute paranoia. And yet the loaded charge of Palestinian paranoia, as we have seen with Nelson's (mis)reading of Puar, is often an opportunity to weaponize anti-Semitism, to use any negative portrayal of Israel as evidence of "blood libel," or more generally as indicating a deep-seated and persistent Palestinian/leftist hatred for the Jewish people. What is missing from the discussion is paranoia's enabling qualities, the ways it fosters an anti-Zionist hermeneutic that actually keeps Palestinians alive, always suspicious of the West's management of the Palestinian problem and its ideological promise of "land for peace" (i.e., peacefully endure your dispossession and you'll be rewarded with a state of your own). Not unlike the public use of *ressentiment*, paranoia, in this latter sense, is something not to overcome/cure but nurture/enact. In this light, we might say that Palestinian paranoia is dialecticized, undergoing a radical mutation. In the Zionist reading paranoia stands for the negation of Palestinian subjectivity/autonomy/sanity; in the anti-colonial reading, we have the negation of negation. What Zionists and their sympathizers consider paranoia is really a *ressentiment*-infused survival attitude, feeding a politics of refusal, a refusal to forget Israel's crimes, and follow or submit to the liberal playbook of "conflict" resolution.

At the same time, Palestinian paranoia is a doubled-edged sword. On the one hand, it calls to be defended, by critiquing its mendacious distortion as anti-Semitic; on the other, it needs to be (re)aligned with the anti-colonial project of "disalienation," which, as Fanon stresses, "implies a brutal awareness of the social and economic realities"[116] and whose goal is nothing less than the destruction of settler colonialism's sick world. "We are aiming for a complete lysis of this morbid universe," writes Fanon.[117] There is a noticeable friction between these two demands. The former pursues an overcoming of a certain understanding of Palestinian paranoia; the latter seeks its end.

Countering colonial forms of reasoning, Fanon, in his reflections on mental disorders in the colonial Algerian war, shifts our critical gaze back to the material conditions of French colonialism: "The criminality of the Algerian, his impulsiveness, the savagery of his murders are not . . . the consequence of how his nervous system is organized or specific character traits, but the direct result of the colonial situation."[118] Under settler/Western eyes, Indigenous "active resistance" is automatically pathologized.[119] But pathologizing the Palestinian body outside the settler context and its racial schema is a grave hermeneutico-political error. This reductive charge ignores the psycho-political dimension of paranoia—the Occupation, and resistance to it, as "a breeding ground for mental disorders"[120]—and repeats the injustices and violence visited on the Native, locking the Palestinian subject eternally in her psychopathology. Put slightly differently, it is not enough to defend Palestinian paranoia, to jettison the settler's Orientalist labels and racial myths, since such a critique risks remaining at the level of *reaction*, and thus inadvertently sustaining Zionism's Manichean thinking. An anti-Zionist hermeneutic worthy of its name critiques the racist and Orientalist representations of Palestinians and Palestinian paranoia *but also* intervenes at the ontological level, and incessantly labors to abolish the sociopolitical conditions that gave rise to paranoia in the first place.[121] And there is really no end to the colonial situation without the public use of *ressentiment*. Again, it takes a village to decolonize an oppressor.

Contrary to the settler's script, then, paranoia is not a mental disorder to which the "Palestinian mind" is naturally prone; instead, Palestinian paranoia, in all of its valences, must be seen as delimited by historical realities, the direct price of egregious Jewish supremacy. It is a symptom of—or an abnormality imposed on—Palestinians by the Occupation, the product of being persecuted and the brutality of settler colonialization. The implication is as clear as it is un-pragmatic: If you (anyone and everyone touched by the Palestinian cause) really want to get rid of Palestinian paranoia—the existential, self-consuming fear of dispossession and elimination—you must, first and last, change the colonial situation and dismantle Israel's vicious regime of control and terror.

4

Sovereignty

Israel established itself by force and insists on maintaining its settler-sovereignty by force. Jewish-Zionist leaders—primarily from Europe—did not come to the Middle East to reestablish their indigenous attachments there. They came as settlers claiming nativity and as conquerors intent on earning acceptance within Europe by establishing a nation-state beyond its shores. Any possible future necessitates an accounting of this history, not simply for the sake of cathartic truth telling, but for the sake of decolonization.

—Noura Erakat[1]

The return of land would in principle signal the end of the settler-colonial regime and inaugurate the condition for Palestinian self-determination and collective sovereignty. In the global imaginary, the idea of the two-state solution still monopolizes what such a land return looks like. Indeed, it is presumably the "desired" solution to the Palestinian question, one that is shared by Western powers, Arab neighbors, liberal Zionists, and the Palestinian Authority itself. And yet, it has lost the support of the majority of Palestinians. A poll conducted in the West Bank and Gaza Strip by the Palestinian Center for Policy and Survey Research in 2021 found that only 39 percent expressed support for the two-state solution.[2] Nevertheless, the two-state solution persists; it is an ideological fantasy that refuses to die. It is dead, however, not only because of the South African-style "bantustanization" of Palestinian land, which has changed the reality on the ground (now splintered into scattered territories), making it practically impossible to create a contiguous Palestinian state, but also because the two-state solution is a racist answer to the Palestinian question that ultimately fails to deliver on the more substantial claims of the Indigenous population. It leaves unanswered the refugee problem and the plight of the Palestinian citizens of Israel, and it ironically divides Palestinians with the promise of sovereignty, with the ideological rewards of the nation-state.

It is time not only to let go of the "two-state hegemon"[3] but also to take inspiration from Chilean protest and claim: *Another end to the two-state solution is possible*.[4] This chapter explores binationalism as that *other* end. Binationalism—a secular and democratic state, or a one-state solution grounded in the axioms of equality and freedom for all—does not follow the nostalgic and redemptive script of a *time before the settler*. Binationalism also rejects the belief that land by itself will heal, or rather address, the colonial wounds of Palestinian sovereignty. It is not about Indigenous sovereignty *restored*, but a future mode of "coexistence" with the Jewish neighbor. And part of binationalism's futurity lies in its unraveling of the metaphysics of sovereignty. This chapter first examines the ideological lure of and libidinal investment in the two-state solution, put on full display in Bartlett Sher's film *Oslo*, which idealizes the promises of the peace process, making superficial gestures of recognition under the liberal heading of bothsidesism. Next, I turn to Larissa Sansour's short sci-fi film *Nation Estate*, which counterbalances her ideological portrait of the colonial situation with a dystopian and hopeless vision of a Palestinian futurity caught within the logic of the two-state hegemon. Finally, I consider binationalism as an ethico-political project for reimagining sovereignty otherwise. ~~Sovereignty~~ (sovereignty under erasure) marks and registers its critical distance toward the category of the human, whose colonial logic legitimized and continues to legitimize anti-Blackness and the subjugation of Indigenous communities all around the world. ~~Sovereignty~~ puts front and center the labor of decolonization and abolition. Binationalism takes up this task, in its struggle not only for racial justice—in its struggle against Zionist/white domination—but also for economic justice: in its struggle against exploitation in Palestine/Israel.

Bothsidesism and Its Discontents

Bartlett Sher's film *Oslo* (2021) tells the story of the secret negotiations between Palestinians and Israelis orchestrated by a Norwegian diplomat couple, Mona Juul (Ruth Wilson) and Terje Rod-Larsen (Andrew Scott), that resulted in the signing of the Declaration of Principles on Interim Self-Government Arrangements, Oslo I Accord, in 1993. The film is adapted from J. T. Rogers's Tony-winning play of the same name. *Oslo* opens with a dream, a primal scene of sorts, that explains Juul's investment in the Israeli-Palestinian conflict. Later, in response to a question posed by Legal Adviser of the Ministry of Foreign Affairs Joel Singer (Igal Naor), "Why are you [she and Rod-Larsen] doing this?"[5] Juul shares a formative experience that occurred during the First Intifada. After taking a wrong turn down an alley in Gaza, she sees "two boys facing each other. One in uniform. One in jeans. But on their faces, the same fear. The same desperate desire to be anywhere but here."[6] We know from an earlier visual account of this scene that the Israeli soldier hesitates to shoot the Palestinian teenager armed with a mere rock, but he is followed by another Israeli soldier who does not. The scene lingers a bit on the first soldier's look of dread at the fallen Palestinian, whose death was also witnessed by Juul, who is herself shaken by what just transpired.

Alongside Juul's traumatic experience, *Oslo* makes Larsen's unconventional approach to conflict resolution a central concern of its portrayal. Larsen stresses the need for trust-building in tough negotiations, the need to maintain a space that fosters empathy and allows you to see your political enemies as fellow human beings, even potential friends. The spatial arrangement of the negotiations, Larsen explains, reinforces this approach; the room where heated policy debates are to take place is kept separate from the one in which the negotiators dine and talk to one another informally and intimately. "Here, here," Larsen asserts, "we are all friends."[7] For Juul and Larsen, the problems fueling the conflict are fundamentally mistrust and misrecognition. Once you see your counterpart as human, the rest will fall into place. This is a version that Eve Tuck and K. Wayne Yang describe as the liberal understanding of decolonization: "Free your mind and the rest will follow."[8] (Re)humanize your enemy—that is, free your mind of hate—and peace will follow. This creates the illusion that Palestinian suffering is the sad result of leaders—from both sides—failing to build a friendly working relation. While any examination of conflict must consider how leaders relate to one another, in *Oslo*, this facet of the war is fetishistically elevated to a primary cause, which means that it is also the solution the film posits: the more the parties can humanize one another, the more they can make concessions, the better the results for all. To critique this approach is not to argue against face-to-face diplomacy, but rather against *Oslo*'s staging of negotiation as unfolding in a neutral space where negotiators can meet as human equals to resolve their problems. *Oslo*'s acknowledgment of the asymmetry of power is kept at a minimum.

In *Oslo*'s moral universe, what matters is mutual respect, empathy, and a willingness to sacrifice for the common good: peace for both sides, for both peoples. Yet in the Oslo negotiations, the two parties did not sacrifice equally. But this objection still does not begin to get at the problem of Oslo (both the accords themselves and the film about their development). The failure of the endeavor was overdetermined. When the Palestinian question is severed from its settler-colonial context, mystified solutions tend to follow, and the Oslo Accords are no exception. In *Oslo*'s dramatization, the colonial situation makes only two brief appearances. It is first evoked as a reaction to the accusation of Palestinian barbarism, when Uri Savir (Jeff Wilbusch), the director-general of the Israeli foreign ministry, says: "You killed our athletes in Munich; murdered our schoolchildren in Ma'alot; invaded us and spilled our blood on Yom Kippur."[9] Ahmed Qurei (Salim Dau), director-general of the PLO's economic branch, counters: "You burned our homes; drove a million people from Palestine; and claimed to this day that there was no such thing as Palestine."[10] Savir neutralizes the exchange by portraying it as mere bravado, and urges both sides to get to the serious business of ending the cycle of violence: "Now that we've both swung our dicks, let me say this. We are tired of being at war with you. We are committed to ending the cycle of violence and enmity. But I want to be clear. Israel will not sacrifice its security."[11] Security takes precedence over peace or reconciliation. Israel's national sovereignty is not to be compromised.

In the second instance, the other Palestinian negotiator Hassan Asfour (Waleed Zuaiter) tries to bring up the colonial situation but to no avail. Addressing Savir, Asfour draws attention to Israel's arrogance and ideological manipulation of its (and Palestinians') global image:

> You sit there, comrade, with your colonial superiority, dictating what our future will or will not be. Yet somehow, with your intelligence service, your army, your nuclear weapons, you are threatened by us. So, are you the master who must be obeyed, or the victim who must be coddled, because you cannot be both![12]

Savir dismisses Asfour's anti-colonial framework as Marxist propaganda, originating from Moscow. But it is precisely this colonial superiority, Israel's Indigenous reason—the *Western/Zionist consciousness of Palestinian Indigeneity*—that the film fails to expose or unravel. As Joseph Fahim rightly avers, "*Oslo* couldn't have been more tone-deaf—a prime emblem of Hollywood's oversimplified treatment of the Israel-Palestine conflict that no longer feels relevant or rings true."[13] Returning to Oslo uncritically can only evoke a sense of nostalgia, as if the Oslo Accords stood for the happy days of diplomacy, the golden age of hope.

The moralism of *Oslo* lies in trying to rectify the overrepresentation of the Zionist perspective by voicing the Palestinian position. This is the film's depoliticized bothsidesism. But what Palestinian voice do we actually hear, and more important, how is it framed by *Oslo*? It is a voice in desperate need of liberal recognition. We see quickly how the Declaration of Principles (DoP), which both parties are meant to hammer out, is met with structural limitations and fierce resistance. The Israeli negotiators repeatedly bat down any genuine demands made on the state of Israel. For example, Qurei's stipulation that "third-party international arbitration" serves as a means of resolving the remaining deadlocks is stricken from the final version of the DoP.[14] What Palestinians get instead is the promise that both parties will return to these substantive and thorny issues—Jerusalem, settlements, borders, and refugees—during "final status" negotiations, during what was later to be called the "Permanent Status Agreement." On the question of Jerusalem, the film gives a rather Machiavellian portrait of Shimon Peres, who enters the negotiations in the last stages. When PLO leader Arafat insists on East Jerusalem as the capital for a future Palestinian state, Peres says to his team, "in the name of constructive ambiguity, we will accept that in the final stage of further negotiations, the future of Jerusalem will be addressed."[15] *Oslo* hints at Peres's disingenuity. And at another key moment in the negotiations, the Palestinians make a demand that falls neatly into the vision of the Israelis. "Mr. Singer, when you are willing to state herein that the Palestine Liberation Organization is the official voice of the Palestinian people, then we will revisit your legitimacy," says Qurei.[16] Palestinians recognize the legitimacy of the state of Israel, whereas Israel only recognizes the PLO as the legitimate voice of the Palestinian people (without a recognition of the right to self-determination, to Palestinian statehood). Worse, Israel sets in motion a Palestinian government in charge of both counterinsurgency (eradicating anti-colonial sentiments) and disciplining (the desires of) its own people, doing the bidding of the occupying force.

The film doubles down on difficult dialogue and concessions for the common good as the arduous labor of peace-making. But nothing in *Oslo* points to the political flaws and limitations in this line of thinking. And this is the film's unmistakable lack of consideration for asymmetry and its impacts. At the time the Oslo Accords were signed, the settler population stood at 200,000, even though the Fourth Geneva Convention prohibits an occupying power like Israel from transferring its own population to areas that it occupies. Unabated by the peace process (worse: it perversely amplified the process by giving the government cover), the number of illegal settlers has continued to balloon. In 2021, there were "between 600,000 and 750,000 Israeli settlers living in at least 250 illegal settlements (130 official, 120 unofficial) in the occupied West Bank and East Jerusalem."[17] Israel systematically violates international law when it authorizes the construction of these settlements on Palestinian land.

Bothsidesism gives the illusion that both parties have the same legitimate claims to the land. It is as if UN Resolution 194, which enshrines the Palestinian right of return, along with UN Resolutions 242 and 338, which "stipulate unequivocally that land acquired by Israel through the war of 1967 must be given back in return for peace,"[18] didn't really exist or limit Israel's national sovereignty, as if the state were immune from their enforcement (the US unconditional support and veto power in the Security Council, of course, feeds Israel's bloated sense of invulnerability and exceptionalism). It is as if Israel, during the negotiations, is being asked to sacrifice part of itself for the greater good of the region. Savir says, "We are shrinking the size of our country!" Qurei rebukes him, cutting through the ideological fantasy: "Hey, this is not land for you to give, but to give back!"[19] If Israel is being asked to give up anything, it is its attachment to a Greater Israel, to a racist Zionist vision devoted to the elimination of the Indigenous population.

While we cannot fault the film for representing what actually took place in the negotiation process, we can scrutinize its commentary, its ideological force and framing, along with its contribution to a nostalgia for Oslo. These elements emerge perhaps most clearly in the film's conclusion, which relates the failures that followed the Oslo Accords. The final minutes of the film present a selective chronology of events through four clips of archival news footage showing Rabin at the White House celebrating the Oslo Accord on September 13, 1993, Rabin's assassination in November 1995 by an Israeli extremist who opposed the Accords, Arafat's public speech condemning the assassination, and scenes from the eruption of the Second Intifada in September 2000.[20] This final clip is preceded by an intertitle informing the audience that the parties failed to reach an agreement on the remaining issues in the July 2000 Camp David summit, while the sequence is narrated in voice-over by Juul, who is shown between clips typing the words we are hearing. This chronological presentation of facts suggests a causal relationship between them, an impression reinforced by Juul's typed reflections on the eventness of the Oslo Accords, which take on the authoritative status of both historical chronicle and prescient prophecy. Following the shot of Rabin at the White House, we hear: "The Oslo channel began with the hopes of creating a dialogue between adversaries. Already, this process has succeeded beyond anything we imagined: The establishment of a Palestinian state. Movement towards a peace treaty between Israel and Jordan. And yet, undoubtedly, objection to this process is coming." Juul's narration continues after the last clip:

For the efforts of any peoples to bridge their hatreds is always met by some with fierce resistance. But whatever mistakes were made, whatever unintended events have been unleashed, I still believe this channel was worth doing. For if we do not sit across from our enemies, and hear them, and see them as human beings, what will become of us?[21]

As we hear her last words, the film returns us to the primal scene of the Israel soldier and Palestinian teenager, which symbolizes the hope of Oslo, a means a breaking the cycle of violence that puts innocent people from both sides into harm's way.

Oslo performs its bothsidesism by its neutral and universal call to humanize the Other. That is, it assumes that Palestinians are not the only ones in need of recognition. Both sides are guilty of demonizing their sworn enemies. The colonized and the colonizers are both caught in the same vicious logic. Bothsidesism is the liberal supplement to the existing Israeli-Palestinian narrative; it indexes the weakening of Israel's rhetoric of the eternal Victim—we have innocent victims on both sides now. Is this a qualitative improvement? For the liberal subject, it undeniably is; both Israeli and Palestinian leaders are to blame for failing to deliver on the promises of Oslo. Bothsidesism signals an incremental step toward a balanced view of the "conflict." But the interpretive and political weakness of this approach is that it tries to fit the—albeit upgraded—image of the Palestinians within an existing framework that obfuscates the dynamics at hand, the antagonisms generated by Israel's status as a settler state and an apartheid regime. However, once Israeli Jews are perceived as settler colonizers, exploiters of Indigenous vitality, matters look much different. The framework of the two-state solution loses any serious credibility. Worse, its disingenuity is exposed. We see the two-state solution for what it is: an ideological lie, "a cynical tool of conflict management never intended to actually resolve the conflict."[22] The belief that both sides deserve a state of their own absent of a political confrontation with Israel's racial settler regime is "like prescribing aspirin to deal with cancer."[23] It does little to question let alone undo "Israel's right to be a racist state [as] guaranteed by the Palestinian leadership."[24] The two-state solution is doomed from its inception.

To see bothsidesism as the fair response to the Israeli-Palestinian conflict thus fails to notice that the cure compounds the problem. The word "conflict" gives the illusion that this is a conflict of equals, a dispute between two parties over land. What gets ideologically distorted is that Palestinians are in a struggle for survival, facing Zionism's eliminative logic. The Oslo Accords may have forced the Israeli government to acknowledge the existence of the Palestinian people, but Israel has subsequently moved, with the help of the Oslo Accords themselves, to shatter Palestinian cohesion, to fragment and seclude the Indigenous population (through check points and siege). The Oslo II Accord, signed on September 28, 1995, carved up the occupied West Bank into three administrative zones (or zones of containment): Area A, where the PA controls civil and security matters; Area B, where the PA controls only civil matters; and Area C, where Israel commands full control. To put matters bluntly: Bothsidesism reeks of interpretive rigidity and sterility. It lives in the realm of the postpolitical, where only the possible and the acceptable (acceptable *because* possible) matter. To get this point across, let's consider Palestinians under Occupation alongside the condition of Black people under the Jim Crow era. Hearing Black voices speaking from their vantage point, as a rebuff to the hegemonic segregationist, was a marked improvement. But bothsidesism on anti-Blackness is today rightly seen as ethically and politically repulsive. The Ku Klux Klan's vision is clearly no longer accepted in dominant discourse as a legitimate perspective that merits entertaining (this, of course, does not mean that anti-Blackness has disappeared, but rather that it can no longer circulate in its habitual ways in public discourse). Isn't today's dominant form of Zionism, which actively promotes Ashkenazi supremacy and ethnonational homogeneity, worthy, at last, of the same scrutiny?

Settling for bothsidesism gives Zionism a lifeline, doing little to challenge Israel's normalized racism. In bothsidesism, symmetry is sought at the expense of justice, ironing out important differences, structural differences between the occupier and the occupied. Occupiers can be traumatized by their exposure to daily violence, but this insight cannot override the settler-colonial context. "We are all victims" in the Israeli-Palestinian conflict is yet another liberal Zionist move to innocence. Bothsidesism may disrupt a settler logic that produces Palestinians as infrahuman, and even solicits a qualified recognition of the Palestinians' humanity. There are, however, significant political limits to bothsidesism. You can relate to Palestinians only as victims (of hate, subjugation) but not as freedom fighters engaged in anti-colonial resistance (which would risk casting Israelis as agents of state terrorism). The colonial situation remains buried in liberal sentimentality. *Free your mind of hate—fill it with love, open yourself to epiphanic encounters—and peace will follow.* Bothsidesism is the new liberal hegemony, and its hermeneutic is ultimately inhospitable to the Palestinian cause.

Settler Recognizes Settler

In its response to *Operation Guardian of the Walls*, the Biden administration asserted its "measured" liberal position that "both sides" need to de-escalate, obfuscating, once again, the asymmetrical situation of power, that is, the colonial situation. Frustrated, angry, and defiant Palestinian protesters in Israel proper are put on the same level as the armed Israeli mobs looking to lynch Palestinians, chanting, as we have seen in Chapter 1, "Death to Arabs!" and wanting to purge their mixed cities of any Palestinian presence. Israeli politicians warn of "civil war"; they denounce the "anarchy" and blame the ungrateful "traitors," Palestinian citizens of Israel—who are unified in solidarity with their brethren in Occupied Palestine—for sparking intracommunal violence and rebelling against Israel's democratic state.[25] But, as Lana Tatour rightly surmised, "the civil war discourse erases the colonial context in which violence against Palestinians takes place. It is designed to mask the reality on the ground: one of settler colonial brutality, state-sanctioned violence, and pogroms by Jewish supremacist groups backed by the state against Palestinians, the Indigenous people of the land."[26] Corporate media's coverage tends to mimic its political leaders' talking points. Indeed, it is *as if* the media lacks the grammar that would portray the Palestinians as the aggrieved party, as legitimate agents of self-defense. Over two decades ago, Slavoj Žižek pointed out how "Palestinian resistance is cited as proof that we are dealing with terrorists. This paradox is inscribed into the very notion of a 'war on terror'—a strange war in which the enemy is criminalised if he defends himself and returns fire with fire."[27] At best, Western media depicts the Palestinian struggle as an unfortunate "conflict," with both parties sharing in the blame (what triggered the struggle, the forced expulsion of Palestinians, is irrelevant or a side note); at worst, Israel is cast as the righteous party, protecting its people from Hamas' indiscriminate rockets (though this narrative is weakening in popularity, it still holds sway with a Western audience invested in safeguarding its citizens from so-called threatening Muslims, *within its borders and without*). Needless to say, the one-dimensionality and hermeneutic poverty of both narratives can only fuel Palestinian paranoia about getting a fair hearing in the Western press.[28]

Whenever Palestinians break from their image as abject victims and resist Israel's ethno-religious belligerence—thwarting, for example, the far-right Israeli extremists' march through the Old City to commemorate "Jerusalem Day," an Israeli national holiday marking the "reunification" of Jerusalem after the 1967 war, meaning a racist day celebrating the ongoing ethnic cleansing and dispossession of the land's Indigenous population—they get labeled terrorists, effortlessly triggering the evocation of Israel's "right to self-defense." Anti-colonial resistance to settler hegemony is overshadowed by endless and numbing talks of Israel's sovereignty and security. The ideological rhetoric of self-defense is, of course, meant to attenuate objections to Israel's disproportionate response in

Gaza—which is mechanically repeated by Western world leaders, with the Biden administration shamelessly leading the charge. This right to self-defense frames Israel's actions as "legitimate" responses to Hamas' "illegitimate" provocations (recall Mourid Barghouti's "Secondly," beginning with the Hamas' rockets rather than the Nakba/Occupation). And as Judith Butler observes, this elevation of self-defense in Israeli propaganda has even replaced the usual slogans, casting Israel as the sole beacon of morality or democracy in the Middle East: "instead of trying to advertise themselves as the only moral or democratic state in the region, which was never true, they [Israelis] now have shifted to a form of self-defense that licenses infinite killing," and this means that "there is no end to that killing because there is no end to the legitimacy of their idea of self-defense."[29] Moreover, this "elevated" right is never afforded to the Indigenous population. *Settler recognizes settler.* Self-defense is a luxury of nation-states: the Israelis possess one, the Palestinians don't.

With more bothsidesism, the Biden administration concedes that Palestinians do have "a right to live in safety and security."[30] This is Biden "evolving" on the Palestinian question. But this right comes with the complete abdication of resistance—violent or otherwise—making a safe and secured Palestinian a Palestinian intrinsically devoid of dignity and will. Safety and security are not to be achieved via a collective struggle for self-determination. No, it is only afforded to them by a greater sovereign power. Palestinians are systematically denied the right to self-defense, the right of survival, the right to refuse Israel's state terrorism and expulsion (the actual *causes* of Palestinian resistance), with Al Aqsa Mosque and the neighborhoods of Sheikh Jarrah and Silwan in Jerusalem serving as the latest flashpoint.[31]

For Israel and its supporters, a Free Palestine is scandalous, terrifying, and intolerable. What is tolerable is only a Palestinian sovereignty, a "ghettoized sovereignty,"[32] a sovereignty muzzled by the occupier's inhospitable sovereignty. But in light of the rise and mainstreaming of the far-right in Israel, we are witnessing in Western media and politics a growing nostalgia for Oslo, anxiety for what used to be the status quo, for the cruel days when the rhetoric of "land for peace" still held purchase. For Israel's more hawkish and cynical Western allies, it is as if Israeli leadership forgot Ideology 101: *Dispossess all you want, but still engage in (fake) peace talks.* Among liberals, keeping alive the racist and discredited two-state solution—a vision that divides the land along strictly ethno-religious lines—is now astonishingly framed as aspirational.[33] As long as there is a *soupçon* of hope, a belief that both sides can still resolve this sad "conflict," the US-led West does not have to step in and exert real pressure on

Israel to decolonize, or, at the very least, make it abide by international law. The Occupation is catastrophic, but not serious, as Žižek might say.[34] Western powers know that Israel is normalizing the Occupation, that it is preparing to annex more Palestinian land (the question is not "is Israel going to annex?" but "how much is it going to annex?"). They know that Palestine is a tragedy, but there is no impetus to marshal a global response and take seriously Israel's egregious Occupation. The Palestinian question is reduced to a local problem—its universal dimension denied. The cry that Palestinian Lives Matter is neutralized, treated as another expression of minority rights rather than a universal push to invent or "recreate the figure of the citizen, or the conditions of democratic politics in Israel and Palestine."[35]

The liberal response to the Palestinian predicament is *to act without acting*. We might say that liberals nostalgically yearn for *a time before Netanyahu*; they pathetically plead for (the promise of) diplomacy. As quintessential liberal Tom Friedman of the *New York Times* writes, "the most important thing for American diplomacy and Israeli politics is to keep one thing alive, and right now it really is in intensive care. The two-state solution. And I see this [anti-Netanyahu] coalition at least potentially doing that because I think there is a common denominator for separation and for real Palestinian autonomy."[36] In this amazing repackaging of the status quo, what "real Palestinian autonomy" translates to is an archipelago of Bantustans, with "separation" (self-governance under Israeli eyes) substituting for genuine Indigenous sovereignty and self-determination. The two-state solution is ideologically rebranded as an ideal; the prospect of independence from the Israeli state is something Palestinians have to work toward, something that they have to "earn" again. The West asks, "Palestinians, isn't a two-state solution better than annexation, non-existence?" But are West Bank annexation and (talks about) the two-state solution really the only two possibilities? This liberal blackmail must be flatly rejected.

Palestinian Futurity

What Oslo ought to produce in us is not hope, but hopelessness—a hopelessness that does not index despair and retreat but motivates indignation and a life-affirming *ressentiment*: there is no just future without a reckoning with the past and present, the ongoing injustice of the Nakba. This hopelessness eschews the normative liberal script that things will get better, that the moral arc of history bends forward. Against the inertia abetted by this belief in progress, hopelessness insists on "the politics of the now,"³⁷ as Jasbir Puar stresses, vigorously rejecting liberal futurity or futurology: refusing, in other words, what is possible from the standpoint of Western liberalism. As Agamben and Žižek observe, it takes courage to be hopeless.³⁸ Indeed, critique draws its strength and inspiration from hopelessness. The "courage of hopelessness," in the context of the Occupation, means that you see Oslo, symbolized by the horizon of the two-state solution, as a dead-end, and that only out of its ruins can something at once emancipatory (a reinvigorated anti-colonial struggle) and inventive (a national struggle beyond the nation-state) be brought into being.

Larissa Sansour's dystopian sci-fi film *Nation Estate* (2012) jolts her audience in that direction. The short film is part of a trilogy including *A Space Exodus* (2009) and *In the Future They Ate from the Finest Porcelain* (2016). *A Space Exodus* reimagines Stanley Kubrick's *2001: A Space Odyssey* as a Palestinian journey into outer space. An astronaut, played by Sansour herself, representing the first Palestinian in space, plants a Palestinian flag on the moon, and nods to Neil Armstrong by uttering "a small step for a Palestinian, a giant leap for mankind."³⁹ "Palestinian" substitutes for "man," and in doing so obliquely signals the universality of the Palestinian cause; the excluded, whose humanity has been systematically degraded under the Occupation, now stand for humanity. This gesture appears at first utopian, confirming Palestinians' inclusion in the human—their ability to go where other men have gone before—and their achievement of national sovereignty over a true *terra nullius*, a land that is really not inhabited by anyone (unlike Palestine itself, which early Zionists framed as empty of a people). Yet it is counterbalanced by a series of dystopian considerations. What kind of national sovereignty is this? Does it exist only in outer space, the stuff of sci-fi fantasy? How can a community come into being in a sterile, lifeless world? The "exodus" in *A Space Exodus* signals that there is no return home (as you have in Homer's *Odyssey*); it also continues to mark the Palestinians as an exiled people, now seemingly expelled to outer space. There is no overcoming or transcendence of their wretchedness: the shift from wretched of the earth to wretched in outer space is hardly an occasion for celebration. Palestinian national sovereignty, if such a thing is to ever materialize, will be out of this world. Underlining this pessimistic mood are the final shots of the Palestinian astronaut losing contact with her vessel and mission control as she drifts, terrifyingly untethered, outward into space. As in the world below, the little hope for national sovereignty is vanishing right before our eyes.

Not unlike Suleiman's staging of Palestinian *ressentiment*, however, Sansour's dystopian musings do not register despair but incite critique, or a feeling of hopelessness that opens to a critical sensibility, a yearning to expand on Palestinian ways of being. Robert Stam puts it succinctly: "as Palestine shrinks on the ground, it expands in cinematic space."[40] Sansour's *In the Future*, codirected with Søren Lind, takes up this very question of narrative space as its site of intervention. In this complex film, a session between a resistance leader and her psychiatrist sparks an exchange about the ideology of myths and counter-myths. In their dialogue—which we hear as a voice-over narrative while opaque, dreamlike tableaux and sequences occupy the visual field—they talk about the patient's sister, who died as a child, and the patient's own plan to interfere with future history by manipulating the carbon-dated age of *keffiyeh*-patterned porcelain bowls and planting them in the earth to be excavated later. The psychiatrist pushes the self-described "narrative terrorist" to justify her guerilla project:

> Psychiatrist: You're dismissing scientific methodology as irrelevant.
> Resistance leader: For all practical purposes, yes. This region has been held captive by myth and fiction for millennia, the convenient narrative of one intruder always followed by that of another. It's all about implementation and sedimentation. Myth hides best out in the open. Its repetition is its camouflage.
> History is by default revisionist. Archival photos don't depict history, history is the story we tell about these photos, and this story was never immune to fiction, religion, folklore or myths.[41]

For the "narrative terrorist," affect trumps cognition: "I used to see archive and documentary as shortcuts to a truth-based countermeasure to the versions of history written by our rulers. Now I don't. Truth is beside the point. Legitimacy is not a rational concept, it's emotional, psychological."[42] As a "terrorist of the imaginary,"[43] she is short-circuiting the affective and identificatory field, contesting the privilege of myth-making. Though Sansour never mentions Palestine or Israel by name in the film, her target might very well be Zionist uses of the science of archeology to shape world opinion and affirm their metaphysical Indigeneity to the Promised Land.[44] Palestinians, the resistance fighter believes, can beat Zionists at their own game. If Palestinians' past and present have both been narrated for them by (hostile) others, she is giving herself the permission to narrate, to narrate the future of her people. But a distinction must be made. Unlike "our rulers," who deploy archeology as a state strategy, as a propaganda machine to naturalize Indigenous dispossession, the protagonist is rusing with archeology (keeping in mind that rusing is a weapon of the weak). Her relation to myth-making is tactical and profoundly ironic: basically, she does not drink the Kool-Aid. She is inventing artifacts out of necessity, because that is the currency that people with power understand. Claiming Indigeneity is now about facticity-making rather than facticity-reporting. Future generations of diasporic Palestinians depend on the creation of counter-myths.

If *A Space Exodus* and *In the Future* posit Palestinian sovereignty as an ideal not only under threat on earth, in the present, but also in outer space and in the future, respectively, *Nation Estate* materializes this threat in a phantasmatic rendering of the two-state solution as a colossal skyscraper assuring its people's vertical enclosure. The short film also succeeds in conveying the continuity of Palestinian enclosure; from the Occupation to the two-state solution, an aura of sameness prevails. *Nation Estate*, of course, evokes nation-state: the Western prize of national belonging. "Estate" brings us into the business of real estate, making Palestine a coveted *property* for its would-be citizens. This short film begins in an underground train tunnel and follows the pregnant protagonist (Sansour) as she returns to her home in Bethlehem. She gets off the Amman Express and enters an immaculate, spacious skyscraper, where an enormous Palestinian flag hangs on display in the glossy lobby. The skyscraper comprises of all of Palestine, with cities and attractions stacked one above the other, as a giant directory next to the elevator indicates. Bethlehem, for example, is on the twenty-first floor, while the "Gaza Shore" restaurant, featuring "the best sushi on the block,"[45] as an elevator advertisement touts, is located on the Mediterranean level (the twenty-eighth floor). The few visitors in this space, dressed in spotless basketweave tunics and quietly trundling small roller bags, nod and smile calmly to one another as they enter the elevator and wait silently for their floor. What kind of Palestine is this? What kind of solution to the Palestinian problem does this estate represent? We get one answer right away, in the form of an announcement to prepare for a security check (fingerprints and retina scan). Surveillance and control are clearly dominant features of this "new" reality. Elevator passengers are reminded that their Nation Estate passports must be validated in order to travel. *Plus ça change . . .*

Eyal Weizman describes Israel's architectural containment and control of Palestinian population as a "politics of verticality" or even "vertical apartheid." Weizman underscores the political function of the illegal settlements: "resettlement projects have been carried out as central components of strategies of 'counter-insurgency' and pacification, demonstrating that the default response to the violence of the colonized has always been increased spatial discipline."[46] They are "optical devices" whose purpose is "the supervision and control of a hostile population."[47] The two-state solution—as imagined in *Nation Estate*—

is not an end to this cruel logic of domination but its full actualization. It has seemingly pacified Palestinian aspiration for national sovereignty, gentrified the Occupation, while keeping the Indigenous population conveniently separated and segregated; indeed, the skyscraper "den[ies] even the possibility of a cognitive encounter" between Palestinians and settlers.[48]

Needless to say, this Palestine is a sterile place, a commodified entity, bearing the tentacles and marks of neoliberal investments. In this capitalist-friendly commercial property, branding is ubiquitous. You can find Nation Estate tote bags for tourists. In the skyscraper's main elevator, Norwegian Fjords advertises its humanitarian contribution to this week's general water supply, and its support of the Water Pipes for Peace program. This corporate advertising obfuscates the ongoing problem of water access. As it does in the Occupation, Israel appears in this future reality to be restricting the Palestinian right to water, which severely qualifies any hope of national sovereignty, forcing political leaders to rely on the goodwill and charity of others and the international aid they provide for its survival and prosperity. Appearances are deceptive. Cutting-edge technological innovations do not yield basic self-sufficiency over essential goods. But then again, is *this* Palestine for Palestinians? Gil Hochberg perspicaciously draws our attention to the skyscraper's fraught relation to the global market:

> Each floor is designated for a city . . ., reachable by a gleaming elevator that opens onto a similarly pristine vista resembling a high-modern airport terminal. The estate high-rise also resembles a museum of Oriental antiquity, wherein the various Palestinian cities are displayed mummified. This idea of preservation contrasts with the futuristic aesthetic of the project in the whole. The clash between the impetus to preserve and the overall hyper-futuristic looks of the "estate" reveals Sansour's political critique of *both* preservation and real-estate development. Both appear in the film as two sides of the same coin: a process through which the livelihood of Palestine is "sold out" to the global market.[49]

The two-state solution delivers Palestine more fully to the market; it offers Palestine either as a relic of the past, locked in an Orientalist framework, or as an ultra-modern, hyper-technological reality, a captive consumer population, a "standing reserve,"[50] in Heideggerian parlance, whose (natural/human) resources are to be ordered, arranged, and developed according to neoliberal fancy.

Is this what Palestinians want? Is this what the protagonist aspires for? The ending of the film answers in the negative. As we follow the protagonist entering her apartment with a keycard in the form of a Palestinian flag (another superficial token of Palestinianness), we sense in her a desire for more. Upon entering the modern flat, she first waters a small olive tree contained to a small plot of earth embedded in the tiled floor, then selects a traditional Palestinian meal (including *marmaon*, *tabbouleh*, and *kibbeh*) from a row of shiny self-heating, prepackaged meal boxes, and serves it on *keffiyeh*-patterned dishes. She puts the food on the table but does not sit down and eat. Instead, she walks over to the nearest window, raises the high-tech frosted-glass blinds with the touch of a button, and stares intently out at the former Palestine, cradling her unborn child, her expression at once grim, determined, and tinged with disbelief. Focusing first on a close-up of her face, the camera zooms out dramatically to reveal the scale of the immense skyscraper, its isolated location, and its enclosure behind a massive security wall.

For queer theorist Lee Edelman, the figure of the Child—which does not refer to actual or historical children but rather to their symbolic function "as the emblem of futurity's unquestioned value"[51]—thematizes the ideological trappings of identity. The Child's phantasmatic appeal is twofold: it points to a pure or innocent existence uncontaminated by the social order, and it also gestures to a more enviable future, a more authentic symbolic space, where society as such is reformed and redeemed, where the transcendent wholeness of the Child is recovered. Edelman opposes queer negativity to this figure of the Child. Queerness declines any integration in the order of beings, never ceding on its heterogeneity; indeed, it rejects all forms of identitarianism: "queerness can never define an identity; it can only ever disturb one."[52] Queer negativity jettisons the Child's putative redemptive value, short-circuiting, in turn, liberal society's heteronormativity and its prospects of "reproductive futurism."[53]

We might be tempted to see *Nation Estate*'s unborn child as an "emblem of futurity,"[54] functioning as fertile ground for nationalist investment. On this reading, the child would intimate a time before the settler, a time before sin, if you will. But this reading effectively ignores the colonial situation, and thus risks hermeneutic distortion. To give the Palestinian child to come an anti-colonial twist is to pay attention to the competing temporalities staged in *Nation Estate*. Within Sansour's ironic and unsentimental universe, this child does not stand for a time of national plenitude, but signals an alternative temporality, a time out-of-joint with Zionist hegemony. The futurity announced by the child takes on a queer dimension, breaking with its prescribed normative function (the reproduction of what *is*), when it is *not* seen as an extension of Zionist futurology, a Zionism that authorizes a Palestinian state on the condition that it be surrounded by an apartheid wall and remain only a simulacrum of national sovereignty.

Nation Estate's child to come invariably gestures to Palestinian futurity, but this futurity cannot be prescribed in advance as in the reified ideal of return to a *time before the settler*. This may become a child of the PA, an authority in the service of reproducing the status quo, of managing the daily business of the skyscraper, or a passive resident of the tower, a stillborn consumer mechanically completing the daily tasks of shopping, eating, and admiring the cleansed surroundings. Yet again, it may become a monstrous child, hungering for more, born of anti-colonial *ressentiment* and rage, unleashing future uprisings and taking on lost causes.

Binationalist Visions

Binationalism might be one such "lost cause" that eschews the cruel politics of pragmatism and the enclosure of Indigenous sovereignty, derailing the paths for Palestinians and Israeli Jews laid out by Zionist futurology. Said asks if "*any* lost cause can ever really be lost,"[55] so long as it is dislodged from "the perspective of realism,"[56] a perspective that can only favor the victors of history. Against this "strict determinist" who cares "about the survival only of powerful nations and peoples,"[57] the champion of lost causes infuses "invention into life."[58] The hopelessness of the cause opens to a refusal of what *is* and a stubborn courage to take it on. Binationalism (or Palestine more generally) as a lost cause joins other "hopeless" causes: "Do many people now believe that the gypsies or the Native Americans can get back what they lost?"[59] If binationalism is going to reconfigure the terms of the debate and upset the coordinates of the "conflict," it must inject invention into Palestinian material existence.

The idea of binationalism was first introduced by early European Zionist intellectuals, including Martin Buber, Judah Magnes, and Arthur Ruppin. They argued against an independent Jewish state in favor of coexistence and cooperation with the Palestinians. But their vision of binationalism was not without shortcomings; it came with an Orientalist understanding of Palestinian Indigeneity, betraying their European/colonial privilege. As settlers, they imagined themselves as bringing "progress," "civilization," and "productivity" to the alleged underdeveloped territory of Palestine and to the "helplessly primitive" Indigenous peasants.[60] Still, unlike what Zionism stands for politically today, their cultural Zionism did not call for the dispossession and elimination of the Natives. On the contrary, they insisted on the principle of coexistence between Palestinians and Jews—what nowadays would be considered self-hating by a large segment of the Zionist population.[61] Though the binationalist vision has been wholly absent in public discourse since the founding of the state of Israel, a few critics have sought to retrieve it from the dustbin of history. Edward Said, of course, led the way in this endeavor, turning to binationalism, freed from its colonial overtones, as a way to think national and political sovereignty otherwise.

Given the decaying status of the two-state solution, which has utterly failed to yield any genuine relief to the Palestinian people (the liberal nostalgia for Oslo and push to revive it notwithstanding), binationalism affirms and enacts that the principle that *another end to the two-state solution is possible*: "One state for two people." For Said, "Oslo set the stage for separation, but real peace can come only with a binational Israeli-Palestinian state."[62] Binationalism sets aside the "achievements" of Oslo, urging Palestinians to begin again. By doing this, the Palestinian question can be raised anew. Like Said and others, I use binationalism and the one-state solution interchangeably. This is not, however, a practice adopted by all. Omar Barghouti has mounted a forceful critique of binationalism and urged its decoupling from the one-state solution: "I am completely and categorically against binationalism because it assumes that there are two nations with equal moral claims to the land."[63] For Barghouti, binationalism rewards the settlers with an equal national claim to the land; another end to the two-state solution can only be achieved in a secular democratic state in historical Palestine:

> Good riddance! The two-state solution for the Palestinian-Israeli conflict is finally dead. But someone has to issue an official death certificate before the rotting corpse is given a proper burial and we can all move on and explore the more just, moral and therefore enduring alternative for peaceful coexistence between Jews and Arabs in Mandate Palestine: the one-state solution.[64]

If the two-state solution is part of a past solution that needs to be mourned and transcended, exorcized from the Palestinian imaginary, binationalism stands for a specious future solution to the Palestinian-Israeli deadlock, falling short in its project of decolonization. For the proponents of the liberal one-state, binationalism is dismissively deemed "a form of Zionism."[65] Without foregrounding the settler-colonial context, binationalism also risks treating Zionism's violence as a problem of "exclusion" rather than as one of "invasion."[66] It would consider Palestinian Indigeneity to be "one among many forms of difference within the state," and thus fail to make it "ethically central" in deliberations about citizenship and statehood.[67] The main point of contention is the status of Jews as a people: their national aspiration and the legitimacy of their special claim to historic Palestine. For Barghouti, binationalism repeats the Zionist script and erroneously assigns a national character to being Jewish as if Jews all over the world shared the same ethos: "Bi-nationalism . . . assumes that Jews around the world form a nation and is consequently premised on a Jewish national right in Palestine, on par and to be reconciled with the *national* right of the indigenous, predominantly Arab population. Bi-nationalism today, despite its variations, still upholds this ahistorical and morally untenable national right of the colonial-settlers."[68] Likewise, Ali Abunimah questions the notion that Jewish settlers constitute a "people," vying for "national self-determination"; they do not possess "a separate 'right' of self-determination."[69] What they are only entitled to in a secular democratic state is to "exercise self-determination as part of the whole in the context of full *decolonization* and unmitigated equality."[70] Barghouti puts the matter clearly if bluntly:

> Accepting modern-day Jewish Israelis as equal citizens and full partners in building and developing a new shared society, free from all colonial subjugation and discrimination, as called for in the democratic state model, is the most magnanimous—rational—offer any oppressed indigenous population can present to its oppressors.[71]

For Barghouti and Abunimah, binationalism concedes too much by accommodating the colonialists' national aspirations: "Recognizing *national* rights of Jewish settlers in Palestine or any part of it cannot but imply accepting the right of colonists to self-determination."[72] Binationalism unfairly grants *political* self-determination to the oppressors, legitimizing the settlers' dispossession and jurisdiction over Palestinian land.

Binationalism, on this account, still bears the mark of Zionism. So what does a decolonized Palestine/Israel then look like for the champions of the secular one-state solution? Do they construe historic Palestine as an *objet petit a*, a land embodying the promise of wholeness regained, returning Palestinians back to the imagined plenitude of precolonial days? No, decolonization does not entail a return to a time prior to the settler. As Barghouti avers, it is not a "blunt and absolute reversal of colonization," dissolving "whatever rights had been acquired to date."[73] Rather, decolonization proposes to dismantle "the aspects of colonialism that deny the rights of the colonized indigenous population and, as a byproduct, dehumanize the colonizers themselves."[74] Decolonization is through and through a universalist project. It liberates the Natives and the settlers from the corrosive viciousness of the colonial situation, from its devastating and life-draining Manichean logic.

Decolonization thus remedies the colonial situation not by depriving the settlers of their rights but by subtracting their "colonial privileges"—their preferred treatment in the allocation of rights under Zionism—where the rights of the settlers are precisely conditioned on the denial, or severe curtailing, of Indigenous rights. This is why decolonization and de-Zionization are one and the same process. The labor of decolonization preserves and sustains "the inalienable rights of the indigenous Palestinian people" (such as the collective right to self-determination) and "the *acquired* rights of the indigenized former colonial settlers to live in peace and security, individually and collectively."[75] Rights without privilege dictate Barghouti's vision of "ethical decolonization."

Other critics working to overcome the divide between binationalism and the democratic one-state solution have sought to recast the right to self-determination in cultural terms, where the Jewish people are no longer driven by a settler logic that breeds superiority over the Indigenous population.[76] Jewish Israelis who disidentify with Israel and distance themselves from the hegemony of Zionism are still a people—not a fetishized and privileged people, but a people nonetheless. Teodora Todorova observes: "Since 1948, Jewish Israelis have shared and been defined by a common language and culture, namely Hebrew. They also share a common territorial identity corresponding to the 1948 borders, with the exception of post-1967 government settler-colonial designs, which have, for the most part, been disputed by a significant number of Israelis."[77] A people remains after the demotion of phantasmatic Jewishness. Acknowledging as much is not intended to repeat and reward the colonists' desire/right to self-determination; rather, it recognizes the peoplehood of Jewish Israelis as a fact of co-inhabitation.

But there is also something stifling, unproductive, and even oppressive about deliberating who is and isn't a people. I find it more generative to discuss what a people *does* (versus what a people *is*), and to consider the type of relationality that a given people adopt in interacting with another. As Edward Said puts it in his last interview, "My Right of Return" (with Ari Shavit), "If enough people think of themselves as a people and need to constitute that, I respect that. But not if it entails the destruction of another people. I cannot accept an attitude of 'You shall die in order for us to rise.'"[78] And such a people are free to consider themselves Zionists. Said avoided the language of de-Zionization; he felt that it was counterproductive to force any groups into abandoning their set of beliefs.[79] He zeroed in on the point of contention. Psychic attachment to the land is by no means illegitimate; what is problematic are chauvinistic attitudes that premise my attachment on exclusivity, on the eradication of the Other's equally legitimate claim to the land and its resources: "I don't like to use words like that [de-Zionization, de-Zionize]. Because that's obviously a signal that I'm asking the Zionists to commit hara-kiri. They can be Zionists, and they can assert their Jewish identity and their connection to the land, so long as it doesn't keep the others out so manifestly."[80] The challenge, as Leila Farsakh formulates it, is "to decolonize Israel without negating the Jewish Israeli culture it has created over the past seventy years."[81] The problem with Zionism lies in its aggressive denial of the Palestinians' right to determine their future. Depriving them of the right to self-rule discloses a willful amnesia about historic Palestine. Said's binationalism bears witness to the land's shared histories, to the coexistence of Palestine's many peoples:

> Palestine is and has always been a land of many histories; it is a radical simplification to think of it as principally or exclusively Jewish or Arab. While the Jewish presence is longstanding, it is by no means the main one.... Palestine is multicultural, multiethnic, multireligious. There is as little historical justification for homogeneity as there is for notions of national or ethnic and religious purity today.[82]

In championing the idea of binationalism, Said returns to Palestine's culturally plural and dynamic past in order to rethink and reinvent the future of this contested land, beyond any claims of sameness and exclusivity.

As colonial and anti-colonial history has taught us, the quest for national identities is often a reactive and fraught enterprise, with fetishization an immanent concern.[83] But the counter to this fetishization in Palestine/Israel, surprisingly, is not an *a priori* dismissal of Jewish sovereignty. Responding to a question about whether Israelis needed to "give up the idea of Jewish sovereignty," Said answers:

> I am not asking people to give up anything. But Jewish sovereignty as an end in itself seems to me not worth the pain and the waste and the suffering it produced. If, on the other hand, one can think of Jewish sovereignty as a step toward a more generous idea of coexistence, of being-in-the-world, then yes, it's worth giving up. Not in the sense of being forced to give it up. Not in the sense of we will conquer you. . . . The better option would be to say that sovereignty should gradually give way to something that is more open and more livable.[84]

But it is worth reiterating with Noura Erakat that "Israel established itself by force and insists on maintaining its settler-sovereignty by force."[85] White supremacy, the settler's collective fantasy, radicalizes the world of Jewish sovereignty by de-worlding that of the Native: "Where there is racism, being-in-the-world is the same thing as being-against-others. The latter are treated as a threat against which one's own existence must be defended. At all cost if necessary."[86] The question, then, is: how ideologically strong is the link between Jewish sovereignty and settler-sovereignty? Said preferred a less rigid identification between the two. Toward that end, he imagines binationalism as a secular process to the extent that "it rejects the transcendental, absolute and exclusive nature of narratives of national-social cohesion."[87]

Against Manichean abstractions, locking Jews and Palestinians in an eternal struggle, Said asks: "Can it ever become the not-so-precarious foundation in the land of Jews and Palestinians of a bi-national state in which Israel and Palestine are parts, rather than antagonists of each other's history and underlying reality?"[88] Like all identities, Jewish sovereignty, Said firmly believed, is not immutable; it is transformable given the appropriate conditions. Jewish sovereignty can both narcissistically close itself in, root itself in the land and make it difficult for non-Jews to thrive (the hegemony of settler-sovereignty), or generously open itself to its Palestinian neighbors and affirm their shared common world. The former is prone to perpetuate Indigenous genocide; the latter prepares the conditions for a binational existence.

So if *Jewish* sovereignty is not the problem, we might ask, with Fred Moten, "what if the problem is sovereignty as such"?[89] To do so reorients our gaze back to the collective unconscious, to society's libidinal economy: it is an invitation to interrogate the racial underpinnings of sovereignty—anti-Blackness's investment in the sovereign and/as human—an opportunity to "understand Palestine not merely as a national liberation struggle *featuring* racism, but rather as a struggle *against* racism."[90]

Sovereignty, Abolition, and the Proletarian Position

Sovereignty is not an ideologically neutral concept. What kind of sovereignty are we talking about when we ask if sovereignty is the problem? It is typically a sovereignty aligned with the ideals of self-possession and self-mastery, self-sameness and indivisibility, with *ipseity*, or selfhood, as the individual expression of absolute power.[91] Carl Schmitt famously defined political sovereignty as the capacity to decide the exception, to determine the friend/enemy dyad.[92] This sovereignty's fortune is indissoluble from that of the free human, the autonomous subject so dear to Western philosophical and political meditations. The elevated ontological status of the latter guarantees the value of the former. To be against *this* sovereignty, or possessive individuality, is to embrace à la Derrida "the idea of a divided, differentiated 'subject,' who cannot be reduced to a conscious, egological intentionality."[93] If "sovereignty" is to be affirmed, it is only on condition that it remains decentered and "under erasure" (*sous rature*), its metaphysical underpinning perpetually scrutinized—whence his aporetic formulation of the subject as an autoimmune sovereign or a "*sovereign without sovereignty.*"[94]

At the same time, the challenge to the metaphysics of sovereignty must be tempered by an account of the colonial situation. The dismissal of sovereignty might strike the colonized as another instantiation of white privilege. The most sustained objections to Indigenous sovereignty, however, have not emanated from Derridean or poststructuralist circles, but from the Afropessimist camp. Political sovereignty—while it allows unrestricted access to land and natural resources, and is crucial for the self-worth of a community—has been accused of trafficking in a specious metaphysics, one that generates the unsovereign, the primitive, the slave/Black as its constitutive Other, unworthy and incapable of (enjoying the fruits of) sovereignty. But for Indigenous communities, destroying any possibility for agency or self-determination would be tantamount to what Glen Coulthard and Leanne Simpson describe as a "form of auto-genocide."[95] To give up claims to Indigenous land and jurisdiction is to embrace nothing short of collective suicide. Affirming the goal of Indigenous sovereignty disrupts the settler's various techniques of pacification, and its ideological agenda for redressing grievances.

The Palestinian struggle for sovereignty and self-determination positions it at the heart of this debate. Palestinians are confronted with a double bind. On the one hand, they must contend with the *vel* or forced choice of the two-state solution, and prevent the *naturalization* of their abjection or "ghettoized sovereignty,"[96] and, on the other, they must maintain a skeptical attitude toward that very sovereignty, keep front and center its violent racial legacy, and never forget the degree to which "freedom and slavery are so bound up with one another";[97] the value of the former is premised on the reality and promulgation of the latter. The initial choice between occupation or national sovereignty may at first appear an obvious and easy choice. But to claim national sovereignty unwittingly subscribes the Palestinian people to a logic of subjectivity that reproduces rather than breaks with an imperial mode of governance. The route of the nation-state, paved by the two-state solution, is an ideological trap; it delimits choice and limits your imagination of alternative modes of Indigenous belonging and coexistence. This forced choice engenders a sense of alienation.

You are as free, Lacan tells us, as an individual getting mugged who confronts the "choice," "*Your money or your life, or freedom or death*."[98] In either case, Palestinians lose; they are "assigned the losing position."[99] Worse, Palestinians are construed as agents in their own ideological ambush: *They chose this!*

~~Sovereignty~~ marks a refusal to proceed as anticipated; to desire an outcome to fit within the reigning ideology of the nation-state. It troubles Zionism's body politics, its ontological values of purity and exceptionality, unraveling the "phantasmatico-theological"[100] character of the sovereign subject/citizen. Claiming ~~sovereignty~~ is reminiscent of tarrying with the exilic,[101] insofar as it holds on to negation, and refuses the appeals of rootedness, insisting on the irreducible gap separating the subject from her organic community as the condition of Palestinian identity. It jams the Other's gaze, what Western powers want from the PA, what it expects from the Palestinian people: play along and follow our script, since we know what's best for you, and, in any case, you lost the war, so this is the best outcome that can be "reasonably" expected.[102] Binationalism does not accept the benefits of territorial partition as a fait accompli; it hungers for something other than ethnonationalism. Haidar Eid perspicuously distinguishes the ideal of "independence" from that of "liberation." The two-state solution might deliver on independence but it falls far short of liberation, necessarily ceding on the Palestinian right of return, and settling for Bantustan-style enclaves.

There are thus two senses of ~~sovereignty~~ that we might generatively read in relation to the two understandings of Indigenous reason—the settler's use and the Native's; the distinction between *Zionist settler consciousness of Palestinian Indigeneity* and *Palestinian consciousness of Palestinian Indigeneity*. In the first instance, Indigenous reason deprives Palestinians of humanity, and arrogantly deems them unworthy of collective sovereignty. As the sole sovereign power, Israel engages in the spatial isolation of Palestinians and annexation of their territory, enabling it to decide "who may live and who must die":[103] Palestinians living in the West Bank, East Jerusalem, and within Israel proper may live (on condition that they fully acquiesce to Israel occupation) but the resistant Gazans must die or, at the very least, be reduced to "the status of *living dead*."[104] Israel proclaims its sovereignty as it defends its right to exist, but as Fred Moten notes, "it's a defense not just of Israel's right to exist, but of the nation state as a political form's right to exist."[105] Israel's belligerent behavior is, in this respect, exemplary, putting on full display the treacherous mechanisms of the nation-state. Against the ideological abstraction of the nation-state's so-called rights, Moten articulates what a state *ought to do* and what it actually *does*: "Nation-states don't have rights. What they're supposed to be are mechanisms to protect the rights of the people who live in them, and that has almost never been the case. And to the extent that they do protect the rights of the people who live with them, it's at the expense of the people who don't."[106]

The nation-state enacts its ethnic and racial sovereignty in its murderous decision concerning who matters and who doesn't, where the latter, as we know, is a precondition for the former. The separation Wall in the West Bank, the unending blockade of Gaza and the "de-development" of its economy, the Israeli settlements on confiscated Palestinian land, the habitual expulsion of Israeli Palestinians, the targeted extrajudicial assassinations of Hamas and Islamic Jihad leaders, and the Iron Dome missile defense system, all work to optimize Jewish life, to maximize overall Israeli well-being. Israel's wicked biopolitics proliferates Jewish lives at the expense of Palestinian lives. It is in fact "nourished by the death of others."[107] Palestinians experience Israel primarily if not exclusively as a necropolitical state. The settler colony's aim is to weaken or kill (physically, psychically, and symbolically) the Native, to introduce insecurity and disorder in the everyday lives of Palestinians so as to make life itself not worth living.

In the second sense, Indigenous reason contests the notion that sovereignty is the prerogative of the settler. Indigenous reason reframes the Natives as the narrators of their anti-colonial struggle, unwilling to compromise on their right to sovereignty and self-determination. Palestinians refuse "to consider their reality as definitive."[108] This version of Indigenous reason still upholds the virtues of sovereignty, hesitant to embrace ~~sovereignty~~ and jettison the protections that come with it. The challenge here is to reimagine ~~sovereignty~~ as an ethico-political response to the complexities of the colonial system, to recast it as a right to refuse rights, exercised in the refusal, in Moten's paradoxical formula, of "what has been refused."[109] In the private use of *ressentiment*, the desire for sovereignty often takes the form of vengeful envy, the kind Fanon ascribes to the Native who is resisting but still caught up in a Manichean logic: "The colonized man is an envious man. The colonist is aware of this as he catches the furtive glance, and constantly on his guard realizes bitterly that: 'They want to take our place.' And it's true there is not one colonized subject who at least once a day does not dream of taking the place of the colonist."[110] In the public use of *ressentiment*, the Native takes up a different attitude toward her envy. *Ressentiment* here does not transcend envy but rechannels it toward a liberatory end. It de-individualizes envy's libidinal grasp on the colonized.[111] Clinging to *ressentiment* counters or derails the impulse to subscribe to the settler's values. It recalls and insists that what has been refused to Palestinians, and other Indigenous peoples, is the right to national sovereignty (not unlike the right to self-defense, the exclusive privilege of nation-states). But this right to sovereignty, as I've argued in this book, is deeply intertwined with the exclusionary grammar of humanity. When the Palestinian "does not claim a radical politics of refusal, but rather, some form of liberal inclusion," as Sarah Ihmoud points out, "s/he too capitulates to the structure of white supremacy."[112] The public use of *ressentiment* compels the colonized not to forget sovereignty's cruel history. Indeed, to choose or embrace Indigenous sovereignty unproblematically is to tacitly endorse a murderous vision of humanity, a humanity predicated on the negation of Black folks, the nonhuman par excellence. Sovereignty or subjugation? No, thanks! Palestinians must refuse this choice as offered.[113]

~~Sovereignty~~, a barred sovereignty, both names coloniality's constitutively excluded Others and embodies a Palestinian politics of refusal. To refuse what Palestinians have been refused is to reject the racist logic intrinsic to Zionism and to the type of Western reasoning whose murderous legacy Fanon powerfully indicts in *The Wretched of the Earth*: "When I look for man in European lifestyles and technology I see a constant denial of man, an avalanche of murders."[114] As witnessed firsthand by Palestinians, full sovereignty, as promised by Zionism, is a collective fantasy, and a violent fantasy at that. Jewish sovereignty, under the ubiquitous and dominant horizon of Zionist supremacy, was/is predicated on the elimination of Indigenous presence, destroying any hope for mutuality and co-belonging. Binationalism must inaugurate another reality, renew a feeling of insurgency, and spell out another end to the two-state solution; it cannot repeat the disastrous logic of the nation-state (my land versus your land), nor adopt an insular mode of Indigeneity as with decoloniality. While Omar Barghouti does not envision the democratic one-state solution as a return to a prior phantasmatic plenitude, he ignores or downplays the persisting role of libidinal and political economies in this new configuration. It is as if this newly restituted Palestine, celebrated for its magnanimity and tolerance of its former occupiers, would join the club of existing liberal democracies, the very same democracies plagued by racial and economic injustices.

Is there an alternative sovereignty, an affirmative or positive rendering of ~~sovereignty~~, if you will? I believe there is, and I want to connect my thoughts further to the extremely rich critical work on sovereignty happening in Critical Black and Indigenous Studies. Kahnawake Mohawk scholar Audra Simpson repeats and extends sovereignty's life-preserving qualities: "The significance of 'sovereignty' to protect land and relationships is not limited to territory, but to bodily integrity and safety as well."[115] Simpson also questions sovereignty's

Western telos, the drive to assert its powers, favoring "sovereignty as a form of relationality rather than a violent claim of property, exclusion, and a right to kill."[116] Upholding sovereignty would mean to reject a necropolitical sovereignty committed to the virtues of immunity and protection, countering and short-circuiting a logic driven by the will to possess and govern. Sovereignty as relationality is a sovereignty forged in refusal; it divests the sovereign of its phantasmatic privileges over Others: the right to decide "who matters and who does not, who is *disposable* and who is not."[117]

As his alternative to the primacy of (Indigenous) sovereignty, Jared Sexton proposes the project of abolition: "Abolition is beyond (the restoration of) sovereignty. Beyond the restoration of a lost commons through radical redistribution (everything for everyone), there is the unimaginable loss of that all too imaginable loss itself (nothing for no one)."[118] Sexton frames the struggle for abolition as "already and of necessity the struggle for the promise of communism, decolonization, and settler decolonization, among other things," standing for the "interminable radicalization of every radical movement."[119] Abolition explodes coloniality and its regimes of overrepresentation. It imagines a radical break with the order of being. There is no end to this anti-Black world without abolition, without a reckoning with the afterlife of slavery. Abolition enacts a courage of hopelessness; indeed, it takes painful courage to decline the privileges of humanity and denounce the moral bankruptcy of reform and incremental change: the promise that the wretched of the earth will be (one day) folded back into the plenitude of the Human. For Sexton, adopting the vantage point of Black existence discloses the totality of racial formation. But this, of course, doesn't mean that everything race-related is reducible to Black existence, only that it is through and from the epistemic and hermeneutic perspective of Blackness that "the whole range of positions within the racial formation is most fully understood."[120] Why? The slave incarnates the "concrete universal"; Black folks dwelling in the zone of nonbeing, in the afterlife of slavery, are not just one group among others, but constitute, quoting Žižek, "'a singularity of the social structure,' that 'relate(s) to the totality,' a point of identification with constitutive—not contingent—exclusion."[121] To do justice to the struggle against anti-Blackness, an anti-racist solidarity must adopt the "vantage of black existence" and engage "black existence [as] the truth of the racial formation."[122] As white civil society's constitutive outsider, the slave stands for "true universality";[123] since the interests of this most wretched of the earth are not predetermined by her subject position, when she seeks to remedy racial wrongs, she speaks to universal concerns—whence the claim that the project of abolition always performs the "interminable radicalization of every radical movement."[124]

What does the struggle for abolition look like in the context of the Palestinian struggle for liberation? What if Palestinian Indigeneity did not align so neatly with the rewards of Western sovereignty, what if it didn't stand for a ready-made, precolonial identity (the phantasmic symbolic identity that a *time before the settler* dreams of)? Wouldn't this in effect make the Palestinian a candidate for concrete universality, committed to the project of abolition? Claiming Indigeneity here would not be a retreat into decolonial particularity (reducing Palestinianness to one symbolic identity among others) but would refer back to a universality "grounded in the 'part of no-part,' the singular universality—an otherwise sovereignty—exemplified in those who lack a determined place in the social totality, who are 'out of place' in it."[125]

Palestinian Indigeneity confronts Zionism/coloniality, and its overrepresentation of Man, with its "'unbearable' example."[126] The dispossessed Indigenous Palestinian is the symptom of the settler colony. As its symptom, she is external to the Zionist order of things, not belonging to the system but holding it together. Zionism, by helping to bring Israel into being, creates this Palestinian who also poses an ultimate threat to the legitimacy of the Jewish state. As we have already seen, the Palestinian is a site of ambivalence. The sheer presence of Palestinians is an offense, and, at the same time, a necessary presence for justifying Israel's muscular form of Judaism. The Palestinian neighbor is the enemy whose life/death must be cruelly managed, validating Israel's hyper-investment in its militarism. The Palestinian symptom is the "constitutive exception" to a Zionist order of things; the symptom expresses the repressed truth of the social order: it is Jewish and *un*democratic. Affirming Palestinian lives and the reproduction of the Zionist order of things are mutually exclusive. The Palestinian is the position of the unthought in Israel. At some level, there is an abondance of discourse about Palestinians/Arabs. There is a hypervisibility of the "Palestinian problem." But the vantage point of Palestinians is for the most part ignored. What would it mean for Israeli Jews to consider the state of affairs from the perspective of Palestinian existence? It would mean to identify with Israel's symptom.

The exclusion of Palestinians discloses Israel's racial matrix. Liberal Zionists might dream of a more inclusive Jewish state that extends more rights to Israeli Palestinians and implements better treatment Palestinians in the Occupied Territories, thus fulfilling the ideals of Israel as a beacon of justice. On this reading, the condition of Palestinians is the fundamental obstacle for true Jewish universalism. Liberal Zionists blame ethno-religious zealots for placing Israel in this unfortunate and compromising position, damaging its brand and its appeal to the Western world. But Jewish universalism within the contours of the nation-state of Israel is an ideological fantasy. The promise of universality lies rather in the Palestinians, in the ostensibly concrete but abject "particular," the embodiment of Zionism's symptomatically excluded.

In this light, Palestinian ~~sovereignty~~ constitutes both a curse and a blessing. It marks the ontological harm of the Occupation that condemns a swath of Palestinians to social death, relegating them to the deleterious zone of nonbeing. But it also points to their revolutionary potential, that is, the promise of abolition. Toward that end, I would argue that Palestinian ~~sovereignty~~ names the Palestinian who comes to occupy the "proletarian position"—a subject who has no proper place within Israel's settler colonialism and apartheid regime—making the Palestinian cause and the genuine dream of binationalism inseparable from the dynamics of class struggle. The benefit of this move is twofold. It grounds binationalism in political economy, casting it as a struggle against exploitation, a struggle irreducible to that against domination (as in the fight to end Palestinophobia); it complicates the Afropessimists' neat delineation between worker, Native, and slave/Black, because it refers neither to an identity nor does it desperately seek to recover one.

What class struggle stands for here is not a conflict with preexisting social groups or class positions. "Against the liberal understanding of the classes," writes Agon Hamza, "we need to affirm the thesis that the proletarian position is constituted in class struggle, that is to say, the position that is occupied within the class struggle determines the class position. There is no class position outside of the class struggle."[127] With class struggle, the very fabric of society is in question; class struggle effectively denaturalizes society and is at war with identitarian solutions (recognition and tolerance of class difference gives you "classism," a "class" version of identity politics[128]). Class struggle shakes Zionism's collective fantasy of a potential Jewish polity free of divisions;[129] it gives the lie to an *ipseic* Israel, pointing to the persistence or irreconcilability of antagonism, casting society as intrinsically lacking "a positive order of being."[130] Needless to say, binationalism, inflected with class struggle, does not consider the struggles against domination and exploitation as constituting two separate fights. *Pace* Mignolo, exploitation is not just a facet of domination; capitalism is not reducible to "*economic* coloniality."[131]

In practicing their public use of *ressentiment*, Palestinians must reimagine what constitutes "co-existence," and not content themselves with an abstract recognition of their equality. In other words, they cannot afford mystifying (peaceful) coexistence as some idyllic existence of Palestinians and Jews—binationalism with a liberal face, dreaming of reconciliation or a "non-antagonistic co-existence"[132] between Natives and settlers—absent a political reckoning. Binationalism, in other words, cannot ratify Israel's historical and ongoing land grab, for *decolonization is not a metaphor*. Reparation or repatriation of land is a precondition for genuine peace. There is no just binationalism that preserves the settlement-blocks in the Occupied Territories, these signs of state criminality. Illegal settlements are the spoils of settler colonialism, and as such, must be dismantled. Yet, ethnonationalists and liberal alarmists within Israel warn of civil war among Jews over the removal of these settlements. The numerous Israeli governments who actively supported the building of settlements along with the Western powers who publicly condemned the illegal practice but neither imposed sanctions, halted financial support, nor advanced any other action to stop it (focusing instead, moreover, on demonizing and raising legal challenges to BDS, as if the latter were the obstacle to peace[133]) are morally and politically responsible for finding a solution to the settlers' predicament.

Binationalism's promise of a coexistence *à venir* must be premised on an immediate co-resistance. Tamer Nafar, founding member of the renowned Palestinian hip-hop group DAM, speaks of the ideological comfort that coexistence (= temporary armistice) entails for many Israeli Jews, a kind of virtue signaling that does little to help the plight of actual Palestinians. He says,

> Israel keeps talking about coexistence. So, I'm thinking to promote a new term that's called "co-resistance" and not coexistence. And when I talk about that, I'm talking about those Jews who are similar to the white people that march with Black Lives Matter. [They're] not trying to tell them "all lives matter." [They're saying] "No, you are what matter now. It's about people that need us in [their] struggle." And so, I think that we, the Palestinians and the anti-apartheid Jews, especially, should start forming a new thing called co-resistance.[134]

Co-resistance puts front and center anti-Palestinian violence. In claiming support for Black Lives Matter, and repeating it with Palestinian Lives Matter, allies bear witness to Blacks and Palestinians as instances of "concrete universality," their anti-racist struggles disclose "the true nature of violence in our society."[135]

The push for co-resistance rejects the multiculturalist appropriation of coexistence as a tolerance of difference, which, while preaching the need to repair relations, ends up becoming a form of "cultural apartheid," the social reality of *separate but unequal*. The political imperative of co-resistance also blocks the moralizing Western account of tolerance, exposing it for what it is, a mere example of abstract universalism. Asserting that "we are all human beings," equally deserving of human rights, may disrupt the sensibility of the ethnonationalists but if it is not followed by a structural intervention, it does little to alter business as usual. Inclusion is never an end in itself. Worse, it lures you into a false sense of belonging—where coexistence (the suspension of struggle, armed or otherwise) takes place alongside a pervasively racist state. The demands of the Indigenous part of no-part can never be accommodated by the settler-colonial social order. And it should be added that a future polity grounded in co-resistance has no truck with racial or ethnic separatism; it shakes national loyalties and reconfigures existing divisions as an invitation to give up Jewish/settler privilege to identify with the Palestinian cause, to defect in *the pursuit of socioeconomic justice*. The rallying cry for co-resistance "change[s] the entire field, introducing a totally different Universal, that of an antagonistic struggle which, rather than taking place between particular communities, splits each community from within, so that the 'trans-cultural' link between communities is one of a shared struggle."[136] Cultivating a transcultural link between Palestinians and Jewish communities impacts the lives of the Natives and the settlers both libidinally and politically. The emancipatory project of ~~sovereignty~~/abolition makes the political economy inseparable from the libidinal economy (and vice versa).

Anti-colonial liberation starts from a Fanonian assumption that the colonial situation alters the Marxist analytic framework by complicating and reconceptualizing the base/superstructure opposition:

> Looking at the immediacies of the colonial context, it is clear that what divides this world is first and foremost what species, what race one belongs to. In the colonies the economic infrastructure is also a superstructure. The cause is effect: You are rich because you are white, you are white because you are rich. This is why a Marxist analysis should always be *slightly stretched* when it comes to addressing the colonial issue.[137]

Fanon refuses to subordinate race to class, but he does so without jettisoning the paradigm of Marxist critique. Foregrounding race by highlighting society's libidinal economy avoids the erroneous treatment of racism as a mere epiphenomenon of global capitalism. Afropessimists have consistently repeated this Fanonian point. Indeed, one of the many virtues of Afropessimism is that it has made the notion of libidinal economy crucial for understanding the workings of racism, more generally, and the specificity of anti-Blackness in contemporary

American society, more specifically.[138] But in their eagerness to displace political economy with libidinal economy, Afropessimists do not stretch Marxism; they effectively *break* with it. Afropessimists abandon an understanding of the economy as "a kind of socio-transcendental a priori."[139] Wilderson can only see marked differences between the worker and the slave: "The time of Blackness is no time at all, because one cannot know a plenitude of Blackness distinct from Slaveness."[140] For the slave, there is no prior reference as for the worker, "a time before the Enclosures."[141] The worker can always dream of overcoming her disequilibrium (capitalist political economy) and retrieving a "spatial-temporal point prior to oppression"[142] (the enjoyment of unalienated labor).

In Wilderson's Afropessimist account, the demands and dreams of the worker and the Native take place firmly within society's existing coordinates. For Palestinians, a solution lies on the horizon: a Palestinian state with a deracialized economy (where the Indigenous population can, once again, flourish and enjoy unrestricted access to land and natural resources). But for Black Americans, social death is their destiny. For Wilderson, Palestinians and Black people do not share the same background. Unlike the latter, the former are not stripped of a just solution putatively embodied in a Palestinian state, a return to a "prior plenitude," to a "spatial place that was lost."[143] Palestinians can legitimately demand their sovereignty, captured in the slogan, "Free Palestine." This demand has an auditor; the world can register and recognize "the spatial coordinates of that demand."[144] But for Black folks, there is a lack of an auditor insofar as "the collective unconscious is not ready to accept that black people had something that could have been appropriated, which is to say that the collective unconscious is not ready to accept that blacks are human."[145]

To return to Fanon via Žižek, the proletarian position *stretches* the classic Marxist identification of the proletariat with the working class. Again, we can no longer think in terms of "a 'predestined' revolutionary subject,"[146] as in the days of Marx; now, we must seek out "*different proletarian positions.*"[147] What ties these proletarian positions together is a shared investment in class struggle, in the political belief that society does *not* exist as "a positive order of being." *There is no return to a time before the settler; there is no post-capitalist utopia/ plenitude.* Systematically deprived of their substance, the racialized Palestinians occupy the proletarian position; their being bears the mark of both political and libidinal economies. They have a co-primacy in Palestinian daily lives, and for this reason, a genuine intervention into the matrix of coloniality—the social-cultural mechanisms that govern who count (the settlers who enjoy the privileges of humanity and sovereignty) and who don't (the Natives who are abandoned and consigned to the status of "superfluous humanity"[148])—cannot afford to elide either economy.

Indeed, there is no chance for a just one-state solution, a new binationalist order of being, if the Palestinian cause does not, simultaneously, address and alter its own insidious structures of socioeconomic privilege (its internal antagonism). Abunimah rightfully draws attention to the PA's complicity with a neoliberal framework that masquerades as advancing national interests but in fact serves to enrich the pockets of a small Palestinian elite class "by deepening its political, economic, and military ties with Israel and the United States, often explicitly undermining efforts by Palestinian civil society to resist."[149] Occupied Palestine is indeed already feeling neoliberalism's infiltrations, evidenced in the widening gap between the haves (the leaders of the PA, their associates, the Palestinian bourgeoisie, etc.) and the have-nots (the permanently unemployed, the low-wage laborers, the living dead of Gaza, etc.). Who benefits from the colonial situation aside from the settlers? Which Palestinian future is less amenable to installing and reproducing what Toufic Haddad names "Palestine Ltd."?[150] Oslo rewarded collaboration and the reification of the status quo.[151] The neoliberalization of Palestine replaces one oppressor with another. Some Palestinians are in fact experiencing a "double colonization"[152] or "double occupation" under the PA's leadership: "If these are indeed the foundations of a future Palestinian state, then a people who have struggled for so long for liberation from Zionism's colonial assault can only look forward to new, more insidious forms of economic and political bondage."[153]

Liberation from such "economic and political bondage" requires a supplement to the critique of colonial power, a reconfiguration of society's antagonism, and an attentiveness to the socioeconomic contradictions of our global economic system, which touches Palestinians and Jewish Israelis alike.[154] No one is fully spared. "*There is no outside to capitalism today*," writes Žižek.[155] Everyone must confront today's racial capitalism, or what Mbembe describes as the "*Becoming Black of the world*,"[156] a generalized logic of enslavement, a global problem affecting *all* human beings on the planet, with Black and Indigenous communities at the top of the list. If democracy's ideological mission once protected its white workers from the (worst of the) ills of capitalism, offering its base white privilege as a libidinal reward for their investment in (the reproduction of) the status quo, the marriage of democracy and capitalism is now visibly hobbled, imploding under neoliberalism's global regime of austerity and its aggressive enclosure of and encroachment on the commons (an understanding of the "commons" that often ignores the prior and dispossessed commons of Indigenous peoples).[157] Only the obscenely wealthy are relatively exempt or immunized from "Blackening," protected from a criminal system that perversely bequeaths luxury to the 1 percent and cannibalizes the rest. The workers, the unsovereigns, the *less than nothing*, those ~~subjectivities~~ deemed lacking the "privilege" of being exploited,[158] are all subjected to the rapacious and inexorable logic of racial capitalism. In this necroeconomy, a merciless process petrifies individuals, robbing them of dignity and respect, reducing them to "units of human capital,"[159] to the status of violable and disposable beings.[160] Domination and exploitation are irremediably interwoven. The struggle against one opens to the other.

Capitalism is surely "economic coloniality," but it is also *more*. Delinking from the colonial West will not succeed in shielding Palestinians and other racialized communities from global neoliberalism's destructive range. Decolonization is not about auto-enclosure, a retreat into one's borders: it is "an agenda for total disorder."[161] What can arrest and counter this assimilative worldwide process are not new moral claims of exceptionalism (Afropessimism and decoloniality) or reformist desires (the liberal hope/collective fantasy of a "woke" capitalism and inclusionary society), but a reframing of the political horizon around class struggle and a renewed investment in transnational solidarity and planetary sensibility, incarnated in the Palestinian cause and its fight for egalitarian justice. An unchecked anti-Blackness, for instance, would (continue to) produce Ethiopian Jews—or other racialized groups—as society's symptom, its disruptive unsovereigns, the excluded part of no-part that incessantly reiterates the universal call for "equality or nothing" within an imagined "harmonious" Palestine/Israel. A binationalism worthy of its name would work tirelessly to derail the neoliberalization of the region, but it would *not* eliminate the symptom; it would inevitably generate its own obstacles but also identifications with new proletarian positions. Binationalism must remain an incomplete, ever-renewed project. Its limits are its strength.

Conclusion

The Palestinian Cause

How to tell the difference between solidarity, slight, and seizure? The challenge is to understand a solidarity that seems to persist, in principle and in practice, despite problems of asymmetry or even antagonism; a solidarity that does not simply join the struggle, but exceeds it from within; a force of solidarity that is in the struggle more *than the struggle itself?*

—Jared Sexton[1]

Settler colonialism is not destiny; this is an axiom of Indigenous refusal. Vladimir Jabotinsky recognized it in 1923 when he—speaking as a conquering Zionist settler—acknowledged that what sustains anti-colonial refusal is the residue of hope in the Native: "Every native population in the world resists colonists as long as it has the slightest hope of being able to rid itself of the danger of being colonised. That is what the Arabs in Palestine are doing, and what they will persist in doing as long as there remains *a solitary spark of hope* that they will be able to prevent the transformation of 'Palestine' into the 'Land of Israel.'"[2] Hope fuels the Palestinian refusal to surrender to the settler's eliminative strategies. The Palestinian cause both reflects and sustains this hope; it is the child of hope but also its father. The Palestinian cause, like any other struggle for justice, is born out of a sense of hope. Hope indexes a breach in the dispossessive project of settler colonialism; the mere fact that the settler has not succeeded in extinguishing hope's flame itself works to prevent this breach from closing. Conversely, proponents of the Palestinian cause paradoxically nurture this fleeting hope by insisting on the situation's epistemic and existential hopelessness, by declaring that the current coordinates are irremediable, that the climate under which the Palestinian question is posed is detrimental to the lives of Palestinians and anathema to the cause of social justice. Hope must traverse hopelessness. Only by seeing the existing state of affairs as hopeless, yielding no promise of transformative change, can a "courage of hopelessness" trigger and renew the need to imagine a genuine solution to the Palestinian question. Only out of this Palestinian courage of hopelessness emerges what Fanon called the "possibility of impossibility,"[3] the possibility of hearing the Palestinian cause anew.

The Palestinian cause obviously speaks to the concerns of the Indigenous Palestinians, to their demands for dignity and self-determination, but it does so in a universal register that allows it to cast the wrongs against its people in a way that resonates with the interests and demands of the racially and economically decimated around the globe. If Israel relied and relies upon (the political leaders of) the United States—its "outsized and enabling evil twin"[4]—for economic and military aid, the Palestinian people draw affective support from the wretched of the earth, from the aggrieved parties of colonialism.[5] Indeed, anti-colonial rage and anti-racist anger mobilize commitment to the Palestinian cause. Edward Said has great faith in its universal appeal, suggesting that you need only grasp the facts of the case to appreciate "the justice of the Palestinian cause," to be persuaded to join the Palestinian in solidarity.[6] The fellow dispossessed, it would seem, do not need much convincing. Nick Estes, a citizen of the Lower Brule Sioux Tribe and Indigenous activist and scholar, similarly sees common cause with the Palestinians, yet he also laments that a significant number of his kin—native politicians, elites, and public figures—do not identify with it. The reasons for this range from anti-Palestinian hostility, reflecting Zionist prejudice, to the shunning of Palestinian protest and resistance due to respectability politics and internalized centrist liberal sensibilities. Zionists capitalize on what Estes calls "anti-Palestinian opportunism."[7] In seeking to legitimize their mystified claims of Indigeneity, Zionists entice native people of Turtle Island "to align with the Zionist project": *we are like you seeking to reclaim our original land*. And by enlisting Indigenous peoples to their cause—*look, we speak with moral authority*—Zionists distract from the dispossession of the Natives of historic Palestine, normalizing, in turn, the Israeli settler project. Against this "Red washing," Estes urges his kin to cut through Zionism's ideological lies and interpellative rewards, and stand with "our Palestinian relatives who struggle for liberation from the same violence that threatens to erase *our* histories and *our* futures."[8] "Palestine is the moral barometer of Indigenous North America," writes Estes.[9] Joining the Palestinian cause even helps to recast Indigenous resistance at home: "Allying with Palestinian nationhood offers an alternative path for anti-colonial Indigenous nationhood that doesn't normalize settler colonial regimes—whether it's Israel, the United States, or Canada."[10] Waziyatawin, a Wahpetunwan Dakota, concurs: "Sometimes it takes seeing the suffering of others to realise the full magnitude of our own suffering."[11] Decolonization is never an isolated endeavor nor a local matter; it is global or it is not. *Indigenous peoples of the world learn from one another and unite.*

Can the same be said of cross-racial solidarity with the cause of Black people? Is there a shared *ressentiment* that can form the basis for a Black-Palestinian solidarity? Yes and no. The ruse of analogy looms large. Co-optation and betrayal take center stage when addressing the likelihood of Black-Palestinian solidarity. Jared Sexton, who has been a key figure in stressing the singularity of Black positionality, inventively recasts solidarity as a challenge rather than a betrayal-in-waiting. Sexton asks us to rethink solidarity as that which persists despite, or rather because of, differences: "a solidarity that does not simply join the struggle, but exceeds it from within; a force of solidarity that is in the struggle *more* than the struggle itself?" The question, "What is in the struggle *more* than the struggle itself?"[12] disturbs a myopic form of politics grounded in identity and the struggle for recognition and accommodation; it declines to pursue the type of struggle sanctioned by liberals. Each group's "commitment is to something greater than [its] own well-being."[13] To align with Palestinians is to risk the charge of anti-Semitism and social ostracization; to align with Blacks is to tempt ontological degradation and white terror. This is a model of solidarity at odds with itself, pointing to a "beyond the pleasure principle," to a politics of the death drive (death drive-as-possibility)—to what lies beyond a conservative and narcissistic logic invested in consensus and self-preservation, "identity-based forms of kinship,"[14] and the reproduction of what is (in one's self-centered interests: a Black agenda or a Palestinian agenda).

This Black-Palestinian solidarity changes the coordinates of the situation; it disrupts the field of power, de-reifying the political landscape. It breaks with cultural destinies, protocols of obligation, and the lure of "identity politics"—which compels each group to prioritize the power of their organic own, to act only according to its narrow economic and libidinal self-interest—transforming, in turn, the preexisting identities of both: whence solidarity's unruly and destabilizing force. This is a coalition of life-affirming unsovereigns, who refuse ideological comfort, de-immunize their identity, and come to terms with the painful reality that anti-Blackness, Islamophobia, anti-Semitism, and other forms of hate affects and infects us all. Fred Moten puts the matter colorfully: "The coalition emerges out of your recognition that it's fucked up for you, in the same way that we've already recognized that it's fucked up for us. I don't need your help. I just need you to recognize that this shit is killing you, too, however much more softly, you stupid motherfucker, you know?"[15]

Wilderson, for his part, moves to call out non-Black coalition partners, to shut down and invalidate dialogue in advance, foreclosing the very possibility of cross-racial solidarity:

> The besetting hobble of multiracial coalitions is manifest in the ways Black members become refugees of the coalition's "universal" agenda. In social movements dedicated, for example, to prison abolition, the "selection of topics, distribution of concerns, framing of issues, filtering of information, emphasis and tone" . . . and the way debate is bound within premises acceptable to non-Black coalition partners, work to crowd out a deeper understanding of captivity and anti-Black violence by limiting the scope of the dialogue to those aspects of state violence and captivity that non-Black coalition partners have in common with Blacks. It's sometimes as blunt and straightforward as our coalition partners simply telling us to "stop playing Oppression Olympics."[16]

Afropessimist futurology: Black difference or specificity will be neglected, marginalized, or cannibalized, that is, appropriated for a non-Black end. In all cases, Black concerns and questions will fall on deaf ears. This is why, for Wilderson, negotiation, let alone dialectics, is *a priori* ruled out. Indeed, a quasi-ontological inability to hear Black suffering and understand anti-Black violence plagues non-Black coalition partners. Despite Wilderson's totalizing assessment, there is much truth in his diagnosis of the ways leftist coalition politics have marginalized the cause of Black folks. But, again, is history destiny? Is Sexton's challenge to consider "what is in the struggle *more* than the struggle itself" an empty exercise, a futile attempt at politics? The validity of the "Oppression Olympics" charge becomes harder to dismiss when a critique of anti-Blackness is made a central structure of a universal politics, such as the one informing Black-Palestinian solidarity.

"The slave's cause is the cause of another world in and on the ruins of this one, in the end of its ends," writes Sexton.[17] This is the cause, as we have seen, of abolition, what is in the Indigenous struggle (for sovereignty) *more* than the struggle itself (for what exceeds *self*-interest). But with the *becoming Black of the world*, an ever-increasing number of humanity's population is entering the Fanonian "zone of nonbeing" along with the diminished prospects of a "new departure" emerging from this forced or unenviable condition:

> There is a zone of nonbeing, an extraordinarily sterile and arid region, an incline stripped bare of every essential from which a genuine new departure can emerge. In most cases, the black man cannot take advantage of this descent into a veritable hell.[18]

Palestinians—especially Gazans—have been dwelling in this condition since the advent of political Zionism in the region. Ontological erasure, or social death, has become the norm rather than the exception of Palestinian life under the Occupation. *Settler colonialism is a structure, not an event.* Can the wretched of the earth ever exit this zone? If Fanon worked meticulously to disclose the specificity of Blackness, he also strenuously argued against the traps of *locking* "the black man in his blackness."[19] Black ~~being~~ is (in most instances) unable to take advantage of this descent into a veritable hell, but it would wrong to ontologically reify this state of nonbeing, to make it, as it were, an unchangeable "fact of Blackness."

This struggle against the *becoming Black of the world* recasts the Palestinian cause in a new ontological and political light. Abolition and sovereignty are not merely competing ideals vying for primacy. What disables—the destruction of social selves and organic communities—also enables insofar as it creates the possibility of new identities, communities, and solidarities. Without the latter, the wretched of the world would effectively remain sealed in a state devoid of agentic potential, none of them would be able "to take advantage of this descent into a veritable hell." Sovereignty as relationality and the abolition of the human go hand in hand. The two come together in Fanon's seemingly uncontentious demand: "I acknowledge one right for myself: the right to demand human behavior from the other [*exiger de l'autre un comportement humain*]."[20] Fanon affirms what appears to be a humanist or even a Kantian demand to be treated not merely as a means but as an end. And yet actually achieving this right would provoke nothing short of an upheaval in the matrix of humanity, recasting the question of Man, and bringing disorder into the current humanist order of being, since this demand springs from a brutalized body, a ~~sovereignty~~ deemed unworthy and unequal by a system that has arrogated to itself the grammar of human worth and suffering.

This "right" of the Palestinian to be treated as a human—that is, not to be "animalized," instrumentalized, or slaughtered with impunity—would in fact interrogate the existing coordinates of the human itself, "seize access to ontology, storming the fortified heaven of *being itself*,"[21] and unsettle the ways Ashkenazi Jews/whites effortlessly define themselves over and against Palestinian bodies. This right would contest Western modernity's overrepresentation of Man: this colonial assemblage of Man that has always been predicated on the not-quite-human and the nonhuman, on the relativization, objectification, and disposability of some marginalized groups deemed unworthy to participate in human life. But as Fanon avers, the "rank of Man" is not a state ever achieved, or achievable, by the white subject/settler/master: "The black man wants to be white. The white man is *desperately trying to achieve the rank of man* [*s'acharne à réaliser une condition d'homme*]."[22] Whiteness continues to be a *fantasy* of self-actualization, plenitude, or wholeness, an undeniable source of anxiety in the dominant subject, the Ashkenazi Jew in the Palestinian context, because no subject can ever embody "Man," the "phantasmatic humanity that whites uphold in the name of a community,"[23] a community without Palestinians. In this respect, achieving the rank of man would coincide with the achievement of a Greater/whiter Israel. But until the rank of man is secured (again, itself an impossibility), doubts about oneself, about one's community, will continue to fester.

Needless to say, racisms of all kinds thrive in these conditions; they redirect the subject away from avowing this reality, where alienation is a constitutive feature of the world, and unleash narratives of blame and scapegoating: *if only Israel were Palestinian-free, purified of any excessive Brownness and Blackness— be it Jewish or not—then Israel would be fully harmonious.* In this scenario, the libidinal economy exerts a crushing pressure on the daily lives of citizens and social members. The anti-colonial labor of disalienation by contrast reorients our gaze to the brutality of "the social and economic realities,"[24] which affect both Natives and settlers, without, of course, ignoring the differential allocation of power that Jewish/white privilege continues to entail. As a mode of intervention, political economy does not work by simply correcting the distortions of the libidinal economy: *don't misrecognize your true enemy (capitalism) for your racialized neighbor (the Palestinian, the Jewish Israeli—the object of scorn and phobia)*. Rather, it heuristically separates alienation provoked by phantasmatic aspirations (pure humanity, becoming white) from alienation rooted in one's material existence. The former involves an overcoming or traversal of the subject's fantasies of plenitude, and the correlative avowal that a degree of alienation is a permanent feature of all human existence (though, in this morbid universe, alienation is also lived differently by differently racialized subjects[25]); the latter a direct confrontation with the crushing realities of capitalism.

Again, *the becoming Black of the world* forces us to intertwine the political and affective economies. Human capital arrives always already translated in a racialized form. Occupied Palestine is a case in point. While some extreme ethnonationalist settlers entertain genocidal fancies about a Greater Israel without Palestinians, some capitalist-driven settlers prioritize economic gain over the pleasures of spiritual superiority—they want *terra nullius* in theory but not quite in practice, so to speak, invested as they are in military capitalism, in the lucrative Israeli military-industrial complex. Economic profit drives the Israeli government's hawkish policies, making the Jewish state the world's eighth-largest weapons exporter according to a 2020 report by the Swedish SIPRI research institute. And Israel ranks first for arms exports per capita.[26] What Israel continues to present as a set of necessary security responses to terrorist incursions by the rogue Hamas masks and distracts from Israel's profitable necropolitics, its war economy, which has become constitutive of its settler-colonial mission. As Haim Bresheeth-Zabner observes, "while Israel may not have planned to become a major weapons developer, obvious commercial and technological vectors propelled it onto the world stage from the start. Israel became a specialized war economy, depending on and benefiting from armed conflict. War became its raison d'être and its organizing principle."[27]

Many of Israel's political and financial elites prefer to keep Palestinians alive, or better yet, blackened and relegated to one of the global order's "death-worlds," to these "new and unique forms of social existence in which vast populations are subjected to conditions of life conferring upon them the status of living dead."[28] This casting of Indigenous land as the site of "deathscapes" earns Occupied Palestine the dreadful designation of being the "most accomplished form of necropower."[29] Israel's necropolitical strategies "produce, invent, and feed the very monstrosity they claim to overcome."[30] In seeking to protect its citizens from "bloodthirsty terrorists," the state creates more bloodthirsty terrorists (and rebellions from within, from its Arab minority). And yet this is not a straightforward case of an immunological disorder. On the one hand, as Derrida insists, the desire for pure immunity—the desire to protect the border, to annex Palestinian land (for security reason, we're repeatedly told), to preserve Israel as an eternal, undivided, and self-enclosed whole—is both phantasmatic and suicidal,[31] but, on the other, the Israeli military-industrial complex exploits this non-coincidence between the fantasy of wholeness and the actuality of Israel, manipulating it in its favor; indeed, Israel financially enjoys its autoimmunity, turning it into a condition of profitability, obscenely capitalizing on the state's vulnerability and exposure, cynically feeding Jewish paranoia (at home and abroad) by fanning the flames of terrorism, generating a "war without end,"[32] and further justifying the indefinite/infinite occupation of Palestinian land. Gaza, in particular, suffers Israel's overlapping libidinal and political economies. The programmatic Gaza wars test and showcase Israeli military superiority for the world, earning the state large profits in global arms sales. Occupation is indeed lucrative *for some*; Israel's political and financial elites benefit from the status quo, from mild anti-colonial resistance. Hamas is a psychically and economically rewarding foe *as long as* the settler nation's military and technological might prevails, as long as there is "war without warfare" (the Colin Powell doctrine), that is, war with casualties overwhelmingly on the Palestinian side.[33] As a profitable laboratory, Gaza is thus purely instrumentalized—Palestinian deaths and social deaths be damned.[34]

The Gazafication of Palestine points to Gaza as a kind of microcosm of *the becoming Black of the world*. Lives rendered superfluous are multiplying. And global capitalism's fingerprints are all over it. If Israel's military-industrial complex thematizes the threat *from without*, colonialism's amenability to neoliberal desires indexes a threat *from within*, since both practice what David Harvey describes as "accumulation by dispossession."[35] On the one hand, the settler regime's illegal dispossession of Palestinian land and extraction of its resources provoke outrage among Palestinians and their supporters. On the other, global capitalism with a "Palestinian" face risks circumventing objections, passing under the radar, and thus normalizing this suffocating and life-draining reality. Transnational capitalism welcomes collaborators.[36] It preaches privatization of the commons as a common good and speaks the language of "neoliberal urbanism," which, as Sami Tayeb explains, "ultimately does little to address Palestinians' most immediate and salient social issues—unemployment, poverty, food and water insecurity—or their struggle for liberation from Israeli occupation."[37] A Palestine free from Occupation may well remain a Palestine enslaved to market forces unless it manages to dismantle the new master's economy. The struggle against both the reality of Israel's military-industrial complex and the neoliberalization of Palestine/Israel characterizes the universality of the Palestinian cause.

Its universal cry for equality and dignity does not stem from a yearning to return to *a time before the settler*. Palestinian Indigeneity is not to be fetishized; "Palestinianism for its own sake"[38] must be resisted. The refusal to comply with the will of the powerful is born from economic precarity and the material conditions of Palestinians. Indigenous resurgence stems from their hunger for life. It is their *prise de conscience* that the status quo is unlivable that fuels their rebellion. Fanon gives a similar materialist explanation for the struggle against French colonialism in Southeast Asia: "It is not because the Indo-Chinese discovered a culture of their own that they revolted. Quite simply this was because it became *impossible for them to breathe*, in more than one sense of the word."[39] In the midst of Black outrage at police brutality, surrounding the lethal choking of Eric Garner by NYPD officer Daniel Pantaleo on Staten Island on July 17, 2014, Black activists adopted and adapted Fanon's words, circulating on social media the quote: "when we revolt it's not for a particular culture. We revolt simply because, for many reasons, we can no longer breathe."[40] *We can no longer breathe* translated and collectivized Eric Garner's "I can't breathe"—the mantra for BLM, the decolonizing and anti-capitalist mantra of the part of no-part.

Breathing as the luxury of the immune and protected is an unsustainable and unacceptable proposition. The *becoming Black of the world* signals that capitalism's ideological fantasy of spreading democracy across the globe—on the backs of Black and Indigenous folks—is coming to a halting end. What comes next is an unfettered form of racial capitalism. A vicious system that feasts on human capital. The liberal solutions of reform and identity politics can, at best, only dream of slowing down the processes of erasure and subjugation; at worst, they cover over the antagonisms and the structural flaws of the system, which, in turn, spur the rise of right-wing governments and their fascistic aspirations. The Palestinian cause takes to heart the precept that "another end of the world is possible," beginning with imagining another end to the flawed, and Western-backed, two-state solution. As a planetary form of commitment, the Palestinian cause hungers for solidarity and relationality as it maintains and underscores the dual but interlocking struggles against racial domination and economic exploitation. This unflinching ethico-political commitment to an alternative world makes the Palestinian cause unapologetically universalist.

Notes

Introduction

1 Omar Barghouti, "Relative Humanity: Identity, Rights, and Ethics: Israel as a Case Study," *PMLA* 121, no. 5 (2006): 1537.
2 For the partisans of Jewish Indigeneity, there are strictly speaking no Occupied Territories—only parts of "Greater Israel."
3 "Beginning and beginning-again are historical whereas origins are divine" (Edward Said, *Beginnings: Intention and Method* [New York: Columbia University Press, 1985], xiii). Jewish Indigeneity emerges as a historical category when Jewish settlers rebrand Zionism as a movement against the British Empire. As Joseph Massad notes, "launching terrorist attacks against the British forces, the Jewish colonists were adamant that Britain had betrayed them. In the period between 1944 and 1948 Jewish terrorism and the British response to it led to the killing of 44 Jewish terrorists and 170 British soldiers and civilians, a ratio of 4 to 1 in favour of the terrorists. Unlike other anti-colonial struggles where the casualty figures would be astronomically in favour of the colonisers, Zionism would begin to call its terrorist war against Britain a 'war of independence,' casting itself as anti-colonial movement" (Joseph Massad, "Zionism, Anti-Semitism and Colonialism," *Al Jazeera*, December 24, 2012. https://www.aljazeera.com/opinions/2012/12/24/zionism-anti-semitism-and-colonialism). Refashioning Zionism, recasting the terrorist attacks of the Haganah as anti-colonial, is a work of pure ideology if there ever was one. Political Zionism's success in colonizing Palestine would have been unthinkable and unrealizable without the active support of Western powers. The state of Israel is the legitimate child of Imperial European nations.
4 The formulation "Israeli Occupation Forces"—as opposed to Israel's self-designated label of "Israeli Defense Forces"—underscores the settler-colonial framework. The IOF/IDF soldiers are not so much heroically defending Israelis as cruelly subjugating Palestinians.
5 Slavoj Žižek, "A Leftist Plea for 'Eurocentrism,'" *Critical Inquiry* 24, no. 4 (1998): 997.
6 Claiming Indigeneity would enable Palestinians to seek remedy for their grievances through an appeal to the UN Declaration on the Rights of Indigenous Peoples (UNDRIP). For an account of the limitations of UNDRIP in addressing the plight of the Palestinian people, see Ahmad Amara and Yara Hawari, "Using

Indigeneity in the Struggle for Palestinian Liberation," *Al Shabaka*, August 8, 2019. https://al-shabaka.org/commentaries/using-indigeneity-in-the-struggle-for-palestinian-liberation/.

7 "A universal cause is not only the cause of victims, the oppressed, it is a cause coinciding with the long-term interest of the oppressors themselves, morally and materially" (Étienne Balibar, "A Complex Urgent Universal Political Cause." Address before the conference of Faculty for Israeli–Palestinian Peace [FFIPP]. Université Libre de Bruxelles, July 3–4, 2004).

8 Frank B. Wilderson III, *Afropessimism* (New York: Liveright, 2020), 217.

9 Pierina Ferretti, "Chile's Six Months of Struggle," trans. Daniel Runnels, *Jacobin*, May 2, 2020. https://www.jacobinmag.com/2020/05/chile-feminism-international-womens-day-october-uprising-coronavirus-covid.

10 Walter D. Mignolo, "Coloniality Is Far from Over and, So Must Be Decoloniality," *Afterall* 43 (spring/summer 2017): 39.

11 Mignolo, "Coloniality Is Far from Over," 39.

12 Wanda Nanibush was actually in Palestine at the time of her exchange with Mignolo. Her remarks about Indigeneity are shaped by the example of Palestine: "I think the physical occupation in Palestine makes the importance of who is enunciating so visible" (Walter Mignolo and Wanda Nanibush, "Thinking and Engaging with the Decolonial: A Conversation between Walter D. Mignolo and Wanda Nanibush," *Afterall* 45 [Spring/Summer, 2018]: 26).

13 Mignolo and Nanibush, "Thinking and Engaging," 27–8.

14 Edward Cavanagh and Lorenzo Veracini, "Editors' Statement," *Settler Colonial Studies* 3, no. 1 (2013): 1.

15 Fayez Sayegh, "Zionist Colonialism in Palestine (1965)," *Settler Colonial Studies* 2, no. 1 (2012): 209.

16 Sayegh, "Zionist Colonialism in Palestine," 217.

17 Lorenzo Veracini, "Introducing Settler Colonial Studies," *Settler Colonial Studies* 1, no. 1 (2011): 1.

18 Mignolo, *The Darker Side of Western Modernity: Global Futures, Decolonial Options* (Durham: Duke University Press, 2011), 143.

19 Eve Tuck and K. Wayne Yang, "Decolonization Is Not a Metaphor," *Decolonization: Indigeneity, Education, and Society* 1, no. 1 (2012): 5.

20 Tuck and Yang, "Decolonization Is Not a Metaphor," 9.

21 Mark Rifkin, "Indigeneity, Apartheid, Palestine: On the Transit of Political Metaphors," *Cultural Critique* 95 (2017): 28.

22 Achille Mbembe, *Critique of Black Reason*, trans. Laurent Dubois (Durham: Duke University Press, 2017), 28.

23 See Steven Salaita, *Inter/Nationalism: Decolonizing Native America and Palestine* (Minneapolis: University of Minnesota Press, 2016); Waziyatawin, "Malice Enough

in their Hearts and Courage Enough in Ours: Reflections on US Indigenous and Palestinian Experiences under Occupation," *Settler Colonial Studies* 2, no. 1 (2012): 172–89.

24 Mbembe, "In Conversation: Achille Mbembe and David Theo Goldberg on *Critique of Black Reason*," *Theory, Culture, and Society*, July 3, 2018. https://www.theoryculturesociety.org/conversation-achille-mbembe-and-david-theo-goldberg-on-critique-of-black-reason/.

25 Tuck and Yang, "Decolonization Is Not a Metaphor," 6.

26 Mbembe, "In Conversation."

27 Edward Said, *On Late Style: Music and Literature Against the Grain* (New York: Vintage, 2007), 85.

28 Seyla Benhabib displays both of these tendencies, shielding Israel from settler-colonial critique—"I do not believe that we will get very far by repeating the formula that 'Zionism is a form of settler colonialism'"—and minimizing the phantasmic appeal of the Zionist slogan, *A land without a people for a people without a land*: "Of course, there were 'people' in Palestine and in old Jerusalem! The crux of the struggle between cultural Zionists such as Martin Buber and political Zionists such as Ben-Gurion was about how to deal with these other 'peoples,' namely the Palestinian Arabs, Armenians, Druze, and others who were Ottoman subjects but who then were subject to the British Protectorate at the end of World War I" (Seyla Benhabib, *Exile, Statelessness and Migration: Playing Chess with History from Hannah Arendt to Isaiah Berlin* [Princeton: Princeton University Press, 2018], 82, 223n.37). This is a case of *"lying in the guise of truth"* (Žižek, "The Subject Supposed to Loot and Rape: Reality and Fantasy in New Orleans," *In These Times*, October 20, 2005. https://inthesetimes.com/article/the-subject-supposed-to-loot-and-rape). Benhabib's historical reminder obfuscates and distracts from the present critique of Zionism. Benhabib's account of the complexity of Zionism, tracking its internal split vis-à-vis "the Palestinian problem," serves as an alibi against the accusation of Zionist settler colonialism, preserving the idea of an innocent and pure Zionism, *as if* untainted by racism and Palestinophobia.

29 Gilles Deleuze and Elias Sanbar, "The Indians of Palestine," in *Two Regimes of Madness: Texts and Interviews 1975–1995*, ed. David Lapoujade (New York: Semiotext(e), 2006), 198.

30 See Martin Heidegger, *The Fundamental Concepts of Metaphysics*, trans. William Mcneill and Nicholas Walker (Bloomington: Indiana University Press, 1995), 197–226.

31 Said, *Orientalism*, 25th anniversary ed. (New York: Vintage, 2003), 307.

32 Christian Zionism also factored in the European support for Jewish nationalism, since the return of the Jews to Palestine "would herald the unfolding of the divine

promise for the end of time," serving as "the precursor of the return of the Messiah and the resurrection of the dead." Behind this support for the Zionist cause, however, lay an unquestionable anti-Semitism: "For pushing Jewish communities in the direction of Palestine was not only a religious imperative; it also helped in the creation of a Europe without Jews. It therefore represented a double gain: getting rid of the Jews in Europe, and at the same time fulfilling the divine scheme in which the Second Coming was to be precipitated by the return of the Jews to Palestine" (Ilan Pappé, *Ten Myths about Israel* [New York: Verso, 2017], 32). Being a European anti-Semite and a staunch defender of Israel are by no means mutually exclusive.

33 Needless to say, Israel was also the preferred choice of many European anti-Semites, since it coincided with their desire for a "Europe without Jews."

34 Israel was also strategically promoted by Western powers, playing a key role in "the post-Holocaust rehabilitation of the West as a civilising force." The fact of Israel indexes the West's atonement for its anti-Semitism along with the reach of white supremacy, that is, "European superiority to occupy and dispossess a people of colour" (Paul Kelemen, "The 'New Antisemitism,' the Left and Palestine: The 'Anti-Imperialism of Fools' or an Invention of Imperial Reason," *Journal of Holy Land and Palestine Studies* 17, no. 2 [2018]: 255).

35 Omri Boehm, "Did Israel Just Stop Trying to Be a Democracy?" *The New York Times*, July 26, 2018. https://www.nytimes.com/2018/07/26/opinion/israel-law-jewish-democracy-apartheid-palestinian.html.

36 See Rey Chow, *The Protestant Ethnic and the Spirit of Capitalism* (New York: Columbia University Press, 2002), 3; Jasbir Puar, *Terrorist Assemblages: Homonationalism in Queer Times* (Durham: Duke University Press, 2007), 30.

37 Theodor Herzl, "The Jewish State" (1896), in *The Zionist Idea: A Historical Analysis and Reader*, ed. Arthur Hertzberg (Philadelphia: Jewish Publication Society, 1997), 222.

38 Qtd. in Jerome Slater, "What Went Wrong? The Collapse of the Israeli-Palestinian Peace Process," *Political Science Quarterly* 116, no. 2 (2001): 180.

39 Said, *Orientalism*, 95.

40 Giorgio Agamben, *Homo Sacer: Sovereign Power and Bare Life*, trans. Daniel Heller-Roazen (Stanford: Stanford University Press, 1998), 28. Said asks similarly: "We allow justly that the Holocaust has permanently altered the consciousness of our time: Why do we not accord the same epistemological mutation in what imperialism has done, and what Orientalism continues to do?" (Said, *Orientalism*, xxii). Orientalism blunts or forecloses revisions in the West's understanding of Palestinian Indigeneity.

41 According to Hannah Arendt, imperialism and chattel slavery create the conditions for the possibility of the Holocaust, enacting a "boomerang effect" of

sorts: "African colonial possessions became the most fertile soil for the flowering of what later was to become the Nazi elite. Here they had seen with their own eyes how peoples could be converted into races and how, simply by taking the initiative in this process, one might push one's own people into the position of the master race" (Hannah Arendt, *The Origins of Totalitarianism* [New York: Harcourt Brace and Co., 1979], 206). Césaire, for his part, frames the matter more starkly, providing an anti-colonial rejoinder to the Western outrage over the Holocaust, disclosing the "universal" subject of that fury as "the very distinguished, the very humanistic, the very Christian bourgeois": "What he cannot forgive Hitler for is not the crime in itself, the crime against man, it is not the humiliation of man as such, it is the crime against the white man, the humiliation of the white man, and the fact that he applied to Europe colonialist procedures which until then had been reserved exclusively for the Arabs of Algeria, the coolies of India, and the blacks of Africa" (Aimé Césaire, *Discourse on Colonialism*, trans. Joan Pinkham [New York: Monthly Review Press, 2000], 36).

42 Agamben, *Means without End*, trans. Vincenzo Binetti and Cesare Casarino (Minneapolis: University of Minnesota Press, 2000), 39.
43 Achille Mbembe, "Necropolitics," *Public Culture* 15, no. 1 (2003): 12.
44 Mbembe, "Necropolitics," 14.
45 Mbembe, "Necropolitics," 25–6.
46 Mbembe, "Necropolitics," 27.
47 In 2006, Dov Weisglass, an adviser to the Israeli prime minister, said: "The idea is to put the Palestinians on a diet, but not to make them die of hunger" (qtd. in Mouin Rabbani, "Israel Mows the Lawn," *London Review of Books*, July 31, 2014. https://www.lrb.co.uk/v36/n15/mouin-rabbani/israel-mows-the-lawn).
48 Nadia Abu El-Haj, "Racial Palestinianization and the Janus-Faced Nature of the Israeli State," *Patterns of Prejudice* 44, no. 1 (2010): 28.
49 Mbembe, "Necropolitics," 26.
50 Mbembe, "Necropolitics," 24.
51 I borrow this formulation from Stefano Harney and Fred Moten who are at once distancing themselves from and jamming the neoliberal logic of the university: "To abuse its hospitality, to spite its mission, to join its refugee colony, its gypsy encampment, to be in but not of—this is the path of the subversive intellectual in the modern university" (Stefano Harney and Fred Moten, *The Undercommons: Fugitive Planning and Black Study* [New York: Autonomedia, 2013], 26).
52 I'm drawing here on Žižek's account of the two ways of negating the statement "he is human." We can say, "he is not human" and "he is inhuman." But as Žižek observes, these claims are not the same: "'He is not human' means simply that he is external to humanity, animal or divine, while 'he is inhuman' means something thoroughly different, namely that he is neither human nor not human, but marked

by a terrifying excess which, although negating what we understand as 'humanity,' is inherent to being human" (Žižek, *Less Than Nothing: Hegel and the Shadow of Dialectical Materialism* [New York: Verso, 2012], 166).

53 Mbembe, "Necropolitics," 21.
54 Denise Ferreira da Silva, "Hacking the Subject: Black Feminism and Refusal beyond the Limits of Critique," *philoSOPHIA* 8, no. 1 (2018): 25.
55 Žižek, "We Need a Socialist Reset, Not a Corporate 'Great Reset,'" *Jacobin*, December 31, 2020. https://jacobinmag.com/2020/12/slavoj-zizek-socialism-great-reset.
56 Žižek, "We Need a Socialist Reset."
57 Massad, "Zionism, Anti-Semitism and Colonialism."
58 Again, the problem is not what Palestinians *do* but who they *are*. Commenting on the peaceful "Great March of Return" from March 2018 to the end of 2019, Noura Erakat exposes how Palestinian nonviolence produces the same forced suppression: "snipers shot down hundreds of Palestinian Gandhis, so to speak—for all those who keep saying, 'If only Palestinians would be peaceful.' We have been nothing but. The question to ask is: How have Palestinians not been more violent, frankly, given this atrocious treatment? They shot hundreds of Palestinians, 90% of which in the head, in the neck, in the back, in the torso, as they were fleeing— medics, children. And the Israeli Supreme Court said that this was justified? Because even the peaceful protests are, quote-unquote, 'Hamas's new tactic' of warfare against Israel. They have securitized our entire life, our entire existence" (Amy Goodman, "Angela Davis & Noura Erakat on Palestinian Solidarity, Gaza & Israel's Killing of Ahmad Erakat," *Democracy Now!*, May 20, 2021. https://www.democracynow.org/2021/5/20/palestinian_solidarity_ahmad_erakat). The Israeli demand for a nonviolent Palestinian partner is an ideological lie. What Israel wants is a servile Palestinian population who accept their inferior position in the Zionist order of things, are available for economic exploitation, and are, ultimately, grateful for not being annihilated by Israeli might.
59 Charles Krauthammer, "Why Was There War in Gaza?" *The Washington Post*, November 22, 2012. https://www.washingtonpost.com/opinions/charles-krauthammer-why-was-there-war-in-gaza/2012/11/22/c77582e8-3412-11e2-bfd5-e202b6d7b501_story.html.
60 Bret Stephens, "Every Time Palestinians Say 'No,' They Lose," *The New York Times*, January 30, 2020. https://www.nytimes.com/2020/01/30/opinion/middle-east-peace-plan.html.
61 In *Except for Palestine*, Marc Lamont Hill and Mitchell Plitnick meticulously document the strange phenomenon of PEP. Their antidote is simple and to the point; liberals and progressives must engage in an honest and robust debate about every aspect of US policy toward Palestine/Israel: "No longer can any position be

'taken for granted,' nor can any solution be viewed as a non-starter. Rather, we must be willing to critically interrogate our entire approach to the current crisis. We must be willing to embrace, or at least consider, any solution that will yield freedom, justice, safety, and self-determination for everyone" (Marc Lamont Hill and Mitchell Plitnick, *Except for Palestine: The Limits of Progressive Politics* [New York: The New Press, 2021], 157). Ultimately, the antidote to PEP is an unabashed commitment to a universal politics: the values that are defended for Palestinians must also be available to Israelis (and vice versa).

62 One 2019 Gallup poll illustrates the significant support that Israel continues to hold in the United States, dwarfing that of the PA: "Sixty-nine percent of U.S. adults view Israel very or mostly favorably, down from 74% last year but within the 66% to 72% range seen between 2010 and 2017: Twenty-one percent view the Palestinian Authority favorably, identical to last year and similar to the finding most years since 2010" (Lydia Saad, "Americans, but Not Liberal Democrats, Mostly Pro-Israel," *Gallup*, March 6, 2019. https://news.gallup.com/poll/247376/americans-not-liberal-democrats-mostly-pro-israel.aspx). At the same time, the poll points out that "While liberal Democrats are no less favorable toward Israel today than they have been over the past two decades, they have grown more favorable toward the Palestinians and, perhaps as a result, less likely to side with Israel in the conflict." The success of the Boycott, Divestment and Sanctions (BDS) movement against Israel at colleges and universities is surely contributing to this shift in perception among a younger generation of voters; a small but enthusiastic activist block—demanding social justice for Palestinians—that the pro-Israel Democratic party is struggling to placate.

63 Michael F. Brown, "US Fails to Acknowledge Gaza has Civilians," *The Electronic Intifada*, April 20, 2018. https://electronicintifada.net/blogs/michael-f-brown/us-fails-acknowledge-gaza-has-civilians.

64 In his biography *The Labyrinth of Exile*, Ernst Pawel stresses Herzl's colonial arrogance in his relation to Palestinians: "his attitude toward the indigenous population was one of benign indifference at best. He never questioned the popular view of colonialism as a mission of mercy that brought the blessings of civilization to stone-age savages. . . . [H]e fully believed that the Palestine Arabs would welcome the Jews with open arms; after all, they only stood to gain from the material and technological progress imported by the Jews. He committed these views to paper in a famous exchange of letters, which have survived and become something of an embarrassment in the context of the current Arab-Israeli conflict" (Ernst Pawel, *The Labyrinth of Exile: A Life of Theodor Herzl* [New York: Farrar, Straus, and Giroux, 1989], 404).

65 Judith Butler, *Parting Ways: Jewishness and the Critique of Zionism* (New York: Columbia University Press, 2012), 36.

66 International Holocaust Remembrance Alliance website, https://www.holocau
stremembrance.com/resources/working-definitions-charters/working-definition
-antisemitism.
67 Alexander Weheliye, *Habeas Viscus: Racializing Assemblages, Biopolitics, and Black Feminist Theories of the Human* (Durham: Duke University Press, 2014).
68 Weheliye, *Habeas Viscus*, 4.
69 Gilles Deleuze and Félix Guattari, *A Thousand Plateaus*, trans. Brian Massumi (Minneapolis: University of Minnesota Press, 1987).
70 Jasbir K. Puar, "'I Would Rather Be a Cyborg Than a Goddess': Becoming-Intersectional in Assemblage Theory," *philoSOPHIA* 2, no. 1 (2012): 57.
71 Jane Bennett, *Vibrant Matter: A Political Ecology of Things* (Durham: Duke University Press, 2010), 34.
72 Weheliye, *Habeas Viscus*, 14. Weheliye is quoting David Scott's gloss of Sylvia Wynter's theorization of race (David Scott and Sylvia Wynter, "The Re-enchantment of Humanism: An Interview with Sylvia Wynter," *Small Axe* 8 [2000]: 183).
73 Mbembe, *Critique of Black Reason*, 33.
74 Nur Masalha, *Expulsion of the Palestinians: The Concept of Transfer in Zionist Political Thought, 1882–1948* (Washington: Institute for Palestine Studies, 1992), 17.
75 Alllnon Kapeliouk, "Begin and the Beasts," *New Statesman*, June 25, 1982.
76 Paul Foot, "In a State of Cruelty," *The Guardian*, May 29, 2000. https://www.theguardian.com/world/2000/may/30/comment.israelandthepalestinians.
77 Agence France-Presse, "Israel Vows to make Hamas Pay for Alleged Murder of Three Teenagers," *The Guardian*, June 30, 2014. http://www.theguardian.com/world/2014/jul/01/israel-vows-hamas-pay-murder-teenagers.
78 Ali Abunimah, "Israeli Lawmaker's Call for Genocide of Palestinians Gets Thousands of Facebook Likes," *The Electronic Intifada*, July 7, 2014. https://electronicintifada.net/blogs/ali-abunimah/israeli-lawmakers-call-genocide-palestinians-gets-thousands-facebook-likes.
79 David Theo Goldberg, *Are We All Postracial Yet?* (Cambridge: Polity, 2015), 54.
80 Sarah Ihmoud, "Mohammed Abu-Khdeir and the Politics of Racial Terror in Occupied Jerusalem," *borderlands* 14, no. 1 (2015): 9.
81 Ronit Lentin, *Traces of Racial Exception: Racializing Israeli Settler Colonialism* (New York: Bloomsbury, 2018), 126. Ihmoud rightly cautions against seeing the violent misogynist imaginary of Gaza as a violable-body-in-waiting as an isolated event: "Zionism's orientalist logics have historically propelled on the one hand, an equation of Palestinian land and the female body, framing the Palestinian body as an inherently 'rapeable' body (or the personification of the Palestinian collective as a single rape-able woman) and on the other, a feminization of the colonized

man or pathologization of his masculinity" (Ihmoud, "Mohammed Abu-Khdeir," 10).
82 Lentin, *Traces of Racial Exception*, 108.
83 Barghouti, "Relative Humanity," 1537.
84 George Bisharat, "The Forced Displacement of Palestinians Never Truly Ended," *The Nation*, April 19, 2018.
85 Mbembe, "Necropolitics," 40.
86 Sylvia Wynter, "Unsettling the Coloniality of Being/Power/Truth/Freedom: Towards the Human, After Man, Its Overrepresentation—An Argument," *CR: The New Centennial Review* 3, no. 3 (2003): 281.
87 Wynter, "Unsettling the Coloniality," 260.
88 Greg Thomas, "PROUD FLESH Inter/Views: Sylvia Wynter," *ProudFlesh: New Afrikan Journal of Culture, Politics, and Consciousness* 4 (2006): 23.
89 C. Heike Schotten, *Queer Terror: Life, Death, and Desire in the Settler Solony* (New York: Columbia University Press, New York, 2018), 141.
90 Walter Benjamin, *Illuminations*, ed. Hannah Arendt, trans. Harry Zohn (New York: Schocken, 1968), 262.
91 Sayegh, "Zionist Colonialism in Palestine," 214.
92 The border police officer has been charged with reckless homicide, which carries up to twelve years in prison. See Josh Breiner, "A Year Later, Israeli Cop Charged Over Killing of Autistic Palestinian Eyad al-Hallaq," *Haaretz*, June 17, 2021. https://www.haaretz.com/israel-news/.premium-indictment-filed-against-cop-who-killed-autistic-palestinian-eyad-al-hallaq-1.9914607.
93 Tia Goldenberg, "Israeli PM: Killing of Palestinian with Autism a 'Tragedy,'" *Associated Press*, June 7, 2020. https://apnews.com/article/75104c37fadeb37b993400c3b7182b3e.
94 Gideon Levy points out the lousy track record of the IDF and Border Police when it comes to disabled Palestinians: "the slightest wrong movement or sound could sentence them to death. . . . None of these unfortunate mentally disabled people were endangering the soldiers or the Border Police personnel at all" (Gideon Levy, "'Being Black in America Shouldn't Be a Death Sentence.' What About Being Palestinian?" *Haaretz*, May 30, 2020. https://www.haaretz.com/opinion/2020-06-02/ty-article-opinion/.premium/being-black-in-america-shouldnt-be-a-death-sentence-what-about-being-palestinian/0000017f-dc13-db5a-a57f-dc7bee470000.
95 Ramzy Baroud, "Palestine Bleeds: Execution of Autistic Man Is Not an Exception but the Norm," *Middle East Monitor*, June 9, 2020. https://www.middleeastmonitor.com/20200609-palestine-bleeds-execution-of-autistic-man-is-not-an-exception-but-the-norm/.
96 The killing of Al Jazeera reporter Shireen Abu Akleh by Israeli gunfire during an IDF special operation in the West Bank city of Jenin on May 11, 2022 attests to

Israel's flagrant disregard for Palestinian lives. Wearing a press vest and helmet did not shield Abu Akleh. Worse, they seemed to have made her a target. The world is once again reminded of the ways Israeli soldiers operate with systemic impunity, aligning Israel's treatment of Palestinian journalists with the practices of unsavory nations-states such as Russia, Myanmar, and Syria. The Israeli government and its supporters will undoubtedly move to isolate this event, labeling it tragic and unfortunate. Top Israelis officials quickly issued a statement calling for an investigation of Abu Akleh's death, but then decided to suspend any actual investigation, since "such an investigation, which would necessitate questioning as potential criminal suspects soldiers for their actions during a military operation, would provoke opposition and controversy within the IDF and in Israeli society in general" (Amos Harel, "Israeli Military Will Not Conduct Criminal Probe Into Al Jazeera Reporter's Death," *Haaretz*, May 19, 2022. https://www.haaretz.com/israel-news/2022-05-19/ty-article/.highlight/israeli-military-will-not-conduct-criminal-probe-into-al-jazeera-reporters-death/00000180-e9f1-d189-af82-f9fd924b0000). Accountability will be wanting until the Occupation—along with the hatred of Palestinians that it breeds in the Israeli military and civil society—is foregrounded in the investigation. The Israeli human rights organization B'Tselem and other groups have documented the government's horrendous track record in prosecuting their own. Is this surprising? The assassination of Palestinians—including journalists—is not an exception but a feature of a cruel and powerful system that posits *all* Palestinians as intrinsic enemies. Witness the viciousness of the Israeli police during Abu Akleh's funeral procession in the Old City of Jerusalem, where they assaulted mourners and the pallbearers who almost dropped her casket (Belen Fernandez, "Israel's Policy: Kill the Messenger, Attack the Mourners," *Al Jazeera*, May 14, 2022. https://www.aljazeera.com/opinions/2022/5/14/israels-policy-kill-the-messenger-attack-the-mourners). The abusers and murderers of Palestinians cannot be trusted to police themselves—whence the need for the International Criminal Court (ICC) to investigate possible war crimes. There is no scenario for a different and just outcome without Israeli accountability, without ICC involvement. See Linah Alsaafin, Umut Uras, Zena Al Tahhan and Farah Najjar, "Thousands Honour Al Jazeera's Shireen Abu Akleh: Live News," *Al Jazeera*, May 11, 2022. https://www.aljazeera.com/news/2022/5/11/veteran-al-jazeera-journalist-killed-by-israeli-forces-live-news.

97 Žižek, *The Courage of Hopelessness: Chronicles of a Year of Acting Dangerously* (New York: Allen Lane, 2017), 247.

98 Nir Hasson, "Why Israelis Care About the Killing of an Autistic Palestinian, but Are Silent About Others," *Haaretz*, October 21, 2020. https://www.haaretz.com/middle-east-news/palestinians/2020-10-21/ty-article/.premium/why-israelis-care-about-killing-of-autistic-palestinian-but-are-silent-about-others/0000017f-e912

-dc7e-adff-f9bfff240000. As with the case of Hallaq, we must also resist the impulse to exceptionalize Shireen Abu Akleh. The universal outrage that her brutal killing rightly generated must be harnessed and channeled back to the countless and faceless Palestinians who systematically fail to register any reaction from Western audiences. Liberals—from politicians to well-minded citizens—can publicly perform their outrage, but to actually do justice to Abu Akleh's legacy, there needs to be a reckoning with Israel's oppressive regime, the normalization of its cruel practices, which Abu Akleh spent a lifetime investigating and documenting. See Gideon Levy, "Is Blood of Iconic Journalist Redder Than Blood of Anonymous Palestinians?" *Haaretz*, May 11, 2022. https://www.haaretz.com/opinion/2022-05-11/ty-article-opinion/.highlight/the-killing-of-shireen-abu-akleh-now-youre-appalled/00000180-d62b-d452-a1fa-d7efc4710000).

99 Saidiya V. Hartman and Frank B. Wilderson III, "The Position of the Unthought," *Qui Parle* 13, no. 2 (2003): 189.
100 Hartman and Wilderson, "The Position of the Unthought," 189.
101 See also Hartman, *Scenes of Subjection: Terror, Slavery, and Self-Making in Nineteenth-Century America* (Oxford: Oxford University Press, 1997), 19.
102 Abunimah, "Israeli Lawmaker's Call for Genocide of Palestinians."
103 Who can forget Ayelet Shaked's controversial and tasteless 2019 campaign ad, where she is modeling for a luxury perfume called "Fascism." https://twitter.com/Ayelet__Shaked/status/1107718043571048450.
104 Shaked's comment that "it's a shame and a disgrace that we transferred vaccines to Gaza, as long as our soldiers and our citizens are held there" resonates with Jewish Israelis at large: the core belief that Jewish bodies (dead or alive) are more valuable than those of Palestinians. What is ideologically astonishing about Shaked's position is the way she casts her demand in the decontextualized language of symmetry and reciprocity: "a humanitarian gesture for a humanitarian gesture" (Tovah Lazaroff, "Shaked: Shameful to give COVID-19 Vaccines to Gaza While IDF Bodies Held," *The Jerusalem Post*, February 21, 2021. https://www.jpost.com/israel-news/shaked-shameful-to-give-covid-19-vaccines-to-gaza-while-idf-bodies-held-659648). It is as if it is Hamas leaders who are being unreasonable or unfair, not the Israeli state who currently choking the life out of the Gazans, leaving the Palestinians with so few bargaining chips. Moreover, under international law, Israel, as an occupying power, is legally obligated to facilitate the distribution of the Covid-19 vaccines to the Palestinian people living under its occupation. Shaked's call for collective punishment during a pandemic—the creation of medical apartheid—is the consequence that Gazans have to endure for their leaders' unwillingness to submit to the Zionist order of things, international law be damned. See "Denying COVID-19 Vaccines to Palestinians Exposes Israel's Institutionalized Discrimination," *Amnesty International*, January 6, 2021.

https://www.amnesty.org/en/latest/news/2021/01/denying-covid19-vaccines-to-palestinians-exposes-israels-institutionalized-discrimination/;

105 Mbembe, *Critique of Black Reason*, 10.
106 Saree Makdisi, *Palestine Inside Out: An Everyday Occupation* (New York: Norton, 2008), 6.
107 Tuck and Yang, "Decolonization Is Not a Metaphor," 10. Settler innocence was also claimed from the beginning of the conquest, when early Zionists dubiously asserted that there was no ethnic cleansing, that "Arabs just left." See Dan Rabinowitz, "'The Arabs Just Left': Othering and the Construction of Self amongst Jews in Haifa Before and After 1948," in *Mixed Towns, Trapped Communities: Spatial Dynamics, Gender Relations and Cultural Encounters in Palestinian-Israeli Towns*, ed. Daniel Monterescu and Dan Rabinowitz (Aldershot: Ashgate, 2007), 51–64.
108 "The subject that is shamed by its racism is . . . also a subject that is proud about its shame. The very claim to feel bad (about this or that) also involved a self-perception of 'being good'" (Sara Ahmed, "The Politics of Bad Feelings," *Australian Critical Race and Whiteness Studies Association Journal* 1 [2005]: 81).
109 Said, *The End of the Peace Process: Oslo and After* (New York: Vintage, 2001), 135.
110 Tikva Honig-Parnass, *False Prophets of Peace: Liberal Zionism and the Struggle for Palestine* (Chicago: Haymarket Books, 2011).
111 Tuck and Yang, "Decolonization Is Not a Metaphor," 17. See also Didier Fassin, "The Humanitarian Politics of Testimony: Subjectification through Trauma in the Israeli: Palestinian Conflict," *Cultural Anthropology* 23, no. 3 (2008): 531–58.
112 Teodora Todorova, "Reframing Bi-Nationalism in Palestine-Israel as a Process of Settler Decolonisation," *Antipode* 47, no. 5 (2015): 1370.
113 Mbembe, *Critique of Black Reason*, 4.
114 Mbembe, *Critique of Black Reason*, 28.
115 Mbembe, "In Conversation."
116 See Seamus Deane, "*Culture and Imperialism*: Errors of a Syllabus," in *After Said: Postcolonial Literary Studies in the Twenty-First Century*, ed. Bashir Abu-Manneh (Cambridge: Cambridge University Press, 2019), 61.
117 Jamil Khader, "Rehumanizing Palestinians? Radicalize the Struggle!" *The Philosophical Salon*, July 9, 2018. https://thephilosophicalsalon.com/rehumanizing-palestinians-radicalize-the-struggle/.
118 "The notion that Palestinians should renounce violence . . . in order to be recognized as 'ethical' subjects subjugates their experiences and priorities. This renders almost impossible the consideration that their actions might be construed as having ethical and moral foundations within a different epistemic and ontological paradigm" (Sunera Thobani, "White Wars: Western Feminism and the 'War on Terror,'" *Feminist Theory* 2, no. 2 [2007]: 178).

119 In settler colonialism, the colonizers have come to stay. There is, strictly speaking, no difference between the master's and the settler's house. Audre Lorde's essay "The Master's Tools Will Never Dismantle the Master's House" speaks to the perpetual challenges of critique, of keeping it from turning into toothless reform, with no genuine material redress in the lives of Black folks (Audre Lorde, "The Master's Tools Will Never Dismantle the Master's House," in *Sister Outsider: Essays and Speeches* [Freedom: Crossing Press, 1984], 110–13). Anishnaabe scholar Leanne Simpson questions, however, the usefulness of dwelling on such challenges. She writes: "I am interested in a different question. I am not so concerned with how we dismantle the master's house, that is, which sets of theories we use to critique colonialism; but I am very concerned with how we (re)build our own house, or our own houses. I have spent enough time taking down the master's house and now I want most of my energy to go into visioning and building our new house. Our Elders and Knowledge Holders have always put a great emphasis into how things are done. This reinforces the idea that it is our own tools, strategies, values and processes and intellect that are going to build our new house" (Leanne Simpson, *Dancing on Our Turtle's Back: Stories of Nishnaabeg Re-creation, Resurgence and a New Emergence* [Winnipeg: Arbeiter Ring Pub., 2011], 32). Though I'm not unsympathetic to Simpson's concerns, I do want to highlight the risk of defining critique too narrowly (as purely destructive, devoid of invention, and something that needs overcoming in order to build or rebuild) and of setting up separatism as an achievable goal (my sovereign Indigenous house as separate from the master's house, as if the master's—and settler's—house no longer constituted a threat to my emergent house). In the context of Palestine/Israel, Palestinians struggle against a ubiquitous settler state, in the Occupied Territories and Israel proper. Envisioning and building a new Palestinian house is coterminous with the dismantling the master's/settler's house; the invention and redeployment of critical tools must play a central role in both projects.

120 "Whoever is not willing to talk about capitalism should also keep quiet about fascism. . . . The totalitarian order differs from its bourgeois predecessor only in that it has lost its inhibitions" (Max Horkheimer, "The Jews and Europe," in *Critical Theory and Society: A Reader*, ed. Stephen Bronner and Douglas Kellner [New York: Routledge, 1989], 78). Žižek also adapts Horkheimer's saying to make his point against critics too quick to level anti-Semitic charges at the BDS supporters without simultaneously objecting to Israel's segregationist logic: "those who are not ready to criticize the apartheid politics of the state of Israel should also keep silent about the possible excesses of BDS" (Žižek, "Labeling BDS 'anti-Semitic' Desecrates the Holocaust in Order to Legitimize Apartheid," *RT*, May 25, 2019. https://www.rt.com/op-ed/460228-anti-semitic-bds-israel-zizek/).

121 Khader, "Rehumanizing Palestinians?"

122 Fanon, *The Wretched of the Earth*, trans. Richard Philcox (New York: Grove Press, 2004), 51.
123 Lara Sheehi and Stephen Sheehi, *Psychoanalysis Under Occupation: Practicing Resistance in Palestine* (New York: Routledge, 2021), 129.
124 Deleuze and Sanbar, "The Indians of Palestine," 194.
125 Mbembe, *Critique of Black Reason*, 28.
126 Said, "Zionism from the Standpoint of Its Victims," *Social Text* 1 (1979): 18.
127 José Medina, "Varieties of Hermeneutical Injustice," in *The Routledge Handbook of Epistemic Injustice*, ed. Ian James Kidd, José Medina and Gaile Pohlhaus (New York: Routledge, 2017), 49. See also Santos de Sousa Boaventura, *Epistemologies of the South: Justice against Epistemicide* (Boulder: Paradigm Publishers, 2014).
128 Elias Sanbar, *The Palestinians: Photographs of a Land and its People from 1839 to the Present Day* (New Haven: Yale University Press, 2015), 33.
129 Mbembe, *Critique of Black Reason*, 29.
130 Amal Jamal, *Arab Minority Nationalism in Israel: The Politics of Indigeneity* (New York: Routledge, 2011), 5.
131 Jodi Byrd, *The Transit of Empire: Indigenous Critiques of Colonialism* (Minneapolis: University of Minnesota Press, 2011), xxiii.
132 Byrd, *The Transit of Empire* xxiii.
133 Tuck and Yang, "Decolonization Is Not a Metaphor," 4. There is, however, a danger here in Settler and Indigenous Studies of affirming too simple of an opposition between Indigeneity and Blackness insofar as what gets eclipsed from the discussion is Black Indigeneity. As Robin Kelley observes, it is as if Indigenous folks "exist only in the Americas and Australasia"; "African Indigeneity" drops out, and all that remains are "Black Americans" (Robin Kelley, "The Rest of Us: Rethinking Settler and Native," *American Quarterly* 69, no. 2 [2017]: 268).
134 Saeb Erekat, "As Long as Israel Continues Its Settlements, a Two-State Solution Is Impossible," *The Washington Post*, October 24, 2016. https://www.washingtonpost.com/news/global-opinions/wp/2016/10/24/as-long-as-israel-continues-its-settlements-a-two-state-solution-is-impossible/.
135 Haidar Eid, "The Two-State Solution: The Opium of the Palestinian People," *Al Jazeera*, December 29, 2020. https://www.aljazeera.com/opinions/2020/12/29/the-two-state-solution-the-opium-of-the-palestinian-people.
136 Eid, "The Two-State Solution."
137 https://twitter.com/rashidatlaib/status/1392552629260144641?lang=en.
138 Glen Sean Coulthard, *Red Skin, White Masks: Rejecting the Colonial Politics of Recognition* (Minneapolis: University of Minnesota Press, 2014), 173.
139 Noura Erakat, "Rethinking Israel-Palestine: Beyond Bantustans, Beyond Reservations," *The Nation*, March 21, 2013. https://www.thenation.com/article/archive/rethinking-israel-palestine-beyond-bantustans-beyond-reservations/.

140 Žižek, *In Defense of Lost Causes* (New York: Verso, 2008), 289.
141 Žižek, *In Defense of Lost Causes*, 424.
142 Žižek, *Demanding the Impossible*, ed. Yong-June Park (Cambridge: Polity Press, 2013), 102.
143 Mignolo, "On Subalterns and Other Agencies," *Postcolonial Studies* 8, no. 4 (2006): 385.
144 "Coloniality is different from colonialism. Colonialism denotes a political and economic relation in which the sovereignty of a nation or a people rests on the power of another nation, which makes such nation an empire. Coloniality, instead, refers to long-standing patterns of power that emerged as a result of colonialism, but that define culture, labor, intersubjective relations, and knowledge production well beyond the strict limits of colonial administrations. Thus, coloniality survives colonialism. It is maintained alive in books, in the criteria for academic performance, in cultural patterns, in common sense, in the self-image of peoples, in aspirations of self, and so many other aspects of our modern experience. In a way, as modern subjects we breathe coloniality all the time and everyday" (Nelson Maldonado-Torres, "On the Coloniality of Being," *Cultural Studies* 21, no. 2–3 [2007]: 243).
145 Mignolo, *The Idea of Latin America* (Malden: Blackwell, 2005), xv.
146 Mignolo, "Yes, We Can: Non-European Thinkers and Philosophers," *Al Jazeera*, February 19, 2013. http://www.aljazeera.com/indepth/opinion/2013/02/20132672747320891.html
147 Mignolo, "Yes, We Can." And it turns out that communism is not the right solution for non-Europeans. Mignolo writes: "In the non-European World, communism is part of the problem rather than the solution" (Mignolo, "Yes, We Can").
148 Žižek, *Trouble in Paradise: From the End of History to the End of Capitalism* (Brooklyn: Melville House, 2014), 191.
149 "The discovery of gold and silver in America, the extirpation, enslavement and entombment in mines of the indigenous population of that continent, the beginnings of the conquest and plunder of India, and the conversion of Africa into a preserve for the commercial hunting of blackskins, are all things which characterize the dawn of the era of capitalist production. These idyllic proceedings are the chief moments of primitive accumulation" (Marx, *Capital: A Critique of Political Economy*, vol. 1, intro. Ernest Mandel, trans. Ben Fowkes [New York: Penguin Books, 1976], 915); see also Nikhil Pal Singh, "On Race, Violence, and 'So-Called Primitive Accumulation,'" in *Futures of Black Radicalism*, ed. Gaye Theresa Johnson and Alex Lubin (New York: Verso, 2017), 39–58.
150 The Standing Rock Sioux Tribe's protest of the Dakota Access Pipeline gained national and international attention in 2016 is a case in point. Mainstream media covered the event, but it was rarely elevated to a structural problem of Indigenous

dispossession. To acknowledge the latter is to acknowledge the US status as an ongoing settler, still engaged in the pursuit of Indigenous elimination; *plus ça change*...

151 Racial capitalism, as Cedric Robinson reminds us, begins in Europe, in its internal order of things: "racism ... was not simply a convention for ordering the relations of European to non-European peoples but has its genesis in the 'internal' relations of European peoples" (Cedric J. Robinson, *Black Marxism: The Making of the Black Radical Tradition* [Chapel Hill: University of North Carolina Press, 2000], 2). The "Negro" is modeled after "the racial fabrications concealing the Slavs (*the* slaves), the Irish and others" (Robinson, *Black Marxism*, 4; see also Kelley, "The Rest of Us," 267–76). In a similar vein, Boaventura de Sousa Santos foregrounds Europe's internal Others by recasting the Global South beyond its geographical designation ("even though the great majority of its populations live in countries of the Southern hemisphere") as "a metaphor for the human suffering caused by capitalism and colonialism on the global level, as well as for the resistance to overcoming or minimising such suffering" (Boaventura de Sousa Santos, "Epistemologies of the South and the Future," *From the European South* 1 [2016]: 18).

152 Žižek, *In Defense of Lost Causes*, 428.

153 Žižek, *Demanding the Impossible*, 60.

154 Khader, "The Living Dead in Palestine and the Failure of International Humanitarian Intervention," *Truthout*, November 8, 2015. https://truthout.org/articles/the-living-dead-in-palestine-and-the-failure-of-international-humanitarian-intervention/.

155 Said, "The Gap Grows Wider," *Al-Ahram Weekly* 471 (March 2–8, 2000).

156 Said, "The Gap Grows Wider."

157 Mbembe, *Critique of Black Reason*, 158.

158 We might contrast the formulation of "time before the settler" with *Négritude*'s "return to Africa" call. Frantz Fanon and Saidiya Hartman caution against the latter's phantasmatic narrative. Hartman describes her own disillusionment in looking for "Afrotopia," her original organic community: "In the jumble of my features, no certain line of origin could be traced. Clearly, I was not Fanti, or Ashanti, or Ewe, or Ga. Then I started to hear it everywhere. It was the buzz in the market. It was the shorthand my new Ghanaian friends used to describe me to their old friends. *Obruni* lurked like an undertone in the hustle of street peddlers. People said it casually in my face, until I sucked my teeth and said 'ehh!' informing the speaker that first, I knew what the word meant, and second, I didn't relish the label. But then I learned to accept it. After all, I was a stranger from across the sea. A black face didn't make me kin" (Saidiya V. Hartman, *Lose Your Mother: A Journey Along the Atlantic Slave Route* [New York: Farrar, Straus and Giroux, 2008], 4). Fanon credits *Négritude*'s anti-colonial attitude for crucially

raising Black political consciousness, but finds its phantasmatic claims of a "golden past" disconcertingly vague and counterproductive; indeed, "to be locked in the substantialized 'tower of the past'" (Fanon, *Black Skin, White Masks*, trans. Richard Philcox [New York: Grove Press, 2008], 201) is detrimental to decolonization and genuine emancipation. But in the case of Palestine, some Palestinians never left Palestine—whence the temptation for a "time before the settler."

159 Fanon, "The white man is locked [*enfermé*] in his whiteness. The black man in his blackness" (Fanon, *Black Skin*, xiii–iv).
160 Tuck and Yang, "Decolonization Is Not a Metaphor," 19.
161 Wynter and Thomas, "Proud Flesh Inter/Views," 5.
162 Hortense J. Spillers, "Mama's Baby, Papa's Maybe: An American Grammar Book," *Diacritics* 17, no. 2 (1987): 68; see also Tapji Garba and Sara-Maria Sorentino, "Slavery Is a Metaphor: A Critical Commentary on Eve Tuck and K. Wayne Yang's 'Decolonization Is Not a Metaphor,'" *Antipode* 52, no. 3 (2020): 776.
163 Slavoj Žižek and Glyn Daly, *Conversations with Žižek* (Cambridge: Polity, 2004), 121; see also Erik Vogt, "Žižek and Fanon: On Violence and Related Matters," in *Žižek Now: Cultural Perspectives in Žižek Studies*, ed. Jamil Khader and Molly Anne Rothenberg (Cambridge: Polity, 2013), 147.
164 Taiaiake Alfred, *Peace, Power, Righteousness: An Indigenous Manifesto* (Don Mills: Oxford University Press, 1999); *Wasáse: Indigenous Pathways of Actions and Freedom* (Peterborough: Broadview Press, 2005); Simpson, *Dancing on Our Turtle's Back*. Brock Pitawanakwat similarly turns to "critical traditionalism" as a means for rehabilitating and strengthening Indigenous cultural identity (Brock Pitawanakwat, "Red-Baiting and Red-Herrings: Indigenous Labour Organizing in Saskatchewan," *New Socialist* 58 [2006]: 33).
165 Coulthard, *Red Skin*, 155.
166 Coulthard, *Red Skin*, 154.
167 Coulthard, *Red Skin*, 154–9.
168 Coulthard, *Red Skin*, 173.
169 Žižek makes a slightly different point. The desire to unplug from Western hegemony, to return "to some pre-colonial indigenous roots mostly fit perfectly global capitalism" (Žižek, "The Need to Traverse the Fantasy," *In These Times*, December 28, 2015. http://inthesetimes.com/article/18722/Slavoj-Zizek-on-Syria-refugees-Eurocentrism-Western-Values-Lacan-Islam). Global capitalism thrives when its detractors are not silenced but contained, when it isn't facing any calls questioning its legitimacy/fairness as a system.
170 Coulthard, *Red Skin*, 170.
171 Coulthard, *Red Skin*, 154. Fanon, for his part, considers the emancipatory path of a return to the past to be of limited value: "The discovery that a black civilization existed in the fifteenth century does not earn me a certificate of humanity. Whether

you like it or not, the past can in no way be my guide in the actual state of things" (Fanon, *Black Skin*, 199–200).
172 Coulthard, *Red Skin*, 65.
173 Žižek offers a cautionary tale against the impulse to fetishize Indigenous cultures, elevating their norms and rules as good without qualification, above critique: "Let us take an example, one that challenges the stance that local customs are sites of resistance. In the autumn of 2016, a 55-year-old former pastor in Santiago Quetzalapa, a remote indigenous community 450 kilometers south of Mexico City, raped an 8-year-old girl, and the local court condemned him to buy the victim's father two crates of beer. Santiago Quetzalapa is in Oaxaca state, where many indigenous communities are ruled by an idiosyncratic system popularly known as *usos y costumbres* ('traditions and customs'), supposed to enshrine the traditions of diverse indigenous populations. Officials in *usos y costumbres* communities have previously used the framework as a pretext to exclude women from local government; for example, Eufrosina Cruz Mendoza, an indigenous woman, won the mayoral election, but was denied office by local leaders because of her gender. Cases like these clearly demonstrate that local popular customs are in no way to be revered as a form of resistance to global imperialism. The task is rather to undermine them by supporting the mobilization against these customs of local indigenous people themselves, as in Mexico where indigenous women are organized in effective networks" (Žižek, *The Courage of Hopelessness*, 13). Indigeneity is not a homogenized category. Within the same culture, fault lines exist. To his credit, Coulthard does acknowledge such divisions, foregrounding, in turn, the works of Indigenous feminists and their fight against heteropatriarchy in native communities (Coulthard, *Red Skin*, 157–9). But this insight does cast culture in a different light, removing it from a potentially self-enclosed decolonial revival project. Indigenous nation-building, driven by such a feminist ethos, would entail as much *invention* as *recovery*, tempering the spell of nostalgia for a time before the settler. Indigenous feminism is and drives a universal project; its critique knows no borders—it "does not discriminate," as Nick Estes puts it (Nick Estes, "Indigenous Feminism Does Not Discriminate," *The Red Nation*, September 7, 2019. http://therednation.org/indigenous-feminism-does-not-discriminate/). Solidarity with Indigenous feminists here would take up the struggle for justice across national and cultural lines.
174 Fanon, *Black Skin*, 201.
175 Bashir Abu-Manneh, "Who Owns Frantz Fanon's Legacy?" *Catalyst* 5, no. 1 (2021): 15.
176 Ruba Salih and Sophie Richter-Devroe, "Palestine beyond National Frames: Emerging Politics, Cultures, and Claims," *South Atlantic Quarterly* 117, no. 1 (2018): 14.

177 Žižek, *Violence: Six Sideways Reflections* (New York: Picador, 2008), 157.
178 Angela Davis bears witness to the generative impact of Palestinian solidarity with Black activists: "I don't know whether the US contemporary black movement would exist as we know it had it not been for the solidarity extended by people in Palestine" (Angela Davis, Gayatri Chakravorty Spivak and Nikita Dhawan, "Planetary Utopias," *Radical Philosophy* no. 2.05 [Autumn 2019]: 72–3).
179 Žižek, "Class Struggle or Postmodernism? Yes, Please!" in *Contingency, Hegemony, Universality: Contemporary Dialogues on the Left*, ed. Judith Butler, Ernesto Laclau, and Slavoj Žižek (New York: Verso, 2000), 102.

Chapter 1

1 Haidar Eid, "On Jared Kushner's Palestinophobia," *Mondoweiss*, November 1, 2019. https://mondoweiss.net/2019/11/on-jared-kushners-palestinophobia/.
2 There is no Zionist desire to lure the Indigenous Palestinians of the Occupied Territories into the settler polity. "Zionism rigorously refused, as it continues to refuse," Patrick Wolfe writes, "any suggestion of Native assimilation." So in this respect Israel breaks with prior models of settler colonialism: "Zionism constitutes a more exclusive exercise of the settler logic of elimination than we encounter in the Australian and US examples" (Patrick Wolfe, *Traces of History: Elementary Structures of Race* [New York: Verso, 2016], 211).
3 Israeli citizenship serves an ideological function. As Lana Tatour powerfully notes, its aim is to "normalize domination, naturalize settler sovereignty, classify populations, produce difference, and exclude, racialize, and eliminate indigenous peoples" (Lana Tatour, "Citizenship as Domination: Settler Colonialism and the Making of Palestinian Citizenship in Israel," *Arab Studies Journal* 27, no. 2 [2019]: 11).
4 Fanon, *Black Skin*, 93.
5 Fanon, *Black Skin*, 89.
6 George Yancy, *Look, A White! Philosophical Essays on Whiteness* (Philadelphia: Temple University Press, 2012), 4.
7 Fanon, *Black Skin*, xii.
8 Lewis R. Gordon, "Through the Hellish Zone of Nonbeing: Thinking through Fanon, Disaster, and the Damned of the Earth," *Human Architecture: Journal of the Sociology of Self-Knowledge* 5, no. 3 (2007): 11.
9 "For Fanon . . . this is a shattering event, the moment when he realizes the extent to which he is not in control of his subjecthood, how he is not who he thought he was" (James R. Martel, *The Misinterpellated Subject* [Durham: Duke University Press, 2017], 98).

10 On Israeli apartheid see Amnesty International, "Israel's Apartheid Against Palestinians: Cruel System of Domination and Crime Against Humanity," February 1, 2022. https://www.amnesty.org/en/wp-content/uploads/2022/02/MDE1551412022ENGLISH.pdf; Human Rights Watch, "A Threshold Crossed Israeli Authorities and the Crimes of Apartheid and Persecution," April 27, 2021. https://www.hrw.org/report/2021/04/27/threshold-crossed/israeli-authorities-and-crimes-apartheid-and-persecution#; B'Tselem, "A Regime of Jewish Supremacy From the Jordan River to the Mediterranean Sea: This is Apartheid," January 12, 2021. https://www.btselem.org/publications/fulltext/202101_this_is_apartheid. On the predictable and immediate charges of anti-Semitism against any group daring to associate Israel with apartheid, Gideon Levy simply asks, "Was Israel not founded on an explicit policy of maintaining Jewish demographic hegemony, while reducing the number of Palestinians within its boundaries? Yes or no? True or false? Does this policy not exist to this day? Yes or no? True or false? Does Israel not maintain a regime of oppression and control of Palestinians in Israel and in the occupied territories for the benefit of Israeli Jews? Yes or no? True or false? Do the rules of engagement with Palestinians not reflect a policy of shoot to kill, or at least maim? Yes or no? True or false? Are the evictions of Palestinians from their homes and the denial of construction permits not part of Israeli policy? Yes or no? True or false? (Gideon Levy, "Tell Me What's Untrue in Amnesty's Report on Israel," *Haaretz*, February 3, 2022. https://www.haaretz.com/opinion/2022-02-03/ty-article-opinion/.highlight/tell-me-whats-untrue-in-amnestys-report-on-israel/0000017f-f30e-d487-abff-f3fe970b0000).

11 "Knesset Basic Law: Israel as the Nation State of the Jewish People," *Israel Studies* 25, no. 3 (2020): 135.

12 Adalah, "Historical Background," https://www.adalah.org/en/content/view/7478.

13 Cornel West, "Black America's Neo-liberal Sleepwalking Is Coming to an End," Interview by George Souvlis. *OpenDemocracy*, June 13, 2016. https://www.opendemocracy.net/en/cornel-west-black-america-s-neo-liberal-sleepwalking-is-coming-to-end/.

14 Michael Warschawski, *Toward an Open Tomb: The Crisis of Israeli Society*, trans. Peter Drucker (New York: Monthly Review Press, 2004), 55.

15 Yancy, *Look, A White!* 4.

16 Yancy, *Look, A White!* 4.

17 Sarah Ihmoud, "Murabata: The Politics of Staying in Place," *Feminist Studies* 45, no. 2–3 (2019): 529.

18 See Yumna Patel, "Israeli Mobs Chant 'Death to Arabs' in Night of Violence in Jerusalem," *Mondoweiss*, April 23, 2021. https://mondoweiss.net/2021/04/israeli-mobs-chant-death-to-arabs-in-night-of-violence-in-jerusalem/; Patrick O. Strickland, "Palestinians in Israel Beaten, Arrested for Gaza Support," *The*

Electronic Intifada, August 19, 2014. https://electronicintifada.net/content/palestinians-israel-beaten-arrested-gaza-support/13774.
19 Ihmoud, "Mohammed Abu-Khdeir," 4.
20 Jared Sexton and Colucciello Barber, "On Black Negativity, or the Affirmation of Nothing," *Society and Space*, September 18, 2017. https://www.societyandspace.org/articles/on-black-negativity-or-the-affirmation-of-nothing.
21 Wilderson, *Red, White & Black: Cinema and the Structure of U.S. Antagonisms* (Durham: Duke University Press, 2010), 58.
22 Calvin Warren, "Onticide: Afro-pessimism, Gay Nigger #1, and Surplus Violence," *GLQ* 23, no. 3 (2017): 407.
23 Wilderson, "An Afropessimist on the Year Since George Floyd Was Murdered: Notes of a (Minneapolis) Native Son," *The Nation*, May 27, 2021. https://www.thenation.com/article/society/george-floyd-afropessimism/. Similarly, Kihana Mireya Ross underscores the specificity of the term "anti-Blackness," stressing its incommensurability with "racism": "The word 'racism' is everywhere. It's used to explain all the things that cause African-Americans' suffering and death: inadequate access to health care, food, housing and jobs, or a police bullet, baton or knee. But 'racism' fails to fully capture what black people in this country are facing. . . . '[R]acism' isn't a meaningless term. But it's a catch-all that can encapsulate anything from black people being denied fair access to mortgage loans, to Asian students being burdened with a 'model minority' label. It's not specific" (Kihana Mireya Ross, "Call It What It Is: Anti-Blackness," *New York Times*, June 4, 2020. https://www.nytimes.com/2020/06/04/opinion/george-floyd-anti-blackness.html.
24 Fredric Jameson, *Representing Capital: A Reading of Volume One* (New York: Verso, 2011), 150. See also Žižek, *Less Than Nothing*, 1003.
25 Žižek, "Attempts to Escape the Logic of Capitalism," *London Review of Books* 21, no. 21 (October 28, 1999). https://www.lrb.co.uk/the-paper/v21/n21/slavoj-zizek/attempts-to-escape-the-logic-of-capitalism.
26 Frank B. Wilderson, III, Saidya Hartman, Steve Martinot, Jared Sexton, Hortense J. Spillers, "Editors' Introduction," in *Afro-Pessimism: An Introduction*, ed. Frank B. Wilderson III, Saidya Hartman, Steve Martinot, Jared Sexton, Hortense J. Spillers (Minneapolis: Racked & Dispatched, 2017), 7n.1.
27 "2015 Black Solidarity Statement with Palestine," http://www.blackforpalestine.com/read-the-statement.html/.
28 Erum Salam, "Black Lives Matter Protesters Make Palestinian Struggle Their Own," *The Guardian*, June 16, 2021. https://www.theguardian.com/world/2021/jun/16/black-lives-matter-palestinian-struggle-us-left.
29 Wilderson, *Afropessimism* (New York: Liveright, 2020), 243–4.
30 Wilderson, *Afropessimism*, 15.

31 Wilderson, *Red, White & Black*, 35–53.
32 Wilderson, "'We're Trying to Destroy the World': Anti-Blackness and Police Violence After Ferguson," in *Shifting Corporealities in Contemporary Performance Danger, Im/mobility and Politics*, ed. Marina Gržinić and Aneta Stojnić (New York: Palgrave, 2018), 52, emphasis added.
33 Wilderson, *Afropessimism*, 244.
34 Wilderson, *Red, White & Black*, xi.
35 Jared Sexton, "The Social Life of Social Death: On Afro-Pessimism and Black Optimism," *InTensions* 5 (2011): 6.
36 Wilderson, *Afropessimism*, 198–9.
37 Christina Sharpe, *In the Wake: On Blackness and Being* (Durham: Duke University Press, 2016), 104.
38 Wilderson, *Red, White & Black*, 38.
39 Wilderson, *Afropessimism*, 217.
40 On Black-Palestinian solidarity, see, for example, Angela Davis, *Freedom Is a Constant Struggle*; Keith Feldman, *A Shadow over Palestine: The Imperial Life of Race in America* (Minneapolis: University of Minnesota Press, 2015); Greg Burris, "Birth of a 'Zionist' Nation: Black Radicalism and the Future of Palestine," in *Futures of Black Radicalism*, ed. Gaye Theresa Johnson and Alex Lubin (New York: Verso, 2017), 120–32; Robin D. G. Kelley, "Yes, I said, 'National Liberation,'" in *Letters to Palestine: Writers Respond to War and Occupation*, ed. Vijay Prashad (New York: Verso, 2015), 139–53; Kristian Davis Bailey, "Black-Palestinian Solidarity in the Ferguson-Gaza Era," *American Quarterly* 67, no. 4 (2015): 1017–26; Michael R. Fischbach, *Black Power and Palestine: Transnational Countries of Color* (Stanford: Stanford University Press, 2018); Noura Erakat and Marc Lamont Hill, "Black-Palestinian Transnational Solidarity: Renewals, Returns, and Practice," *Journal of Palestine Studies* 48, no. 4 (2019): 7–16. Michelle Alexander, "Time to Break the Silence on Palestine," *The New York Times*, January 19, 2019. https://www.nytimes.com/2019/01/19/opinion/sunday/martin-luther-king-palestine-israel.html.
41 Linette Park, "Afropessimism and Futures of . . .: A Conversation with Frank Wilderson," *The Black Scholar* 50, no. 3 (2020): 36.
42 Park, "Afropessimism," 40.
43 Mbembe, *Necropolitics*, trans. Steven Corcoran (Durham: Duke University Press, 2019), 163.
44 Wilderson, *Red, White & Black*, 28.
45 Park, "Afropessimism," 29.
46 Wilderson, "An Afropessimist on the Year."
47 Wilderson, "An Afropessimist on the Year."
48 Wilderson, "An Afropessimist on the Year."

49 Wilderson, "'We're Trying to Destroy the World,'" 50.
50 "We cannot enter into a structure of recognition as a being, an incorporation into a community of beings, without recognition and incorporation being completely destroyed. We know that we are the antithesis of recognition and incorporation" (Wilderson, "We're Trying to Destroy the World," 48).
51 Wilderson, "Afropessimism and the Ruse of Analogy: Violence, Freedom Struggles, and the Death of Black Desire," in *Antiblackness*, ed. Moon-Kie Jung and João H. Costa Vargas (Durham: Duke University Press, 2021), 39.
52 In *Afropessimism*, Wilderson alerts his readers that the "names and other potentially identifying characteristics of some people in this book have been changed. Some people depicted are composites." In Wilderson's discourse, "Sameer Bishara" stands for the "Arab psychic life." This move is not unproblematic to the extent that it overdetermines the image of his Palestinian friend, rendering him an example of and lesson in Arab anti-Blackness, effacing any potential enigmaticity or ambivalence that such a position could entail.
53 Wilderson, *Afropessimism*, 11.
54 Tiffany Lethabo King refers to another "origin story" when the young Frank accompanied his father to a meeting at the University of Minnesota dealing with a dispute about reservation lands. As a representative of the university, Frank's father was met with hostility by the tribal leaders who objected not so much to his authoritative status as a stand-in for the university as to his Blackness, evidenced by their unsettling dismissal of not what he had to say but of his being, "We don't want you, a *nigger man*, telling us what to do!" (Wilderson, *Afropessimism*, 44; quoted in Frank Wilderson and Tiffany Lethabo King, "Staying Ready for Black Study: A Conversation," in *Otherwise Worlds: Against Settler Colonialism and Anti-Blackness*, ed. Tiffany Lethabo King Jenell Navarro Andrea Smith [Durham: Duke University Press, 2020], 55).
55 Patrick Wolfe, "Settler Colonialism and the Elimination of the Native," *Journal of Genocide Research* 8, no. 4 (2006): 387–409.
56 As Charlene Carruthers avers, "It is important to take great care and not compare oppression. That does not serve the goal of collective liberation. No one, besides our oppressors, wins in an argument about who got whipped the worst. Eradicating oppression requires us to identify connections, not sameness" (Charlene A. Carruthers, *Unapologetic: A Black, Queer, and Feminist Mandate for Radical Movements* [Boston: Beacon Press, 2018], 31).
57 Tuck and Yang tend to reify projects of social justice as instantiations of "settler moves to innocence," in a way that is reminiscent of the Afropessimists' dismissals of competing critical models (Tuck and Yang, "Decolonization Is Not a Metaphor," 21).
58 Nick Mitchell, "The View from Nowhere: On Frank Wilderson's *Afropessimism*," *Specter*, no. 2 (Fall 2020): 119.

59 "Even the ability to be a minority citizen in the settler nation means an option to become a brown settler. For many people of color, becoming a subordinate settler is an option even when becoming white is not" (Tuck and Yang, "Decolonization Is Not a Metaphor," 18). Similarly, Zainab Amadahy and Bonita Lawrence names Afro-Canadians "ambiguous settlers" (Zainab Amadahy and Bonita Lawrence, "Indigenous Peoples and Black People in Canada: Settlers or Allies?" in *Breaching the Colonial Contract: Anti-Colonialism in the US and Canada*, ed. Arlo Kempf [New York: Springer, 2009], 121).

60 Mitchell, "The View from Nowhere," 118.

61 Expansion of Jewish privilege is also possible for some Jews. This helps to explain the virulent anti-Palestinian racism of some Sephardi and Mizrahi Jews. Seeking their own ascendency to whiteness, caught in a state of in-betweeness, they work hard to disavow their "Arabness," their proximity to Palestinians (as a racially discriminated group), undergoing an alchemical transformation, a process of "Ashkenazification," which, in turn, upholds and reproduces Ashkenazi supremacy along with its necessary corollate: Palestinian racialization. See Orna Sasson-Levy and Avi Shoshana, "'Passing' as (Non) Ethnic: The Israeli Version of Acting White," *Sociological Inquiry* 83, no. 3 (2013): 448–72.

62 Wilderson, *Afropessimism*, 13.

63 A further point that does not cross Wilderson's mind is the existence of Afro-Palestinians, which complicates his foundational Black/non-Black binary. This is obviously not to say Afro-Palestinians are free of Palestinian anti-Blackness, only that insisting on the ontological difference, as Wilderson does, excises an ambivalent, and potentially enlightening, positionality from consideration, revealing the limitations of a US-centric vision of Black peoples. See Isma'il Kushkush, "'Afro-Palestinians' Forge a Unique Identity in Israel," *Associated Press*, January 11, 2017. https://apnews.com/article/f6bf554b21d04b56be9d6385fbf36d31.

64 Greg Burris, "Black Skin, White Cameras: African Asylum-Seekers in Israeli Documentary Film," *Lateral* 10, no. 1 (2021). https://csalateral.org/forum/cultural-constructions-race-racism-middle-east-north-africa-southwest-asia-mena-swana/black-skin-white-cameras-african-asylum-seekers-israeli-documentary-film-burris/.

65 Yossi Mekelberg, "The Plight of Ethiopian Jews in Israel," *BBC News*, May 25, 2015. https://www.bbc.com/news/world-middle-east-32813056. Amelia Smith similarly observes: "Racism in Israel towards non-white Jews is not subtle. There is abundant evidence of blatant institutionalised racism in schools, hospitals, housing associations and within the workforce. This racism and open discrimination also pervade Israeli society at a grassroots level. From a bus driver in 2009 refusing to let a black woman on the bus, saying: 'I don't allow Kushim [derogatory term for black people] on board. Were there buses

in Ethiopia? In Ethiopia you didn't even have shoes and here you do, so why don't you walk?'; to reports of settlers becoming hostile if arrested by a black IDF soldier; Israeli children throwing stones at Ethiopian soldiers; and ethnic slurs being directed at Ethiopians, including frequent reports of jeers such as, 'You are just niggers'" (Amelia Smith, "Israel: Promised Land for Jews . . . As Long as They're Not Black?" *Middle East Monitor*, May 4, 2014. https://www.middleeastmonitor.com/20140504-israel-promised-land-for-jews-as-long-as-they-re-not-black/).

66 Mekelberg, "The Plight of Ethiopian Jews." See also David M. Halbfinger and Isabel Kershner, "After a Police Shooting, Ethiopian Israelis Seek a 'Black Lives Matter' Reckoning," *New York Times*, July 13, 2019.

67 Theo Goldberg, *Are We All Postracial Yet?*, 136. See also Hana Chehata, "Israel: Promised Land for Jews as Long as They're Not Black," *Race and Class* 53, no. 4 (2012): 67–77; Puar, *The Right to Maim: Debility, Capacity, Disability* (Durham: Duke University Press, 2017), 100.

68 Hedva Eyal, the author of the report, comments: "We believe it is a method of reducing the number of births in a community that is black and mostly poor" ("Furore in Israel Over Birth Control Drugs for Ethiopian Jews," *The New Humanitarian*, January 28, 2013. https://www.thenewhumanitarian.org/news/2013/01/28/furore-israel-over-birth-control-drugs-ethiopian-jews).

69 Harriet Sherwood, "Israel PM: Illegal African Immigrants Threaten Identity of Jewish State," *The Guardian*, May 20, 2012. https://www.theguardian.com/world/2012/may/20/israel-netanyahu-african-immigrants-jewish.

70 Sherwood, "Israel Turns on Its Refugees," *The Guardian*, June 4, 2012. https://www.theguardian.com/world/2012/jun/04/israel-migrant-hate.

71 Sherwood, "Israelis Attack African Migrants During Protest Against Refugees," *The Guardian*, May 24, 2012. https://www.theguardian.com/world/2012/may/24/israelis-attack-african-migrants-protest.

72 Sherwood, "Israel PM."

73 Lahav Harkov, "Netanyahu Fixates on African Migrants—But Likud Has No Policy," *The Jerusalem Post*, March 21, 2021. https://www.jpost.com/israel-elections/netanyahu-fixates-on-african-migrants-but-likud-has-no-policy-662683.

74 Harkov, "Netanyahu Fixates," emphasis added.

75 While some countries like France profess an affinity with their former colonies, the relation with Africa remains a purely instrumentalist one. To be clear: the indifference relates to the lives of Africans and not to their natural resources. See Achille Mbembe, *On the Postcolony* (Berkeley: University of California Press, 2001).

76 Wilderson, "'The Inside-Outside of Civil Society': An Interview with Frank B. Wilderson, III," Interview by Samira Spatzek, and Paula von Gleich, *Black Studies*

Papers 2, no. 1 (2016): 17. Commenting on *Time* magazine's 2006 cover story "The Deadliest War in the World," detailing how around 4 million people had died in the Democratic Republic of Congo due to political violence over the preceding decade, Žižek focuses on the story's failure to alter the "symbolic space" of its readership: "To put it cynically, *Time* picked the wrong victim in the struggle for hegemony in suffering. It should have stuck to the list of usual suspects: Muslim women and their plight, or the families of 9/11 victims and how they have coped with their losses. The Congo today has effectively re-emerged as a Conradean 'heart of darkness.' No one dares to confront it head on. The death of a West Bank Palestinian child, not to mention an Israeli or an American, is mediatically worth thousands of times more than the death of a nameless Congolese" (Žižek, *Violence*, 3). The "nonhumanity" of the Congolese disqualifies them from Western care; the "not-quite-humanity" of the Palestinian child affords her some care (although Žižek inflates the outrage that the death of Palestinian child would produce, since the Orientalist gaze frames Palestinians as responsible for their own tragic reality); the humanity of the Israeli or American child entitles her to absolute care. But as the *Time*'s story reveals, the problem is not the absence of extensive coverage. The media's coverage both reflects and reinforces their societies' racial regime (who matters and who doesn't). The coverage of two recent massacres in the Democratic Republic of the Congo and Burkina Faso makes this point. The stories only manage to convey the horrific facts of the massacres: 55 civilians were savagely killed (some burned alive) in DR Congo and 132 in Burkina Faso by jihadi groups, associated with the Islamic State and/or al-Qaeda, vying for power and territory ("At Least 55 Killed in Eastern Congo Massacres, U.N. Says," *Reuters*, May 31, 2021. https://www.reuters.com/world/africa/least-50-killed-eastern-congo-massacres-research-group-2021-05-31/; "At Least 132 Civilians Killed in Burkina Faso's Worst Attack in Years," *Reuters*, June 6, 2021. https://www.reuters.com/world/africa/armed-attackers-kill-100-civilians-burkina-faso-village-raid-2021-06-05/). There is no confrontation with the frame of anti-Blackness that structures the West's relation to Africa. In this vicious circle, the reception of Black suffering is overdetermined. It is as if the devastation of African lives were somehow already anticipated by the rest of the world. Western coverage—when it does report on the "dark continent"—tends to reify Africa as the eternal site of catastrophe and inhumanity.

77 Halbfinger and Kershner, "After a Police Shooting."
78 Weheliye, *Habeas Viscus*, 19.
79 Bruce Fink, *A Clinical Introduction to Lacanian Psychoanalysis: Theory and Technique* (Cambridge: Harvard University Press, 1997), 61.
80 Fink, *A Clinical Introduction*, 61.
81 See Robert K. Beshara, "Islamophobia as a Fundamental Fantasy," *International Journal of Žižek Studies* 13, no. 3 (2019): 6–7.

82 Žižek, *The Plague of Fantasies* (New York: Verso, 1997), 9.
83 Žižek, "The Palestinian Question: The Couple Symptom/Fetish," *Lacan.com*, 2009. http://www.lacan.com/essays/?page_id=261.
84 Žižek, *The Parallax View* (Cambridge, MA: MIT Press, 2006), 255.
85 Žižek, *Disparities* (New York: Bloomsbury, 2016), 183.
86 See Max Nordau, *Degeneration* (Lincoln: University of Nebraska, 1993).
87 Jacqueline Rose, *The Question of Zion* (Princeton: Princeton University Press, 2007), 17.
88 Žižek, *The Sublime Object of Ideology* (New York: Verso, 1989), 5.
89 Žižek, "The Seven Veils of Fantasy," in *Key Concepts of Lacanian Psychoanalysis*, ed. Dany Nobus (New York: Other Press, 1998), 190.
90 See, for example, Rashid Khalidi, *Palestinian Identity: The Construction of Modern National Consciousness* (New York: Columbia University Press, 2010).
91 Rose resists the description of Zionism as merely "delusion," preferring to stress its perplexities, how "something can be both a delusion and actual; effective and insane." Zionism, she adds, "is a violation of reality that knows its own delusion. And runs with it" (Rose, *The Question of Zion*, 15, 16).
92 Rose, *The Question of Zion*, 44.
93 Žižek, *Less Than Nothing*, 859.
94 Žižek, *Violence*, 53.
95 "The IDF is the most moral army in the world," said Defense Minister Avigdor Lieberman in 2018 after the death of a Palestinian journalist at the hands of an Israeli soldier (Jeff Barak, "Reality Check: The Most Moral Army in the World. Really?" *The Jerusalem Post*, April 15, 2018. https://www.jpost.com/opinion/reality-check-the-most-moral-army-in-the-world-really-549906).
96 Said, "Politics of Knowledge," in *Race, Identity, and Representation in Education*, ed. Cameron McCarthy, Warren Crichlow (New York: Routledge, 1993), 313.
97 Sari Hanafi, "Spacio-cide: Colonial Politics, Invisibility and Rezoning in Palestinian territory," *Contemporary Arab Affairs* 2, no. 1 (2009): 106–21.
98 Nadia Abu El-Haj, "Zoom Webinar: Said's Palestine," moderated by Judith Butler. *University of California Humanities Research Institute*, June 1, 2021. https://uchri.org/events/saids-palestine/.
99 Jacqueline Rose, *Proust Among the Nations: From Dreyfus to the Middle East* (Chicago: University of Chicago Press, 2011), 66.
100 Said, "Zionism from the Standpoint of Its Victims."
101 Liberal Zionists aspire to occupy the position of the liberal Canadian, which, as Stephen Marche points out, is wholly inadequate: "We say, over and over, that we want desperately to atone for a crime while we're still in the middle of committing it" (Stephen Marche, "Canada's Impossible Acknowledgment," *The New Yorker*, September 7, 2017. https://www.newyorker.com/culture/culture-desk/canadas-impossible-acknowledgment).

102 With Israel's noticeable shift to the Right, the commonplace view that Israelis have more robust political discussions at home about the "conflict" is losing credibility and ideological currency. Does it really matter if Israelis have "richer" discussions when, in practice, they keep electing more and more extremist prime ministers who basically all agree on the continued dispossession of the Palestinian people and the colonial program of annexation?

103 Jeremy Sharon and Idan Zonshine, "Lapid Condemns Flag March Slurs: 'This is Not Judaism and Not Israeli,'" June 15, 2021. https://www.jpost.com/arab-israeli-conflict/raam-leader-abbas-on-jerusalem-flag-march-were-against-any-provocation-671068.

104 Sharon and Zonshine, "Lapid Condemns Flag March Slurs."

105 Robert Mackey, "Israel's New Leaders Won't Stop 'Death to Arabs' Chants, but They Will Feel Bad About Them," *The Intercept*, June 16, 2021. https://theintercept.com/2021/06/16/israels-new-leaders-wont-stop-death-arabs-chants-will-feel-bad/.

106 Raz Yosef, *The Politics of Loss and Trauma in Contemporary Israeli Cinema* (New York: Routledge, 2011), 25.

107 Baruch Kimmerling, *Politicide: Ariel Sharon's War against the Palestinians* (New York: Verso, 2003), 35–42.

108 Žižek, "Israelis' SHAME over What Their State Is Doing in West Bank Would Be Sign of Truly Belonging to Israel," *RT*, May 17, 2021. https://www.rt.com/op-ed/524075-israelis-shame-west-bank-palestinians/.

109 Nimer Sultany, "Colonial Realities: From Sheikh Jarrah to Lydda," *Mondoweiss*, May 12, 2021. https://mondoweiss.net/2021/05/colonial-realities-from-sheikh-jarrah-to-lydda/.

110 Žižek, "Israelis' SHAME."

111 "Jewish Electoral Institute: National Jewish Survey," June 28–July 1, 2021. https://www.jewishelectorateinstitute.org/wp-content/uploads/2021/07/JEI-National-Jewish-Survey-Topline-Results-July-2021.pdf.

112 James Baldwin, "A Report from Occupied Territory," in *James Baldwin: Collected Essays*, ed. Toni Morrison (New York: Library of America, 1998), 730; see also Timothy Seidel, "'Occupied Territory is Occupied Territory': James Baldwin, Palestine and the Possibilities of Transnational Solidarity," *Third World Quarterly* 37, no. 9 (2016); 1644–60.

113 Wilderson, *Red, White & Black*, 82.

114 Park, "Afropessimism," 34.

115 Wilderson, *Red, White & Black*, 55.

116 Fanon, *Black Skin, White Masks*, trans. Charles Lam Markmann (New York: Grove Press, 1967), 100.

117 Wilderson, "We're Trying to Destroy the World," 52.

118 David Marriott, "Black Cultural Studies," *The Year's Work in Critical and Cultural Theory* 20 (2012): 47.
119 Jacques Derrida, "'Eating Well,' or the Calculation of the Subject: An Interview with Jacques Derrida," in *Who Comes After the Subject?* ed. Eduardo Cadava, Peter Connor, and Jean-Luc Nancy (New York: Routledge, 1991), 115.
120 Derrida, "Avowing—The Impossible: 'Returns,' Repentance, and Reconciliation," in *Living Together: Jacques Derrida's Communities of Violence and Peace*, ed. Elisabeth Weber (New York: Fordham University Press, 2013), 28.
121 Derrida, "Avowing," 27.
122 Wilderson, *Red, White & Black*, 58.
123 Wilderson, "Afropessimism," 39.
124 Wilderson, *Red, White & Black*, 28.
125 Arabs For Black Lives Collective, June 2, 2020. https://www.mpowerchange.org/culture-blog/arabs-for-black-lives. It must be noted that the convenience store that alerted the police to Floyd's suspected counterfeit $20 bill was owned by Mahmoud Abumayyaleh, a Palestinian-American man. "The Arabs for Black Lives Collective" does not consider this to be an isolated episode but symptomatic of a general Arab attitude that puts Black lives in danger. The collective further states: "In many major cities across the US, Arab-owned corner stores are concentrated in predominantly black working-class neighborhoods. We need to examine how we are showing up to support the black community, and what steps we are taking that do not involve reliance on law enforcement."
126 Robin D. G. Kelley, Jack Amariglio, and Lucas Wilson, "'Solidarity Is Not a Market Exchange': An RM Interview with Robin D. G. Kelley, Part 1," *Rethinking Marxism* 30, no. 4 (2018): 592.
127 Bailey, "Black-Palestinian Solidarity in the Ferguson-Gaza Era," 1019.
128 https://www.facebook.com/linaabojaradehart/videos/923911664738203/.
129 Jared Sexton, "People-of-Color-Blindness: Notes on the Afterlife of Slavery," *Social Text* 28, no. 2 103 (2010): 48.
130 Conversely, Abojaradeh's artwork might be said to ignore Indigenous concerns, subordinating them to anti-Black violence, treating white supremacy as the ultimate obstacle to belonging or inclusion in the (settler) state. But this is to grossly misconstrue the politics of BLM as identitarian in spirit rather than universalist. BLM is not after inclusion but a reconfiguration of the state as such.
131 Che Gossett, "A Wall is Just a Wall: Anti-Blackness and the Politics of Black and Prison Abolitionist Solidarity with Palestinian Struggle," *Decolonization* (blog), June 16, 2014. https://decolonization.wordpress.com/2014/06/16/a-wall-is-just-a-wall-anti-blackness-and-the-politics-of-black-and-prison-abolitionist-solidarity-with-palestinian-struggle/.
132 Sexton, "People-of-Color-Blindness," 56n.75.

133 As Žižek argues, the paradoxical answer "Yes, Please!" affirms a "refusal of choice," jamming the overdetermined character of a question. Responding to the question of Blackness or Indigeneity? with "Yes, Please!" declines the expected type of answer that would rank the suffering of Blacks and Indigenous peoples. See Žižek, "Class Struggle or Postmodernism," 90.

134 Nadera Shalhoub, "Roundtable on Anti-Blackness and Black-Palestinian Solidarity," *Jadaliyya*, June 3, 2015. https://www.jadaliyya.com/Details/32145/Roundtable-on-Anti-Blackness-and-Black-Palestinian-Solidarity.

135 Saidiya Hartman chides the white liberal subject for whom caring for non-whites is predicated on phantasmatic empathy or narcissistic identification, the notion that "only if I can see myself in that position can I understand the crisis of that position" (Hartman and Wilderson, "The Position of the Unthought," 189). The liberal ally is again the model to avoid. In relating to Black trauma, Palestinian allies must also resist the temptation of innocence (only care for the innocent—which ultimately means white—individual), since, as Hartman adds, the "[white] sympathetic ally… in some ways is actually no more able to see the slave than the person who is exploiting him or her as their property" (Hartman and Wilderson, "The Position of the Unthought," 189).

136 Robin D. G. Kelley, "From the River to the Sea to Every Mountain Top: Solidarity as Worldmaking," *Journal of Palestine Studies* 48, no. 4 (2019): 73.

137 Tiffany Lethabo King, Jenell Navarro, and Andrea Smith, "Beyond Incommensurability: Toward an Otherwise Stance on Black and Indigenous Relationality," in *Otherwise Worlds: Against Settler Colonialism and Anti-Blackness*, ed. Tiffany Lethabo King, Jenell Navarro, and Andrea Smith (Durham: Duke University Press, 2020), 6.

138 It is terribly difficult to avoid the affective language of humanism. Rallying people behind the Palestinian cause often begins with a plea to bear witness to the *humanity* of Palestinians: "To move beyond the current limits, progressives must embrace a more principled politics, one that begins by recognizing the fundamental humanity of Palestinians" (Hill and Plitnick, *Except for Palestine*, 155). Unless this move is situated in a simultaneous (anti-racist, anti-speciesist) critique of what and who constitutes the human, there is a danger that a defense of the Palestinian cause will remain complicit in an anti-Black project, libidinally bonded to a vision of the human cleansed, as it were, of its Blackness and animality. While taking up the question of animality and settler colonialism is beyond the scope of this book, I would note that to object to colonial life as an instantiation of animal life is not so much a call to alter the situation of the former by humanizing the life of the racialized being; rather, it involves a reckoning with anthropocentrism and speciesism, that is, a ceaseless contestation of the privilege of the human in all its forms.

139 "For Europe, for ourselves and for humanity, comrades, we must make a new start, develop a new way of thinking, and endeavor to create a new man" (Fanon, *The Wretched of the Earth*, 239). This "new man" will serve as the basis for a "New Humanism" (Fanon, *Black Skin*, xi). See Ato Sekyi-Otu, *Fanon's Dialectic of Experience* (Cambridge, MA: Harvard University Press, 1996), 182.

Chapter 2

1 Walter Mignolo, "I Am Where I Think: Remapping the Order of Knowing," in *The Creolization of Theory*, ed. Françoise Lionnet and Shu-mei Shi (Durham: Duke University Press, 2011), 161. Copyright 2011, Duke University Press. All rights reserved. Reprinted by permission of the publisher. www.dukeupress.edu.
2 Saree Makdisi, "For a Secular Democratic State," *The Nation*, June 18, 2007. https://www.thenation.com/article/archive/secular-democratic-state/.
3 Edward Said, *After the Last Sky: Palestinian Lives*, with photographs by Jean Mohr (New York: Pantheon, 1986), 53.
4 Makdisi, "For a Secular Democratic State."
5 Mignolo, "I Am Where I Think," 159–92.
6 Mignolo, "Decoloniality and Phenomenology: The Geopolitics of Knowing and Epistemic/Ontological Colonial Differences," *The Journal of Speculative Philosophy* 32, no. 3 (2018): 382.
7 Said, *The Question of Palestine* (New York: Pantheon Books, 1979), xxxi.
8 "It is a peculiar sensation, this double-consciousness, this sense of always looking at one's self through the eyes of others, of measuring one's soul by the tape of a world that looks on in amused contempt and pity. One ever feels his two-ness,—an American, a Negro; two souls, two thoughts, two unreconciled strivings" (W. E. B. Du Bois, *The Souls of Black Folk* [New Haven: Yale University Press, 2015], 5). See Lewis R. Gordon, "Theory in Black: Teleological Suspensions in Philosophy of Culture," *Qui Parle* 18, no. 2 (2010): 193–214.
9 Denise Ferreira da Silva, *Toward a Global Idea of Race* (Minneapolis: University of Minnesota Press, 2007).
10 Walter D. Mignolo, "The Decolonial Option and the Meaning of Identity in Politics," *Anales Nueva Época* 9, no. 10 (2007): 43–72.
11 Mignolo, "Foreword: Yes, We Can," in *Can Non-Europeans Think?*, by Hamid Dabashi (London: Zed Books, 2015), xi.
12 Ta-Nehisi Coates, *Between the World and Me* (New York: Spiegel and Grau, 2015), 7.
13 As Mbembe puts it, "We must therefore consider race as being both beside and beyond being. It is an *operation of the imagination*, the site of an encounter with

the shadows and hidden zones of the unconscious" (Mbembe, *Critique of Black Reason*, 32, emphasis added).

14 Commenting on Fanon's rhetorical use of the Native, Neil Lazarus rightfully says, "the figure of the native is not autochthonous, but is rather a construction of colonialism—actually, of the settler" (Neil Lazarus, "Disavowing Decolonization: Fanon, Nationalism, and the Problematic of Representation in Current Theories of Colonial Discourse," *Research in African Literatures* 24, no. 4 [1993]: 75).

15 Mignolo, *The Darker Side of Western Modernity*, 3.

16 Mignolo, "Decolonizing the Nation-State: Zionism in the Colonial Horizon of Modernity," in *Deconstructing Zionism: A Critique of Political Metaphysics*, ed. Gianni Vattimo and Michael Marder (New York: Bloomsbury, 2013), 58.

17 Mignolo, *The Darker Side of Western Modernity*, 121.

18 Mignolo, "Decolonizing the Nation-State," 65.

19 Mignolo, "Decolonizing the Nation-State," 71.

20 Ilan Pappé thoroughly documents Zionists' systematic plan to eradicate Palestinians from Jewish land. The Plan D (Dalet in Hebrew) "was both the inevitable product of the Zionist ideological impulse to have an exclusively Jewish presence in Palestine, and a response to developments on the ground once the British cabinet had decided to end the mandate. Clashes with local Palestinian militias provided the perfect context and pretext for implementing the ideological vision of an ethnically cleansed Palestine. The Zionist policy was first based on retaliation against Palestinian attacks in February 1947, and it transformed into an initiative to ethnically cleanse the country as a whole in March 1948. Once the decision was taken, it took six months to complete the mission. When it was over, more than half of Palestine's native population, close to 800,000 people, had been uprooted, 531 villages had been destroyed, and eleven urban neighbourhoods emptied of their inhabitants. The plan decided upon on March 10, 1948, and above all its systematic implementation in the following months, was a clear-cut case of an ethnic cleansing operation, regarded under international law today as a crime against humanity" (Pappé, *The Ethnic Cleansing of Palestine* [Oxford: Oneworld, 2006], xii). See also Walid Khalidi, "Plan Dalet: Master Plan for the Conquest of Palestine," *Journal of Palestine Studies* 18, no. 1 (1988): 4–33.

21 Mignolo, "Decolonizing the Nation-State," 61.

22 "Inside Israel, the difference that counts is that between Jew and non-Jew. So far as land in Israel is concerned, for instance, much of it (nearly 90 percent) is held in trust for the Jewish people, whereas non-Jews, simply because they are not Jews, cannot juridically derive equal benefits from it" (Said, "An Ideology of Difference," *Critical Inquiry* 12, no. 1 [1985]: 41).

23 "Racial discrimination against the indigenous Palestinian people who became citizens of the state of Israel was formalized and institutionalized through the

creation by law of a 'Jewish nationality' that is distinct from Israeli citizenship. No 'Israeli' nationality exists in Israel, and the Supreme Court has persistently refused to recognize one, as it would end the system of Jewish supremacy in Israel" (Omar Barghouti, *Boycott Divestment Sanctions: The Global Struggle for Palestinian Rights* [Chicago: Haymarket, 2011], 200).

24 Mignolo, "Decolonizing the Nation-State," 68.
25 Mbembe, *Necropolitics*, 96.
26 Mbembe, *Necropolitics*, 97.
27 Mbembe, *Necropolitics*, 97.
28 Dov Weisglass, "Oslo Deal Was Good for the Jews," *Ynetnews*, August 21, 2012. https://www.ynetnews.com/articles/0,7340,L-4270970,00.html. On Israel's dubious neglect or refusal of responsibility in the Occupied Territories, see also Darryl Li, "The Gaza Strip as Laboratory: Notes in the Wake of Disengagement," *Journal of Palestine Studies* 35, no. 2 (2006): 38–55.
29 Mbembe, *Necropolitics*, 97.
30 Anshel Pfeffer, "Israel Has Abandoned All Its Citizens, Not Just Its Arab Ones," *Haaretz*, May 19, 2021. https://www.haaretz.com/israel-news/2021-05-19/ty-article/.highlight/israel-has-abandoned-all-its-citizens-not-just-its-arab-ones/0000017f-f469-ddde-abff-fc6d649f0000.
31 As Pfeffer observes, "Awad, a Muslim teenager, was meant to represent Israeli citizens at risk of rocket fire. However, Israel contributed to her death by neglecting for decades her tiny unrecognized village, Dahmash (right next to Lod), which was hit by the rocket. Seven years ago, the High Court ruled that Dahmash should get essential services, but bomb shelters are yet to be erected there" (Pfeffer, "Israel Has Abandoned All Its Citizens, Not Just Its Arab Ones"). Abstract equality works ideologically when there is no will on the government's part to actually treat all of its citizens with decency and dignity. Occasional legal victories for the Palestinian minority give the *illusion* of justice for all; until the legal system confronts the colonial situation under which it operates, its judgments can never be taken at face value.
32 Mignolo, "Decolonizing the Nation-State," 61.
33 Sumaya Awad and Annie Levin, "Roots of the Nakba: Zionist Settler Colonialism," in *Palestine: A Socialist Introduction*, ed. Sumaya Awad and Brian Bean (Chicago: Haymarket Books, 2020), 19.
34 Ilan Pappé, "Indigeneity as Cultural Resistance: Notes on the Palestinian Struggle within Twenty-First-Century Israel," *The South Atlantic Quarterly* 117, no. 1 (2018): 170.
35 As'ad Ghanem, "'Identity and Belonging': A Pioneering Project, Which Must Be the Starting Point for an Alternative, Comprehensive Educational Plan," *Adalah's Newsletter* 27 (2006). https://www.adalah.org/uploads/oldfiles/newsletter/eng/jul-aug06/ar2.pdf.

36 Mahmood Jrere, Tamer Nafar, and Udi Aloni, "'We Don't Want What Happened in 1948 to Happen to Us Again,'" *The Nation*, May 26, 2021. https://www.thenation.com/article/activism/dam-palestine-protest/.
37 Medina, "Varieties of Hermeneutical Injustice," 49.
38 Ghanem, "'Identity and Belonging.'"
39 Amal Jamal, "Nationalizing States and the Constitution of 'Hollow Citizenship': Israel and its Palestinian Citizens," *Ethnopolitics* 6, no. 4 (2007): 473. Majid al-Haj also writes: "The education system has been used by the Israeli establishment as a mechanism of control over the Arab population. The segregated education system that separates Arabs and Jews is also reflected in a segregated curriculum. Although the main theme of the curriculum for Jewish schools focuses on national content, the curriculum in Arab schools has been sanitized of any national content. Throughout Israel's existence, the message internalized by Jewish students is that Israel is a state of, by, and for Jews; there has been no attempt to foster a civic culture in which the Arab citizens are a separate but equal component" (Majid al-Haj "National Ethos, Multicultural Education, and the New History Textbooks in Israel," *Curriculum Inquiry* 35 [2005]: 52).
40 Pappé, "Indigeneity as Cultural Resistance," 170.
41 Pappé, "Indigeneity as Cultural Resistance," 165.
42 Pappé, "Indigeneity as Cultural Resistance," 162.
43 Ghanem, "'Identity and Belonging.'"
44 Michel de Certeau, *The Practice of Everyday Life*, trans. Steven Rendall (Berkeley: University of California Press, 1984), xix.
45 de Certeau, *The Practice of Everyday Life*, xix.
46 de Certeau, *The Practice of Everyday Life*, 37.
47 de Certeau, *The Practice of Everyday Life*, 37.
48 Nicole Simek, "Trading Well," *symplokē* 27, no. 1–2 (2019): 407.
49 Dina Kraft and Laura King, "'Second Front' for Israel: Violence Among Arab Citizens and Jews Comes as a Wartime Test," *Los Angeles Times*, May 14, 2021. https://www.latimes.com/world-nation/story/2021-05-14/israel-jewish-arab-tension.
50 Israel Democracy Institute Researcher Arik Rudnitzky and one of the two authors of the report on non-formal education in the Arab community, qtd. in Shoshanna Solomon, "To Help Arabs Integrate, Israel Should Help Strengthen Arab Identity—Study," *The Times of Israel*, September 16, 2018. https://www.timesofisrael.com/to-help-arabs-integrate-israel-should-help-strengthen-arab-identity-study/.
51 To fully unpack the meaning of colonial difference is to put it "in relation to the very dynamics of imperial and colonial power, in short, in relation to the coloniality of power, knowledge, and being" (Nelson Maldonado-Torres, "Levinas's Hegemonic Identity Politics, Radical Philosophy, and the Unfinished Project of Decolonization," *Levinas Studies* 7 [2012]: 70).

52 Hillel Cohen, *Good Arabs: The Israeli Security Agencies and the Israeli Arabs, 1948–1967* (Berkeley: University of California Press, 2010), 3, emphasis added.

53 Amal Helow extends the need to teach the Nakba to Jewish children as well, proposing what we might describe as a de-centralizing pedagogy of the Other, which would function as an antidote to Israel's anachronistic and insular practices: "Israeli Jews need to recognize that only when our narrative is taught to Jewish children just as the Jewish narrative is taught in Arab schools, will Israel be on its way to becoming a true democracy. Displaying Palestinian symbols does not negate Jewish symbols; quite the opposite: it sends a strong and true message of mutual respect. A state based on religious affiliation is archaic in today's world. When a state affords democratic rights to only some of its citizens it is not democratic" (Amal Helow, "Challenging Israel to Become Democratic," *bitterlemons.org*, January 29, 2007. http://www.bitterlemons.org/previous/bl290107ed4.html#pal2).

54 "Israel's New Government Fails to Renew Disputed Citizenship Law," *Reuters*, July 6, 2021. https://www.reuters.com/world/middle-east/israels-new-government-dealt-blow-controversial-citizenship-vote-2021-07-06/.

55 Jonathan Ofir, "Israel's Ban on Palestinian Spouses Becomes Permanent Law—a Triumph for 'Jewish State,'" *Mondoweiss*, March 11, 2022. https://mondoweiss.net/2022/03/israels-ban-on-palestinian-spouses-becomes-permanent-law-a-triumph-for-jewish-state/.

56 Warschawski, *Toward an Open Tomb*, 56.

57 Said, "Introduction," in *Blaming the Victims: Spurious Scholarship and the Palestine Question*, ed. Edward Said and Christopher Hitchens (New York: Verso, 1988), 3.

58 In a similar vein, Abu El-Haj asks, "Why is denying Israel's right to exist objectionable in the first place?" (El-Haj, "Racial Palestinianization and the Janus-Faced Nature of the Israeli State," 34).

59 Commenting on the differences between Israel's and the United States' forms of settler colonialism, Indigenous scholar Waziyatawin writes, "with our populations thoroughly subjugated, it is now safe for them to acknowledge that Indigenous people were here first, while feeling no sense of obligation for accompanying actions toward justice. They do not perceive us as a serious threat" (Waziyatawin, "Malice Enough in their Hearts and Courage Enough in Ours," 180–1).

60 Walter Benjamin, "Critique of Violence," in *Selected Writings, vol. 1*, ed. Marcus Bullock and Michael W. Jennings, trans. Edmund Jephcott et al. (Cambridge, MA: Harvard University Press, 1996), 236–52.

61 Žižek, *Violence*, 117.

62 Derrida, *On Cosmopolitanism and Forgiveness*, trans. Mark Dooley and Michael Hughes (New York: Routledge, 2001), 57. As mentioned in Chapter 1 though,

with the rise of ethnonationalism in Israel, an alarming number of right-wing fascists are belligerently avowing the Nakba, yearning to complete the Palestinian catastrophe and thus realize the eliminative project of Zionism.

63 I take my inspiration for this metaphor from Elias Sanbar's statement, "Palestine is a bone stuck in the world's throat; no one will manage to swallow it [*La Palestine est une arête plantée dans la gorge du monde. Personne ne parviendra à l'avaler*]" (Elias Sanbar, *Le bien des absents* [Paris: Actes Sud, 2001], 61).

64 Gayatri Spivak, *An Aesthetic Education in the Era of Globalization* (Cambridge, MA: Harvard University Press, 2013), 154.

65 Fanon gives us an account of white civil society's "good Negro": "look how handsome that Negro is, the handsome Negro says, 'fuck you,' madame" (Fanon, *Black Skin*, 94). The "good Negro" is the exception that proves the rule of Black abjection. *Look how nonviolent that Palestinian is* . . .

66 Nadim Rouhana, "Homeland Nationalism and Guarding Dignity in a Settler Colonial Context: The Palestinian Citizens of Israel Reclaim Their Homeland," *borderlands* 14, no. 1 (2015): 1–37.

67 Mignolo, "I Am Where I Think," 161.

68 Mignolo, "I Am Where I Think," 174.

69 See Anibal Quijano, "Coloniality of Power, Eurocentrism and Latin America," *Nepantla: Views from South* 1, no. 3 (2000): 533–80.

70 See Mignolo, *The Darker Side of Western Modernity*.

71 Mignolo, *Local Histories/Global Designs: Coloniality, Subaltern Knowledges, and Border Thinking* (Princeton: Princeton University Press, 2000), 22.

72 Linda Martín Alcoff, "Mignolo's Epistemology of Coloniality," *CR: The New Centennial Review* 7, no. 3 (2007): 84.

73 Alcoff, "Mignolo's Epistemology of Coloniality," 99.

74 "The 'myth of modernity' . . . is simultaneous with the emergence of modern subjectivity itself: freedom and the ensuing sense of rationality that emanates from it were tied to a peculiar conception of power that is premised on the alleged superiority of some subjects over others" (Maldonado-Torres, *Against War: Views from the Underside of Modernity* [Durham: Duke University Press, 2008], 213).

75 Denise Ferreira da Silva sketches a similar narrative, opposing the "transparent I" of the post-Enlightenment to the "affectable I" of the "others of Europe" (that is, the colonized and the enslaved of the world). The "transparent I" reflects Europe's long investment in self-determination (ever since the Stoics and Augustine, "self-determination would be added as the rational thing's exclusive (moral) attribute" [da Silva, *Toward a Global Idea of Race*, 40]). However, self-determination only became a European privilege after the conquest of the Americas. This genocidal encounter brought the "transparent I" to full fruition, giving it a global dimension, as "the kind of mind that is able to know, emulate, and control powers of universal reason." And, at the same time, this

catastrophic encounter is also responsible for producing its European counterpart: the "affectable I": "the one that emerged in other global regions, the kind of mind subjected to both the exterior determination of the 'laws of nature' and the superior force of European minds" (da Silva, *Toward a Global Idea of Race*, 117).

76 Mignolo, *The Darker Side of Western Modernity*, 113. As postcolonial theory's offshoot or rebellious variant, decoloniality's relation to Western modernity is far more combative than that of its forerunner. Unlike postcolonial theory, which relies heavily on continental philosophers (Derrida, Foucault, Deleuze, etc.), decoloniality, as we have seen, hungers for (a return to) the local, a precolonial, authentic reality untainted or uncorrupted by Western thought and the hegemony of global market democracy.

77 Mbembe, "Thoughts on the Planetary: An interview with Achille Mbembe," in *Decolonising the Neoliberal University: Law, Psychoanalysis and the Politics of Student Protest*, ed. Jaco Barnard-Naudé (New York: Routledge, 2022), 125.

78 Said, "Backlash and Backtrack," *Counterpunch*, September 28, 2003. https://www.counterpunch.org/2001/09/28/backlash-and-backtrack/. More generally, decoloniality suffers from an un-Fanonian idealization of a prior, pristine time before the colonial encounter: "I concede the fact that the actual existence of an Aztec civilization has done little to change the diet of today's Mexican peasant. I concede that whatever proof there is of a once mighty Songhai civilization does not change the fact that the Songhais today are undernourished, illiterate, abandoned to the ashes and water, with a blank mind and glazed eyes" (Fanon, *The Wretched of the Earth*, 148).

79 Wilderson, "The Black Liberation Army and the Paradox of Political Engagement," in *Postcoloniality-Decoloniality-Black Critique: Joints and Fissures*, ed. Sabine Broeck and Carsten Junker (Frankfurt: Campus Verlag, 2014), 178.

80 I take my inspiration for "tarrying in the exilic" from Žižek's appropriation of Hegel's formulation of "tarrying with the negative." See Žižek, *Tarrying with the Negative: Kant, Hegel, and the Critique of Ideology* (Durham: Duke University Press, 1993).

81 Arjun Appadurai, "Beyond Domination: The Future and Past of Decolonization," *The Nation*, March 9, 2021. https://www.thenation.com/article/world/achille-mbembe-walter-mignolo-catherine-walsh-decolonization/.

82 Said, *Reflections on Exile* and Other Essays (Cambridge, MA: Harvard University Press, 2000), 173.

83 It should be noted that Said is himself critical of the notion of diaspora which he aligns—perhaps too restrictively—with a myth-making narrative (Said, "*Orientalism*, Arab Intellectuals, Marxism, and Myth in Palestinian History," in *Power, Politics, and Culture: Interviews with Edward W. Said*, ed. Gauri Viswanathan [New York: Vintage, 2001], 441–2).

84 Rehnuma Sazzad, *Edward Said's Concept of Exile: Identity and Cultural Migration in the Middle East* (New York: I.B.Tauris & Co. Ltd, 2017), 220.
85 Said, *Reflections on Exile*, 186.
86 Said, *Reflections on Exile*, 186.
87 Gordon, "Theory in Black," 197.
88 Said, *Out of Place: A Memoir* (New York: Knopf, 1999), 295.
89 Said, *Culture and Imperialism* (New York: Vintage, 1994), 336.
90 Gordon, "Theory in Black," 206.
91 Du Bois, *The Souls of Black Folks*, 5.
92 Said, *Reflections on Exile*, 173.
93 Said, *Reflections on Exile*, 174.
94 Reflecting on his dividedness as an Arab and an American, Said displays his contrapuntal sensibility: "to think and write contrapuntally, using the disparate halves of my experience, as an Arab and as an American, to work with and also against each other" (Said, *Reflections on Exile*, 562). Elsewhere, Said generalizes this condition as an open dialectic of self and other: "All cultures spin out a dialectic of self and other, the subject 'I' who is native, authentic, at home, and the object 'it' or 'you,' who is foreign, perhaps threatening, different, out there" (Said, *After the Last Sky*, 40).
95 Said, *Out of Place*, 293.
96 Anna Bernard, *Rhetorics of Belonging: Nation, Narration, and Israel/Palestine* (Liverpool: Liverpool University Press, 2013), 47.
97 Zionism, which lacked any sense of contrapuntal consciousness, managed to convert the "proverbial people of exile, the Jews," into ethnonational sovereigns while simultaneously producing a new people of exile, the Palestinians (Said, *Reflections on Exile*, 178). One of the challenges for Said is to avoid this phantasmatic transformation for the Palestinian people.
98 Said, *Representations of the Intellectual: The 1993 Reith Lectures* (New York: Vintage Books, 1996), 44.
99 Said, *Culture and Imperialism*, 278.
100 Said, "Backlash and Backtrack."
101 Said, "Forward," in *I Saw Ramallah*, xi, emphasis added.
102 Judith Butler, *Frames of War: When is Life Grievable* (New York: Verso, 2009), 25.
103 Said, "Forward," xi.
104 Bernard, *Rhetorics of Belonging*, 83.
105 Bernard, *Rhetorics of Belonging*, 79.
106 Bernard, *Rhetorics of Belonging*, 69.
107 Bernard, *Rhetorics of Belonging*, 82.
108 Bernard, *Rhetorics of Belonging*, 69, 83. Nivedita Majumdar makes a similar point: "To present the Palestinian situation under the banner of exile is to marginalize the lived

realities of the millions who live *in* Palestine" (Nivedita Majumdar, *World in a Grain of Sand: Postcolonial Literature and Radical Universalism* [New York: Verso, 2021], 173).
109 Barghouti, *I Saw Ramallah*, 131, xi.
110 Barghouti, *I Saw Ramallah*, 133. Elsewhere, Barghouti describes the exile/stranger as plagued with social death, a seemingly permanent condition of being Palestinian: "Displacement is like death. . . . [T]he stranger can never go back to what he was. Even if he returns. It is over. A person gets 'displacement' as he gets asthma, and there is no cure for either" (Barghouti, *I Saw Ramallah*, 3, 4).
111 Bernard, *Rhetorics of Belonging*, 80.
112 Barghouti, *I Saw Ramallah*, 131.
113 Bernard, *Rhetorics of Belonging*, 79.
114 Said, "What Israel Has Done," *The Nation*, April 18, 2002, emphasis added. https://www.thenation.com/article/archive/what-israel-has-done/. Said shares Fanon's observation that "For a colonized people the most essential value, because the most concrete, is first and foremost the land: the land which will bring them bread, and above all, dignity" (Fanon, *The Wretched of the Earth*, 9). An investment in land does not, however, commit Said or Fanon to a mythical past when the Indigenous population enjoyed the plenitude of the land.
115 Makdisi, "Said, Palestine, and the Humanism of Liberation," *Critical Inquiry* 31 (2005): 443–61.
116 In Chapter 4, we will take up the importance of centering political economy, along with land repatriation, in any vision of a future Palestine.
117 Said, *Culture and Imperialism*, 14.
118 Said, *Culture and Imperialism*, 277.
119 Said, *Representations of the Intellectual*, 32.
120 Majumdar, *World in a Grain of Sand*, 174.
121 Barghouti, *I Saw Ramallah*, 126.
122 Barghouti, *I Saw Ramallah*, 42, 43.
123 Barghouti, *I Saw Ramallah*, 43–4.
124 Žižek, *For They Know Not What They Do: Enjoyment as a Political Factor* (New York: Verso, 2002), 70.
125 Barghouti, *I Saw Ramallah*, 7.
126 Barghouti, *I Saw Ramallah*, 38.
127 Barghouti, *I Saw Ramallah*, 62, 69.
128 Barghouti, *I Saw Ramallah*, 147.
129 Barghouti, *I Saw Ramallah*, 69.
130 Barghouti, *I Saw Ramallah*, 13.
131 Barghouti, *I Saw Ramallah*, 38.
132 Said, *Peace and it Discontents: Essays on Palestine in the Middle East Peace Process* (New York: Vintage, 1995); Said, *The End of the Peace Process*.

133 Barghouti, *I Saw Ramallah*, 178. For Donna Nevel, the retort "But Hamas..." functions much in the same way. Hamas is the phobic object *par excellence*. It is moral baseness incarnate. Hamas is the boogeyman of liberal Zionists. Its name derails the framing of the Palestinian cause as an anti-colonial struggle (armed or otherwise): "In conversations about Gaza, I have heard many thoughtful people in the Jewish community lament the loss of Palestinian lives in Gaza but then say, 'But Hamas...' as if that were the heart of the problem. I'd like to suggest that, when we have these conversations about Hamas and Israel's bombing campaign, we begin with the necessary context and historical perspective" (Donna Nevel, "Conversations About Gaza: 'But Hamas...'" *Fair Observer*, August 18, 2014. https://www.fairobserver.com/region/middle_east_north_africa/conversations-about-gaza-but-hamas-12739/).

134 For Said, "For the intellectual the task... is explicitly to universalize the crisis" (Said, *Representations of the Intellectual*, 44).

135 Qtd in "Introduction," in *Palestine: A Socialist Introduction*, ed. Sumaya Awad and Brian Bean (Chicago: Haymarket Books, 2020), 1.

136 Said, "Politics of Knowledge," 313.

137 Žižek, *First as Tragedy, Then as Farce* (New York: Verso, 2009), 92.

138 Žižek, *In Defense of Lost Causes*, 424.

139 See Yvonne Ridley, "Palestinian Lives Do Matter," *Middle East Monitor*, June 15, 2021. https://www.middleeastmonitor.com/20210615-palestinian-lives-do-matter/; Sarah Aziza, "Can Palestinian Lives Matter?" May 13, 2021. https://theintercept.com/2021/05/13/israel-palestinian-lives-matter-blm/; Ronit Lentin, "Palestinian Lives Matter: Racialising Israeli Settler-Colonialism," *Journal of Holy Land and Palestine Studies* 19, no. 2 (2020): 133–49.

140 Barghouti, *I Saw Ramallah*, 7.

141 "The opening pages of the first issue of your journal [*La Revue d'études palestiniennes*] contain a manifesto: we are 'a people like any other people'" (Deleuze and Sanbar, "The Indians of Palestine," 199).

142 Adi Ophir, "The Identity of the Victims and the Victims of Identity: A Critique of Zionist Ideology for a Post-Zionist Age," in *Mapping Jewish Identities*, ed. Laurence J. Silberstein (New York: New York University Press, 2000), 174–200.

143 "A subtext of the Holocaust uniqueness claim is that the Holocaust is uniquely evil. However terrible, the suffering of others simply does not compare" (Norman G. Finkelstein, *The Holocaust Industry Reflections on the Exploitation of Jewish Suffering* [New York: Verso, 2003], 47). The reception of the Shoah points up the fault lines brought to light by the decolonial turn. What is at stake here is the West's investment in the human as white, with the non-European racialized as subhuman. This decolonial sensibility and outrage is visible in Aimé Césaire's pointed observation about Hitler's crimes. In

Discourse on Colonialism, Césaire can now be seen as presenting a decolonial supplement to the subject of modernity, the white, Christian, humanist, bourgeois European: "What he cannot forgive Hitler for is not the *crime* in itself, *the crime against man*, it is not *the humiliation of man as such*, it is the crime against the white man, the humiliation of the white man, and the fact that he applied to Europe colonialist procedures which until then had been reserved exclusively for the Arabs of Algeria, the coolies of India, and the blacks of Africa" (Césaire, *Discourse on Colonialism*, 36). Colonialism and chattel slavery are evoked together to counterbalance the prevailing ethico-political weight of the Shoah in the European imaginary, masterfully exploited by the Israeli government and its supporters. Here Césaire affirms a virtual solidarity among the unrecognized and marginalized, the enslaved and colonized of Western modernity: the excluded (the Indigenous, indentured laborers, and slaves), those racialized bodies deemed unworthy of being mourned.

144 Deleuze and Sanbar, "The Indians of Palestine," 198.
145 Here the category of "people" must also undergo metaphysical scrutiny. As with the grammar of humanity/humanism, we need to ask, Is what makes a people matter not premised on anti-Blackness? The claim to unexceptional status—a "people like any other people"—may thus still be implicated in the circulation of anti-Blackness.
146 The universality of the Palestinian cause derives from their plight being intertwined with those of other Indigenous peoples. Palestinian activists stand in support of Idle No More, an Indigenous grassroots movement in Canada that has touched Indigenous communities across the world, including North African Tuaregs and New Zealand Maoris. Idle No More also displayed their support for Palestinians, stating: "Idle No More stands in solidarity with Palestinian people against ongoing Israeli attacks and enforced settler colonialism. The actions of the Israeli government is genocide against Palestinian people. Idle No More calls upon the Canadian and US governments, along with the United Nations to Boycott, Divest and Sanction the Israeli government for international crimes against humanity. The silence of the Canadian government on these events is complicity with genocide" ("Idle No More Stands in Solidarity with Palestinian People," *Idle No More*. https://idlenomore.ca/idle-no-more-stands-in-solidarity-with-palestinian-people/).
147 Barghouti, *I Saw Ramallah*, 29.
148 Barghouti, *I Saw Ramallah*, 29–30.
149 Chemi Shalev, "Full Transcript of Interview With Palestinian Professor Rashid Khalidi," *Haaretz*, December 5, 2011. https://www.haaretz.com/1.5216535.

Chapter 3

1 Jasbir Puar, "Speaking of Palestine: Solidarity and Its Censors," *Jadaliyya*, March 16, 2016. https://www.jadaliyya.com/Details/33095/Speaking-of-Palestine-Solidarity-and-Its-Censors.
2 Said, *Oslo to Iraq and the Road Map* (New York: Vintage, 2004), 292; Said, *The Politics of Dispossession: The Struggle for Palestinian Self-Determination 1969–1994* (New York: Vintage, 1994), 419.
3 Said, *Reflections on Exile*, 178.
4 As Glen Coulthard notes, "in settler-colonial contexts such as Canada . . . state-sanctioned approaches to reconciliation tend to ideologically fabricate such a transition by narrowly situating the abuses of settler colonization firmly *in the past*" (Coulthard, *Red Skin*, 22).
5 Said, *Culture and Imperialism*, 18.
6 Jean Améry, *At the Mind's Limits: Contemplations by a Survivor on Auschwitz and Its Realities*, trans. Sidney Rosenfeld and Stella P. Rosenfeld (Bloomington: Indiana University Press, 1980), 72.
7 It should be noted that Améry himself didn't extend this right to *ressentiment* to Palestinians, let alone entertain solidarity with them. Quite the contrary, he took a staunchly Zionist stance. In 1978, Améry writes: "The only connection between me and most Jews the world over is a sense of solidarity with the state of Israel, a commitment that has long since ceased to be a duty of which I need to remind myself. Not that I would want to live there. The country is too hot, too loud, in every respect too alien. Nor do I approve of everything that is done there. I abhor the theocratic tendencies, the religiously inflected nationalism. I have only visited the country once for a short period of time and may never return. Yet even though I do not speak their language and could never adopt their way of life, I am inextricably connected to the people who inhabit this unholy spot and who have been abandoned by the rest of the world. For me, Israel is not an auspicious promise, not a biblically legitimized territorial claim, no Holy Land. It is simply the place where survivors have gathered, a state in which every inhabitant still, and for a long time to come, must fear for his life. My solidarity with Israel is a means of staying loyal to those of my comrades who perished" (Améry, "My Jewishness," in *Essays on Antisemitism, Anti-Zionism, and the Left*, ed. Marlene Gallner [Bloomington: Indiana University Press, 2022], 85). Though nobody would accuse Améry of romanticizing Israel, he does demonstrate a lack of sensitivity to the plight of the dispossessed Palestinians, failing to see Zionism/Israel as a settler-colonial project installing a genocidal horizon for the Indigenous population. Palestinians are erased in this view of Israel as a state in which "every inhabitant" is a Jewish survivor who has "simply" gathered

there with other survivors. Though Améry does on occasion acknowledge the legitimacy of Palestinian resistance to a powerful occupying presence, he neutralizes his concession by adding that "Israelis too are engaged in a struggle for national liberation and that this struggle is inordinately more dangerous and inordinately more tragic than that of the Palestinian Arabs" (Améry, "The New Left's Approach to 'Zionism,'" in *Essays on Antisemitism, Anti-Zionism, and the Left*, ed. Marlene Gallner [Bloomington: Indiana University Press, 2022], 44). What matters above else for Améry is the lives of Jews, and these lives can only be secured by Israel, which we are told "was created with just as much legitimacy under international law as any other" (Améry, "The New Left," 43). Améry's unconditional defense of Israel at once effaces and normalizes the ongoing Nakba; it is as if the Palestinians were now being asked to forgive and forget the atrocities of the Zionist settlers, the very form of coerced amnesia that provoked Améry's active form of *ressentiment* in the first place. See also Améry, "Virtuous Antisemitism: Address on the Occasion of Jewish-Christian Brotherhood Week," in *Essays on Antisemitism, Anti-Zionism, and the Left*, ed. Marlene Gallner (Bloomington: Indiana University Press, 2022), 58–73.

8 Mignolo, "Foreword: On Pluriversality and Multipolarity," in *Constructing the Pluriverse: The Geopolitics of Knowledge*, ed. Bernd Reiter (Durham: Duke University Press, 2018), xiv.

9 Coulthard, *Red Skin*, 110.

10 Puar, "Speaking of Palestine."

11 In 2015, the Palestinian Authority raised, at the United Nations, this accusation of illegal organ harvesting. It was met by a similar denial/counter-accusation from Danny Danon, then Israel's U.N. Ambassador: "This blood libel by the Palestinian representative exposes his anti-Semitic motives and his true colors" (Louis Charbonneau, "Israel Blasts Palestinians After Accusations Of Organ-Harvesting," *Reuters*, November 4, 2015. https://www.reuters.com/article/us-israel-palestinians-un/israel-blasts-palestinians-after-accusations-of-organ-harvesting-idUSKCN0ST32420151104). The charge of blood libel is repeatedly leveled to silence Israel's critics. For instance, after the *New York Times* (a journal that can hardly be considered anti-Israeli in its coverage of the Occupation) published, under the title "They Were Only Children" (on May 28, 2021), the pictures and names of the sixty-six Palestinian children who were killed in Israel's recent bombings of Gaza, Abraham Foxman, former Anti-Defamation League head, accused the NYT of printing a "blood libel" on its front page.

12 Friedrich Nietzsche, *On the Genealogy of Morals*, trans. Walter Kaufmann (New York: Vintage, 1989), I, 14, 48.

13 Michel de Montaigne, *The Complete Works of Montaigne*, trans. Donald Frame (Stanford: Stanford University Press, 1957), 136.

14. Steve Erickson, "A Breakdown of Communication: Elia Suleiman Talks About *Divine Intervention*," *Indiewire*, January 15, 2003. https://www.indiewire.com/2003/01/a-breakdown-of-communication-elia-suleiman-talks-about-divine-intervention-80022/.
15. Erickson, "A Breakdown of Communication."
16. *Divine Intervention: A Chronicle of Love and Pain* [Yadon Ilaheyya], dir. Elia Suleiman (New York: Avatar Films, 2002).
17. Said, "Preface," in *Dreams of a Nation: On Palestinian Cinema*, ed. Hamid Dabashi (New York: Verso, 2006), 3.
18. Fulvia Carnevale and John Kelsey, "Art of the Possible: Fulvia Carnevale and John Kelsey in Conversation with Jacques Rancière," *Artforum* 45, no. 7 (2007): 263.
19. Carnevale and Kelsey, "Art of the Possible," 259.
20. In another instance of striking at the enemy, E.S., semi-consciously, tosses an apricot pit out of his car, which magically blows up an Israeli tank. This scene visualizes a Palestinian imaginary uncompliant with Zionist ideology, refusing its colonization, gesturing to what is in E.S. more than E.S., to a deep-seated *ressentiment*: an undeniable yearning for the destruction of the occupier.
21. Robert Stam, *World Literature, Transnational Cinema, and Global Media: Towards a Transartistic Commons* (New York: Routledge, 2019), 165.
22. John Menick, "The Occupied Imagination of Elia Suleiman," *John Menick Blog*, June 2003. https://www.johnmenick.com/writing/the-occupied-imagination-of-elia-suleiman.html.
23. Gil Z. Hochberg raises an important point about whose fantasy the spectator is actually witnessing: "While one could certainly claim that it expresses a Palestinian collective fantasy of revenge, one could just as convincingly argue that it represents an Israeli, or broader Western, projected fantasy of Palestinian violence" (Gil Z. Hochberg, *Visual Occupations: Violence and Visibility in a Conflict Zone* [Durham: Duke University Press, 2015], 72). Suleiman may well be staging Palestinian violence as an object of parody, visualizing what Israel's fears the most, a giant-killer, a reversal of the David versus Goliath narrative, where Israel/David becomes the bullish occupier and the Palestinians/Goliath fighting the righteous cause against all odds, robbing Jews of their eternal underdog status.
24. Dennis Grunes, "Divine Intervention (Elia Suleiman, 2001)," February 15, 2007. https://grunes.wordpress.com/2007/02/15/divine-intervention-elia-sulieman-2001/.
25. Grunes, "Divine Intervention."
26. In contrast to the liberal stance on the question of Palestinian non/violence, Marc Lamont Hill adopts a far more nuanced position: "We must prioritize peace, but we must not romanticize or fetishize it. We must advocate and promote nonviolence at every opportunity, but we cannot endorse a narrow politics of respectability that

shames Palestinians for resisting, for refusing to do nothing in the face of state violence and ethnic cleansing" (Eli Day, "Marc Lamont Hill Has Secured His Place in the Proud Black Anti-Colonial Tradition," *In These Times*, December 11, 2018. https://inthesetimes.com/article/marc-lamont-hill-cnn-palestine-israel-apartheid-jim-crow-black-radical.

27 Grunes, "Divine Intervention."
28 Fanon, *The Wretched of the Earth*, 51.
29 Grunes, "Divine Intervention."
30 Grunes, "Divine Intervention."
31 Somdeep Sen, *Decolonizing Palestine: Hamas between The Anticolonial and the Postcolonial* (Ithaca: Cornell University Press, 2020), 32.
32 Žižek, "Anti-Semitism and Its Transformations," in *Deconstructing Zionism: A Critique of Political Metaphysics*, ed. Gianni Vattimo and Michael Marder (New York: Bloomsbury, 2013), 11.
33 "My response to racism is anger. I have lived with that anger, on that anger, beneath that anger, on top of that anger, ignoring that anger, feeding upon that anger, learning to use that anger before it laid my visions to waste, for most of my life. Once I did it in silence, afraid of the weight of that anger. My fear of that anger taught me nothing. Your fear of that anger will teach you nothing, also" (Audre Lorde, "The Uses of Anger: Women Responding to Racism," in *Sister Outsider: Essays and Speeches* [Freedom: Crossing Press, 1984], 124).
34 Spivak, *An Aesthetic Education in the Era of Globalization*, 154.
35 Žižek, *Violence*, 60.
36 Immanuel Kant, "An Answer to the Question: What Is Enlightenment?" in *What Is Enlightenment? Eighteenth-Century Answers and Twentieth-Century Questions*, ed. James Schmidt (Berkeley: University of California Press, 1996), 60.
37 Žižek, *Violence*, 143.
38 Žižek, *Violence*, 143.
39 "The native, formerly battered and dehumanized, jealous, resentful and angry, simply wanted to take the place of the colonizer" (Nigel Gibson, *Fanon: The Postcolonial Imagination* [Cambridge: Polity, 2003], 13).
40 Fanon, *Black Skin*, 160. See also Gibson, *Fanon*, 6–7.
41 Fanon, *Black Skin*, 197, translation modified.
42 Améry, *At the Mind's Limits*, 70. Drawing on Améry, Žižek also rehabilitates *ressentiment*, decoupling it from the reactive and vindictive morality of the weak, by introducing the paradoxical notion of "authentic resentment" (Žižek, *Violence*, 190). In its authentic form, *ressentiment* no longer signifies spiritual sickness but points to an active ethico-political resistance. *True ressentiment*—or what Žižek now dubs "a Nietzschean heroic resentment" (Žižek, *Violence*, 190)—is not after ideological resolution but the inconvenient exposures of persistent antagonisms.

43 Améry himself was an engaged reader of Fanon's work, especially his reflections on France's practice of torture during the war in Algeria. See Victoria Fareld, "Entangled Memories of Violence: Jean Améry and Frantz Fanon," *Memory Studies* 14, no. 1 (2021): 58–67.
44 Said, *Culture and Imperialism*, 228–9.
45 Said, *Culture and Imperialism*, 228. The private use of *ressentiment* is also at work in international media coverage of war zones. For instance, in the context of the Kosovo war, it authorizes the designation of the Balkan Other as an "anonymous victim," an "abstract suffering," devoid of any agency. This imposed form of *ressentiment* transforms freedom fighters into abject victims. The West feels compassion for the latter but fears the former. The private use of *ressentiment* functions to stabilize the geopolitical scene, paving the way for the Western solution to war: more tolerance of cultural differences among the factions. This use of *ressentiment* effectively covers over the true social antagonisms (Slavoj Žižek and Christopher Hanlon, "Psychoanalysis and the Post-Political: An Interview with Slavoj Žižek," *New Literary History* 32, no. 1 [2001]: 18).
46 See Wendy Brown, *States of Injury: Power and Freedom in Late Modernity* (Princeton: Princeton University Press, 1995).
47 Fareld, "Entangled Memories," 64.
48 Ilan Kapoor, *Confronting Desire: Psychoanalysis and International Development* (Ithaca: Cornell University Press, 2020), 114.
49 Jadaliyya Reports, "Black, Palestinian Artists and Activists Affirm Solidarity in New Video," *Jadaliyya*, October 14, 2015, https://www.jadaliyya.com/Details/32588/Black,-Palestinian-Artists-and-Activists-Affirm-Solidarity-in-New-Video.
50 Fanon, *The Wretched of the Earth*, 89.
51 "Equaliberty is an all-or-nothing notion" (Étienne Balibar, *Politics and the Other Scene* [New York: Verso, 2002], 165). In his engagement with the notion of *ressentiment*, Žižek more frequently relies on a strictly Nietzschean understanding, critically tying the affect to postmodernity's cult of victimhood: "Postmodern identity politics involves the logic of *ressentiment*, of proclaiming oneself a victim and expecting the dominant social Other to pay for the damage, while *égaliberté* breaks out of the vicious cycle of *ressentiment*" (Žižek, "A Leftist Plea for 'Eurocentrism,'" 1006–7). But in our use, the public use of *ressentiment* aligns firmly with the emancipatory value of *égaliberté*.
52 Stefano Harney and Fred Moten, *The Undercommons: Fugitive Planning & Black Study* (New York: Minor Compositions, 2013), 42.
53 A recent vote in Minneapolis is a cautionary reminder of the status quo's resilience. The bill to remove the Minneapolis Police Department from the city charter and to replace it with a "public-health oriented" Department of Public Safety was rejected by voters. Defunding the police is a nice slogan for white liberal American, but

don't let it actually change anything; don't let it contribute to the dismantling of white privilege (Mitch Smith and Tim Arango, "'We Need Policemen': Even in Liberal Cities, Voters Reject Scaled-Back Policing," *The New York Times*, November 3, 2021. https://www.nytimes.com/2021/11/03/us/police-reform-minneapolis-election.html). And if there was any doubt about a backlash to BLM's call to "Defund the Police" in the aftermath of George Floyd's murder, take stock of President Biden's 2022 State of the Union address, in which he confidently asserted that "We should all agree. The answer is not to defund the police. It's to fund the police. Fund them. Fund them. Fund them with resources and training. Resources and training they need to protect their communities" (Jamelle Bouie, "Biden Says 'Fund the Police.' Well, They Aren't Exactly Hurting for Cash," *The New York Times*, March 4, 2022. https://www.nytimes.com/2022/03/04/opinion/the-police-arent-exactly-running-out-of-cash.html). The wager in this political calculation is that acknowledging white fear of crime (a thin veil for negrophobia) garners more votes than insisting on the struggle against anti-Blackness.

54 Mbembe, *Critique of Black Reason*, 6. I discuss this point in greater depth in Chapter 4.
55 Ilan Kapoor and Zahi Zalloua, *Universal Politics* (Oxford: Oxford University Press, 2021), 137–48.
56 Žižek, "Disputations: Who Are You Calling Anti-Semitic?" *The New Republic*, January 6, 2009. https://newrepublic.com/article/62376/disputations-who-are-you-calling-anti-semitic; see also Zahi Zalloua, *Žižek on Race: Toward an Anti-Racist Politics* (New York: Bloomsbury, 2020), 118.
57 Amy Goodman, "Rashid Khalidi: Israel & UAE Deal to Normalize Relations Is New Chapter in 100-Year War on Palestine," *Democracy Now!*, August 14, 2020. https://www.democracynow.org/2020/8/14/israel_uae_agreement_trump_palestine.
58 Fanon, *The Wretched of the Earth*, 233.
59 Sheehi and Sheehi, *Psychoanalysis Under Occupation*, 157n.70.
60 For Jeffrey Goldberg, it is an error to blame the current standoff between Israelis and Palestinians on the rise of settlements; rather, he astonishingly blames the victims of settler colonialism, the Palestinians, for their religious paranoia and intolerance, "the unwillingness of many Muslim Palestinians to accept the notion that Jews are a people who are indigenous to the land Palestinians believe to be exclusively their own" (Jeffrey Goldberg, "The Paranoid, Supremacist Roots of the Stabbing Intifada," *The Atlantic*, October 16, 2015. https://www.theatlantic.com/international/archive/2015/10/the-roots-of-the-palestinian-uprising-against-israel/410944/). For Goldberg, there is a constant Palestinian paranoia of Jews taking over Muslim religious sites from the early twentieth century to the present. Palestinian pathology is simultaneously decontextualized and depoliticized, elevated to a

transhistorical explanation for the violence. This pathologized Palestinian violence discloses "something profound about the inner psyche of every Palestinian (paranoid, supremacist)," which "has led to disastrous consequences time and time again, [and] yet it remains popular because it allows us to avoid meaningful changes that are costly and complicated" (Noam Sheizaf, "Jerusalem, in Context," *+972 Magazine*, October 19, 2015. https://www.972mag.com/jerusalem-in-context/).

61 Said, *Orientalism*, 72.
62 Said, *Representations of the Intellectual*, 373.
63 Slavoj Žižek, *Pandemic! 2: Chronicles of a Lost Time* (New York: OR Books, 2020), 128.
64 Žižek, *Pandemic! 2*, 128.
65 Žižek, *Enjoy Your Symptom!: Jacques Lacan in Hollywood and Out* (New York: Routledge, 2001), 216.
66 Puar, *The Right to Maim*, 153.
67 Puar, "Speaking of Palestine."
68 Puar, "Speaking of Palestine."
69 Puar, "Speaking of Palestine."
70 Puar, "Speaking of Palestine."
71 Puar, "Speaking of Palestine."
72 Netanyahu tried to demonize the Palestinians by making them worse than Hitler. He recycled a debunked story about how it was a Palestinian, Haj Amin al-Husseini, the Grand Mufti of Jerusalem, who birthed the idea to exterminate the Jews. In this narrative, the "Final Solution" has Palestinian fingerprints all over it. But this was ultimately a failed attempt at controversy. Nazism as the pure and endless well for the spread of anti-Semitism—which provided, and continues to provide, a justification for the existence of Israel—was a narrative too few Israeli Jews and political leaders wanted to alter or qualify. Netanyahu miscalculated in aligning Palestinians with Nazis and thereby diminishing the pure evil of Hitler. See Jodi Rudoren, "Netanyahu Denounced for Saying Palestinian Inspired Holocaust," *The New York Times*, October 21, 2015. https://www.nytimes.com/2015/10/22/world/middleeast/netanyahu-saying-palestinian-mufti-inspired-holocaust-draws-broad-criticism.html.
73 Seyla Benhabib, *Exile, Statelessness and Migration*, 97. Jaqueline Rose provides a far more rewarding psychoanalytic account of Israeli paranoia: "Israel is now the fourth most militarily powerful nation in the world. It is a nuclear power. It is not in danger. The fear that Israel will be destroyed is groundless. But that does not mean that it isn't real. The fear is real and it is understandable. This is the difficult territory: you have to say both things at once. But . . . when the fear becomes an identity that justifies itself by a violence that cannot acknowledge itself as violence, something has gone terribly wrong" (Jacqueline Rose, "Nation as Trauma, Zionism

as Question: Jacqueline Rose Interviewed," *Open Democracy*, August 17, 2005. https://www.opendemocracy.net/en/zionism_2766jsp/). Paranoia is what happens when fear of annihilation becomes an identity, and when Palestinians, as the external/internal enemy, a Nazi in the making, is constitutive of such a paranoid identity.

74 We can observe Israeli paranoia in the mechanical response to any US congressional resistance to unconditional economic aid for Israel's Iron Dome; a principled objection to funding the militarization of an apartheid state is interpreted as an expression of anti-Semitism, as a "license to kill Jews." See Michael Arria, "Bowman Tries to Explain His Iron Dome Vote," *Mondoweiss*, October 7, 2021. https://mondoweiss.net/2021/10/bowman-tries-to-explain-his-iron-dome-vote/.

75 Cary Nelson, *Israel Denial: Anti-Zionism, Anti-Semitism, & the Faculty Campaign Against the Jewish State* (Bloomington: Indiana University Press, 2019), 50–2, 97–8.

76 Nelson, *Israel Denial*, 100. Nelson also maintains that the Palestinian right of return can only be treated metaphorically—as a "symbolic statement"—for the implementation of an actual right of return would put an end to Israel as a Jewish majority state (Nelson, *Israel Denial*, 99).

77 Nelson, *Israel Denial*, 208.

78 Nelson seeks to immunize Israel from any critique from without but if the critique comes from within, it is left unchallenged; Ultra-Orthodox Jews, as conscientious objectors, are not guilty of distorting the facts. There is a clear double standard: when Palestinians find the instrumentalization of their dead ethically repulsive, their reaction is deemed anti-Semitic; but when Ultra-Orthodox Jews find it equally repulsive on strictly religious grounds—since it violates Halakhic (religious) law—this objection is accepted as valid, beyond reproach. Nelson can remain neutral here because, as he sees it, Ultra-Orthodox Jews are objecting to the practice of organ harvesting whereas Palestinians are using the practice to condemn Jewish identity as such. The former are invested in a certain religious image of Jewishness; the latter reject a Jewish identity that seemingly operates with impunity in its mistreatment of the enemy's bodies.

79 Nelson, *Israel Denial*, 209.

80 Nelson, *Israel Denial*, 449n.312. According to Sternberg, "One needs only passing familiarity with Israelis of Hiss's generation to know that they have not read Edward Said and instead use the word to mean 'Oriental Jews,' as the adjoining discussion of funerary ritual makes clear—the context discussed Sephardic customs of putting sand into the eyes of the deceased. Nonetheless, the damage was done: Israel-hating propagandists would now widely claim that Hiss had confirmed the *Aftonbladet* report on the murder of Palestinians for the theft of their organs" (Ernest Sternberg, "Fanatical Anti-Zionism and the Degradation

of the University: What I Have Learned in Buffalo," in *Anti-Zionism on Campus: The University, Free Speech, and BDS*, ed. Doron S. Ben-Atar and Andrew Pessin [Bloomington: Indiana University Press, 2018], 341). Does ignorance of Said's *Orientalism* absolve their racist use of the term "Oriental"? Or does it, on the contrary, disclose to what degree the Israelis of Hiss's generation had thoroughly naturalized their racist views of Palestinians and Arab Jews? Eliding race and settler coloniality enables Sternberg and Nelson to provide a narrow and rather simplistic account of "Oriental."

81 Nancy Scheper-Hughes, "The Body of the Terrorist: Blood Libels, Bio-Piracy, and the Spoils of War at the Israeli Forensic Institute," *Social Research* 78, no. 3 (2011): 858.
82 Scheper-Hughes, "The Body of the Terrorist," 860.
83 Mark Lavie, "Israel Harvested Organs in '90s Without Permission," *Associated Press*, December 20, 2009.
84 Scheper-Hughes, "The Body of the Terrorist," 880.
85 Scheper-Hughes, "The Body of the Terrorist," 869.
86 Scheper-Hughes, "The Body of the Terrorist," 873, emphasis in the original. Nelson conveniently dismisses Kugel (whom he doesn't name) as Hiss's "disgruntled" former employee (213) and does not bother to take up Weiss's testimony. He repeats the point that what Hiss did was not very widespread and that other Western nations do it and legally allow it. Nelson blames Scheper-Hughes for her wild speculations, that is, for indulging in "anti-Semitic conspiracy theorizing" (214), stemming from her self-described "'militant anthropology'" (450n.141). But what Nelson misses in his rebuttal to Scheper-Hughes is her emphasis on the symbolic significance of Israel's use of the bodies of its dead enemy for organs and tissues: "When the bodies of the enemy—Palestinian 'stone throwers,' 'trouble makers,' enemy combatants (all of them classified as 'terrorists')—are subject to tissue and organ theft that includes taking sheets of skin from the back or the back of the legs (even when done 'carefully,' as Hiss explained, 'not like skinning a rabbit') in order to supply the national skin bank at Hadassah Hospital, we can speak of crimes against humanity" (Scheper-Hughes, "The Body of the Terrorist," 881).
87 Noura Erakat, "Whiteness as Property in Israel: Revival, Rehabilitation, and Removal," *Harvard Journal of Racial and Ethnic Justice* 31 (2015): 99.
88 Ella Shohat, *Taboo Memories, Diasporic Voices: Columbus, Palestine, and Arab-Jews* (Durham: Duke University Press, 2006), 217.
89 Jamil Khader, "The Living Dead in Palestine and the Failure."
90 Lacan, *The Ethics of Psychoanalysis, 1959–1960, The Seminar of Jacques Lacan, Book VII*, ed. Jacques-Alain Miller, trans. Dennis Porter (New York: Norton, 1992), 320.
91 Puar, "Speaking of Palestine."

92 Scheper-Hughes, "The Body of the Terrorist," 854.
93 Nelson, *Israel Denial*, 214.
94 We can observe in a similar displacement of Palestinian victimization when the charge of Israeli apartheid is deflected by talks of anti-Semitism. The anchor of *Face the Nation*, John Dickerson, recently asked Senator Sanders about the anti-Semitic consequences of a critical discourse on Israel:

> JOHN DICKERSON: There are a number of liberals who use the word apartheid to describe Israel's treatment of the Palestinians, a number of them liberals in the House who use that language. The executive director of the American Jewish Congress, who handled Jewish outreach for your campaign, has said that that word, Joel Rubin, has said that using that word has increased the level of vitriol that has contributed to this anti-Semitism. Do you think those who—who share your view should not use that kind of language?
>
> SEN. SANDERS: Well, I think we should tone down the rhetoric. I think our goal is very simple. It is to understand that what's going on in Gaza today is unsustainable when you have 70% of the young people unemployed, when people cannot leave the community, when hospitals and wastewater plants have been destroyed. That is unsustainable. And the job of the United States is to bring people together. And that is what we have got to try to do. ("Transcript: Senator Bernie Sanders on 'Face the Nation,'" May 23, 2021. https://www.cbsnews.com/news/transcript-senator-bernie-sanders-face-the-nation-05-23-2021/.)

Sanders's answer disappoints. To be sure, the question was ideologically loaded. The connection between the word "apartheid" and "anti-Semitism," once made, makes it difficult to sustain a critical focus on Israel's brutal occupation of Palestinians. To Dickerson's question, Sanders should have decoupled the two terms. A dual critique is required. Support for the Palestinian cause is never attained via anti-Semitism. Moreover, to blame all Jews is to perpetuate the myth that Israel stands for all Jews. A just response to the Palestinian question cannot be premised on an unjust response to the Jewish question. Palestinian paranoia, though, is only fueled when any mention of apartheid in relation to Israel is quickly associated in mainstream media with anti-Semitism; critics (including activists, artists, academics, and journalists) are told that discussing Israeli apartheid fosters anti-Semitism, and that therefore critics should be reasonable and "tone down the rhetoric": *if you really care about reducing anti-Semitism, then don't accuse Israel of being an apartheid regime.* Palestinian paranoia insists on telling things like they are, declining the liberal framework of toothless critique: *Yes, we're with you, but tone down the rhetoric.* This implicit blackmail—either you stand with Israel or you are an anti-Semite—must be flatly rejected.

95 See Edward W. Said and Christopher Hitchens, ed. *Blaming the Victims: Spurious Scholarship and the Palestinian Question* (New York: Verso, 1988).
96 Puar, "Speaking of Palestine."
97 Nelson, *Israel Denial*, 210.
98 On the protocols governing the disposal of the dead, internal humanitarian law is clear: "IHL Rule 115. Disposal of the Dead—The dead must be disposed of in a respectful manner and their graves respected and properly maintained" (qtd. in Chris Moore-Backman, "Why Did Israel Withhold Bodies of Slain Palestinians, Denying the Right to Mourn?" *Truthout*, January 5, 2016. https://truthout.org/articles/why-did-israel-withhold-bodies-of-slain-palestinians-denying-the-right-to-mourn/).
99 Moore-Backman, "Why Did Israel Withhold Bodies." Puar cites Moore-Backman's article, so Nelson would have been familiar with Moore-Backman's analysis, if he bothered to read her attentively.
100 Adalah, "Israeli Cabinet Declares: We Won't Return Bodies of Palestinians to their families for Burial," September 2, 2020. https://www.adalah.org/en/content/view/10109.
101 Goodman, "Angela Davis & Noura Erakat on Palestinian Solidarity, Gaza & Israel's Killing of Ahmad Erekat."
102 Richard Falk, "The Goldstone Report and the Battle for Legitimacy," *The Electronic Intifada*, September 22, 2009. https://electronicintifada.net/content/goldstone-report-and-battle-legitimacy/8456. See also Ali Abunimah, *The Battle for Justice in Palestine* (Chicago: Haymarket Books, 2014). In the West, the figure of the Israeli Jew as colonizer and dispossessor of Palestinian land doesn't have much circulation outside leftist and anti-colonial circles (where BDS is making great headway). The image of the Israeli Jewish state as a beacon of democracy still dominates Western mainstream media. A similar split is visible among the Democratic party in the US Whereas establishment leaders from Clintonites to Biden systematically shield Israel from any international scrutiny of its war crimes and atrocities, politicians supported, and spurred, by grassroot activists (Rashida Tlaib, Ilhan Omar, Alexandria Ocasio-Cortez, Cori Bush, and Bernie Sanders, among a growing list) are starting to take up the Palestinian cause and call out Israel's state-sanctioned violence and abusive practices (although the commitment to the cause varies considerably, from acknowledging Israeli racist policies to denouncing Israel as an apartheid regime and settler-colonial state). See Ryan Grim, "As Israel Attacked Gaza, It Heard Something New: Opposition from Congress," *The Intercept*, May 13, 2021. https://theintercept.com/2021/05/14/israel-palestine-congress-criticism-democrats/?utm_medium=email&utm_source=The%20Intercept%20Newsletter.
103 Benhabib should be making a plea on behalf of the weak, a plea for understanding Palestinian paranoia, urging those in power to start taking responsibility for the colonial situation, to start the laborious work of decolonizing Israel.

104 Nelson, *Israel Denial*, 210.
105 Said, "An Ideology of Difference," 43.
106 Qtd. in Jacqueline Rose, "Apocalypse/Emnity/Dialogue: Negotiating the Depths," in *The Arab and Jewish Questions Geographies of Engagement in Palestine and Beyond*, ed. Bashir Bashir and Leila Farsakh (New York: Columbia University Press, 2020), 202.
107 Hartman and Wilderson, "The Position of the Unthought," 196.
108 Calvin L. Warren, *Ontological Terror: Blackness, Nihilism, and Emancipation* (Durham: Duke University Press, 2018), 130.
109 Žižek, "The Subject Supposed to Loot and Rape Reality and Fantasy in New Orleans."
110 Judith Butler, "Endangered/Endangering: Schematic Racism and White Paranoia," *Reading Rodney King/Reading Urban Uprising*, ed. Robert Gooding-Williams (New York: Routledge, 1993), 20.
111 Fanon, *Black Skin*, 165.
112 Fanon, *The Wretched of the Earth*, 182.
113 Ignorance of Palestinian suffering is not the absence of knowledge (a failure to be educated on the subject, which, for instance, a teach-in on the brutality of the Occupation could readily fix) but reflects a different form of knowledge; this alternative mode of cognition "assumes the positive form of a special insider-knowledge, of an insight into what most of the people don't see" (Žižek, *Pandemic! 2*, 142). This is especially the case in academia where the Palestinian question has received a boost from the BDS campaign. Those who are ignorant of Palestinian suffering, deny or minimize its seriousness and relevance, "know" something more important, more fundamental: the rhetoric about Palestinian suffering is an ideological smokescreen, a plot to harm Jews. For them, it masks a secret anti-Semitic narrative aimed at brainwashing college students, controlling their minds for the purpose of delegitimizing and destroying the state of Israel. When people talk about Palestinian suffering they are really talking about the Jewish problem, using Palestine as a pretext for spewing their *Judeophobia*. These are the "pseudo-facts invisible to others" (Žižek, *Pandemic! 2*, 143). For those who possess this "excess knowledge" (Žižek, *Pandemic! 2*, 142), the rhetoric surrounding Palestinian suffering is part of a general pattern, contributing to the "new" face anti-Semitism, which we are told, finds its home among the global Left, the warriors of social justice.
114 As Palestinian-American Congresswoman Rashida Tlaib reminds us in a pointed tweet on May 10, 2021: "The Nakba never ended. From Jaffa in 1948 to Sheikh Jarrah, Jerusalem today, we must recognize the forced displacement and violent dispossession faced by Palestinians for over 70 years."
115 The Shoah can also condition the opposite response of compassion for the suffering of Palestinians and shame at the actions the Israeli state carries out in the name of Jews. As a response to *Operation Protective Edge*, the 2014 Gaza war, hundreds of Holocaust survivors and descendants of survivors denounced, in an ad in the *New*

York Times, "the massacre of Palestinians in Gaza and the ongoing occupation and colonization of historic Palestine." They make their objections to the Israeli status quo crystal clear: "We are alarmed by the extreme, racist dehumanization of Palestinians in Israeli society, which has reached a fever-pitch" (Matthew Kassel, "NY Times Runs Ad from Holocaust Survivors Condemning Israel, Attacking Elie Wiesel," *Observer*, August 25, 2014. https://observer.com/2014/08/ny-times-runs-ad-from-holocaust-survivors-condemning-israel-attacking-elie-wiesel/). Žižek praises the courage of the Jewish dissidents but limits his focus to the Occupation as a source of shame: "Hopefully today, more Israelis will gather the courage to feel shame apropos the politics enacted by leaders . . . for what Israel's policies in the West Bank are doing to the most precious legacy of Judaism itself" (Žižek, *Heaven in Disorder* [New York: OR Books, 2021], 190–1). However, it is important to note that the letter also names the racialization of Palestinian Israelis as a grave concern. It is the treatment of the Palestinian neighbor that is at stake, inside and outside the Green Line. In other words, shame is not simply an ethico-political response to '67 (the Occupation as an embarrassment to a democracy); rather, it touches the very idea of a Jewish state premised on Zionist supremacy.

116 Fanon, *Black Skin*, xiv. Disalienation also begins with "refusing to consider [the colonized's] reality as definitive" (Fanon, *Black Skin*, 201). The material life of Palestinians is not destiny—whence the possibility of revolutionary politics.
117 Fanon, *Black Skin*, xiv.
118 Fanon, *The Wretched of the Earth*, 233.
119 Sheehi and Sheehi, *Psychoanalysis Under Occupation*, 96.
120 Fanon, *The Wretched of the Earth*, 182–3.
121 I follow Gavin Arnall here in stressing the importance of the "but also" logic in contrast to those of "either . . . or" and "both . . . and" (Gavin Arnall, *Subterranean Fanon: An Underground Theory of Radical Change* [New York: Columbia University Press, 2020], 32). The former speaks to the "relationship of disjuncture" dear to the Martinican philosopher, illustrated in Moten's comment on Fanon's aim: "to critique but also to destroy and disintegrate the ground on which the settler stands, the standpoint from which the violence of colonialism and racism emanates" (Fred Moten and Stefano Harney, *The Undercommons: Fugitive Planning & Black Study* [New York: Minor Compositions, 2013], 132; qtd. in Arnall, *Subterranean Fanon*, 32).

Chapter 4

1 Noura Erakat, *Justice for Some: Law and the Question of Palestine* (Stanford: Stanford University Press, 2019), 236.

2 "Palestinian Center for Policy and Survey Research," *The Palestinian Center for Policy and Survey Research*, June 15, 2021. https://www.pcpsr.org/sites/default/files/Poll%2080%20English%20press%20release%20June2021.pdf.
3 Bashir Bashir and Rachel Busbridge, "The Politics of Decolonisation and Bi-Nationalism in Israel/Palestine," *Political Studies* 67, no. 2 (2019): 389.
4 "During the protests that erupted in Chile in October 2019, there was graffiti on a wall which read, '*Another end of the world is possible*'. This should be our answer to an establishment obsessed by apocalyptic scenarios. Yes, your old world is coming to an end, but the options envisaged by you are not the only ones: another end of the world is possible" (Žižek, "Covid Crisis Sparked Fear of Communism & China's Rise As Superpower. But Best Way To Prevent Communism is to FOLLOW China," *RT*, October 7, 2020. https://www.rt.com/op-ed/502825-china-communism-covid-follow/.
5 *Oslo*, screenplay by J. T. Rogers, dir. Bartlett Sher (HBO, 2021).
6 *Oslo*.
7 *Oslo*.
8 Tuck and Yang, "Decolonization Is Not a Metaphor," 19.
9 *Oslo*.
10 *Oslo*.
11 *Oslo*.
12 *Oslo*.
13 Joseph Fahim, "Why the Movie Oslo is a Missed Opportunity For Hollywood," *Middle East Eye*, June 10, 2021. https://www.middleeasteye.net/discover/oslo-hbo-review-film-neutrality-catch.
14 Hilde Henriksen Waage, "Norway's Role in the Middle East Peace Talks: Between a Strong State and a Weak Belligerent," *Journal of Palestine Studies* 34, no. 4 (2005): 10.
15 *Oslo*.
16 *Oslo*.
17 Mohammed Haddad, "Mapping Israeli occupation," *Al Jazeera*, May 18, 2021. https://www.aljazeera.com/news/2021/5/18/mapping-israeli-occupation-gaza-palestine.
18 Said, *Oslo to Iraq and the Road Map*, 10.
19 *Oslo*.
20 The Second Intifada also marks the "neo-Zionist" backlash in Israel. Against the post-Zionist movement and the promises to decolonize Israel, neo-Zionism circulated the narrative that Israelis tried peace (the Oslo Accords) and they got the Second Intifada (Palestinian violence) (Ilan Pappé, *The Idea of Israel: A History of Power and Knowledge* [New York: Verso, 2014], 8).
21 *Oslo*.

22 Jeff Halper, *Decolonizing Israel, Liberating Palestine: Zionism, Settler Colonialism, and the Case for One Democratic State* (London: Pluto Press, 2021), 6.
23 Erakat, "Rethinking Israel-Palestine."
24 Joseph Massad, "'The 'Deal of the Century': The Final Stage of the Oslo Accords," *Al Jazeera*, November 6, 2018. https://studies.aljazeera.net/en/reports/2018/11/181106114236864.html.
25 The charge of treason leveled against Palestinian Israelis is, of course, not new; it was widely circulated in Israeli media and the parliament during the Second Intifada (Warschawski, *Toward an Open Tomb*, 58).
26 Lana Tatour, "This Isn't a Civil War, It is Settler-Colonial Brutality," *Mondoweiss*, May 13, 2021. https://mondoweiss.net/2021/05/this-isnt-a-civil-war-it-is-settler-colonial-brutality/.
27 Žižek, "Are We in a War? Do We Have an Enemy?" *London Review of Books* 24, no. 10 (May 23, 2002). https://www.lrb.co.uk/the-paper/v24/n10/slavoj-zizek/are-we-in-a-war-do-we-have-an-enemy.
28 See also Ali Harb, "Jerusalem: Biden Administration's 'Bothsidesism' Angers Palestinians," *Middle East Eye*, May 9, 2021. https://www.middleeasteye.net/news/jerusalem-biden-administration-both-sides-palestinians-israel; Branko Marcetic, "On Palestine, the Media Is Allergic to the Truth," *Jacobin*, May 12, 2021. https://www.jacobinmag.com/2021/05/media-press-palestine-israel-gaza-violence-hamas?mc_cid=cfe48687a5&mc_eid=0317ccf9ee.
29 Butler, "Zoom Webinar: Said's Palestine," moderated by Judith Butler. *University of California Humanities Research Institute*, June 1, 2021. https://uchri.org/events/saids-palestine/.
30 Deirdre Shesgreen, "Amid Warnings Of a 'Full Scale war,' Biden Administration Dispatches Envoy to Middle East," *USA Today*, May 12, 2021. https://www.usatoday.com/story/news/politics/2021/05/12/israel-palestine-full-scale-war-feared-us-without-ambassador/5053344001/.
31 The right to self-defense, for example, is readily and rightly afforded to Ukrainians in their active resistance against Russian forces, who are invading and occupying their territory. But Palestinians are repeatedly denied that right by the same Western powers that support Ukraine's righteous defense. In its drive to dispossess and subjugate its Palestinian neighbor, Israel behaves like Russia all the time, but Western powers, led by the United States government, shield the Israeli state from any political and legal accountability. Western states do not consider Palestinians freedom fighters engaged in a heart-wrenching struggle against a much stronger settler-colonial state. Whereas Russian aggression is, again rightly, met with global calls for boycotts, divestment and sanctions, the same spirit captured by the BDS movement is systematically discredited, demonized, and criminalized. The *reason* for Palestinian resistance is almost always read through

the lens of suspicion, perceived as sinister, mendaciously tied to their anti-Semitism. Let's call this by its right name. More than mere hypocrisy, this double standard hides a racist vision of the Palestinian/non-European. The "best" that the West can offer Palestinians is humanitarian aid, which is, of course, premised on their permanent abjection and self-inflicted victimization. See Yousef Munayyer, "On Watching Ukraine Through Palestinian Eyes," *The Nation*, March 3, 2022. https://www.thenation.com/article/world/ukraine-palestine-occupation/; Chris McGreal, "US Accused of Hypocrisy for Supporting Sanctions Against Russia but Not Israel," *The Guardian*, March 7, 2022. https://www.theguardian.com/world/2022/mar/07/us-sanctions-against-russia-but-not-israel; Žižek, "L'Ukraine et la Troisième Guerre mondiale," *L'Obs*, March 1, 2022. https://www.nouvelobs.com/guerre-en-ukraine/20220301.OBS55119/l-ukraine-et-la-troisieme-guerre-mondiale-par-slavoj-zizek.html.

32 Erakat, *Justice for Some*, 160.
33 As Haidar Eid observes, "the two-state solution is a racist solution that calls for a 'pure Jewish state,' and a 'pure Palestinian state,' both of which would be based on ethno-religious identities" (Haidar Eid, "Interview with Dr. Haidar Eid: 'The Palestinian Struggle Is Not About Independence—It Is About Liberation,'" *Mondoweiss*, December 2, 2013. http://mondoweiss.net/2013/12/palestinian-independence-liberation.
34 Žižek, *Less Than Nothing*, 996.
35 Balibar, "A Complex Urgent Universal Political Cause."
36 Fareed Zakaria, *CNN*, May 30, 2021. http://transcripts.cnn.com/TRANSCRIPTS/2105/30/fzgps.01.html.
37 Puar, *The Right to Maim*, 7.
38 See Žižek, *The Courage of Hopelessness*; Giorgio Agamben, "Thought is the Courage of Hopelessness: An Interview with Philosopher Giorgio Agamben," Interview by Jordan Skinner, *Verso Books*, June 17, 2014. https://www.versobooks.com/blogs/1612-thought-is-the-courage-of-hopelessness-an-interview-with-philosopher-giorgio-agamben.
39 *A Space Exodus*, dir. Larissa Sansour (Mec Film, 2009).
40 Stam, *World Literature*, 164.
41 *In the Future They Ate from the Finest Porcelain*, dir. Larissa Sansour and Søren Lind (Mec Film, 2016).
42 *In the Future*.
43 I am drawing on Martinican novelist Patrick Chamoiseau's formulation of "warrior of the imaginary." See Chamoiseau, *Un dimanche au cachot* (Paris: Gallimard, 2007), 182.
44 On the political use of archeology in securing and inventing a link between cultural remains and national identity in Israel, see Nadia Abu El-Haj's magistral

study, *Facts on the Ground: Archaeological Practice and Territorial Self-Fashioning in Israeli Society* (Chicago: University of Chicago Press, 2001).
45 *Nation Estate*, dir. Larissa Sansour, manuscript and co-director Søren Lind (Mec Film, 2012).
46 Eyal Weizman, *Hollow Land: Israel's Architecture of Occupation* (New York: Verso, 2007), 229.
47 Weizman, *Hollow Land*, 131, 105.
48 Weizman, *Hollow Land*, 181.
49 Gil Hochberg, "'Jerusalem, We Have a Problem': Larissa Sansour's Sci-Fi Trilogy and the Impetus of Dystopic Imagination," *Arab Studies Journal* 26, no. 1 (2018): 42.
50 Martin Heidegger, *The Question Concerning Technology and Other Essays*, trans. William Lovett (New York, 1977), 17.
51 Lee Edelman, *No Future: Queer Theory and the Death Drive* (Durham: Duke University Press, 2004), 4.
52 Edelman, *No Future*, 17.
53 Edelman, *No Future*, 3.
54 Edelman, *No Future*, 4.
55 Said, *Reflections on Exile*, 553.
56 Richard Falk, "On 'Lost Causes' and the Future of Palestine," *The Nation*, December 16, 2014. https://www.thenation.com/article/archive/lost-causes-and-future-palestine/.
57 Said, *Reflections on Exile*, 527.
58 Fanon, *Black Skin*, 204.
59 Said, *Reflections on Exile*, 552.
60 Martin Buber, *Letters of Martin Buber: A Life of Dialogue* (Syracuse: Syracuse University Press, 1991), 483.
61 According to Zionist ideology, if Jews reject or disidentify with Israel (as a Jewish majority state), then they have betrayed their people, irresponsibly forgotten about the Holocaust, about the ongoing global anti-Semitism, and thus are, at the very least, complicit in its spread.
62 Said, "The One State Solution," *New York Times Magazine*, January 10, 1999. https://www.nytimes.com/1999/01/10/magazine/the-one-state-solution.html.
63 Ali Mustafa, "'Boycotts Work': An interview with Omar Barghouti," *The Electronic Intifada*, May 31, 2009. https://electronicintifada.net/content/boycotts-work-interview-omar-barghouti/8263. Similarly, Haidar Eid objects to the Zionist-friendly politics of binationalism: "A bi-national state by definition is a state made up of two nations. These two nations are historically entitled to the land. But Jews do not constitute a nation. Israeli Jews constitute a settler-colonialist community, not unlike the whites of South Africa or the French in Algeria. Settler colonists are not entitled to self-determination. However, the indigenous people of Palestine,

Muslims, Christians and Jews, are all entitled to self-determination and they do constitute a nation" (David Letwin and Haidar Eid, "Interview with Dr. Haidar Eid: 'The Palestinian Struggle Is Not About Independence—It Is About Liberation,'" *Mondoweiss*, December 2, 2013. http://mondoweiss.net/2013/12/palestinian-independence-liberation).

64 Omar Barghouti, "Relative Humanity: The Essential Obstacle to a Just Peace in Palestine," *Counterpunch*, December 13–14, 2003. https://web.archive.org/web/20100619212701/http://counterpunch.org/barghouti12132003.html.

65 Moshe Behar, "Competing Marxism, Cessation of (Settler) Colonialism, and the One-State Solution in Israel-Palestine," in *The Arab and Jewish Questions Geographies of Engagement in Palestine and Beyond*, ed. Bashir Bashir and Leila Farsakh (New York: Columbia University Press, 2020), 243.

66 Rifkin, "Indigeneity, Apartheid, Palestine," 56.

67 Rifkin, "Indigeneity, Apartheid, Palestine," 48, 55.

68 Barghouti, "What Comes Next: A Secular Democratic State in Historic Palestine—a Promising Land," *Mondoweiss*, October 21, 2013. https://mondoweiss.net/2013/10/democratic-palestine-promising/.

69 Ali Abunimah, "ICAHD Endorses One-State solution, Warns Against "Warehousing" of Palestinians," *The Electronic Intifada*, September 14, 2012. https://electronicintifada.net/blogs/ali-abunimah/icahd-endorses-one-state-solution-warns-against-warehousing-palestinians.

70 Abunimah, "ICAHD."

71 Barghouti, "What Comes Next."

72 Barghouti, "What Comes Next."

73 Barghouti, "What Comes Next."

74 Barghouti, "What Comes Next."

75 Barghouti, "What Comes Next."

76 Bashir and Busbridge, "The Politics of Decolonisation."

77 Teodora Todorova, *Decolonial Solidarity in Palestine-Israel: Settler Colonialism and Resistance from Within* (New York: Zed Books, 2021), 72.

78 Said, "My Right of Return," in *Power, Politics, and Culture*: Interviews with Edward W. Said, ed. Gauri Viswanathan (New York: Vintage, 2001), 452. Pappé makes a similar point: "People are entitled to invent themselves, as so many national movements have done in their moment of inception. But the problem becomes acute if the genesis narrative leads to political projects such as genocide, ethnic cleansing, and oppression" (Pappé, *Ten Myths*, 21).

79 Said never believed that the antidote to Zionism and its cult of exclusionary sovereignty lies purely in its demystification of Zionism, its disclosure and exposure as a racist ideology. Here we might recall the UN General Assembly Resolution 3379, passed in 1975 at the United World Conference against Racism,

held in Durban, which stated that "Zionism is a form of racism and racial discrimination." This resolution was formally revoked by UN General Assembly in 1991 as the result of a fierce but dubious campaign by Israel and the United States to recast the anti-colonial spirit that birthed the resolution as anti-Semitic (and, to contextualize a bit, Israel had made the revocation of the resolution a precondition for its involvement in the "Madrid Peace Conference"). Omar Barghouti laments with good reason this heavy-handed intervention in safeguarding Israel's well-manicured global image as the untouchable Victim. While the link between Zionism and racism highlighted Israel's settler-colonial roots, its severance did not make the world simply forget about the Palestinian problem; no, it did something worse: it explained it away as a mere border or territorial dispute, normalizing, in turn, Israel's status as *a nation like other nations*. No democracy is perfect, and territorial disputes with neighbors happen and do not typically delegitimize a nation. This form of reasoning gave Western liberals a way out. They could still feel bad about the condition of Palestinians, but they could, at the same time, put their faith in international law and its mechanisms for finding a just resolution. The disastrous Oslo Accords, that followed the inconsequential Madrid Conference, with the promise of "land for peace" further placated liberal sensibilities.

Much of the support for the Palestinian cause has been mobilized around reviving the anti-colonial claim that "Zionism is racism," as a powerful way to mount international pressure on Israel. Throughout this book I've repeatedly evoked the idea of "Zionist supremacy": the belief that Jews—or to be more precise Ashkenazi Jews—are ontologically superior to Arabs, the Indigenous population of historic Palestine. At the same time, I am mindful of Edward Said's counterintuitive resistance to Resolution 3379 "Zionism is Racism." In *The Question of Palestine*, Said writes, "Racism is too vague a term: Zionism is Zionism" (Said, *The Question of Palestine*, 112). Now Said was by no means shy about exposing the racist ethos of Zionism, how Zionism embodied what he called "an ideology of difference," how it calcified differences by abstracting them from their worldliness, from the shifting dynamics of meaning and history, how it elevated Jews and devalued non-Jews (and to a lesser extent Oriental Jews), and, of course, how it both produced and silenced its many victims. But still there was something else going on with Zionism. Said was sensitive to what Jacqueline Rose describes as the "affective dimension" of Zionism (Rose, *The Last Resistance* [New York: Verso, 2007], 197), to the fact that we do the concept—and the Palestinian cause—a disservice if we reduce Zionism to an "insult" (Rose, *The Question of Zion*, 10). Moreover, Said himself didn't want to reify Zionism, to do what he accused some Zionists of doing. Declining to endorse the reasonable charge "Zionism is racism" is, of course, not to uphold "Zionism isn't racism," or worse, "Zionism is liberation"; rather, it suggests, "Zionism is *more* than racism." As we saw in Chapter 1, Zionism operates not only as a racist ideology, which asserts an exclusive sovereignty over historic Palestine, but as a fundamental fantasy that at once reflects and cultivates Israel's libidinal economy. See also Feldman, *A Shadow over Palestine*, 226–7.

80 Said, "My Right of Return," 451.
81 Leila H. Farsakh, "Alternatives to Partition in Palestine: Rearticulating the State-Nation Nexus," in *Rethinking Statehood in Palestine Self-Determination and Decolonization Beyond Partition*, ed. Leila H. Farsakh (Oakland: University of California Press, 2021), 186.
82 Said, "The One State Solution."
83 Said, "Criticism and the Art of Politics," in *Power, Politics, and Culture*: Interviews with Edward W. Said, ed. Gauri Viswanathan (New York: Vintage, 2001), 129.
84 Said, "My Right of Return," 452–3.
85 Erakat, *Justice for Some*, 236.
86 Mbembe, "Thoughts on the Planetary," 126.
87 Aamir R. Mufti, "The Missing Homeland of Edward Said," in *Conflicting Humanities*, ed. Rosi Braidotti and Paul Gilroy (New York: Bloomsbury, 2016), 181.
88 Said, *Freud and the Non-European* (New York: Verso, 2004), 55.
89 Fred Moten, *Stolen Life* (Durham: Duke University Press, 2018), 212; qtd. in Sexton, "The *Vel* of Slavery: Tracking the Figure of the Unsovereign," *Critical Sociology* 42, no. 4–5 (2016): 593.
90 Erakat and Hill, "Black-Palestinian Transnational Solidarity," 14.
91 As Derrida puts it, "the *ipseity* of the *ipse* . . . implies the exercise of power by someone it suffices to designate as *himself, ipse*. The sovereign, in the broadest sense of the term, is he who has the right and the strength to be and be recognized as *himself, the same, properly the same as himself*" (Derrida, *The Beast and the Sovereign, vol. 1*, ed. Michel Lisse, Marie-Louise Mallet, and Ginette Michaud, trans. Geoffrey Bennington [Chicago: University of Chicago Press, 2009], 66).
92 Carl Schmitt, *Political Theology: Four Chapters on the Concept of Sovereignty*, trans. George Schwab (Cambridge, MA: MIT Press, 1985), 7; Schmitt, *The Concept of the Political*, trans. George Schwab (Chicago: University of Chicago Press, 1996), 26.
93 Jacques Derrida and Elisabeth Roudinesco, *For What Tomorrow . . .: A Dialogue*, trans. Jeff Fort (Stanford: Stanford University Press, 2004), 176.
94 Derrida, "Autoimmunity: Real and Symbolic Suicides—A Dialogue with Jacques Derrida," in *Philosophy in a Time of Terror: Dialogues with Jürgen Habermas and Jacques Derrida*, ed. Giovanna Borradori (Chicago: University of Chicago Press, 2004), 191n.14. Derrida defines autoimmunity as a process through which "a living being, in a quasi-*suicidal* fashion, 'itself' works to destroy its own protection, to immunise itself *against* its 'own' immunity" (Derrida, "Autoimmunity," 94). Derrida also submits autoimmunity to a transvaluation of values; it is not an illness

or disability to lament or overcome; rather, it is an ontological condition that involves vulnerability to harm, but that also makes relationality as such possible: "Autoimmunity is not an absolute ill or evil. It enables an exposure to the other, to *what* and to *who* comes—which means that it must remain incalculable. Without autoimmunity, with absolute immunity, nothing would ever happen or arrive; we would no longer wait, await, or expect, no longer expect one another, or expect any event" (Derrida, *Rogues: Two Essays on Reason*, trans. Pascale-Anne Brault and Michael Naas [Stanford: Stanford University Press, 2005], 152). Simply put, the logic of autoimmunity unravels the desire to wall off a self, community, or nation from external forces and influences.

95 Glen Coulthard and Leanne Betasamosake Simpson, "Grounded Normativity / Place-Based Solidarity," *American Quarterly* 68, no. 2 (2016): 254.

96 Erakat, *Justice for Some*, 160.

97 Nehal El-Hadi, "Ensemble: An Interview with Dr. Fred Moten," *Mice Magazine*, Summer 2018. https://micemagazine.ca/issue-four/ensemble-interview-dr-fred-moten.

98 Lacan, *The Four Fundamental Concepts of Psycho-analysis*, trans. Alan Sheridan (New York: Routledge, 2018), 246.

99 Bruce Fink, *The Lacanian Subject: Between Language and Jouissance* (Princeton: Princeton University Press, 1995), 51.

100 Derrida, *The Death Penalty, vol. 1*, trans. Peggy Kamuf (Chicago: University of Chicago Press, 2013), 5.

101 Mufti captures well Said's desire for an alternative form of statehood grounded in the generative experience of the exilic: "Said envisions a state, not of national, but exilic and homeless peoples and attempts to transform the Palestinian attempt to wrest a state from the global system of nation-states into a permanent rebuke to this system itself—an exilic state, as it were, not a nation-state. This is of course a position formulated from and with the experience of those 'outside,' but it also reveals the profoundly dialectical nature of the production of outside and inside" (Mufti, "The Missing Homeland of Edward Said," 181). See also Butler, *Parting Ways*, 110–11.

102 While some might object that this formulation is no different from Barghouti's message to settlers concerning what they can reasonably expect from the Natives in a new decolonized Palestine, the comparison must nonetheless be scrutinized, since Barghouti's notion of justice is grounded on the universal principle of equal rights for all of the land's citizens. Unlike the voice of ideological reason that only seek to reproduce the status quo, to legalize Israel's transgressions of international law, Barghouti—though I disagree with his delimitations about what constitutes a people—lays out a just vision of a polity *à venir* that binationalists ought to embrace.

103 Mbembe, "Necropolitics," 17.

104 Mbembe, "Necropolitics," 40.

105 Afua Cooper and Rinaldo Walcott, "Robin D. G. Kelley and Fred Moten in Conversation," *Critical Ethnic Studies* 4, no. 1 (2018): 160.
106 Cooper and Walcott, "Robin D. G. Kelley," 161.
107 Roberto Esposito, *Bios: Biopolitics and Philosophy*, trans. Timothy Campbell (Minneapolis: University of Minnesota Press, 2008), 39.
108 Fanon, *Black Skin*, 201.
109 Moten, *Stolen Life*, 180. Moten is drawing on Gayatri Spivak's observation that "at the bottom, the first right is the right to refuse" (Steve Paulson, "Critical Intimacy: An Interview with Gayatri Chakravorty Spivak," *Los Angeles Review of Books*, July 29, 2016. https://lareviewofbooks.org/article/critical-intimacy-interview-gayatri-chakravorty-spivak/).
110 Fanon, *The Wretched*, 5.
111 Kapoor and Zalloua, *Universal Politics*, 194.
112 Sarah Ihmoud, "Roundtable on Anti-Blackness and Black-Palestinian Solidarity," *Jadaliyya*, June 3, 2015. https://www.jadaliyya.com/Details/32145/Roundtable-on-Anti-Blackness-and-Black-Palestinian-Solidarity.
113 Jack Halberstam, "The Wild Beyond: With and for the Undercommons," in *The Undercommons: Fugitive Planning & Black Study*, by Fred Moten and Stefano Harney (New York: Minor Compositions, 2013), 8.
114 Fanon, *The Wretched of the Earth*, 236.
115 Audra Simpson, "The Sovereignty of Critique," *The South Atlantic Quarterly* 119, no. 4 (2020): 688. Simpson struggles with using the grammar of sovereignty ("Is sovereignty the right thing, then, for us to think with?"), all too cognizant of its settler origins (how it "is more than merely an ancestor to white, western political ordering confined only to Europe but is a language game that historically been played under conditions of imperial settler coloniality" (Simpson, "The Sovereignty of Critique," 689, 687). She opts to engage with "the two-faced Janus of sovereignty" (Simpson, "The Sovereignty of Critique," 689).
116 Simpson, "The Sovereignty of Critique," 689.
117 Mbembe, "Necropolitics," 27.
118 Sexton, "The *Vel* of Slavery," 593.
119 Sexton, "The *Vel* of Slavery," 593.
120 Sexton, "People-of-Color-Blindness," 48.
121 Sexton, "People-of-Color-Blindness," 56n.75. Sexton draws a key parallel between the insights that a Black critical framework discloses about racial formation with those of feminism and queer theory and their capacity to make sense of "the range of gender and sexual variance under patriarchal and heteronormative regimes" (Sexton, "People-of-Color-Blindnes," 48). Iyko Day questions the legitimacy of this analogy, pointing out that "unlike the way feminist and queer critical theory interrogate heteropatriarchy from a subjectless standpoint, Sexton's

entire point seems to rest on the very specificity and singularity—rather than subjectlessness—of black critical theory's capacity to understand race" (Iyko Day, "Being or Nothingness: Indigeneity, Antiblackness, and Settler Colonial Critique," *Critical Ethnic Studies* 1, no. 2 [2015]: 112). I frame the problem differently. What's problematic is not so much Sexton's failure to adopt a "subjectless" standpoint as *ontologizing* the "concrete universal," the contingent particular as the site of the true nature of racial violence. In this formulation, Blackness is absolutized and exempt from change and displacement. It is substantialized and rendered permanently Other. And most importantly, no other racialized group can become candidates for "concrete universality" or the part of no-part. Their epistemic position can never yield exemplary insights into racial formation.

122 Sexton, "People-of-Color-Blindness," 56n.75. A cross-racial coalition could, for example, take up mass incarceration as a fundamental problem and contest how Black bodies are treated as socially and legally insignificant, "meant to be warehoused and die" (Wilderson, "Gramsci's Black Marx: Whither the Slave in Civil Society?," *Social Identities* 9, no. 2 [2003]: 238).

123 Elsewhere Sexton puts the matter of Black universality in Lacanian terms, underlying Blackness's extimacy to universality, its perpetually interrupted proximity to the universal: "If blackness is . . . about a sort of dehiscent 'everywhere,' then I would add only that this dimension that is '"more" universal than universality,' this excessive or . . . this *extimate* relation to universality is not simply incommensurate—which designation might preserve and protect universality from the threat of blackness. It is also antagonistic, we might even say *protagonistic*, toward universality . . . [A] black universality, the universality of blackness, is one that cannot settle or rest or accept what is universal within it. It is a ceaselessly universalizing universality, attentive to, insistent on, *and* skeptical about every particularity, every local situation through which it is articulated" (Barber, "On Black Negativity, Or The Affirmation Of Nothing").

124 Saidiya Hartman says something similar apropos Mbembe: "That's what's so interesting for me about Achille Mbembe's work, the way he thinks about the position of the formerly colonized subject along the lines of the slave as an essential way of defining the predicament. Essentially, he says, the slave is the object to whom anything can be done, whose life can be squandered with impunity" (Hartman and Wilderson, "The Position of the Unthought," 188).

125 Žižek, *Less Than Nothing*, 83.

126 Žižek, *The Parallax View*, 13.

127 Agon Hamza, "On Love," *The Philosophical Salon*, July 26, 2021. http://thephilosophicalsalon.com/the-r-files-6-a-hamza-on-love/.

128 Žižek, *Heaven in Disorder*, 161.

129 Daphna Thier, "Not an Ally: The Israeli Working Class," in *Palestine: A Socialist Introduction*, ed. Sumaya Awad and Brian Bean (Chicago: Haymarket Books, 2020), 94.

130 Žižek credits Althusser for this insight: "'Class struggle' paradoxically precedes classes as determinate social groups . . . every class position and determination is already an effect of the 'class struggle.' This is why 'class struggle' is another name for the fact that 'society does not exist'—it does not exist as a positive order of being" (Žižek, *Living in the End Times* [New York: Verso, 2011], 198).
131 Mignolo, "'Coloniality is not over, it's all over.' Interview with Dr. Walter Mignolo (Nov. 2014. Part I)," *Transmodernity* (Spring 2016): 176, emphasis added.
132 Žižek, *Heaven in Disorder*, 164.
133 Incidentally, the spread and adoption of anti-BDS legislation in the United States and Canada speaks volumes about the fakeness or ideological character of land acknowledgment: how do you take seriously these states' attempts to reckon with their genocidal and racial past (and present) when they actively support and protect Israel as a settler-colonial state?
134 Jrere, Nafar and Aloni, "We Don't Want What Happened in 1948 to Happen to Us Again."
135 Žižek, "Forward: The Importance of Theory," in *Žižek on Race: Toward an Antiracist Future*, by Zahi Zalloua (New York: Bloomsbury, 2020), xii.
136 Žižek, *Living in the End of Times*, 53.
137 Fanon, *The Wretched of the Earth*, 5, emphasis added.
138 Wilderson exposes the limits of a Gramscian Marxist understanding of antiBlackness as a mere effect of the base rather than constituting the base itself: "Exploitation (wage slavery) is the only category of oppression which concerns Gramsci: society, Western society, thrives on the exploitation of the Gramscian subject. Full stop. Again, this is inadequate, because it would call white supremacy 'racism' and articulate it as a derivative phenomenon of the capitalist matrix, rather than incorporating white supremacy as a matrix constituent to the base, if not the base itself" (Wilderson, "Gramsci's Black Marx," 231).
139 Žižek, "Afterword: Lenin's Choice," in V. I. Lenin, *Revolution at the Gates: Selected Writings of Lenin from 1917*, ed. Slavoj Žižek (New York: Verso, 2002), 271.
140 Wilderson, *Afropessimism*, 217.
141 Wilderson, *Afropessimism*, 217.
142 Wilderson, "The Black Liberation Army," 178.
143 Wilderson, "We're Trying to Destroy the World," 58.
144 Wilderson, "We're Trying to Destroy the World," 58.
145 Wilderson, "We're Trying to Destroy the World," 58.
146 Žižek, *In Defense of Lost Causes*, 289.
147 Žižek, *Demanding the Impossible*, 60.
148 Mbembe, *Critique of Black Reason*, 3.
149 Abunimah, *The Battle for Justice in Palestine*, 78. See also Andy Clarno, *Neoliberal Apartheid: Palestine/Israel and South Africa after 1994* (Chicago: University of Chicago Press, 2017).

150 Toufic Haddad, *Palestine Ltd.: Neoliberalism and Nationalism in the Occupied Territories* (London: I.B. Tauris, 2016).
151 "The Oslo period was the period of the most classically colonial relationship with the natives: favors, a class of go-betweens to manage the occupied population's daily life, and a native police to keep order" (Warschawski, *Toward an Open Tomb*, 74).
152 Ahmad Qabaha and Bilal Hamamra, "The Nakba Continues: The Palestinian Crisis from the Past to the Present," *Janus Unbound* 1, no. 1 (2021): 30.
153 Abunimah, *The Battle for Justice in Palestine*, 78–9.
154 Abunimah, *The Battle for Justice in Palestine*, 71.
155 Žižek, *Living in the End of Times*, 198. As Žižek further argues, "Apart from some tribes in the Amazon jungle who have not yet established contact with modern societies, all communities today are part of global civilization in the sense that their very autonomy itself has to be accounted for in terms of global capitalism" (Žižek, *Like A Thief In Broad Daylight: Power in the Era of Post-Humanity* [New York: Allen Lane, 2018], 139).
156 Mbembe, *Critique of Black Reason*, 6.
157 Žižek, *Demanding the Impossible*, 30.
158 The *less than nothing* belong to global capitalism's "geo-social class"; they are not so much exploited "in what they are doing" (the classic Marxist worker) as exploited "in their very existence, . . . exploited via the material conditions of their life: their access to clean water and air, their health, their safety" (Žižek, "May 1 in the Viral World Is a Holiday for the New Working Class," *RT*, May 1, 2020. https://www.rt.com/op-ed/487517-slavoj-zizek-new-working-class/.) See also Bruno Latour and Nikolaj Schultz, "A Conversation with Bruno Latour and Nikolaj Schultz: Reassembling the Geo-social," *Theory, Culture & Society* 36, no. 7–8 (2019): 215–30.
159 Halper, *Decolonizing Israel*, 165.
160 Sobhi Samour, "Covid-19 and the Necroeconomy of Palestinian Labor in Israel," *Journal of Palestine Studies* 49, no. 4 (2020): 53–64.
161 Fanon, *The Wretched of the Earth*, 2.

Conclusion

1 Sexton, "Roundtable on Anti-Blackness and Black-Palestinian Solidarity," *Jadaliyya*, June 3, 2015. https://www.jadaliyya.com/Details/32145/Roundtable-on-Anti-Blackness-and-Black-Palestinian-Solidarity.
2 Vladimir Ze'ev Jabotinsky, "The Iron Wall," November 4, 1923, emphasis added. https://www.jewishvirtuallibrary.org/quot-the-iron-wall-quot.

3   Fanon, *Black Skin*, 193.
4   Fred Moten, "The New International of Insurgent Feeling," *BDS*, November 16, 2009. https://bdsmovement.net/news/new-international-insurgent-feeling.
5   To be clear, the Palestinian cause does not only appeal to the excluded or globally marginalized. As Said points out, "Remember the solidarity here and everywhere in Latin America, Africa, Europe, Asia and Australia, and remember also that there is a cause to which many people have committed themselves, difficulties and terrible obstacles notwithstanding. Why? Because it is a just cause, a noble ideal, a moral quest for equality and human rights" (Said, *Oslo to Iraq and the Road Map*, 292).
6   Said, *Oslo to Iraq and the Road Map*, 290.
7   Nick Estes, "The Liberation of Palestine Represents an Alternative Path for Native Nations," *The Red Nation*, September 7, 2019. http://therednation.org/the-liberation-of-palestine-represents-an-alternative-path-for-native-nations/.
8   Estes, "The Liberation of Palestine." Palestinians also stood in solidarity with the Standing Rock Sioux in their protest of the Dakota Access Pipeline. As a Palestinian activist put it, "Although we are of different color, religion, culture and place, I have learned, as I read about the protests at Standing Rock, that we have much more in common than differences.... When I read your history, I can see myself and my people reflected in yours. I feel in my core that your fight is my fight, and that I am not alone in the battle against injustice" (Ben Norton, "Palestinians Support Indigenous Dakota Pipeline Protests: 'We stand with Standing Rock,'" *Salon*, November 18, 2016. https://www.salon.com/2016/11/18/palestinians-support-indigenous-nodapl-protests-we-stand-with-standing-rock/).
9   Estes, "The Liberation of Palestine."
10 Estes, "The Liberation of Palestine."
11 Waziyatawin, "Malice Enough," 172.
12 Sexton's formulation of "what is in the struggle *more* than the struggle itself" is modeled after Lacan's "in you more than you" (Lacan, *The Four Fundamental Concepts of Psycho-analysis*, 263–76), which attests to "the ineradicable nature of the subject" (Žižek and Daly, *Conversations with Žižek*, 6), to this "strange body in my interior ... which is radically interior and at the same time already exterior" (Žižek, *The Sublime Object*, 180).
13 Derek Hook, "Death-Bound Subjectivity: Fanon's Zone of Nonbeing and the Lacanian Death Drive," *Subjectivity* 13 (2020): 367.
14 Erakat and Hill, "Black-Palestinian Transnational Solidarity," 12.
15 Moten and Harney, *The Undercommons*, 140–1.
16 Wilderson, "An Afropessimist on the Year."
17 Sexton, "All Black Everything," *e-flux* 79 (2017). https://www.e-flux.com/journal/79/94158/all-black-everything/.
18 Fanon, *Black Skin*, xii.
19 Fanon, *Black Skin*, xiv.

20 Fanon, *Black Skin*, 204.
21 George Ciccariello-Maher, "Jumpstarting the Decolonial Engine: Symbolic Violence from Fanon to Chávez," *Theory & Event* 13, no. 1 (2010).
22 Fanon, *Black Skin*, xiii, emphasis added.
23 Étienne Balibar, *Citizen Subject: Foundations for Philosophical Anthropology*, trans. Steven Miller (New York: Fordham University Press, 2017), 285.
24 Fanon, *Black Skin*, xiv.
25 As Fanon reminds his white existentialist interlocutor: "Sartre forgets that the black man suffers in his body quite differently from the white man" (Fanon, *Black Skin*, 117).
26 SIPRI Fact Sheet, "Trends in International Arms Transfers, 2020," https://www.sipri.org/sites/default/files/2021-03/fs_2103_at_2020_v2.pdf. But as Susan Abulhawa carefully points out, the data about Israel's arms sales is probably a "gross underestimation," since Israel "doesn't actually report its arms deals—many of which occur through covert deals via independent arms hustlers, often retired Israeli military generals" (Susan Abulhawa, "Israel: More Than Apartheid," *The Washington Report on Middle East Affairs* 38, no. 3 [May 2019]. https://www.wrmea.org/2019-may/page-14.html). Israel's arms export is also not free of scandals; indeed, its track record leaves much to be desired. Israel has sold arms to "Chile under Pinochet, South Africa under apartheid, [and] Guatemala during the civil war." This series of shady sales "has given the country's arms sector a reputation for providing weapons without asking questions" (Shir Hever, "Israel Arms Sales: Court Decision Ends Hopes for Transparency," *Middle East Eye*, July 1, 2021. https://www.middleeasteye.net/news/israel-arms-sales-transparency-court-decision-ends-hopes).
27 Haim Bresheeth-Zabner, *An Army Like No Other: How the Israeli Defence Forces Made a Nation* (New York: Verso, 2020), 294.
28 Mbembe, "Necropolitics," 40.
29 Mbembe, "Necropolitics," 40, 27.
30 Derrida, "Autoimmunity," 99.
31 Derrida, *Learning to Live Finally: The Last Interview*, trans. Pascale-Anne Brault and Michael Naas (Hoboken: Melville House, 2007), 39.
32 Mbembe, "Necropolitics," 23.
33 Žižek, "From Politics to Biopolitics . . . and Back," *South Atlantic Quarterly* 103, no. 2–3 (2004): 507.
34 BDS challenges Israel's economic prosperity by jeopardizing both its military-industrial complex and its 3.8 billion security aid from the US administration. If subsidizing Israel's occupation of Palestine halts, and the export of Israeli tested weapons dwindles, the settler government might be forced to decolonize or, at the very least, reassess its brutal policies toward the Palestinian people.

35 David Harvey, *The New Imperialism* (Oxford: Oxford University Press, 2003).
36 Chandni Desai, "Disrupting Settler-Colonial Capitalism: Indigenous Intifadas and Resurgent Solidarity from Turtle Island to Palestine," *Journal of Palestine Studies* 50, no. 2 (2021): 58.
37 Sami Tayeb, "The Palestinian McCity in the Neoliberal Era," *Middle East Report* 290 (2019): 25.
38 Said, *After the Last Sky*, 112.
39 Fanon, *Black Skin*, 201, emphasis added. Fanon also states: "To fight is the only solution. And he will undertake and carry out this struggle not as the results of a Marxist or idealistic analysis but because quite simply he cannot conceive his life otherwise than as a kind of combat against exploitation, poverty, and hunger" (Fanon, *Black Skin*, 199).
40 Jean-Thomas Tremblay, "Being Black and Breathing: On 'Blackpentecostal Breath,'" *Los Angeles Review of Books*, October 19, 2016. https://lareviewofbooks.org/article/being-black-and-breathing-on-blackpentecostal-breath/.

Bibliography

Abulhawa, Susan. "Israel: More Than Apartheid." *The Washington Report on Middle East Affairs* 38, no. 3 (May 2019). https://www.wrmea.org/2019-may/page-14.html.

Abu-Manneh, Bashir. "Who Owns Frantz Fanon's Legacy?" *Catalyst* 5, no. 1 (2021): 11–39.

Abunimah, Ali. "ICAHD Endorses One-State Solution, Warns Against 'Warehousing' of Palestinians." *The Electronic Intifada*, September 14, 2012. https://electronicintifada.net/blogs/ali-abunimah/icahd-endorses-one-state-solution-warns-against-warehousing-palestinians.

Abunimah, Ali. "Israeli Lawmaker's Call for Genocide of Palestinians Gets Thousands of Facebook Likes." *The Electronic Intifada*, July 7, 2014. https://electronicintifada.net/blogs/ali-abunimah/israeli-lawmakers-call-genocide-palestinians-gets-thousands-facebook-likes.

Abunimah, Ali. *The Battle for Justice in Palestine*. Chicago: Haymarket Books, 2014.

Adalah. "Historical Background." https://www.adalah.org/en/content/view/7478.

Adalah. "Israeli Cabinet Declares: We Won't Return Bodies of Palestinians to Their Families for Burial." September 2, 2020. https://www.adalah.org/en/content/view/10109.

Agamben, Giorgio. *Homo Sacer: Sovereign Power and Bare Life*. Translated by Daniel Heller-Roazen. Stanford: Stanford University Press, 1998.

Agamben, Giorgio. *Means without End*. Translated by Vincenzo Binetti and Cesare Casarino. Minneapolis: University of Minnesota Press, 2000.

Agamben, Giorgio. "Thought is the Courage of Hopelessness: An Interview with Philosopher Giorgio Agamben." Interview by Jordan Skinner, *Verso Books*, June 17, 2014. https://www.versobooks.com/blogs/1612-thought-is-the-courage-of-hopelessness-an-interview-with-philosopher-giorgio-agamben.

Agence France-Presse. "Israel Vows to Make Hamas Pay for Alleged Murder of Three Teenagers." *The Guardian*, June 30, 2014. http://www.theguardian.com/world/2014/jul/01/israel-vows-hamas-pay-murder-teenagers.

Alexander, Michelle. "Time to Break the Silence on Palestine." *The New York Times*, January 19, 2019. https://www.nytimes.com/2019/01/19/opinion/sunday/martin-luther-king-palestine-israel.html.

Alfred, Taiaiake. *Peace, Power, Righteousness: An Indigenous Manifesto*. Don Mills: Oxford University Press, 1999.

Alfred, Taiaiake. *Wasáse: Indigenous Pathways of Actions and Freedom*. Peterborough: Broadview Press, 2005.

Al-Haj, Majid. "National Ethos, Multicultural Education, and the New History Textbooks in Israel." *Curriculum Inquiry* 35 (2005): 47–71.

Alsaafin, Linah, Umut Uras, Al Tahhan and Farah Najjar. "Thousands Honour Al Jazeera's Shireen Abu Akleh: Live News." *Al Jazeera*, May 11, 2022. https://www.aljazeera.com/news/2022/5/11/veteran-al-jazeera-journalist-killed-by-israeli-forces-live-news.

Amadahy, Zainab and Bonita Lawrence. "Indigenous Peoples and Black People in Canada: Settlers or Allies?" In *Breaching the Colonial Contract: Anti-Colonialism in the US and Canada*, edited by Arlo Kempf, 105–36. New York: Springer, 2009.

Améry, Jean. *At the Mind's Limits: Contemplations by a Survivor on Auschwitz and Its Realities*. Translated by Sidney Rosenfeld and Stella P. Rosenfeld. Bloomington: Indiana University Press, 1980.

Améry, Jean. "The New Left's Approach to 'Zionism.'" In *Essays on Antisemitism, Anti-Zionism, and the Left*, edited by Marlene Gallner, 41–5. Bloomington: Indiana University Press, 2022.

Améry, Jean. "My Jewishness." In *Essays on Antisemitism, Anti-Zionism, and the Left*, edited by Marlene Gallner, 78–86. Bloomington: Indiana University Press, 2022.

Améry, Jean. "Virtuous Antisemitism: Address on the Occasion of Jewish-Christian Brotherhood Week." In *Essays on Antisemitism, Anti-Zionism, and the Left*, edited by Marlene Gallner, 58–73. Bloomington: Indiana University Press, 2022.

Amnesty International. "Israel's Apartheid Against Palestinians: Cruel System of Domination and Crime Against Humanity." February 1, 2022. https://www.amnesty.org/en/wp-content/uploads/2022/02/MDE1551412022ENGLISH.pdf.

Amnesty International. "Denying COVID-19 Vaccines to Palestinians Exposes Israel's Institutionalized Discrimination." January 6, 2021. https://www.amnesty.org/en/latest/news/2021/01/denying-covid19-vaccines-to-palestinians-exposes-israels-institutionalized-discrimination/.

Appadurai, Arjun. "Beyond Domination: The Future and Past of Decolonization." *The Nation*, March 9, 2021. https://www.thenation.com/article/world/achille-mbembe-walter-mignolo-catherine-walsh-decolonization/.

Arabs For Black Lives Collective. June 2, 2020. https://www.mpowerchange.org/culture-blog/arabs-for-black-lives.

Arendt, Hannah. *The Origins of Totalitarianism*. New York: Harcourt Brace and Co., 1979.

Arnall, Gavin. *Subterranean Fanon: An Underground Theory of Radical Change*. New York: Columbia University Press, 2020.

Arria, Michael. "Bowman Tries to Explain His Iron Dome Vote." *Mondoweiss*, October 7, 2021. https://mondoweiss.net/2021/10/bowman-tries-to-explain-his-iron-dome-vote/.

Awad, Sumaya and Annie Levin. "Roots of the Nakba: Zionist Settler Colonialism." In *Palestine: A Socialist Introduction*, edited by Sumaya Awad and Brian Bean, 15–38. Chicago: Haymarket Books, 2020.

Aziza, Sarah. "Can Palestinian Lives Matter?" *The Intercept*, May 13, 2021. https://theintercept.com/2021/05/13/israel-palestinian-lives-matter-blm/.

Bailey, Kristian Davis. "Black-Palestinian Solidarity in the Ferguson-Gaza Era." *American Quarterly* 67, no. 4 (2015): 1017–26.

Baldwin, James. "A Report from Occupied Territory." In *James Baldwin: Collected Essays*, edited by Toni Morrison, 728–38. New York: Library of America, 1998.

Balibar, Étienne. "A Complex Urgent Universal Political Cause." Address before the conference of Faculty for Israeli–Palestinian Peace (FFIPP). Université Libre de Bruxelles, July 3–4, 2004.

Balibar, Étienne. *Citizen Subject: Foundations for Philosophical Anthropology*. Translated by Steven Miller. New York: Fordham University Press, 2017.

Balibar, Étienne. *Politics and the Other Scene*. New York: Verso, 2002.

Barak, Jeff. "Reality Check: The Most Moral Army in The World. Really?" *The Jerusalem Post*, April 15, 2018. https://www.jpost.com/opinion/reality-check-the-most-moral-army-in-the-world-really-549906.

Barghouti, Mourid. *I Saw Ramallah*. Translated by Ahdaf Soueif. New York: Anchor Books, 2003.

Barghouti, Omar. *Boycott Divestment Sanctions: The Global Struggle for Palestinian Rights*. Chicago: Haymarket, 2011.

Barghouti, Omar. "Relative Humanity: Identity, Rights, and Ethics: Israel as a Case Study." *PMLA* 121, no. 5 (2006): 1536–43.

Barghouti, Omar. "Relative Humanity: The Essential Obstacle to a Just Peace in Palestine." *Counterpunch*, December 13–14, 2003. https://web.archive.org/web/20100619212701/http://counterpunch.org/barghouti12132003.html.

Barghouti, Omar. "What Comes Next: A Secular Democratic State in Historic Palestine—A Promising Land." *Mondoweiss*, October 21, 2013. https://mondoweiss.net/2013/10/democratic-palestine-promising/.

Baroud, Ramzy. "Palestine Bleeds: Execution of Autistic Man Is Not an Exception but the Norm." *Middle East Monitor*, June 9, 2020. https://www.middleeastmonitor.com/20200609-palestine-bleeds-execution-of-autistic-man-is-not-an-exception-but-the-norm/.

Bashir, Bashir and Rachel Busbridge. "The Politics of Decolonisation and Bi-Nationalism in Israel/Palestine." *Political Studies* 67, no. 2 (2019): 388–405.

Behar, Moshe. "Competing Marxism, Cessation of (Settler) Colonialism, and the One-State Solution in Israel-Palestine." In *The Arab and Jewish Questions Geographies of Engagement in Palestine and Beyond*, edited by Bashir Bashir and Leila Farsakh, 220–49. New York: Columbia University Press, 2020.

Benhabib, Seyla. *Exile, Statelessness and Migration: Playing Chess with History from Hannah Arendt to Isaiah Berlin*. Princeton: Princeton University Press, 2018.

Benjamin, Walter. "Critique of Violence." In *Selected Writings, vol. 1*, edited by Marcus Bullock and Michael W. Jennings, translated by Edmund Jephcott et al., 236–52. Cambridge: Harvard University Press, 1996.

Benjamin, Walter. *Illuminations*. Edited by Hannah Arendt. Translated by Harry Zohn. New York: Schocken, 1968.

Bennett, Jane. *Vibrant Matter: A Political Ecology of Things*. Durham: Duke University Press, 2010.

Bernard, Anna. *Rhetorics of Belonging: Nation, Narration, and Israel/Palestine*. Liverpool: Liverpool University Press, 2013.

Beshara, Robert K. "Islamophobia as a Fundamental Fantasy." *International Journal of Žižek Studies* 13, no. 3 (2019): 1–10.

Bisharat, George. "The Forced Displacement of Palestinians Never Truly Ended." *The Nation*, April 19, 2018.

"2015 Black Solidarity Statement with Palestine." http://www.blackforpalestine.com/read-the-statement.html/.

Boehm, Omri. "Did Israel Just Stop Trying to Be a Democracy?" *The New York Times*, July 26, 2018. https://www.nytimes.com/2018/07/26/opinion/israel-law-jewish-democracy-apartheid-palestinian.html.

Bouie, Jamelle. "Biden Says 'Fund the Police.' Well, They Aren't Exactly Hurting for Cash." *The New York Times*, March 4, 2022. https://www.nytimes.com/2022/03/04/opinion/the-police-arent-exactly-running-out-of-cash.html.

Breiner, Josh. "A Year Later, Israeli Cop Charged Over Killing of Autistic Palestinian Eyad al-Hallaq." *Haaretz*, June 17, 2021. https://www.haaretz.com/israel-news/.premium-indictment-filed-against-cop-who-killed-autistic-palestinian-eyad-al-hallaq-1.9914607.

Bresheeth-Zabner, Haim. *An Army Like No Other: How the Israeli Defence Forces Made a Nation*. New York: Verso, 2020.

Brown, Michael F. "US Fails to Acknowledge Gaza has Civilians." *The Electronic Intifada*, April 20, 2018. https://electronicintifada.net/blogs/michael-f-brown/us-fails-acknowledge-gaza-has-civilians.

B'Tselem. "A Regime of Jewish Supremacy from the Jordan River to the Mediterranean Sea: This is Apartheid." January 12, 2021. https://www.btselem.org/publications/fulltext/202101_this_is_apartheid.

Buber, Martin. *Letters of Martin Buber: A Life of Dialogue*. Syracuse: Syracuse University Press, 1991.

Burris, Greg. "Birth of a 'Zionist' Nation: Black Radicalism and the Future of Palestine." In *Futures of Black Radicalism*, edited by Gaye Theresa Johnson and Alex Lubin, 120–32. New York: Verso, 2017.

Burris, Greg. "Black Skin, White Cameras: African Asylum-Seekers in Israeli Documentary Film." *Lateral* 10, no. 1 (2021). https://csalateral.org/forum/cultural-constructions-race-racism-middle-east-north-africa-southwest-asia-mena-swana/black-skin-white-cameras-african-asylum-seekers-israeli-documentary-film-burris/.

Butler, Judith. "Endangered/Endangering: Schematic Racism and White Paranoia." In *Reading Rodney King/Reading Urban Uprising*, edited by Robert Gooding-Williams, 15–22. New York: Routledge, 1993.

Butler, Judith. *Frames of War: When is Life Grievable*. New York: Verso, 2009.
Butler, Judith. *Parting Ways: Jewishness and the Critique of Zionism*. New York: Columbia University Press, 2012.
Byrd, Jodi. *The Transit of Empire: Indigenous Critiques of Colonialism*. Minneapolis: University of Minnesota Press, 2011.
Carruthers, Charlene A. *Unapologetic: A Black, Queer, and Feminist Mandate for Radical Movements*. Boston: Beacon Press, 2018.
Cavanagh, Edward and Lorenzo Veracini. "Editors' Statement." *Settler Colonial Studies* 3, no. 1 (2013): 1.
Certeau, Michel de. *The Practice of Everyday Life*. Translated by Steven Rendall. Berkeley: University of California Press, 1984.
Césaire, Aimé. *Discourse on Colonialism*. Translated by Joan Pinkham. New York: Monthly Review Press, 2000.
Chamoiseau, Patrick. *Un dimanche au cachot*. Paris: Gallimard, 2007.
Charbonneau, Louis. "Israel Blasts Palestinians After Accusations of Organ-Harvesting." *Reuters*, November 4, 2015. https://www.reuters.com/article/us-israel-palestinians-un/israel-blasts-palestinians-after-accusations-of-organ-harvesting-idUSKCN0ST3 2420151104.
Chebata, Hana. "Israel: Promised Land for Jews as Long as They're Not Black." *Race and Class* 53, no. 4 (2012): 67–77.
Chow, Rey. *The Protestant Ethnic and the Spirit of Capitalism*. New York: Columbia University Press, 2002.
Ciccariello-Maher, George. "Jumpstarting the Decolonial Engine: Symbolic Violence from Fanon to Chávez." *Theory & Event* 13, no. 1 (2010).
Clarno, Andy. *Neoliberal Apartheid: Palestine/Israel and South Africa after 1994*. Chicago: University of Chicago Press, 2017.
Coates, Ta-Nehisi. *Between the World and Me*. New York: Spiegel and Grau, 2015.
Cohen, Hillel. *Good Arabs: The Israeli Security Agencies and the Israeli Arabs, 1948–1967*. Berkeley: University of California Press, 2010.
Colucciello Barber, Daniel. "On Black Negativity, Or The Affirmation Of Nothing: Jared Sexton, interviewed by Daniel Barber." *Society and Space*, September 18, 2017. https://www.societyandspace.org/articles/on-black-negativity-or-the-affirmation-of-nothing.
Cooper, Afua and Rinaldo Walcott. "Robin D. G. Kelley and Fred Moten in Conversation." *Critical Ethnic Studies* 4, no. 1 (2018): 154–72.
Coulthard, Glen Sean and Leanne Betasamosake Simpson. "Grounded Normativity / Place-Based Solidarity." *American Quarterly* 68, no. 2 (2016): 249–55.
Coulthard, Glen Sean and Leanne Betasamosake Simpson. *Red Skin, White Masks: Rejecting the Colonial Politics of Recognition*. Minneapolis: University of Minnesota Press, 2014.
Davis, Angela, Gayatri Chakravorty Spivak and Nikita Dhawan. "Planetary Utopias." *Radical Philosophy*, no. 2.05 (Autumn 2019): 67–77.

Day, Eli. "Marc Lamont Hill Has Secured His Place in the Proud Black Anti-Colonial Tradition." *In These Times*, December 11, 2018. https://inthesetimes.com/article/marc-lamont-hill-cnn-palestine-israel-apartheid-jim-crow-black-radical.

Day, Iyko. "Being or Nothingness: Indigeneity, Antiblackness, and Settler Colonial Critique." *Critical Ethnic Studies* 1, no. 2 (2015): 102–21.

Deane, Seamus. "*Culture and Imperialism*: Errors of a Syllabus." In *After Said: Postcolonial Literary Studies in the Twenty-First Century*, edited by Bashir Abu-Manneh, 53–68. Cambridge: Cambridge University Press, 2019.

Deleuze, Gilles and Felix Guattari. *A Thousand Plateaus*. Translated by Brian Massumi. Minneapolis: University of Minnesota Press, 1987.

Deleuze, Gilles, Felix Guattari and Elias Sanbar. "The Indians of Palestine." In *Two Regimes of Madness: Texts and Interviews 1975–1995*, edited by David Lapoujade, 194–200. New York: Semiotext(e), 2006.

Derrida, Jacques. "Autoimmunity: Real and Symbolic Suicides—A Dialogue with Jacques Derrida." In *Philosophy in a Time of Terror: Dialogues with Jürgen Habermas and Jacques Derrida*, edited by Giovanna Borradori, 85–136. Chicago: University of Chicago Press, 2004.

Derrida, Jacques. "Avowing—The Impossible: 'Returns,' Repentance, and Reconciliation." In *Living Together: Jacques Derrida's Communities of Violence and Peace*, edited by Elisabeth Weber, 18–41. New York: Fordham University Press, 2013.

Derrida, Jacques. *On Cosmopolitanism and Forgiveness*. Translated by Mark Dooley and Michael Hughes. New York: Routledge, 2001.

Derrida, Jacques. "'Eating Well,' or the Calculation of the Subject: An Interview with Jacques Derrida." In *Who Comes After the Subject?* edited by Eduardo Cadava, Peter Connor, and Jean-Luc Nancy, 96–119. New York: Routledge, 1991.

Derrida, Jacques. *Learning to Live Finally: The Last Interview*. Translated by Pascale-Anne Brault and Michael Naas. Hoboken: Melville House, 2007.

Derrida, Jacques. *Rogues: Two Essays on Reason*. Translated by Pascale-Anne Brault and Michael Naas. Stanford: Stanford University Press, 2005.

Derrida, Jacques. *The Beast and the Sovereign, vol. 1*. Edited by Michel Lisse, Marie-Louise Mallet, and Ginette Michaud. Translated by Geoffrey Bennington. Chicago: University of Chicago Press, 2009.

Derrida, Jacques. *The Death Penalty, vol. 1*. Translated by Peggy Kamuf. Chicago: University of Chicago Press, 2013.

Derrida, Jacques and Elisabeth Roudinesco. *For What Tomorrow . . . : A Dialogue*. Translated by Jeff Fort. Stanford: Stanford University Press, 2004.

Desai, Chandni. "Disrupting Settler-Colonial Capitalism: Indigenous Intifadas and Resurgent Solidarity from Turtle Island to Palestine." *Journal of Palestine Studies* 50, no. 2 (2021): 43–66.

Divine Intervention: A Chronicle of Love and Pain [Yadon Ilaheyya]. Dir. Elia Suleiman. New York: Avatar Films, 2002.

Du Bois, W. E. B. *The Souls of Black Folk*. New Haven: Yale University Press, 2015.

Edelman, Lee. *No Future: Queer Theory and the Death Drive*. Durham: Duke University Press, 2004.

Eid, Haidar. "Interview with Dr. Haidar Eid: 'The Palestinian Struggle Is Not About Independence—It Is About Liberation.'" *Mondoweiss*, December 2, 2013. http://mondoweiss.net/2013/12/palestinian-independence-liberation.

Eid, Haidar. "On Jared Kushner's Palestinophobia." *Mondoweiss*, November 1, 2019. https://mondoweiss.net/2019/11/on-jared-kushners-palestinophobia/.

Eid, Haidar. "The Two-State Solution: The Opium of the Palestinian People." *Al Jazeera*, December 29, 2020. https://www.aljazeera.com/opinions/2020/12/29/the-two-state-solution-the-opium-of-the-palestinian-people.

El-Hadi, Nehal. "Ensemble: An Interview with Dr. Fred Moten." *Mice Magazine*, Summer 2018. https://micemagazine.ca/issue-four/ensemble-interview-dr-fred-moten.

El-Haj, Nadia Abu. *Facts on the Ground: Archaeological Practice and Territorial Self-Fashioning in Israeli Society*. Chicago: University of Chicago Press, 2001.

El-Haj, Nadia Abu. "Racial Palestinianization and the Janus-Faced Nature of the Israeli State." *Patterns of Prejudice* 44, no. 1 (2010): 27–41.

El-Haj, Nadia Abu. "Zoom Webinar: Said's Palestine." Moderated by Judith Butler. *University of California Humanities Research Institute*, June 1, 2021. https://uchri.org/events/saids-palestine/.

Erakat, Noura. *Justice for Some: Law and the Question of Palestine*. Stanford: Stanford University Press, 2019.

Erakat, Noura. "Rethinking Israel-Palestine: Beyond Bantustans, Beyond Reservations." *The Nation*, March 21, 2013. https://www.thenation.com/article/archive/rethinking-israel-palestine-beyond-bantustans-beyond-reservations/.

Erakat, Noura. "Whiteness as Property in Israel: Revival, Rehabilitation, and Removal." *Harvard Journal of Racial and Ethnic Justice* 31 (2015): 69–103.

Erakat, Noura and Marc Lamont Hill. "Black-Palestinian Transnational Solidarity: Renewals, Returns, and Practice." *Journal of Palestine Studies* 48, no. 4 (2019): 7–16.

Erekat, Saeb. "As Long As Israel Continues Its Settlements, a Two-State Solution Is Impossible." *The Washington Post*, October 24, 2016. https://www.washingtonpost.com/news/global-opinions/wp/2016/10/24/as-long-as-israel-continues-its-settlements-a-two-state-solution-is-impossible/.

Erickson, Steve. A Breakdown of Communication: Elia Suleiman Talks About Divine Intervention." *Indiewire*, January 15, 2003. https://www.indiewire.com/2003/01/a-breakdown-of-communication-elia-suleiman-talks-about-divine-intervention-80022/.

Esposito, Roberto. *Bios: Biopolitics and Philosophy*. Translated by Timothy Campbell. Minneapolis: University of Minnesota Press, 2008.

Estes, Nick. "Indigenous Feminism Does Not Discriminate." *The Red Nation*, September 7, 2019. http://therednation.org/indigenous-feminism-does-not-discriminate/.

Estes, Nick. "The Liberation of Palestine Represents an Alternative Path for Native Nations." *The Red Nation*, September 7, 2019. http://therednation.org/the-liberation-of-palestine-represents-an-alternative-path-for-native-nations/.

Eyal, Hedva. "Furore in Israel Over Birth Control Drugs for Ethiopian Jews." *The New Humanitarian*, January 28, 2013. https://www.thenewhumanitarian.org/news/2013/01/28/furore-israel-over-birth-control-drugs-ethiopian-jews.

Fahim, Joseph. "Why the Movie Oslo Is a Missed Opportunity for Hollywood." *Middle East Eye*, June 10, 2021. https://www.middleeasteye.net/discover/oslo-hbo-review-film-neutrality-catch.

Falk, Richard. "On 'Lost Causes' and the Future of Palestine." *The Nation*, December 16, 2014. https://www.thenation.com/article/archive/lost-causes-and-future-palestine/.

Falk, Richard. "The Goldstone Report and the Battle for Legitimacy." *The Electronic Intifada*, September 22, 2009. https://electronicintifada.net/content/goldstone-report-and-battle-legitimacy/8456.

Fanon, Frantz. *Black Skin, White Masks*. Translated by Charles Lam Markmann. New York: Grove Press, 1967.

Fanon, Frantz. *Black Skin, White Masks*. Translated by Richard Philcox. New York: Grove Press, 2008.

Fanon, Frantz. *The Wretched of the Earth*. Translated by Richard Philcox. New York: Grove Press, 2004.

Fareld, Victoria. "Entangled Memories of Violence: Jean Améry and Frantz Fanon." *Memory Studies* 14, no. 1 (2021): 58–67.

Farsakh, Leila H. "Alternatives to Partition in Palestine: Rearticulating the State-Nation Nexus." In *Rethinking Statehood in Palestine Self-Determination and Decolonization Beyond Partition*, edited by Leila H. Farsakh, 173–91. Oakland: University of California Press, 2021.

Feldman, Keith. *A Shadow over Palestine: The Imperial Life of Race in America*. Minneapolis: University of Minnesota Press, 2015.

Fernandez, Belen. "Israel's Policy: Kill the Messenger, Attack the Mourners." *Al Jazeera*, May 14, 2022. https://www.aljazeera.com/opinions/2022/5/14/israels-policy-kill-the-messenger-attack-the-mourners.

Fink, Bruce. *A Clinical Introduction to Lacanian Psychoanalysis: Theory and Technique*. Cambridge: Harvard University Press, 1997.

Fink, Bruce. *The Lacanian Subject: Between Language and Jouissance*. Princeton: Princeton University Press, 1995.

Finkelstein, Norman G. *The Holocaust Industry Reflections on the Exploitation of Jewish Suffering*. New York: Verso, 2003.

Fischbach, Michael R. *Black Power and Palestine: Transnational Countries of Color*. Stanford: Stanford University Press, 2018.

Foot, Paul. "In a State of Cruelty." *The Guardian*, May 29, 2000. https://www.theguardian.com/world/2000/may/30/comment.israelandthepalestinians.

Garba, Tapji and Sara-Maria Sorentino. "Slavery Is a Metaphor: A Critical Commentary on Eve Tuck and K. Wayne Yang's 'Decolonization Is Not a Metaphor.'" *Antipode* 52, no. 3 (2020): 764–82.

Gibson, Nigel. *Fanon: The Postcolonial Imagination*. Cambridge: Polity, 2003.

Ghanem, As'ad. "'Identity and Belonging': A Pioneering Project, Which Must Be the Starting Point for an Alternative, Comprehensive Educational Plan." *Adalah's Newsletter* 27 (2006). https://www.adalah.org/uploads/oldfiles/newsletter/eng/jul-aug06/ar2.pdf.

Goldberg, David Theo. *Are We All Postracial Yet?* Cambridge: Polity, 2015.

Goldberg, Jeffrey. "The Paranoid, Supremacist Roots of the Stabbing Intifada." *The Atlantic*, October 16, 2015. https://www.theatlantic.com/international/archive/2015/10/the-roots-of-the-palestinian-uprising-against-israel/410944/.

Goldenberg, Tia. "Israeli PM: Killing of Palestinian With Autism a 'Tragedy.'" *Associated Press*, June 7, 2020. https://apnews.com/article/75104c37fadeb37b993400c3b7182b3e.

Goodman, Amy. "Angela Davis & Noura Erakat on Palestinian Solidarity, Gaza & Israel's Killing of Ahmad Erekat." *Democracy Now!*, May 20, 2021. https://www.democracynow.org/2021/5/20/palestinian_solidarity_ahmad_erekat.

Goodman, Amy. "Rashid Khalidi: Israel & UAE Deal to Normalize Relations Is New Chapter in 100-Year War on Palestine." *Democracy Now!*, August 14, 2020. https://www.democracynow.org/2020/8/14/israel_uae_agreement_trump_palestine.

Gordon, Lewis R. "Theory in Black: Teleological Suspensions in Philosophy of Culture." *Qui Parle* 18, no. 2 (2010): 193–214.

Gordon, Lewis R. "Through the Hellish Zone of Nonbeing: Thinking through Fanon, Disaster, and the Damned of the Earth." *Human Architecture: Journal of the Sociology of Self-Knowledge* 5, no. 3 (2007): 5–11.

Gossett, Che. "A Wall is Just a Wall: Anti-Blackness and the Politics of Black and Prison Abolitionist Solidarity with Palestinian Struggle." *Decolonization* (blog), June 16, 2014. https://decolonization.wordpress.com/2014/06/16/a-wall-is-just-a-wall-anti-blackness-and-the-politics-of-black-and-prison-abolitionist-solidarity-with-palestinian-struggle/.

Grim, Ryan. "As Israel Attacked Gaza, It Heard Something New: Opposition from Congress." *The Intercept*, May 13, 2021. https://theintercept.com/2021/05/14/israel-palestine-congress-criticism-democrats/?utm_medium=email&utm_source=The%20Intercept%20Newsletter.

Grunes, Dennis. "Divine Intervention (Elia Suleiman, 2001)." February 15, 2007. https://grunes.wordpress.com/2007/02/15/divine-intervention-elia-sulieman-2001/.

Haddad, Mohammed. "Mapping Israeli Occupation." *Al Jazeera*, May 18, 2021. https://www.aljazeera.com/news/2021/5/18/mapping-israeli-occupation-gaza-palestine.

Haddad, Toufic. *Palestine Ltd.: Neoliberalism and Nationalism in the Occupied Territories*. London: I.B. Tauris, 2016.

Halberstam, Jack. "The Wild Beyond: With and for the Undercommons." In *The Undercommons: Fugitive Planning & Black Study*, edited by Fred Moten and Stefano Harney, 2–12. New York: Minor Compositions, 2013.

Halbfinger, David M. and Isabel Kershner. "After a Police Shooting, Ethiopian Israelis Seek a 'Black Lives Matter' Reckoning." *The New York Times*, July 13, 2019. https://www.nytimes.com/2019/07/13/world/middleeast/ethiopian-israeli-protests-racism.html.

Halper, Joseph. *Decolonizing Israel, Liberating Palestine: Zionism, Settler Colonialism, and the Case for One Democratic State*. London: Pluto Press, 2021.

Hamza, Agon. "On Love." *The Philosophical Salon*, July 26, 2021. http://thephilosophicalsalon.com/the-r-files-6-a-hamza-on-love/.

Hanafi, Sari. "Spacio-cide: Colonial Politics, Invisibility and Rezoning in Palestinian territory." *Contemporary Arab Affairs* 2, no. 1 (2009): 106–21.

Harb, Ali. "Jerusalem: Biden Administration's 'Bothsidesism' Angers Palestinians." *Middle East Eye*, May 9, 2021. https://www.middleeasteye.net/news/jerusalem-biden-administration-both-sides-palestinians-israel.

Harel, Amos. "Israeli Military Will Not Conduct Criminal Probe Into Al Jazeera Reporter's Death." *Haaretz*, May 19, 2022. https://www.haaretz.com/israel-news/2022-05-19/ty-article/.highlight/israeli-military-will-not-conduct-criminal-probe-into-al-jazeera-reporters-death/00000180-e9f1-d189-af82-f9fd924b0000.

Harkov, Lahav. "Netanyahu Fixates on African Migrants—But Likud Has No Policy." *The Jerusalem Post*, March 21, 2021. https://www.jpost.com/israel-elections/netanyahu-fixates-on-african-migrants-but-likud-has-no-policy-662683.

Harney, Stefano and Fred Moten. *The Undercommons: Fugitive Planning and Black Study*. New York: Autonomedia, 2013.

Harvey, David. *The New Imperialism*. Oxford: Oxford University Press, 2003.

Hartman, Saidiya V. *Lose Your Mother: A Journey Along the Atlantic Slave Route*. New York: Farrar, Straus and Giroux, 2008.

Hartman, Saidiya V. *Scenes of Subjection: Terror, Slavery, and Self-Making in Nineteenth-Century America*. Oxford: Oxford University Press, 1997.

Hartman, Saidiya V. and Frank B. Wilderson III. "The Position of the Unthought." *Qui Parle* 13, no. 2 (2003): 183–201.

Hasson, Nir. "Why Israelis Care About the Killing of an Autistic Palestinian, but Are Silent About Others." *Haaretz*, October 21, 2020. https://www.haaretz.com/middle-east-news/palestinians/2020-10-21/ty-article/.premium/why-israelis-care-about-killing-of-autistic-palestinian-but-are-silent-about-others/0000017f-e912-dc7e-adff-f9bfff240000.

Heidegger, Martin. *The Fundamental Concepts of Metaphysics*. Translated by William Mcneill and Nicholas Walker. Bloomington: Indiana University Press, 1995.

Heidegger, Martin. *The Question Concerning Technology and Other Essays*. Translated by William Lovett. New York, 1977.

Helow, Amal. "Challenging Israel to Become Democratic." *bitterlemons.org*, January 29, 2007. http://www.bitterlemons.org/previous/bl290107ed4.html#pal2.

Henriksen Waage, Hilde. "Norway's Role in the Middle East Peace Talks: Between a Strong State and a Weak Belligerent." *Journal of Palestine Studies* 34, no. 4 (2005): 6–24.

Herzl, Theodor. "The Jewish State." (1896). In *The Zionist Idea: A Historical Analysis and Reader*, edited by Arthur Hertzberg, 204–26. Philadelphia: Jewish Publication Society, 1997.

Hever, Shir. "Israel Arms Sales: Court Decision Ends Hopes for Transparency." *Middle East Eye*, July 1, 2021. https://www.middleeasteye.net/news/israel-arms-sales-transparency-court-decision-ends-hopes.

Hochberg, Gil Z. "'Jerusalem, We Have a Problem': Larissa Sansour's Sci-Fi Trilogy and the Impetus of Dystopic Imagination." *Arab Studies Journal* 26, no. 1 (2018): 34–57.

Hochberg, Gil Z. *Visual Occupations: Violence and Visibility in a Conflict Zone*. Durham: Duke University Press, 2015.

Honig-Parnass, Tikva. *False Prophets of Peace: Liberal Zionism and the Struggle for Palestine*. Chicago: Haymarket Books, 2011.

Hook, Derek. "Death-Bound Subjectivity: Fanon's Zone of Nonbeing and the Lacanian Death Drive." *Subjectivity* 13 (2020): 355–75.

Horkheimer, Max. "The Jews and Europe." In *Critical Theory and Society: A Reader*, edited by Stephen Bronner and Douglas Kellner, 77–94. New York: Routledge, 1989.

Human Rights Watch. "A Threshold Crossed Israeli Authorities and the Crimes of Apartheid and Persecution." April 27, 2021. https://www.hrw.org/report/2021/04/27/threshold-crossed/israeli-authorities-and-crimes-apartheid-and-persecution#.

"Idle No More Stands in Solidarity with Palestinian People." *Idle No More*. https://idlenomore.ca/idle-no-more-stands-in-solidarity-with-palestinian-people/.

Ihmoud, Sarah. "Mohammed Abu-Khdeir and the Politics of Racial Terror in Occupied Jerusalem." *borderlands* 14, no. 1 (2015): 1–28.

Ihmoud, Sarah. "Murabata: The Politics of Staying in Place." *Feminist Studies* 45, no. 2–3 (2019): 512–40.

Ihmoud, Sarah. "Roundtable on Anti-Blackness and Black-Palestinian Solidarity." *Jadaliyya*, June 3, 2015. https://www.jadaliyya.com/Details/32145/Roundtable-on-Anti-Blackness-and-Black-Palestinian-Solidarity.

In the Future They Ate from the Finest Porcelain. Dir. Larissa Sansour and Søren Lind. Mec Film, 2016.

International Holocaust Remembrance Alliance website. https://www.holocaustremembrance.com/resources/working-definitions-charters/working-definition-antisemitism.

Jabotinsky, Vladimir Ze'ev. "The Iron Wall." November 4, 1923. https://www.jewishvirtuallibrary.org/quot-the-iron-wall-quot.

Jadaliyya Reports. "Black, Palestinian Artists and Activists Affirm Solidarity in New Video." *Jadaliyya*, October 14, 2015. https://www.jadaliyya.com/Details/32588/Black,-Palestinian-Artists-and-Activists-Affirm-Solidarity-in-New-Video.

Jamal, Amal. *Arab Minority Nationalism in Israel: The Politics of Indigeneity*. New York: Routledge, 2011.

Jamal, Amal. "Nationalizing States and the Constitution of 'Hollow Citizenship': Israel and its Palestinian Citizens." *Ethnopolitics* 6, no. 4 (2007): 471–93.

Jameson, Fredric. *Representing Capital: A Reading of Volume One*. New York: Verso, 2011.

"Jewish Electoral Institute: National Jewish Survey." June 28–July 1, 2021. https://www.jewishelectorateinstitute.org/wp-content/uploads/2021/07/JEI-National-Jewish-Survey-Topline-Results-July-2021.pdf.

Jrere, Mahmood, Tamer Nafar and Udi Aloni. "'We Don't Want What Happened in 1948 to Happen to Us Again.'" *The Nation*, May 26, 2021. https://www.thenation.com/article/activism/dam-palestine-protest/.

Kant, Immanuel. "An Answer to the Question: What Is Enlightenment?" In *What Is Enlightenment? Eighteenth-Century Answers and Twentieth-Century Questions*, edited by James Schmidt, 58–64. Berkeley: University of California Press, 1996.

Kapeliouk, Amnon. "Begin and the Beasts." *New Statesman*, June 25, 1982.

Kapoor, Ilan. *Confronting Desire: Psychoanalysis and International Development*. Ithaca: Cornell University Press, 2020.

Kapoor, Ilan and Zahi Zalloua. *Universal Politics*. Oxford: Oxford University Press, 2021.

Kassel, Matthew. "NY Times Runs Ad from Holocaust Survivors Condemning Israel, Attacking Elie Wiesel." *Observer*, August 25, 2014. https://observer.com/2014/08/ny-times-runs-ad-from-holocaust-survivors-condemning-israel-attacking-elie-wiesel/.

Kelemen, Paul. "The 'New Antisemitism,' the Left and Palestine: The 'Anti-Imperialism of Fools' or an Invention of Imperial Reason." *Journal of Holy Land and Palestine Studies* 17, no. 2 (2018): 235–57.

Kelley, Robin D. G. "From the River to the Sea to Every Mountain Top: Solidarity as Worldmaking." *Journal of Palestine Studies* 48, no. 4 (2019): 69–91.

Kelley, Robin D. G. "The Rest of Us: Rethinking Settler and Native." *American Quarterly* 69, no. 2 (2017): 267–76.

Kelley, Robin D. G. "Yes, I said, 'National Liberation.'" In *Letters to Palestine: Writers Respond to War and Occupation*, edited by Vijay Prashad, 139–53. New York: Verso, 2015.

Kelley, Robin D. G. Jack Amariglio, and Lucas Wilson. "'Solidarity Is Not a Market Exchange': An RM Interview with Robin D. G. Kelley, Part 1." *Rethinking Marxism* 30, no. 4 (2018): 568–98.

Khader, Jamil. "Rehumanizing Palestinians? Radicalize the Struggle!" *The Philosophical Salon*, July 9, 2018. https://thephilosophicalsalon.com/rehumanizing-palestinians-radicalize-the-struggle/.

Khader, Jamil. "The Living Dead in Palestine and the Failure of International Humanitarian Intervention." *Truthout*, November 8, 2015. https://truthout.org/

articles/the-living-dead-in-palestine-and-the-failure-of-international-humanitarian-intervention/.

Khalidi, Rashid. *Palestinian Identity: The Construction of Modern National Consciousness*. New York: Columbia University Press, 2010.

Khalidi, Walid. "Plan Dalet: Master Plan for the Conquest of Palestine." *Journal of Palestine Studies* 18, no. 1 (1988): 4–33.

Kimmerling, Baruch. *Politicide: Ariel Sharon's War against the Palestinians*. New York: Verso, 2003.

King, Tiffany Lethabo, Jenell Navarro, and Andrea Smith. "Beyond Incommensurability: Toward an Otherwise Stance on Black and Indigenous Relationality." In *Otherwise Worlds: Against Settler Colonialism and Anti-Blackness*, edited by Tiffany Lethabo King, Jenell Navarro, and Andrea Smith, 1–23. Durham: Duke University Press, 2020.

Kraft, Dina and Laura King. "'Second front' for Israel: Violence Among Arab Citizens and Jews Comes as a Wartime Test." *Los Angeles Times*, May 14, 2021. https://www.latimes.com/world-nation/story/2021-05-14/israel-jewish-arab-tension.

Krauthammer, Charles. "Why Was There War in Gaza?" *The Washington Post*, November 22, 2012. https://www.washingtonpost.com/opinions/charles-krauthammer-why-was-there-war-in-gaza/2012/11/22/c77582e8-3412-11e2-bfd5-e202b6d7b501_story.html.

Kushkush, Isma'il. "'Afro-Palestinians' Forge a Unique Identity in Israel." *Associated Press*, January 11, 2017. https://apnews.com/article/f6bf554b21d04b56be9d6385fbf36d31.

Lacan, Jacques. *The Ethics of Psychoanalysis, 1959–1960, The Seminar of Jacques Lacan, Book VII*. Edited by Jacques-Alain Miller. Translated by Dennis Porter. New York: Norton, 1992.

Lacan, Jacques. *The Four Fundamental Concepts of Psycho-analysis*. Translated by Alan Sheridan. New York: Routledge, 2018.

Lamont Hill, Marc and Mitchell Plitnick. *Except for Palestine: The Limits of Progressive Politics*. New York: The New Press, 2021.

Lavie, Mark. "Israel Harvested Organs in '90s Without Permission." *Associated Press*, December 20, 2009.

Lazaroff, Tovah. "Shaked: Shameful to give COVID-19 Vaccines to Gaza While IDF Bodies Held." *The Jerusalem Post*, February 21, 2021. https://www.jpost.com/israel-news/shaked-shameful-to-give-covid-19-vaccines-to-gaza-while-idf-bodies-held-659648.

Lazarus, Neil. "Disavowing Decolonization: Fanon, Nationalism, and the Problematic of Representation in Current Theories of Colonial Discourse." *Research in African Literatures* 24, no. 4 (1993): 69–98.

Lentin, Ronit. "Palestinian Lives Matter: Racialising Israeli Settler-Colonialism." *Journal of Holy Land and Palestine Studies* 19, no. 2 (2020): 133–49.

Lentin, Ronit. *Traces of Racial Exception: Racializing Israeli Settler Colonialism*. New York: Bloomsbury, 2018.

Letwin, David and Haidar Eid. "Interview with Dr. Haidar Eid: 'The Palestinian Struggle Is Not About Independence—It Is About Liberation.'" *Mondoweiss*, December 2, 2013. http://mondoweiss.net/2013/12/palestinian-independence-liberation.

Levy, Gideon. "'Being Black in America Shouldn't Be a Death Sentence.' What About Being Palestinian?" *Haaretz*, May 30, 2020. https://www.haaretz.com/opinion/2020-06-02/ty-article-opinion/.premium/being-black-in-america-shouldnt-be-a-death-sentence-what-about-being-palestinian/0000017f-dc13-db5a-a57f-dc7bee470000.

Levy, Gideon. "Is Blood of Iconic Journalist Redder Than Blood of Anonymous Palestinians?" *Haaretz*, May 11, 2022. https://www.haaretz.com/opinion/2022-05-11/ty-article-opinion/.highlight/the-killing-of-shireen-abu-akleh-now-youre-appalled/00000180-d62b-d452-a1fa-d7efc4710000.

Levy, Gideon. "Tell Me What's Untrue in Amnesty's Report on Israel." *Haaretz*, February 3, 2022. https://www.haaretz.com/opinion/2022-02-03/ty-article-opinion/.highlight/tell-me-whats-untrue-in-amnestys-report-on-israel/0000017f-f30e-d487-abff-f3fe970b0000.

Li, Darryl. "The Gaza Strip as Laboratory: Notes in the Wake of Disengagement." *Journal of Palestine Studies* 35, no. 2 (2006): 38–55.

Lorde, Audre. "The Master's Tools Will Never Dismantle the Master's House." In *Sister Outsider: Essays and Speeches*, 110–13. Freedom: Crossing Press, 1984.

Lorde, Audre. "The Uses of Anger: Women Responding to Racism." In *Sister Outsider: Essays and Speeches*, 124–33. Freedom: Crossing Press, 1984.

Mackey, Robert. "Israel's New Leaders Won't Stop 'Death to Arabs' Chants, but They Will Feel Bad About Them." *The Intercept*, June 16, 2021. https://theintercept.com/2021/06/16/israels-new-leaders-wont-stop-death-arabs-chants-will-feel-bad/.

Majumdar, Nivedita. *World in a Grain of Sand: Postcolonial Literature and Radical Universalism*. New York: Verso, 2021.

Makdisi, Saree. "For a Secular Democratic State." *The Nation*, June 18, 2007. https://www.thenation.com/article/archive/secular-democratic-state/.

Makdisi, Saree. *Palestine Inside Out: An Everyday Occupation*. New York: Norton, 2008.

Makdisi, Saree. "Said, Palestine, and the Humanism of Liberation." *Critical Inquiry* 31 (2005): 443–61.

Maldonado-Torres, Nelson. *Against War: Views from the Underside of Modernity*. Durham: Duke University Press, 2008.

Maldonado-Torres, Nelson. "Levinas's Hegemonic Identity Politics, Radical Philosophy, and the Unfinished Project of Decolonization." *Levinas Studies* 7 (2012): 63–94.

Maldonado-Torres, Nelson. "On the Coloniality of Being." *Cultural Studies* 21, no. 2–3 (2007): 240–70.

Marcetic, Branko. "On Palestine, the Media Is Allergic to the Truth." *Jacobin*, May 12, 2021. https://www.jacobinmag.com/2021/05/media-press-palestine-israel-gaza-violence-hamas?mc_cid=cfe48687a5&mc_eid=0317ccf9ee.

Marche, Stephen. "Canada's Impossible Acknowledgment." *The New Yorker*, September 7, 2017. https://www.newyorker.com/culture/culture-desk/canadas-impossible-acknowledgment.

Marriott, David. "Black Cultural Studies." *The Year's Work in Critical and Cultural Theory* 20 (2012): 37–66.

Martel, James R. *The Misinterpellated Subject*. Durham: Duke University Press, 2017.

Martin Alcoff, Linda. "Mignolo's Epistemology of Coloniality." *CR: The New Centennial Review* 7, no. 3 (2007): 79–101.

Marx, Karl. *Capital: A Critique of Political Economy, vol. 1*. Intro. Ernest Mandel. Translated by Ben Fowkes. New York: Penguin Books, 1976.

Masalha, Nur. *Expulsion of the Palestinians: The Concept of Transfer in Zionist Political Thought, 1882–1948*. Washington: Institute for Palestine Studies, 1992.

Massad, Joseph. ""The 'Deal of the Century': The Final Stage of the Oslo Accords." *Al Jazeera*, November 6, 2018. https://studies.aljazeera.net/en/reports/2018/11/181106114236864.html.

Massad, Joseph. "Zionism, Anti-Semitism and Colonialism." *Al Jazeera*, December 24, 2012. https://www.aljazeera.com/opinions/2012/12/24/zionism-anti-semitism-and-colonialism.

Mbembe, Achille. *Critique of Black Reason*. Translated by Laurent Dubois. Durham: Duke University Press, 2017.

Mbembe, Achille. "In Conversation: Achille Mbembe and David Theo Goldberg on *Critique of Black Reason*." *Theory, Culture, and Society*, July 3, 2018. https://www.theoryculturesociety.org/conversation-achille-mbembe-and-david-theo-goldberg-on-critique-of-black-reason/.

Mbembe, Achille. "Necropolitics." *Public Culture* 15, no. 1 (2003): 11–40.

Mbembe, Achille. *Necropolitics*. Translated by Steven Corcoran. Durham: Duke University Press, 2019.

Mbembe, Achille. *On the Postcolony*. Berkeley: University of California Press, 2001.

Mbembe, Achille. "Thoughts on the Planetary: An interview with Achille Mbembe." In *Decolonising the Neoliberal University: Law, Psychoanalysis and the Politics of Student Protest*, edited by Jaco Barnard-Naudé, 122–36. New York: Routledge, 2022.

McGreal, Chris. "US Accused of Hypocrisy for Supporting Sanctions Against Russia But Not Israel." *The Guardian*, March 7, 2022. https://www.theguardian.com/world/2022/mar/07/us-sanctions-against-russia-but-not-israel.

Medina, José. "Varieties of Hermeneutical Injustice." In *The Routledge Handbook of Epistemic Injustice*, edited by Ian James Kidd, José Medina and Gaile Pohlhaus, 41–52. New York: Routledge, 2017.

Mekelberg, Yossi. "The Plight of Ethiopian Jews in Israel." *BBC News*, May 25, 2015. https://www.bbc.com/news/world-middle-east-32813056.

Menick, John. "The Occupied Imagination of Elia Suleiman." *John Menick Blog*, June 2003. https://www.johnmenick.com/writing/the-occupied-imagination-of-elia-suleiman.html.

Mignolo, Walter D. "Coloniality Is Far from Over and, So Must Be Decoloniality." *Afterall* 43 (spring/summer 2017): 38–45.

Mignolo, Walter D. "'Coloniality is Not Over, It's All Over.' Interview with Dr. Walter Mignolo (Nov. 2014. Part I)." *Transmodernity* (Spring 2016): 175–84.

Mignolo, Walter D. "Decoloniality and Phenomenology: The Geopolitics of Knowing and Epistemic/Ontological Colonial Differences." *The Journal of Speculative Philosophy* 32, no. 3 (2018): 360–87.

Mignolo, Walter D. "Decolonizing the Nation-State: Zionism in the Colonial Horizon of Modernity." In *Deconstructing Zionism: A Critique of Political Metaphysics*, edited by Gianni Vattimo and Michael Marder, 57–74. New York: Bloomsbury, 2013.

Mignolo, Walter D. "Foreword: On Pluriversality and Multipolarity." In *Constructing the Pluriverse: The Geopolitics of Knowledge*, edited by Bernd Reiter, ix–xvi. Durham: Duke University Press, 2018.

Mignolo, Walter D. "Foreword: Yes, We Can." In *Can Non-Europeans Think?*, by Hamid Dabashi, viii–xlii. London: Zed Books, 2015.

Mignolo, Walter D. "I Am Where I Think: Remapping the Order of Knowing." In *The Creolization of Theory*, edited by Françoise Lionnet and Shu-mei Shi, 159–92. Durham: Duke University Press, 2011.

Mignolo, Walter D. *Local Histories/Global Designs: Coloniality, Subaltern Knowledges, and Border Thinking*. Princeton: Princeton University Press, 2000.

Mignolo, Walter D. "On Subalterns and Other Agencies." *Postcolonial Studies* 8, no. 4 (2006): 381–407.

Mignolo, Walter D. *The Darker Side of Western Modernity: Global Futures, Decolonial Options*. Durham: Duke University Press, 2011.

Mignolo, Walter D. "The Decolonial Option and the Meaning of Identity in Politics." *Anales Nueva Época* 9, no. 10 (2007): 43–72.

Mignolo, Walter D. *The Idea of Latin America*. Malden: Blackwell, 2005.

Mignolo, Walter D. "Yes, We Can: Non-European Thinkers and Philosophers." *Al Jazeera*, February 19, 2013. https://www.aljazeera.com/opinions/2013/2/19/yes-we-can-non-european-thinkers-and-philosophers/.

Mignolo, Walter and Wanda Nanibush. "Thinking and Engaging with the Decolonial: A Conversation between Walter D. Mignolo and Wanda Nanibush." *Afterall* 45 (Spring/Summer, 2018): 24–9.

Mitchell, Nick. "The View from Nowhere: On Frank Wilderson's *Afropessimism*." *Specter*, no. 2 (Fall 2020): 110–22.

Moore-Backman, Chris. "Why Did Israel Withhold Bodies of Slain Palestinians, Denying the Right to Mourn?" *Truthout*, January 5, 2016. https://truthout.org/articles/why-did-israel-withhold-bodies-of-slain-palestinians-denying-the-right-to-mourn/.

Montaigne, Michel de. *The Complete Works of Montaigne*. Translated by Donald Frame. Stanford: Stanford University Press, 1957.

Moten, Fred. *Stolen Life*. Durham: Duke University Press, 2018.

Moten, Fred. "The New International of Insurgent Feeling." *BDS*, November 16, 2009. https://bdsmovement.net/news/new-international-insurgent-feeling.

Mufti, Aamir R. "The Missing Homeland of Edward Said." In *Conflicting Humanities*, edited by Rosi Braidotti and Paul Gilroy, 165–84. New York: Bloomsbury, 2016.

Munayyer, Yousef. "On Watching Ukraine Through Palestinian Eyes." *The Nation*, March 3, 2022. https://www.thenation.com/article/world/ukraine-palestine-occupation/.

Mustafa, Ali. "'Boycotts Work': An interview with Omar Barghouti." *The Electronic Intifada*, May 31, 2009. https://electronicintifada.net/content/boycotts-work-interview-omar-barghouti/8263.

Nation Estate. Dir. Larissa Sansour. Manuscript and co-director Søren Lind. Mec Film, 2012.

Nelson, Cary. *Israel Denial: Anti-Zionism, Anti-Semitism, & the Faculty Campaign Against the Jewish State*. Bloomington: Indiana University Press, 2019.

Nevel, Donna. "Conversations About Gaza: 'But Hamas . . .'" *Fair Observer*, August 18, 2014. https://www.fairobserver.com/region/middle_east_north_africa/conversations-about-gaza-but-hamas-12739/.

Nietzsche, Friedrich. *On the Genealogy of Morals*. Translated by Walter Kaufmann. New York: Vintage, 1989.

Nordau, Max. *Degeneration*. Lincoln: University of Nebraska, 1993.

Norton, Ben. "Palestinians Support Indigenous Dakota Pipeline Protests: 'We stand with Standing Rock.'" *Salon*, November 18, 2016. https://www.salon.com/2016/11/18/palestinians-support-indigenous-nodapl-protests-we-stand-with-standing-rock/.

Ofir, Jonathan. "Israel's Ban on Palestinian Spouses Becomes Permanent Law—a Triumph for 'Jewish State.'" *Mondoweiss*, March 11, 2022. https://mondoweiss.net/2022/03/israels-ban-on-palestinian-spouses-becomes-permanent-law-a-triumph-for-jewish-state/.

Ophir, Adi. "The Identity of the Victims and the Victims of Identity: A Critique of Zionist Ideology for a Post-Zionist Age." In *Mapping Jewish Identities*, edited by Laurence J. Silberstein, 174–200. New York: New York University Press, 2000.

Oslo. Screenplay by J. T. Rogers. Dir. Bartlett Sher. HBO, 2021.

"Palestinian Center for Policy and Survey Research." *The Palestinian Center for Policy and Survey Research*, June 15, 2021. https://www.pcpsr.org/sites/default/files/Poll%2080%20English%20press%20release%20June2021.pdf.

Pappé, Ilan. "Indigeneity as Cultural Resistance: Notes on the Palestinian Struggle within Twenty-First-Century Israel." *The South Atlantic Quarterly* 117, no. 1 (2018): 157–78.

Pappé, Ilan. *The Ethnic Cleansing of Palestine*. Oxford: Oneworld, 2006.

Pappé, Ilan. *The Idea of Israel: A History of Power and Knowledge*. New York: Verso, 2014.

Pappé, Ilan. *Ten Myths about Israel*. New York: Verso, 2017.

Park, Linette. "Afropessimism and Futures of . . . : A Conversation with Frank Wilderson." *The Black Scholar* 50, no. 3 (2020): 29–41.
Patel, Yumna. "Israeli Mobs Chant 'Death to Arabs' in Night of Violence in Jerusalem." *Mondoweiss*, April 23, 2021. https://mondoweiss.net/2021/04/israeli-mobs-chant-death-to-arabs-in-night-of-violence-in-jerusalem/.
Paulson, Steve. "Critical Intimacy: An Interview with Gayatri Chakravorty Spivak." *Los Angeles Review of Books*, July 29, 2016. https://lareviewofbooks.org/article/critical-intimacy-interview-gayatri-chakravorty-spivak/.
Pawel, Ernst. *The Labyrinth of Exile: A Life of Theodor Herzl*. New York: Farrar, Straus, and Giroux, 1989.
Pfeffer, Anshel. "Israel Has Abandoned All Its Citizens, Not Just Its Arab Ones." *Haaretz*, May 19, 2021. https://www.haaretz.com/israel-news/2021-05-19/ty-article/.highlight/israel-has-abandoned-all-its-citizens-not-just-its-arab-ones/0000017f-f469-ddde-abff-fc6d649f0000.
Pitawanakwat, Brock. "Red-Baiting and Red-Herrings: Indigenous Labour Organizing in Saskatchewan." *New Socialist* 58 (2006): 32–3.
Puar, Jasbir. "'I Would Rather be a Cyborg than a Goddess': Becoming-Intersectional in Assemblage Theory." *philoSOPHIA* 2, no. 1 (2012): 49–66.
Puar, Jasbir. "Speaking of Palestine: Solidarity and Its Censors." *Jadaliyya*, March 16, 2016. https://www.jadaliyya.com/Details/33095/Speaking-of-Palestine-Solidarity-and-Its-Censors.
Puar, Jasbir. *Terrorist Assemblages: Homonationalism in Queer Times*. Durham: Duke University Press, 2007.
Puar, Jasbir. *The Right to Maim: Debility, Capacity, Disability*. Durham: Duke University Press, 2017.
Qabaha, Ahmad and Bilal Hamamra. "The Nakba Continues: The Palestinian Crisis from the Past to the Present." *Janus Unbound* 1, no. 1 (2021): 30–42.
Quijano, Anibal. "Coloniality of Power, Eurocentrism and Latin America." *Nepantla: Views from South* 1, no. 3 (2000): 533–80.
Rabbani, Mouin. "Israel Mows the Lawn." *London Review of Books*, July 31, 2014. https://www.lrb.co.uk/v36/n15/mouin-rabbani/israel-mows-the-lawn.
Rabinowitz, Dan. "'The Arabs Just Left': Othering and the Construction of Self amongst Jews in Haifa Before and After 1948." In *Mixed Towns, Trapped Communities: Spatial Dynamics, Gender Relations and Cultural Encounters in Palestinian-Israeli Towns*, edited by Daniel Monterescu and Dan Rabinowitz, 51–64. Aldershot: Ashgate, 2007.
Reuters. "At Least 55 Killed in Eastern Congo Massacres, U.N. Says." *Reuters*, May 31, 2021. https://www.reuters.com/world/africa/least-50-killed-eastern-congo-massacres-research-group-2021-05-31/.
Reuters. "At Least 132 Civilians Killed in Burkina Faso's Worst Attack in Years." *Reuters*, June 6, 2021. https://www.reuters.com/world/africa/armed-attackers-kill-100-civilians-burkina-faso-village-raid-2021-06-05/.

Reuters. "Israel's New Government Fails to Renew Disputed Citizenship Law." *Reuters*, July 6, 2021. https://www.reuters.com/world/middle-east/israels-new-government-dealt-blow-controversial-citizenship-vote-2021-07-06/.

Ridley, Yvonne. "Palestinian Lives Do Matter." *Middle East Monitor*, June 15, 2021. https://www.middleeastmonitor.com/20210615-palestinian-lives-do-matter/.

Rifkin, Mark. "Indigeneity, Apartheid, Palestine: On the Transit of Political Metaphors." *Cultural Critique* 95 (2017): 25–70.

Robinson, Cedric J. *Black Marxism: The Making of the Black Radical Tradition*. Chapel Hill: University of North Carolina Press, 2000.

Rose, Jacqueline. "Apocalypse/Emnity/Dialogue: Negotiating the Depths." In *The Arab and Jewish Questions Geographies of Engagement in Palestine and Beyond*, edited by Bashir Bashir and Leila Farsakh, 201–19. New York: Columbia University Press, 2020.

Rose, Jacqueline. "Nation as Trauma, Zionism as Question: Jacqueline Rose Interviewed." *Open Democracy*, August 17, 2005. https://www.opendemocracy.net/en/zionism_2766jsp/.

Rose, Jacqueline. *Proust Among the Nations: From Dreyfus to the Middle East*. Chicago: University of Chicago Press, 2011.

Rose, Jacqueline. *The Last Resistance*. New York: Verso, 2007.

Rose, Jacqueline. *The Question of Zion*. Princeton: Princeton University Press, 2007.

Ross, Kihana Mireya. "Call It What It Is: Anti-Blackness." *The New York Times*, June 4, 2020. https://www.nytimes.com/2020/06/04/opinion/george-floyd-anti-blackness.html.

Rouhana, Nadim. "Homeland Nationalism and Guarding Dignity in a Settler Colonial Context: The Palestinian Citizens of Israel Reclaim Their Homeland." *borderlands* 14, no. 1 (2015): 1–37.

Rudoren, Jodi. "Netanyahu Denounced for Saying Palestinian Inspired Holocaust." *The New York Times*, October 21, 2015. https://www.nytimes.com/2015/10/22/world/middleeast/netanyahu-saying-palestinian-mufti-inspired-holocaust-draws-broad-criticism.html.

Saad, Lydia. "Americans, but Not Liberal Democrats, Mostly Pro-Israel." *Gallup*, March 6, 2019. https://news.gallup.com/poll/247376/americans-not-liberal-democrats-mostly-pro-israel.aspx.

Said, Edward W. *After the Last Sky: Palestinian Lives*, with photographs by Jean Mohr. New York: Pantheon, 1986.

Said, Edward W. "An Ideology of Difference." *Critical Inquiry* 12, no. 1 (1985): 38–58.

Said, Edward W. "Backlash and Backtrack." *Counterpunch*, September 28, 2003. https://www.counterpunch.org/2001/09/28/backlash-and-backtrack/.

Said, Edward W. *Beginnings: Intention and Method*. New York: Columbia University Press, 1985.

Said, Edward W. "Criticism and the Art of Politics." In *Power, Politics, and Culture*: Interviews with Edward W. Said, edited by Gauri Viswanathan, 118–63. New York: Vintage, 2001.

Said, Edward W. *Culture and Imperialism.* New York: Vintage, 1994.
Said, Edward W. *The End of the Peace Process: Oslo and After.* New York: Vintage, 2001.
Said, Edward W. *Freud and the Non-European.* New York: Verso, 2004.
Said, Edward W. "The Gap Grows Wider." *Al-Ahram Weekly* 471 (March 2–8, 2000).
Said, Edward W. "Introduction." In *Blaming the Victims: Spurious Scholarship and the Palestine Question*, edited by Edward Said and Christopher Hitchens, 1–19. New York: Verso, 1988.
Said, Edward W. "My Right of Return." In *Power, Politics, and Culture: Interviews with Edward W. Said*, edited by Gauri Viswanathan, 443–58. New York: Vintage, 2001.
Said, Edward W. *On Late Style: Music and Literature Against the Grain.* New York: Vintage, 2007.
Said, Edward W. "The One State Solution." *The New York Times Magazine*, January 10, 1999. https://www.nytimes.com/1999/01/10/magazine/the-one-state-solution.html.
Said, Edward W. *Orientalism.* 25th anniversary ed. New York: Vintage, 2003.
Said, Edward W. "Orientalism, Arab Intellectuals, Marxism, and Myth in Palestinian History." In *Power, Politics, and Culture: Interviews with Edward W. Said*, edited by Gauri Viswanathan, 437–42. New York: Vintage, 2001.
Said, Edward W. *Oslo to Iraq and the Road Map.* New York: Vintage, 2004.
Said, Edward W. *Peace and it Discontents: Essays on Palestine in the Middle East Peace Process.* New York: Vintage, 1995.
Said, Edward W. *The Politics of Dispossession: The Struggle for Palestinian Self-Determination 1969–1994.* New York: Vintage, 1994.
Said, Edward W. "The Politics of Knowledge." In *Race, Identity, and Representation in Education*, eds. Cameron McCarthy and Warren Crichlow, 306–14. New York: Routledge, 1993.
Said, Edward W. "Preface." In *Dreams of a Nation: On Palestinian Cinema*, edited by Hamid Dabashi, 1–5. New York: Verso, 2006.
Said, Edward W. *The Question of Palestine.* New York: Pantheon Books, 1979.
Said, Edward W. *Reflections on Exile and Other Essays.* Cambridge: Harvard University Press, 2000.
Said, Edward W. *Representations of the Intellectual: The 1993 Reith Lectures.* New York: Vintage Books, 1996.
Said, Edward W. "What Israel Has Done." *The Nation*, April 18, 2002. https://www.thenation.com/article/archive/what-israel-has-done/.
Said, Edward W. "Zionism from the Standpoint of Its Victims." *Social Text* 1 (1979): 7–58.
Said, Edward and Christopher Hitchens, ed. *Blaming the Victims: Spurious Scholarship and the Palestinian Question.* New York: Verso, 1988.
Salam, Erum. "Black Lives Matter Protesters Make Palestinian Struggle Their Own." *The Guardian*, June 16, 2021. https://www.theguardian.com/world/2021/jun/16/black-lives-matter-palestinian-struggle-us-left.

Salih, Ruba and Sophie Richter-Devroe. "Palestine beyond National Frames: Emerging Politics, Cultures, and Claims." *South Atlantic Quarterly* 117, no. 1 (2018): 1–20.

Samour, Sobhi. "Covid-19 and the Necroeconomy of Palestinian Labor in Israel." *Journal of Palestine Studies* 49, no. 4 (2020): 53–64.

Sanbar, Elias. *Le bien des absents*. Paris: Actes Sud, 2001.

Sanbar, Elias. *The Palestinians: Photographs of a Land and its People from 1839 to the Present Day*. New Haven: Yale University Press, 2015.

Sasson-Levy, Orna and Avi Shoshana. "'Passing' as (Non) Ethnic: The Israeli Version of Acting White." *Sociological Inquiry* 83, no. 3 (2013): 448–72.

Sayegh, Fayez. "Zionist Colonialism in Palestine (1965)." *Settler Colonial Studies* 2, no. 1 (2012): 206–25.

Sazzad, Rehnuma. *Edward Said's Concept of Exile: Identity and Cultural Migration in the Middle East*. New York: I.B.Tauris & Co. Ltd, 2017.

Scheper-Hughes, Nancy. "The Body of the Terrorist: Blood Libels, Bio-Piracy, and the Spoils of War at the Israeli Forensic Institute." *Social Research* 78, no. 3 (2011): 849–86.

Schmitt, Carl. *Political Theology: Four Chapters on the Concept of Sovereignty*. Translated by George Schwab. Cambridge: MIT Press, 1985.

Schmitt, Carl. *The Concept of the Political*. Translated by George Schwab. Chicago: University of Chicago Press, 1996.

Schotten, C. Heike. *Queer Terror: Life, Death, and Desire in the Settler Colony*. New York: Columbia University Press, 2018.

Scott, David and Sylvia Wynter. "The Re-enchantment of Humanism: An Interview with Sylvia Wynter." *Small Axe* 8 (2000): 119–207.

Seidel, Timothy. "'Occupied Territory is Occupied Territory': James Baldwin, Palestine and the Possibilities of Transnational Solidarity." *Third World Quarterly* 37, no. 9 (2016): 1644–60.

Sekyi-Out, Ato. *Fanon's Dialectic of Experience*. Cambridge: Harvard University Press, 1996.

Sen, Somdeep. *Decolonizing Palestine: Hamas between The Anticolonial and the Postcolonial*. Ithaca: Cornell University Press, 2020.

Sexton, Jared. "All Black Everything." *e-flux* 79 (2017). https://www.e-flux.com/journal/79/94158/all-black-everything/.

Sexton, Jared. "People-of-Color-Blindness: Notes on the Afterlife of Slavery." *Social Text* 28, no. 2 103 (2010): 31–56.

Sexton, Jared. "Roundtable on Anti-Blackness and Black-Palestinian Solidarity." *Jadaliyya*, June 3, 2015. https://www.jadaliyya.com/Details/32145/Roundtable-on-Anti-Blackness-and-Black-Palestinian-Solidarity.

Sexton, Jared. "The Social Life of Social Death: On Afro-Pessimism and Black Optimism." *InTensions* 5 (2011): 1–47.

Sexton, Jared. "The *Vel* of Slavery: Tracking the Figure of the Unsovereign." *Critical Sociology* 42, no. 4–5 (2016): 583–97.

Sexton, Jared and Daniel Colucciello Barber. "On Black Negativity, or the Affirmation of Nothing." *Society and Space*, September 18, 2017. https://www.societyandspace.org/articles/on-black-negativity-or-the-affirmation-of-nothing.

Shalev, Chemi. "Full Transcript of Interview With Palestinian Professor Rashid Khalidi." *Haaretz*, December 5, 2011. https://www.haaretz.com/1.5216535.

Shalhoub, Nadera. "Roundtable on Anti-Blackness and Black-Palestinian Solidarity." *Jadaliyya*, June 3, 2015. https://www.jadaliyya.com/Details/32145/Roundtable-on-Anti-Blackness-and-Black-Palestinian-Solidarity.

Sharon, Jeremy and Idan Zonshine. "Lapid Condemns Flag March Slurs: 'This is not Judaism and not Israeli.'" *The Jerusalem Post*, June 15, 2021. https://www.jpost.com/arab-israeli-conflict/raam-leader-abbas-on-jerusalem-flag-march-were-against-any-provocation-671068.

Sharpe, Christina. *In the Wake: On Blackness and Being*. Durham: Duke University Press, 2016.

Sheehi, Lara and Stephen Sheehi. *Psychoanalysis Under Occupation: Practicing Resistance in Palestine*. New York: Routledge, 2021.

Sheizaf, Noam. "Jerusalem, in Context." *+972 Magazine*, October 19, 2015. https://www.972mag.com/jerusalem-in-context/.

Sherwood, Harriet. "Israel PM: Illegal African Immigrants Threaten Identity of Jewish State." *The Guardian*, May 20, 2012. https://www.theguardian.com/world/2012/may/20/israel-netanyahu-african-immigrants-jewish.

Sherwood, Harriet. "Israelis Attack African Migrants During Protest Against Refugees." *The Guardian*, May 24, 2012. https://www.theguardian.com/world/2012/may/24/israelis-attack-african-migrants-protest.

Sherwood, Harriet. "Israel Turns On Its Refugees." *The Guardian*, June 4, 2012. https://www.theguardian.com/world/2012/jun/04/israel-migrant-hate.

Shesgreen, Deidre. "Amid Warnings Of a 'Full Scale War.' Biden Administration Dispatches Envoy to Middle East." *USA Today*, May 12, 2021. https://www.usatoday.com/story/news/politics/2021/05/12/israel-palestine-full-scale-war-feared-us-without-ambassador/5053344001/.

Shohat, Ella. *Taboo Memories, Diasporic Voices: Columbus, Palestine, and Arab-Jews*. Durham: Duke University Press, 2006.

Silva, Denise Ferreira da. *Toward a Global Idea of Race*. Minneapolis: University of Minnesota Press, 2007.

Silva, Denise Ferreira da. "Hacking the Subject: Black Feminism and Refusal beyond the Limits of Critique." *philoSOPHIA* 8, no. 1 (2018): 19–41.

Simek, Nicole. "Trading Well." *symplokē* 27, no. 1–2 (2019): 405–8.

Simpson, Audra. "The Sovereignty of Critique." *The South Atlantic Quarterly* 119, no. 4 (2020): 685–99.

Simpson, Leanne. *Dancing on Our Turtle's Back: Stories of Nishnaabeg Re-creation, Resurgence and a New Emergence*. Winnipeg: Arbeiter Ring Pub., 2011.

Singh, Nikhil Pal. "On Race, Violence, and 'So-Called Primitive Accumulation.'" In *Futures of Black Radicalism*, edited by Gaye Theresa Johnson and Alex Lubin, 39–58. New York: Verso, 2017.

SIPRI Fact Sheet. "Trends in International Arms Transfers, 2020." https://www.sipri.org/sites/default/files/2021-03/fs_2103_at_2020_v2.pdf.

Slater, Jerome. "What Went Wrong? The Collapse of the Israeli-Palestinian Peace Process." *Political Science Quarterly* 116, no. 2 (2001): 171–99.

Smith, Amelia. "Israel: Promised Land For Jews . . . As Long As They're Not Black?" *Middle East Monitor*, May 4, 2014. https://www.middleeastmonitor.com/20140504-israel-promised-land-for-jews-as-long-as-they-re-not-black/.

Smith, Mitch and Tim Arango. "'We Need Policemen': Even in Liberal Cities, Voters Reject Scaled-Back Policing." *The New York Times*, November 3, 2021. https://www.nytimes.com/2021/11/03/us/police-reform-minneapolis-election.html.

Solomon, Shoshanna. "To Help Arabs Integrate, Israel Should Help Strengthen Arab Identity—Study." *The Times of Israel*, September 16, 2018. https://www.timesofisrael.com/to-help-arabs-integrate-israel-should-help-strengthen-arab-identity-study/.

de Sousa Santos, Boaventura. "Epistemologies of the South and the Future." *From the European South* 1 (2016): 17–29.

de Sousa Santos, Boaventura. *Epistemologies of the South: Justice against Epistemicide*. Boulder: Paradigm Publishers, 2014.

A Space Exodus. Dir. Larissa Sansour. Mec Film, 2009.

Spillers, Hortense J. "Mama's Baby, Papa's Maybe: An American Grammar Book." *Diacritics* 17, no. 2 (1987): 64–81.

Spivak, Gayatri. *An Aesthetic Education in the Era of Globalization*. Cambridge: Harvard University Press, 2013.

Stephens, Bret. "Every Time Palestinians Say 'No,' They Lose." *The New York Times*, January 30, 2020. https://www.nytimes.com/2020/01/30/opinion/middle-east-peace-plan.html.

Sternberg, Ernest. "Fanatical Anti-Zionism and the Degradation of the University: What I Have Learned in Buffalo." In *Anti-Zionism on Campus: The University, Free Speech, and BDS*, edited by Doron S. Ben-Atar and Andrew Pessin, 333–47. Bloomington: Indiana University Press, 2018.

Strickland, Patrick O. "Palestinians in Israel Beaten, Arrested for Gaza Support." *The Electronic Intifada*, August 19, 2014. https://electronicintifada.net/content/palestinians-israel-beaten-arrested-gaza-support/13774.

Sultany, Nimer. "Colonial Realities: From Sheikh Jarrah to Lydda." *Mondoweiss*, May 12, 2021. https://mondoweiss.net/2021/05/colonial-realities-from-sheikh-jarrah-to-lydda/.

Tatour, Lana. "Citizenship as Domination: Settler Colonialism and the Making of Palestinian Citizenship in Israel." *Arab Studies Journal* 27, no. 2 (2019): 8–39.

Tatour, Lana. "This Isn't a Civil War, It is Settler-Colonial Brutality." *Mondoweiss*, May 13, 2021. https://mondoweiss.net/2021/05/this-isnt-a-civil-war-it-is-settler-colonial-brutality/.
Tayeb, Sami. "The Palestinian McCity in the Neoliberal Era." *Middle East Report* 290 (2019): 24–8.
Thier, Daphna. "Not an Ally: The Israeli Working Class." In *Palestine: A Socialist Introduction*, edited by Sumaya Awad and Brian Bean, 79–98. Chicago: Haymarket Books, 2020.
Thobani, Sunera. "White Wars: Western Feminism and the "War on Terror."" *Feminist Theory* 2, no. 2 (2007): 169–85.
Thomas, Greg. "PROUD FLESH Inter/Views: Sylvia Wynter." *ProudFlesh: New Afrikan Journal of Culture, Politics, and Consciousness* 4 (2006): 1–35.
Todorova, Teodora. *Decolonial Solidarity in Palestine-Israel: Settler Colonialism and Resistance from Within*. New York: Zed Books, 2021.
Todorova, Teodora. "Reframing Bi-Nationalism in Palestine-Israel as a Process of Settler Decolonisation." *Antipode* 47, no. 5 (2015): 1367–87.
"Transcript: Senator Bernie Sanders on 'Face the Nation.'" May 23, 2021. https://www.cbsnews.com/news/transcript-senator-bernie-sanders-face-the-nation-05-23-2021/.
Tremblay, Jean-Thomas. "Being Black and Breathing: On 'Blackpentecostal Breath.'" *Los Angeles Review of Books*, October 19, 2016. https://lareviewofbooks.org/article/being-black-and-breathing-on-blackpentecostal-breath/.
Tuck, Eve and K. Wayne Yang. "Decolonization Is Not a Metaphor." *Decolonization: Indigeneity, Education, and Society* 1, no. 1 (2012): 1–40.
Vogt, Erik. "Žižek and Fanon: On Violence and Related Matters." In *Žižek Now: Cultural Perspectives in Žižek Studies*, edited by Jamil Khader and Molly Anne Rothenberg, 140–58. Cambridge: Polity, 2013.
Warren, Calvin L. "Onticide: Afro-pessimism, Gay Nigger #1, and Surplus Violence." *GLQ* 23, no. 3 (2017): 391–418.
Warren, Calvin L. *Ontological Terror: Blackness, Nihilism, and Emancipation*. Durham: Duke University Press, 2018.
Warschawski, Michael. *Toward an Open Tomb: The Crisis of Israeli Society*. Translated by Peter Drucker. New York: Monthly Review Press, 2004.
Waziyatawin. "Malice Enough in their Hearts and Courage Enough in Ours: Reflections on US Indigenous and Palestinian Experiences under Occupation." *Settler Colonial Studies* 2, no. 1 (2012): 172–89.
Weheliye, Alexander. *Habeas Viscus: Racializing Assemblages, Biopolitics, and Black Feminist Theories of the Human*. Durham: Duke University Press, 2014.
Weisglass, Dov. "Oslo Deal Was Good for the Jews." *Ynetnews*, August 21, 2012. https://www.ynetnews.com/articles/0,7340,L-4270970,00.html.
Weizman, Eyal. *Hollow Land: Israel's Architecture of Occupation*. New York: Verso, 2007.
West, Cornel. "Black America's Neo-liberal Sleepwalking Is Coming to an End." Interview by George Souvlis. *OpenDemocracy*, June 13, 2016. https://www

.opendemocracy.net/en/cornel-west-black-america-s-neo-liberal-sleepwalking-is-coming-to-end/.

Wilderson, Frank B. III. *Afropessimism.* New York: Liveright, 2020.

Wilderson, Frank B. III. "An Afropessimist on the Year Since George Floyd Was Murdered: Notes of a (Minneapolis) Native Son." *The Nation,* May 27, 2021. https://www.thenation.com/article/society/george-floyd-afropessimism/.

Wilderson, Frank B. III. "Gramsci's Black Marx: Whither the Slave in Civil Society?" *Social Identities* 9, no. 2 (2003): 225–40.

Wilderson, Frank B. III. *Red, White & Black: Cinema and the Structure of U.S. Antagonisms.* Durham: Duke University Press, 2010.

Wilderson, Frank B. III. "The Black Liberation Army and the Paradox of Political Engagement." In *Postcoloniality-Decoloniality-Black Critique: Joints and Fissures,* edited by Sabine Broeck and Carsten Junker, 175–210. Frankfurt: Campus Verlag, 2014.

Wilderson, Frank B. III. "'The Inside-Outside of Civil Society': An Interview with Frank B. Wilderson, III." Interview by Samira Spatzek, and Paula von Gleich, *Black Studies Papers* 2, no. 1 (2016): 4–22.

Wilderson, Frank B. III. "'We're Trying to Destroy the World': Anti-Blackness and Police Violence After Ferguson." In *Shifting Corporealities in Contemporary Performance Danger, Im/mobility and Politics,* edited by Marina Gržinić and Aneta Stojnić, 45–59. New York: Palgrave, 2018.

Wilderson, Frank and Tiffany Lethabo King. "Staying Ready for Black Study: A Conversation." In *Otherwise Worlds: Against Settler Colonialism and Anti-Blackness,* edited by Tiffany Lethabo King, Jenell Navarro and Andrea Smith, 52–73. Durham: Duke University Press, 2020.

Wilderson, Frank, Saidiya Hartman, Steve Martinot, Jared Sexton, Hortense J. Spillers. "Editors' Introduction." In *Afro-Pessimism: An Introduction,* edited by Frank B. Wilderson III, Saidya Hartman, Steve Martinot, Jared Sexton, Hortense J. Spillers, 7–13. Minneapolis: Racked & Dispatched, 2017.

Wolfe, Patrick. *Traces of History: Elementary Structures of Race.* New York: Verso, 2016.

Wolfe, Patrick. "Settler Colonialism and the Elimination of the Native." *Journal of Genocide Research* 8, no. 4 (2006): 387–409.

Wynter, Sylvia. "Unsettling the Coloniality of Being/Power/Truth/Freedom: Towards the Human, After Man, Its Overrepresentation—An Argument." *CR: The New Centennial Review* 3, no. 3 (2003): 257–337.

Yancy, George. *Look, A White! Philosophical Essays on Whiteness.* Philadelphia: Temple University Press, 2012.

Yosef, Raz, *The Politics of Loss and Trauma in Contemporary Israeli Cinema.* New York: Routledge, 2011.

Zakaria, Fareed. *CNN,* May 30, 2021. http://transcripts.cnn.com/TRANSCRIPTS/2105/30/fzgps.01.html.

Zalloua, Zahi. *Žižek on Race: Toward an Anti-Racist Politics*. New York: Bloomsbury, 2020.

Žižek, Slavoj. "Afterword: Lenin's Choice." In *Revolution at the Gates: Selected Writings of Lenin from 1917*, edited by Slavoj Žižek, trans. V. I. Lenin, 165–336. New York: Verso, 2002.

Žižek, Slavoj. "A Leftist Plea for 'Eurocentrism.'" *Critical Inquiry* 24, no. 4 (1998): 988–1009.

Žižek, Slavoj. "Anti-Semitism and Its Transformations." In *Deconstructing Zionism: A Critique of Political Metaphysics*, edited by Gianni Vattimo and Michael Marder, 1–13. New York: Bloomsbury, 2013.

Žižek, Slavoj. "Are We in a War? Do We Have an Enemy?" *London Review of Books*, 24, 10, May 23, 2002. https://www.lrb.co.uk/the-paper/v24/n10/slavoj-zizek/are-we-in-a-war-do-we-have-an-enemy.

Žižek, Slavoj. "Attempts to Escape the Logic of Capitalism." *London Review of Books*, 21, October 28, 1999. https://www.lrb.co.uk/the-paper/v21/n21/slavoj-zizek/attempts-to-escape-the-logic-of-capitalism

Žižek, Slavoj. "Class Struggle Against Classism." *The Philosophical Salon*, May 10, 2021. http://thephilosophicalsalon.com/class-struggle-against-classism/.

Žižek, Slavoj. "Class Struggle or Postmodernism? Yes, Please!" In *Contingency, Hegemony, Universality: Contemporary Dialogues on the Left*, edited by Judith Butler, Ernesto Laclau, and Slavoj Žižek, 90–135. New York: Verso, 2000.

Žižek, Slavoj. "Covid Crisis Sparked Fear of Communism & China's Rise as Superpower. But Best Way to Prevent Communism is to FOLLOW China." *RT*, October 7, 2020. https://www.rt.com/op-ed/502825-china-communism-covid-follow/.

Žižek, Slavoj. *Demanding the Impossible*. Edited by Yong-June Park. Cambridge: Polity, 2013.

Žižek, Slavoj. *Disparities*. New York: Bloomsbury, 2016.

Žižek, Slavoj. "Disputations: Who Are You Calling Anti-Semitic?" *The New Republic*, January 6, 2009. https://newrepublic.com/article/62376/disputations-who-are-you-calling-anti-semitic.

Žižek, Slavoj. *Enjoy Your Symptom!: Jacques Lacan in Hollywood and Out*. New York: Routledge, 2001.

Žižek, Slavoj. *For They Know Not What They Do: Enjoyment as a Political Factor*. New York: Verso, 2002.

Žižek, Slavoj. "Forward: The Importance of Theory." In *Žižek on Race: Toward an Anti-Racist Future*, by Zahi Zalloua, x–xiii. New York: Bloomsbury, 2020.

Žižek, Slavoj. "From Politics to Biopolitics . . . and Back." *South Atlantic Quarterly* 103, no. 2–3 (2004): 501–21.

Žižek, Slavoj. *Heaven in Disorder*. New York: OR Books, 2021.

Žižek, Slavoj. *In Defense of Lost Causes*. London: Verso, 2008.

Žižek, Slavoj. "Israelis' SHAME Over What Their State Is Doing In West Bank Would Be Sign Of Truly Belonging To Israel." *RT*, May 17, 2021. https://www.rt.com/op-ed/524075-israelis-shame-west-bank-palestinians/.

Žižek, Slavoj. "Labeling BDS 'Anti-Semitic' Desecrates the Holocaust in Order to Legitimize Apartheid." *RT*, May 25, 2019. https://www.rt.com/op-ed/460228-anti-semitic-bds-israel-zizek/.

Žižek, Slavoj. *Less Than Nothing: Hegel and the Shadow of Dialectical Materialism*. New York: Verso, 2012.

Žižek, Slavoj. *Like A Thief In Broad Daylight: Power in the Era of Post-Humanity*. New York: Allen Lane, 2018.

Žižek, Slavoj. *Living in the End Times*. New York: Verso, 2011.

Žižek, Slavoj. "May 1 in the Viral World Is a Holiday for the New Working Class." *RT*, May 1, 2020. https://www.rt.com/op-ed/487517-slavoj-zizek-new-working-class/.

Žižek, Slavoj. *Pandemic! 2: Chronicles of a Lost Time*. New York: OR Books, 2020.

Žižek, Slavoj. *Tarrying with the Negative: Kant, Hegel, and the Critique of Ideology*. Durham: Duke University Press, 1993.

Žižek, Slavoj. *The Courage of Hopelessness: Chronicles of a Year of Acting Dangerously*. New York: Allen Lane, 2017.

Žižek, Slavoj. "The Need to Traverse the Fantasy." *In These Times*, December 28, 2015. https://inthesetimes.com/article/Slavoj-Zizek-on-Syria-refugees-Eurocentrism-Western-Values-Lacan-Islam.

Žižek, Slavoj. "The Palestinian Question: The Couple Symptom/Fetish." *Lacan.com*, 2009. https://www.lacan.com/essays/?page_id=261.

Žižek, Slavoj. *The Parallax View*. Cambridge: MIT Press, 2006.

Žižek, Slavoj. *The Plague of Fantasies*. New York: Verso, 1997.

Žižek, Slavoj. "The Subject Supposed to Loot and Rape: Reality and Fantasy in New Orleans." *In These Times*, October 20, 2005. https://inthesetimes.com/article/the-subject-supposed-to-loot-and-rape.

Žižek, Slavoj. *The Sublime Object of Ideology*. New York: Verso, 1989.

Žižek, Slavoj. *Trouble in Paradise: From the End of History to the End of Capitalism*. Brooklyn: Melville House, 2014.

Žižek, Slavoj. "L'Ukraine et la Troisième Guerre mondiale." *L'Obs*, March 1, 2022. https://www.nouvelobs.com/guerre-en-ukraine/20220301.OBS55119/l-ukraine-et-la-troisieme-guerre-mondiale-par-slavoj-zizek.html.

Žižek, Slavoj. *Violence: Six Sideways Reflections*. New York: Picador, 2008.

Žižek, Slavoj. "We Need a Socialist Reset, Not a Corporate 'Great Reset.'" *Jacobin*, December 31, 2020. https://jacobinmag.com/2020/12/slavoj-zizek-socialism-great-reset.

Žižek, Slavoj and Glyn Daly. *Conversations with Žižek*. Cambridge: Polity, 2004.

Žižek, Slavoj and Christopher Hanlon. "Psychoanalysis and the Post-Political: An Interview with Slavoj Žižek." *New Literary History* 32, no. 1 (2001): 1–21.

Index

Abojaradeh, Lina 63–5, 197 n.130
abolition 35, 107, 126, 151–3, 155, 162–3
Abraham Accords 108
Abu Akleh, Shireen 177–8 n.96, 179 n.98
Abu Kabir Institute of Forensic Medicine 112, 115–16, 119, 120, 122
Abulhawa, Susan 236 n.26
Abu-Manneh, Bashir 31
Abumayyaleh, Mahmoud 197 n.25
Abunimah, Ali 143, 157
Adalah 39–40, 73, 119
"affectable I" 204–5 n.75
Africa, world perception of 52, 194 n.76
African migrants to Israel
    Ethiopian Jews 47–51
    non-Jewish 51–3
Afro-Palestinians 192 n.63
Afropessimism
    anti-Blackness, concept of 42–6, 52
    Black exceptionalism and 42–6, 50, 158
    dismissal of competing critical models by 191 n.57
    futurology in 162
    on idea/l of the human 41, 44–6, 53, 62, 65, 66, 151
    Il faut bien détruire ensemble and 62, 64
    on Israeli anti-Blackness 52–3
    libidinal economy, concept of 42–3, 48–50, 53–5, 155–6
    Palestinian cause complicating delineations of 153
    on sovereignty 147
    suspicion of Black-Palestinian alignment in 32–3, 43–5, 60–1
Aftonbladet 115, 217 n.80
Agamben, Giorgio 9, 136
Alcoff, Linda Martin 79
Alfred, Taiaiake 30

Algeria/Algerian War 83, 123, 173, 209, 214 n.43, 226 n.63
al-Haj, Majid 202 n.39
Althusser, Louis 82, 233 n.130
Amadahy, Zainab 192 n.59
Améry, Jean 96–7, 108, 210–11 n.7, 213–14 nn.42–3
anger, politicized 97, 213 n.33
anti-Blackness. *See* Black Studies and Black-Palestinian solidarity
anti-colonialism. *See also* decoloniality; decolonization
    anti-capitalism and 26–31
    "decolonizing the mind" 29–30
    hope and 159–60
    recognizing Zionist settler colonialism as problem of Palestinian Indigeneity 21–32
    "time before the settler," nostalgia for 3, 25, 29, 45, 80, 90, 126, 140–1, 152, 156, 166, 184–5 n.158, 186 n.173
    Zionist movement against British Empire cast as 168 n.3
anti-Semitism
    apartheid, decoupling from 219 n.94
    blood libel charges and organ harvesting controversy 34, 98, 111–13, 115, 117, 211 n.11
    critiques of Israel viewed as 14, 114, 188 n.10, 219 n.94
    European 8, 172 nn.32–3
    European atonement for 172 n.34
    Palestinian Indigeneity/Palestinian cause viewed as 7, 12, 13, 54
    Palestinophobia compared 122
    ressentiment/paranoia viewed as 97–8, 111–13, 119–23
    revenge fantasies in *Divine Intervention* and 102

UN Resolution on Zionism as racism recast as 228 n.79
anti-Zionist hermeneutic 34, 96–7, 111, 114, 123, 124
apartheid
   anti-Semitism, decoupling from 219 n.94
   Citizenship Law (Israel) and 76
   Israel as apartheid state 2, 24–6, 39, 69, 187 n.10
   Palestinian consciousness of Palestinian Indigeneity and 24–5
   universality and 17
   verticalization of 138–9
Apartheid Wall 32, 149
Arabs/Arab Israelis, Palestinians viewed as 8, 37, 51–2, 72
Arabs for Black Lives Collective 62–3, 197 n.25
Arabwashing 72
Arafat, Yasir 12, 103, 129, 130
archaeology, Zionist uses of 137, 225–6 n.44
Arendt, Hannah 9, 172–3 n.41
armed resistance. *See* violent/armed resistance
Armstrong, Neil 136
Arnall, Gavin 222 n.121
Asfour, Hassan 128
Ashkenazi Jews 16–17, 49–53, 64, 66, 72, 91, 114, 132, 163, 164, 192 n.61, 227 n.79
assemblages 14–15
autoimmunity 147, 165, 229–30 n.94
Awad, Nadine 72, 201 n.31

Baldwin, James 59
Balfour Declaration 65
Balibar, Étienne 107, 170 n.7
Barghouti, Mourid 33, 68, 80, 83–6, 88–93, 103, 134, 207 n.110
Barghouti, Omar 1, 16, 142–3, 150, 228 n.79, 230 n.102
BDS. *See* Boycott, Divestment and Sanctions (BDS) movement
becoming Black of the world 107, 156, 162–4, 166, 167
Begin, Menachem 15
Ben-Gurion, David 171 n.28

Benhabib, Seyla 113, 120, 171 n.28, 220 n.103
Benjamin, Walter 17, 78
Bennett, Naftali 76, 77, 103
Bernard, Anna 84–6, 88
bestialization of Palestinian collective body 15
Biden, Joseph 132–4, 215 n.53, 220 n.102
binationalism 34, 45, 126, 141–6, 153, 154, 157, 158
biopolitics and biopower 9–10, 24, 71, 149
Black exceptionalism 42–6, 50
Black Lives Matter (BLM) movement 3, 32, 40, 43, 52, 64, 92, 106–8, 154, 167, 197 n.130, 215 n.53
Black Reason 6
Black Skin, White Masks (Fanon) 38
Black Studies and Black-Palestinian solidarity 32–3, 37–66. *See also* Afropessimism
   Abojaradeh's artwork and 63–5, 64
   Afro-Palestinians 192 n.63
   anti-Blackness theory 3, 19, 25, 29, 42–6, 52, 189 n.23
   bothsidesism on anti-Blackness 132
   Critical Black Studies 3, 41
   double consciousness 81, 199 n.8
   Ethiopian Jews 47–51, 54, 59, 158, 193 n.65
   Il faut bien détruire ensemble, as basis for Black/Indigenous cooperation 62–6, 64
   Israel, anti-Blackness in 50–3, 192–3 n.65
   Marxism and 42, 45, 233 n.138
   non-Jewish African migrants to Israel 51–3
   "Oppression Olympics," avoiding 48, 162, 191 n.56
   Palestinian anti-Blackness 44, 47–9, 60
   paranoia and anger, Black 95
   possibility of Black-Palestinian alignment 161–7
   reciprocal support between Black and Occupied Palestine activists 32, 43, 62–3, 106, 154, 187 n.178
   recognizing differences between Black and Palestinian experience 32, 44, 64, 156

relationships between Blackness, anti-Blackness, and Indigeneity 3, 182 n.33
settler colonialism, Palestinian context of 47–50, 59–60
sovereignty, concept of 126, 146, 147, 150–2, 231–2 n.131
suspicion of Black-Palestinian alignment 32–3, 43–5, 60–1
Wilderson on 42–50, 52, 59–61
Zionist gaze analogized from Fanon on French/white gaze 38–9, 41
Black universality 151, 232 n.123
blame, politics of 96, 97, 105
blaming the victim 12, 13, 103, 106, 118, 133, 215 n.60
BLM. *See* Black Lives Matter (BLM) movement
blood libel 34, 98, 111–13, 115, 117, 211 n.11
Border Police (Israel) 17, 177 n.92, 177 n.94
Boström, Donald 115
bothsidesism, problem of 128, 130–5
Boycott, Divestment and Sanctions (BDS) movement 120, 173 n.51, 181 n.120, 209 n.146, 220 n.102, 221 n.113, 224 n.31, 233 n.133, 236 n.34
Bresheeth-Zabner, Haim 165
B'Tselem 178 n.96
Buber, Martin 14, 141, 171 n.28
Burkina Faso 194 n.76
Bush, Cori 220 n.102
Butler, Judith 84, 113, 134
Byrd, Jodi 25

Camp David summit (July 2000) 130
Canada 192 n.59, 195 n.101, 209 n.146, 210 n.4, 233 n.133
capitalism
  anti-Blackness and 42
  anti-colonialism and 26–31
  liberal democratic ideology's investment in 107–8
  racial 28, 29, 107, 157–8, 167, 184 n.151
Carruthers, Charlene 191 n.56
Cartesianism 33, 68
Cavanagh, Edward 4

Certeau, Michel de 74
Césaire, Aimé 9, 62, 173 n.41, 208–9 n.143
Chamoiseau, Patrick 225 n.43
Chilean protests (2019) 223 n.4, 3, 126
Christian Zionism 171–2 n.32
Chronicles of a Disappearance (film) 99
cinema
  Chronicles of a Disappearance 99
  Divine Intervention 33–4, 98–104, 108, 212 n.20
  In the Future They Ate from the Finest Porcelain 136–8
  Nation Estate 34, 126
  Oslo 34, 126–32
  A Space Exodus 136
  2001: A Space Odyssey 136
  visualization of Palestinianness in 100–1
citizenship in Israel 70–1, 73, 76–9, 187 n.3, 200–1 nn.22–3
Citizenship Law (Israel) 72, 76–9
class struggle 53, 153, 156, 158, 233 n.130
Clinton, Hilary 106
Coates, Ta-Nehisi 70
coexistence/co-resistance 154–5
Cohen, Roger 121
coloniality versus colonialism 183 n.144. *See also* anti-colonialism; decoloniality; postcolonialism; settler colonialism; Zionist settler ideology
contrapuntal consciousness 81–2, 86–7, 92–3, 206 n.94, 206 n.97
Coulthard, Glen 26, 28, 30–1, 97, 147, 186 n.73, 210 n.4
COVID-19 vaccines in Gaza 179 n.104
Critical Black Studies 3, 41
cross-racial solidarity. *See* solidarity
cultural aspects of Indigeneity 30–1, 185 n.64
cultural Zionism 14, 141
Culture and Imperialism (Said) 87

Daher, Nayef Fahoum 99
Dakota Access Pipeline, Native American protest of 183–4 n.150, 235 n.8
DAM (hip-hop group) 73, 154

Danon, Danny 211 n.11
Darwish, Mahmoud 73
Dau, Salim 128
Davis, Angela 187 n.178
Day, Iyko 231–2 n.121
Declaration of Principles on Interim Self-Government Arrangements. *See* Oslo Accords
decoloniality 33, 68, 69–79, 80, 84, 92, 126, 127, 205 n.76, 205 n.78, 208–9 n.143
decolonization
  binationalism and 142–5
  Palestinian Indigeneity/Palestinian cause and 13, 29–30, 35
  ressentiment/paranoia and 96, 124
  sovereignty, concept of 151, 154, 158
  thinking under Occupation and 75, 78, 80, 87, 92
  two-state solution and 125–7, 135
  universality of Palestinian cause and 160, 167
"decolonizing the mind" 29–30
defunding police, in US 56, 107, 214–15 n.53
Deleuze, Gilles 14, 92
Democratic Republic of Congo 194 n.76
Derrida, Jacques 61–2, 147, 165, 229–30 n.94, 229 n.91
Descartes, René 33, 68
de Sousa Santos, Boaventura 184 n.151
de-Zionization 144–5
diaspora. *See* exile/diaspora
Dickerson, John 219 n.94
Divine Intervention (film) 33–4, 98–104, 108, 212 n.20
double consciousness 81, 199 n.8
Du Bois, W. E. B. 68

East Jerusalem 12, 17, 18, 25, 56, 57, 71, 93, 101, 129, 148
Edelman, Lee 140
education system in Israel 73–6, 202 n.39
égaliberté (equaliberty) 107, 214 n.51
Eid, Haidar 25, 37, 40, 148, 225 n.33, 226–7 n.63
Eitan, Rafael 15
El-Haj, Nadia Abu 10, 56, 203 n.58, 225–6 n.44

Elitzur, Uri 19
enclosure as condition of Indigeneity 71–2
epistemic disobedience 79
epistemic reconstitution 68
Erakat, Ahmad 119
Erakat, Noura 26, 65, 116, 119, 125, 145, 174 n.58
Erdan, Gilan 71–2
Erekat, Saeb 25
Estes, Nick 160, 186 n.73
Ethiopian Jews 47–51, 54, 59, 158, 193 n.65
ethnic cleansing 20, 41, 55, 56, 70, 93, 108, 114, 133, 180 n.107, 200 n.20, 213 n.26, 227 n.78
ethnonationalism 34, 56–8, 76, 114, 132, 148, 154, 155, 164, 204 n.62, 206 n.97
European anti-Semitism and Zionism 8
European exceptionalism 4
European Indigeneity 3–4
exceptionalism
  Black/Afropessimist 42–6, 50, 158
  European 4
  Jewish 7, 20, 92, 130
  moral claims of 158
  as oppressor's rhetoric 92
  origins of 83
  Palestinian need to resist 28–9
exile/diaspora 33, 80–93
  alternative forms of statehood and 148, 230 n.101
  Mourid Barghouti on 68, 83–6, 88–93, 207 n.110
  Said on 68, 80–8, 90, 93, 205 n.83, 206 n.94, 207 n.114, 208 n.134
  thinking under Occupation and 33, 68–9, 80–1
Eyal, Hedva 193 n.68

Face the Nation (TV show) 219 n.94
Fahim, Joseph 128
Falk, Richard 120
Fanon, Frantz
  Black-Palestinian solidarity and 48, 59, 62, 66, 187 n.9, 199 n.139
  Black Skin, White Masks 38
  Palestinian Indigeneity and 22–3, 29, 31–2, 184–5 n.158, 185–6 n.171

ressentiment/paranoia and 103, 105, 109, 123–4, 214 n.43, 222 n.116, 222 n.121
 on sovereignty 149, 150, 155, 156
 thinking under Occupation and 83, 200 n.14, 204 n.65, 205 n.78, 207 n.114
 universality of Palestinian cause and 162, 163, 166, 236 n.25, 237 n.39
 The Wretched of the Earth 29, 150
 Zionist gaze analogized from 38–42
Farsakh, Leila 145
feminization of Palestinian collective body 15, 176–7 n.81
Ferguson 43–5, 63, 106
film. *See* cinema
Fink, Bruce 53
First Intifada 127
Flag March (2021) 57
Floyd, George 18, 63, 197 n.125, 215 n.53
Foxman, Abraham 211 n.11
France/French colonialism 38, 39, 83, 123–4, 166, 173, 193 n.75, 209, 214 n.43, 226 n.63
Friedman, Tom 135
futurology 11, 13, 32, 136, 140, 141, 162

Gandhi, Mohandas 12, 91, 174 n.51
Garner, Eric 166–7
Gaza
 Black-Palestinian solidarity and 40, 43, 55, 56, 208 n.133
 COVID-19 vaccines in 179 n.104
 feminization of Palestinian collective body of 15, 176–7 n.81
 Israel-Gaza War (2014) (*see Operation Protective Edge*)
 Palestinian Indigeneity/Palestinian cause and 1, 2, 10, 12, 13, 15–16, 19, 25
 ressentiment/paranoia in 103, 106, 108, 211 n.11, 219 n.94
 thinking under Occupation in 71, 74, 76, 86, 90
 two-state solution and 125, 127, 134, 138, 148, 149, 157, 163, 165, 166
Gazafication 71, 166
Gaza War (2021). *See Operation Guardian of the Walls*

genocide 37, 56, 59, 67, 73, 108, 146, 147, 209 n.146, 227 n.78
geo-social class 234 n.158
Godard, Jean-Luc 100
Goldberg, David Theo 15, 50
Goldberg, Jeffrey 216–17 n.60
Gramsci, Antonio 233 n.138
"Great March of Return" (2018-2019) 174 n.58
Green Line 24, 56, 58, 67, 77, 79, 98, 121, 222 n.115
Grunes, Dennis 102, 103
Guattari, Félix 14

Haddad, Toufic 157
Haj Amin al-Husseini 216 n.72
Hallaq, Eyad 17–19, 177 n.92, 179 n.98
Hamas 12, 21, 24, 72, 102, 133, 134, 149, 165, 174 n.58, 179 n.104, 208 n.133
Hamza, Agon 153
Hanafi, Sari 56
Harney, Stefano 107, 173 n.51
Hartman, Saidiya 18–19, 184–5 n.158, 198 n.135, 232 n.124
Harvey, David 166
hasbara 12, 72
Hegel, Georg Wilhelm Friedrich 205 n.80
Heidegger, Martin 139
Helow, Amal 203 n.53
Herzl, Theodor 9, 73, 175 n.64
Hill, Marc Lamont 174–5 n.61, 198 n.138, 212–13 n.26
Hiss, Yehuda 112, 114–16, 122, 217–18 n.80, 218 n.86
Hochberg, Gil Z. 139, 212 n.23
Holocaust/Shoah 8, 9, 83, 95, 113, 122, 172–3 nn.40–1, 208–9 n.143, 221–2 n.115
Homer's *Odyssey* 136
Horkheimer, Max 22, 102, 181 n.120
humanism 23, 26, 41, 46, 62, 64–6, 163, 173, 198 n.138, 209 n.145
humans/humanity
 Afropessimism on idea/l of 41, 44–6, 53, 62, 65, 66, 151
 decolonial understanding of 208–9 n.143
 grammar of 41, 66, 198 n.138, 209 n.145

ontological paradox of 163–4
organ harvesting controversy and 116
sovereignty under erasure and 126
structural interventions needed to support rhetoric of 155

ICC (International Criminal Court) 178 n.96
identificatory impulse 19–21, 198 n.135
identity in politics 69
identity politics 32, 45, 59, 69, 83, 91, 106, 107, 153, 161, 167, 214 n.51
IDF. *See* Israeli Defense Forces
Idle No More 209 n.146
Ihmoud, Sarah 150, 176–7 n.81
IHRA (International Holocaust Remembrance Alliance) 14, 114
Il faut bien détruire ensemble 61–6
Indigeneity. *See also* Palestinian Indigeneity and Palestinian cause
 concept of 3–11
 cultural aspects of 30–1, 185 n.64
 enclosure as condition of 71–2
 European 3–4
 fetishizing, avoidance of 166, 186 n.73
 Jewish 168 n.3
Indigenous and Native American Studies 1, 4, 25, 26, 42, 74, 147, 150–1, 160, 181 n.119, 185 n.164, 203 n.59
Indigenous reason 2, 6–7, 9–12, 14, 17–18, 22–6, 29, 31, 69, 128, 148, 149
Indigenous sovereignty 126, 136, 141, 147, 150, 151
innocence, move to 20, 51, 57, 75, 87, 102, 132, 171 n.28, 180 n.107, 191 n.57
International Criminal Court (ICC) 178 n.96
International Holocaust Remembrance Alliance (IHRA) 14, 114
In the Future They Ate from the Finest Porcelain (film) 136–8
IOF (Israeli Occupation Forces) 2, 168 n.4
I Saw Ramallah (Barghouti) 68, 83–93
Isha le'Isha 50

Islamic Jihad 101–2, 149
Israel. *See also* Zionist gaze; Zionist settler ideology; *specific laws*
 anti-Blackness in 50–3, 192–3 n.65
 anti-Semitism, critiques viewed as 14, 114, 188 n.10, 219 n.94
 as apartheid state 2, 24–6, 39, 69, 187 n.10
 citizenship in 70–1, 73, 76–9, 187 n.3, 200–1 nn.22–3
 demographics in 50–1
 education system in 73–6, 202 n.39
 European anti-Semitism, Zionism, and founding of 8
 legal position of Palestinians in 39–40
 necropolitics of 10
 paranoia, Israeli/Zionist 109–10, 113, 117, 120, 216–17 nn.73–4
 political shift to right in 196 n.102, 204 n.62, 223 n.20
 racism of state of 19, 24, 53, 132
 right to exist 12, 65, 77, 148, 203 n.58
 right to self-defense 103, 112, 128, 133, 224–5 n.31
 "un-mattering" of Palestinians in 11–21
 war economy of 165–6, 236 n.26, 236 n.34
 Western liberal [loss of] support for 58–9, 120, 175 n.62, 220 n.102
 as white Jewish state 50
Israel Denial (Nelson) 113–14
Israel-Gaza War (2014). *See Operation Protective Edge*
Israeli Defense Forces (IDF) 17, 43, 49, 63, 91, 101, 112, 169 n.4, 177–8 n.96, 177 n.94, 193 n.65, 195 n.95
Israeli Occupation Forces (IOF) 2, 168 n.4

Jabotinsky, Vladimir 159
Jamal, Amal 24
Jameson, Fredric 42
Jerusalem Day marches 133
Jewish exceptionalism 7, 20, 92, 130
Jewish Indigeneity 168 n.3
Jewish universalism, Palestinians' condition as fundamental obstacle for 152–3

Jews. *See also* anti-Semitism
   Ashkenazi 16–17, 49–53, 64, 66, 72, 91, 114, 132, 163, 164, 192 n.61, 227 n.79
   Ethiopian 47–51, 54, 59, 158, 193 n.65
   Eurocentric conception of 16–17
   Mizrahi 49–50, 52, 114, 192 n.61
   Nakba, education about 203 n.53
   Nazi social fantasy of Jewish plot 53–4
   "New Jew" 55
   Palestinian Indigeneity recasting narrative of 1
   "self-hating" 14, 54, 142
   Sephardi 49–50, 192 n.61, 217 n.80
   Shoah/Holocaust and 8, 9, 83, 95, 113, 122, 172–3 nn.40–1, 208–9 n.143, 221–2 n.115
   Ultra-Orthodox 114, 217 n.78
Jrere, Mahmood 73
Juul, Mona 126–7, 130–1

Kanafani, Ghassan 91
Kant, Immanuel 34, 105, 163
Kelley, Robin D. G. 66, 182 n.33
Khader, Jamil 22, 28
Khader, Manal 98
King, Martin Luther, Jr. 37, 107–8
King, Tiffany Lethabo 181 n.54
Krauthammer, Charles 12
Kubrick, Stanley 136
Kugel, Chen 116, 218 n.86

Lacan, Jacques 110, 148, 232 n.123, 235 n.12
land repatriation 25, 29, 75, 86–7, 125, 130
Lapid, Yair 57, 77
Lawrence, Bonita 192 n.59
Lazarus, Neil 200 n.14
Levy, Gordon 177 n.94, 188 n.10
LGBTQ community 46, 140
liberal democratic ideology
   bothsidesism, problem of 128, 130–5
   capitalism, investment in 107–8
   citizenship in Israel, continuing coloniality of 70–1, 73, 76–9, 187 n.3, 200–1 nn.22–3
   decolonization, liberal understanding of 127
   identificatory impulse in 19–21, 198 n.135

   Indigenous reason and 24–5
   Israeli master narrative, [loss of] Western support for 58–9, 120, 175 n.62, 220 n.102
   neoliberalism 4, 27–8, 35, 63, 121, 139, 157–8, 166, 173 n.51
   non-violence, insistence on Palestinian embrace of 22, 103–4
   Palestinian Indigeneity, advantages and disadvantages of claiming 1–3
   two-state solution, support for 34
   "un-mattering" of Palestinians and 12–13, 16
liberal Zionism 2, 16, 19–22, 34, 57, 96, 114, 125, 132, 152–3, 195 n.101, 208 n.133
libidinal economy 42–3, 48–50, 53–5, 57, 59, 60, 146, 155–6, 164–5, 229 n.79
Lieberman, Avigdor 13, 195 n.95
living dead, Palestinians as 65, 117, 148, 157, 165
Locke, John 13
Lorde, Audre 104, 181 n.119, 213 n.33
Lund, Søren 137

Magnes, Judah 141
Majumdar, Nivedita 88, 206–7 n.108
Makdisi, Saree 20, 67, 68
Maldonado-Torres, Nelson 183 n.144, 202 n.51, 204 n.74
Mandela, Nelson 37
Manichean reason/logic 11, 32, 49, 66, 83, 96, 97, 105, 118, 124, 144, 146, 149
Manifest Destiny 1, 6, 70
Marche, Stephen 195 n.101
Marriott, David 60
Martel, James R. 187 n.9
Marxism 26–9, 42, 45, 128, 133 n.138, 155–6, 183 n.149, 236 n.39
Massad, Joseph 168 n.3
matrix of rules 71
Mbembe, Achille
   on *becoming Black of the world* 107, 156, 162–4, 166, 167
   on Black struggle 46
   on decoloniality 71, 80, 199 n.13
   Palestinian Indigeneity and 6, 9–10
   on sovereignty 157, 232 n.124
Mekelberg, Yossi 50

Menick, John   102
Mignolo, Walter
  on decoloniality   67–70, 79, 80, 84
  on exploitation and capitalism   153
  Palestinian Indigeneity and   3, 4, 27–8, 33, 170 n.12, 183 n.147
  ressentiment of Palestinian communities and   97
Mizrahi Jews   49–50, 52, 114, 192 n.61
modernity
  decoloniality and   205 n.76
  identity determination in   69
  settler colonialism and concept of nation-state   70
  subjectivity of   204 n.74
  transmodernity versus   79
Montaigne, Michel de   99
Moore-Backman, Chris   119
Moten, Fred   107, 146, 148–9, 161, 173 n.51, 222 n.121, 231 n.109
move to innocence   20, 51, 57, 75, 87, 102, 132, 171 n.28, 180 n.107, 191 n.57
movies. *See* cinema
Mufti, Aamir R.   230 n.101

Nafar, Tamer   154
Nakba
  of 1948   3, 56, 88
  education about   76, 203 n.53
  liberal versus religious/political Zionist attitudes toward   56–8, 204 n.62
  as ongoing   26, 48, 135, 211 n.7, 221 n.114
  ressentiment/paranoia and   99, 108
  Shoah versus   83
Nakba Day   16, 72
Nakba Law (Israel)   72, 76, 78, 96
Nakba survivors   5, 37, 40
Nanibush. Wanda   4, 170 n.12
Naor, Igal   126
Nation Estate (film)   34, 126, 136–41
nation-state
  ideological abstraction of rights of   148–9
  modernity and   70
  Palestinian Indigeneity inside framework of   2, 3, 25
  self-defense as luxury of   134

  sovereignty, concept of   34–5, 126, 146–58
  Zionism and   8, 70
Nation-State Law (Israel 2018)   8, 39, 51, 108
Native American and Indigenous Studies   1, 4, 25, 26, 42, 74, 147, 150–1, 160, 181 n.119, 185 n.164, 203 n.59
Native Americans
  Abojaradeh, Lina, artwork of   63–5, 64, 197 n.130
  protest of Dakota Access Pipeline   183–4 n.150, 235 n.8
  solidarity with Palestinian cause   160, 235 n.8
  Wilderson's experience of anti-Blackness from   191 n.54
Nazis and Nazism   53–4, 216 n.72
necropolitics and necropower   9, 10, 24, 52, 119, 121, 122, 149, 151, 165
Négritude   184–5 n.158
Nelson, Cary   113–15, 117–21, 123, 217 n.76, 217 n.78, 218 n.80, 218 n.86
neoliberalism   4, 27–8, 35, 63, 121, 139, 157–8, 166, 173 n.51
neo-Zionism   223 n.20
Netanyahu, Benjamin   15, 17–19, 51–2, 74, 76, 77, 103, 114, 135, 216 n.72
Nevel, Donna   208 n.133
"New Jew"   55
New York Times   135, 211 n.11, 215 n.53
Nietzsche, Friedrich   95, 98, 104, 213 n.42, 214 n.51
nonviolence. *See* violent/armed resistance

objet petit a   53, 143
Ocasio-Cortez, Alexandria   220 n.102
Occupied Territories. *See also* East Jerusalem; Gaza; West Bank
  Black-Palestinian solidarity and   37, 39, 48, 49, 58, 187 n.2
  as "Greater Israel"   169 n.2
  Palestinian Indigeneity/Palestinian cause and   7, 16, 24, 25, 181 n.119
  ressentiment/paranoia in   99, 108, 121
  settlements in   20, 57, 92, 93, 108, 129, 138, 139, 154, 215 n.60

thinking under Occupation in 67, 68, 71, 73, 78, 90, 93
  two-state solution and 152, 154
Odyssey (Homer) 136
one-state solution
  Barghouti on 142, 150
  binationalism as democratic version of 126, 142 (*see also* binationalism)
  Greater Israel as racist version of 13
On the Genealogy of Morals (Nietzsche) 98
Operation Guardian of the Walls (Gaza War 2021) 26, 43, 58, 71–2, 74, 103, 132–3
Operation Protective Edge (Israeli-Gaza War 2014) 15, 221–2 n.115
"Oppression Olympics," avoiding 48, 162, 191 n.56
organ harvesting/body holding controversy 34, 97–8, 111–21, 211 n.11
"Oriental," use of 114–15, 218 n.80
Orientalism 8–9, 19, 23, 45, 77, 100, 104, 109, 139, 172 n.40, 194 n.76
Orientalism (Said) 8, 115, 172 n.40, 217–18 n.80
Oslo (film) 34, 126–32
Oslo (play) 126
Oslo Accords 24, 26, 71, 83, 89, 90, 99, 108, 126–32, 135–6, 142, 157

Palestinian Authority (PA) 16, 24, 34, 104, 132, 141, 148, 157, 175 n.62, 211 n.11
Palestinian Indigeneity and Palestinian cause 1–35, 159–67
  advantages and consequences of claiming 1–3
  anti-Semitism, viewed as 7, 12, 13, 54
  Black Studies/Black-Palestinian solidarity and 32–3, 37–66 (*see also* Black Studies and Black-Palestinian solidarity)
  concept of 3–11
  cultural aspects of 30–1
  exile/diaspora and 33, 68–9, 80–93 (*see also* exile/diaspora)
  fetishizing, avoidance of 166, 186 n.73

hope and anti-colonial resistance 159–60
  liberal Zionist approach to 16, 19–22, 34
  Palestinian consciousness of 7, 22–5, 29, 148
  reimagining/reinventing 29–31
  ressentiment/paranoia and 33–4 (*see also ressentiment*/paranoia)
  sovereignty and 152–8
  thinking under Occupation 33, 67–9 (*see also* decoloniality; thinking under Occupation)
  two-state solution to 34–5, 125–58 (*see also* binationalism; two-state solution)
  universality of Palestinian cause 1–3, 32, 135, 136, 160–7, 209 n.146, 235 n.5 (*see also* universality)
  "un-mattering" of Palestinians 11–21
  violent/armed resistance, reclaiming right to 22–3
  Zionist consciousness of 6, 8, 14, 128, 148
  Zionist gaze and 32–3 (*see also* Zionist gaze)
  Zionist settler colonialism as problem of 21–32, 152–3 (*see also* Zionist settler ideology)
Palestinian Liberation Organization (PLO) 25, 129
Palestinian Lives Matter 91, 101, 135, 154
Palestinophobia 17, 19, 21, 30, 53, 57, 59, 67, 108, 109, 122, 153, 171 n.29
Pantaleo, Daniel 166
Pappé, Ilan 73–4, 200 n.20, 227 n.78
paranoia. *See ressentiment*/paranoia
Parting Ways (Butler) 113
Pawel, Ernst 175 n.64
PEP (Progressives Except for Palestine) 13, 174–5 n.61
Peres, Shimon 129
Pfeffer, Anshel 201 n.31
Pitawanakwat, Brock 185 n.164
Plan D 200 n.20
Plitnick, Mitchell 174–5 n.61, 198 n.138
PLO (Palestinian Liberation Organization) 25, 129

police, defunding, in US 56, 107, 214–15 n.53
police brutality, in US 42, 49, 56, 166. *See also* Black Lives Matter; Floyd, George; Garner, Eric
political Zionism 8, 14, 19–20, 46–8, 56–8, 109, 163, 169 n.3, 171 n.28
positionality 4, 28, 42, 46, 50, 59–60, 79, 84, 86, 90, 161, 192 n.63
postcolonialism 42, 45, 205 n.76
Powell, Colin 166
precarity 84, 86, 95, 166
private use of *ressentiment* 149, 214 n.45
Progressives Except for Palestine (PEP) 13, 174–5 n.61
proletarian position 26–9, 153, 156
Puar, Jasbir 14, 34, 95, 97–8, 111–17, 120–1, 123, 136
public use of *ressentiment* 34, 97, 104–8, 149–50

queer theory 140
Qurei, Ahmed 128–30

Rabin, Yitzhak 90–1, 130
race. *See also* Black Studies and Black-Palestinian solidarity
  as operation of the imagination 199–200 n.13
  as product of racism 70
  as socio-political process 14
racial capitalism 28, 29, 107, 157, 158, 167, 184 n.151
racialization
  Holocaust survivors' ad condemning 222 n.115
  identificatory impulse and 19
  Indigeneity and 4, 6
  modernity and 69
  in Zionist settler ideology 8–11, 13, 15, 17
racism
  as anti-Blackness 3, 19, 25, 29, 42–6, 52, 189 n.23
  concept of Indigeneity and 4–11
  of Israeli state 19, 24, 53, 132
  Mignolo's definition of 69
  Palestinian anti-Blackness 44, 47–9, 60
  Palestinian cause as struggle against 146

Palestinian Indigeneity, advantages and consequences of 2–3
politicized anger as response to 97, 213 n.33
race as product of 70
shame about, and self-perception as good 180 n.108
of two-state solution 125, 225 n.33
UN Resolution on Zionism as 227–9 n.79
Rancière, Jean 100–1
Red washing 160
Regev, Miri 51
Resolution 922 (Israel) 74–6
Resolutions, UN. *See* UN Resolutions
ressentiment/paranoia 33–4, 95–124
  anti-Semitism charges against 97–8, 111–13, 119–23
  anti-Zionist hermeneutic of 34, 96–7, 111, 114, 123, 124
  binationalism and 141, 154
  bothsidesism and 133
  Divine Intervention (film) on 33–4, 98–104, 108, 212 n.20
  Israeli/Zionist paranoia 109–10, 113, 117, 120, 216–17 nn.73–4
  Nietzschean formulation of 95, 98, 104, 213 n.42, 214 n.51
  organ harvesting/body holding controversy 34, 97–8, 111–21, 211 n.11
  othering of/control over Palestinian bodies and 116–17, 121, 218 n.86
  Palestinian paranoia 108–11, 113, 120–4, 215–16 n.60
  private use of *ressentiment* 149, 214 n.45
  public use of *ressentiment* 34, 97, 104–8, 149–50
  relationship between 96
  revenge fantasies 101–2, 104, 212 n.20, 212 n.23
  social breakdown and 99–100
  two-state solution and 133, 135, 141
  whitewashing Israeli violence in treatment of 113–17
  Zionist settler-colonial context of 96–7, 117–29
Rhetorics of Belonging (Bernard) 84
Rifkin, Mark 5

right of return   12, 21, 25, 28, 71, 77, 130, 148, 217 n.76
right to exist   12, 65, 77, 148, 203 n.58
right to self-defense   103, 112, 128, 133, 224–5 n.31
Robinson, Cedric   184 n.151
Rod-Larsen, Terje   126–7
Rogers, J. T.   126
Rose, Jacqueline   55, 195 n.91, 216 n.73
Ross, Kihana Mireya   189 n.23
Rubin, Joel   219 n.94
Rudnitzky, Arik   202 n.50
Ruppin, Arthur   141
Russian/Ukrainian immigrants to Israel   116
Russia/Ukraine conflict   224 n.31

Said, Edward   160, 235 n.5
   on exile/diaspora   68, 80–8, 90, 93, 205 n.83, 206 n.94, 207 n.114, 208 n.134
   on Jewish/non-Jewish binary in Israel   200 n.22
   Orientalism   8, 115, 172 n.40, 217–18 n.80
   Palestinian Indigeneity and   1, 8, 20, 23, 28, 33, 172 n.40
   on *ressentiment*/paranoia   95, 96, 100, 105, 115, 117, 121, 217–18 n.80
   on thinking under Occupation   67, 208 n.134
   on two-state solution, binationalism, and sovereignty   141, 142, 144–6, 227–8 n.79, 230 n.101
   on universality of Palestinian cause   160, 208 n.134, 235 n.5
   on victimhood and moral superiority   55–6
"Sameer Bishara"   47, 49, 191 n.52
Sanbar, Elias   23, 92, 204 n.63
Sanders, Bernie   219 n.94, 220 n.102
Sansour, Larissa   34, 126, 136–41
Sartre, Jean-Paul   236 n.25
Savir, Uri   128, 130
Sayegh, Sayez   5, 17
Scheper-Hughes, Nancy   114–18, 218 n.86
Schmitt, Carl   146
Schumer, Chuck   13
Scott, Andrew   126

Scott, David   176 n.72
Second Intifada (2000)   76, 98, 103, 112, 130, 223 n.20, 224 n.25
self-defense, right to   103, 112, 128, 133, 224–5 n.31
self-determination, Western goal of   204–5 n.75
"self-hating" Jews   14, 54, 142, 226 n.61
Sephardi Jews   49–50, 192 n.61, 217 n.80
settlements   20, 57, 92, 93, 108, 129, 138, 139, 154, 215 n.60
settler colonialism
   Black Studies, Black-Palestinian solidarity, and Palestinian context of   47–50, 59–60
   citizenship in Israel, continuing coloniality of   70–1, 187 n.3
   concept of Indigeneity and   4–8
   decoloniality as counter to   33, 68–80, 84, 92
   exceptionalism as rhetoric of   92
   futurology in   11, 13
   hope and resistance to   159–60
   liberal Zionism and   20–1
   modernity and   70
   "native" as product of   70, 200 n.14
   necropolitics at core of   9–10
   Palestinian Indigeneity, advantages and consequences of claiming   3
   subordinate or "junior" settlers, marginalized groups as   46, 49, 192 n.59
   "time before the settler," nostalgia for   3, 25, 29, 45, 80, 90, 126, 140–1, 152, 156, 166, 184–5 n.158, 186 n.173
   "un-mattering" of Palestinians and   11–21
   Zionism as   5–9 (*see also* Zionist settler ideology)
   Zionist gaze in context of   47–50
Sexton, Jerod   64, 151, 159, 161, 162, 231–2 n.121, 232 n.123, 235 n.12
Shaked, Ayelet   15, 19–20, 76, 179 nn.103–4
Shalhoub-Kevorkian, Nadera   65
Sharon, Ariel   103
Shavit, Ari   144
Sheehi, Lara and Stephen   22–3, 109
Sher, Bartlett   34, 126

Shin Bet 76
Shoah/Holocaust 8, 9, 83, 95, 113, 122, 172–3 nn.40–1, 208–9 n.143, 221–2 n.115
Shohat, Ella 117
Silva, Denise Ferreira da 11, 204 n.75
Simek, Nicole 74
Simpson, Audra 150–1, 231 n.115
Simpson, Leanne 30, 147, 181 n.119
Singer, Joel 126, 129
SIPRI research institute 165
Six Day War (1967) 14, 24, 82, 114, 130
Smith, Amelia 192–3 n.65
social death 21, 33, 44, 60, 65, 116, 153, 156, 162, 207 n.110
solidarity. *See also* Black Studies and Black-Palestinian solidarity
  effects of 161
  global commitments to 235 n.5
  Native American/Palestinian 160, 235 n.8
  "Oppression Olympics," avoiding 48, 162, 191 n.56
sovereignty and alternative forms of statehood 34–5, 126, 146–58. *See also* binationalism; nation-state; two-state solution
A Space Exodus (film) 136
Spillers, Hortense 30
Spivak, Gayatri 231 n.109
Stam, Robert 102, 137
Stephens, Bret 12
Sternberg, Ernest 217–18 n.80
Suleiman, Elia 33–4, 98–104, 136, 212 n.23

Tatour, Lana 133, 187 n.3
Tayeb, Sami 166
terra nullius 7–8, 55, 56, 136
terrorists, Palestinians dis-figured as 9, 12, 15, 17, 19, 22, 40–1, 77–8, 90, 100, 104, 109, 133
thinking under Occupation 33, 67–9
  contrapuntal consciousness 81–2, 86–7, 92–3, 206 n.94, 206 n.97
  decoloniality as means of 33, 68–80, 84, 92
  education system in Israel and 73–6
  exile/diaspora and 33, 80–1 (*see also* exile/diaspora)

Mignolo's "I am where I think" 33, 68, 69, 79, 80, 84, 92
  rejection of "being told" from perspective of privileged viewpoint 70
  "transparent I" and "affectable I" 204–5 n.75
Thobani, Sunera 180 n.118
"time before the settler," nostalgia for 3, 25, 29, 45, 80, 90, 126, 140–1, 152, 156, 166, 184–5 n.158, 186 n.173
Tlaib, Rashida 26, 220 n.102, 221 n.114
Todorova, Teodora 21, 144
transmodernity 79
"transparent I" 204–5 n.75
Trump, Donald 13
Tuck, Eve 5, 20, 21, 29, 87, 127, 191 n.57, 192 n.59
two-state solution 34–5, 125–58
  binationalism versus 34, 45, 126, 141–6, 153, 154, 157, 158
  bothsidesism, problem of 128, 130–5
  Cary Nelson's support for 114, 119
  impracticality of/failure to solve Palestinian problems 125, 148
  lack of Palestinian support for 125
  land repatriation and 25, 29, 75, 86–7, 125, 130
  Nation Estate (film) and 34, 126, 136–41
  in *Oslo* (film) 34, 126–32
  Oslo Accords and 126–32, 135–6
  Palestinian Indigeneity and 2, 13, 20, 25–6
  racism of 125, 225 n.33
  sovereignty, concept of 34–5, 126, 146–58
  in Suleiman's *Divine Intervention* 99
  Zionist settler ideology, failure to account for 131–5
2001: A Space Odyssey (film) 136

Ukraine/Russia conflict 224 n.31
Ukrainian/Russian immigrants to Israel 116
Ultra-Orthodox Jews 114, 217 n.78
UN Declaration on the Rights of Indigenous Peoples (UNDRIP) 169 n.6
United States. *See* liberal democratic ideology

universality
  Balibar's definition of a universal
    cause 170 n.7
  Black 151, 232 n.123
  European Indigeneity
    counteracting 3–4
  identificatory impulse of liberal
    ideology and 19–21
  Jewish universalism, Palestinians'
    condition as fundamental obstacle
    for 152–3
  of Palestinian cause 1–3, 32, 135,
    136, 160–7, 208 n.134, 209 n.146,
    235 n.5
  of public use of *ressentiment* 105, 107
  reimagining/reinventing 32
"un-mattering" of Palestinians 11–21
UN Resolutions
  194 130
  242 and 338 130
  922 74–5
  3379 227–8 n.79

Veracini, Lorenzo 4
violent/armed resistance
  anti-colonial struggle displaced by
    objections to 101–3, 208 n.133
  Marc Lamont Hill on 212–13 n.26
  nonviolence, insistence on Palestinian
    embrace of 22, 102–3, 174 n.57,
    180 n.118
  reclaiming right to 22–3, 103
  right to self-defense of Israel versus
    Palestinians 103, 112, 128, 133,
    224–5 n.31
  terrorists, Palestinians disfigured
    as 9, 12, 15, 17, 19, 22, 40–1,
    77–8, 90, 100, 104, 109, 133
  whitewashing Israeli violence 113–17
visualization of Palestinianness 100–1

War on Terror 17, 133
Warren, Calvin 42
Warschwaski, Michael 77–8, 234 n.151
Waziyatawin 160, 203 n.59
Weheliye, Alexander 14, 176 n.72
Weisglass, Dov 173 n.47
Weiss, Meira 116
Weizman, Eyal 138
Weizmann, Chaim 15

West, Cornel 40
West Bank
  Black-Palestinian solidarity and 43
  Palestinian Indigeneity/Palestinian
    cause and 1, 2, 16, 25, 34
  ressentiment/paranoia in 97, 111,
    114, 222 n.115
  thinking under Occupation in 71, 76,
    83, 85, 86, 90, 93
  two-state solution and 125, 129, 132,
    135, 148, 149
Western liberalism. *See* liberal democratic
  ideology
"When I See Them, I See Us"
  (video) 106
white civil society and anti-
  Blackness 42–6
white Jewish state, Israel's identity as 50
Wilbusch, Jeff 128
Wilderson, Frank 42–50, 52, 59–62,
  80, 156, 162, 181 n.54, 191 n.50,
  191 n.52, 192 n.63, 232 n.122,
  233 n.138
Wilson, Ruth 126
Wolfe, Patrick 187 n.2
women/women's rights 46, 186 n.173
The Wretched of the Earth (Fanon) 29,
  150
Wynter, Sylvia 174 n.58

Yaalon, Moshe 119
Yancy, George 38, 40
Yang, K. Wayne 5, 20, 21, 29, 87, 127,
  191 n.57, 192 n.59
Yishai, Eli 51

Zionism as racism, UN Resolution
  on 227–9 n.79
Zionist gaze 32–3
  concept of 37–41
  contrapuntal consciousness and 82
  Fanon on French/white gaze,
    analogized from 38–42 (*see also*
    Black Studies and Black-Palestinian
    solidarity)
  need of Zionism for the
    Palestinian 53–60
  Other, casting Palestinian as 37–8
  Palestinian Indigeneity as means of
    redirecting 41

settler context of 47–50
  visualization of Palestinianness 100–1
Zionist settler ideology 5–9
  binationalism and 142–6
  Christian Zionism and 171–2 n.32
  Citizenship Law (Israel) and 77–8
  consciousness of Palestinian
    Indigeneity 6, 8, 14, 128, 148
  contrapuntal consciousness, lack
    of 206 n.97
  cultural Zionism versus 14, 141
  decoloniality as counter to 69–79
  European anti-Semitism and 8
  fantasy separatist master narrative
    of 54–8, 195 n.91
  futurology in 11, 141
  Indigeneity claims in 160
  Jewish Indigeneity, origins of 168 n.3
  liberal Zionism and 2, 16, 19–22,
    34, 57, 96, 114, 125, 132, 152–3,
    195 n.101, 208 n.133
  as Manifest Destiny 1, 6, 70
  nation-state and 8, 70
  native assimilation, absence
    of 187 n.2
  neo-Zionism 223 n.20
  Palestinian *ressentiment*/paranoia in
    context of 96–7, 117–29
  paranoia of 109–10, 113, 117, 120,
    216–17 nn.73–4
  political Zionism 8, 14, 19–20, 46–8,
    56–8, 109, 163, 169 n.3, 171 n.28
  as problem of Palestinian
    Indigeneity 21–32, 152–3
  racialization in 8–11, 13, 15, 17
  ressentiment/paranoia, coupling of 33
  two-state solution's failure to account
    for 131–5
  "un-mattering" of Palestinians
    by 11–21
Žižek, Slavoj
  on anti-Blackness and Black-
    Palestinian solidarity 42, 55,
    194 n.76, 198 n.33
  Palestinian Indigeneity and 11,
    18, 26–8, 173–4 n.52, 181 n.120,
    185 n.169, 186 n.173
  on *ressentiment*/paranoia 105, 110,
    213 n.42, 214 n.51, 221 n.113,
    222 n.115
  on "tarrying in the exilic" 205 n.80
  on two-state solution, binationalism,
    and sovereignty 133, 135, 136,
    151, 156, 157, 223 n.4, 233 n.130,
    234 n.155, 234 n.158
Zuaiter, Waleed 128

www.ingramcontent.com/pod-product-compliance
Lightning Source LLC
Chambersburg PA
CBHW052216300426
44115CB00011B/1711